D1117238

BEE COUNTY COLLEGE
DATE DUE

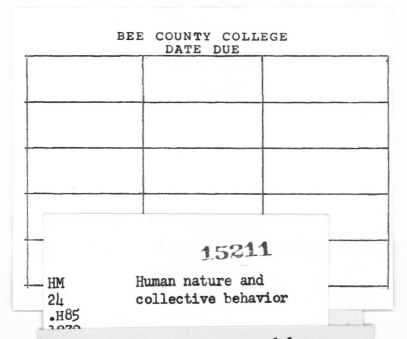

15211

HM
24
.H85
1970

Human nature and
collective behavior

15211

HM
24
.H85
1970

Human nature and collective
behavior

BEE COUNTY COLLEGE LIBRARY
3800 CHARCO ROAD
BEEVILLE, TEXAS 78102
(512) 354-2740

LIBRARY
BEE COUNTY
COLLEGE

HUMAN NATURE
AND
COLLECTIVE BEHAVIOR

PAPERS IN HONOR OF HERBERT BLUMER

HM 24 .H 85 1970

HUMAN NATURE
AND
COLLECTIVE BEHAVIOR

PAPERS IN HONOR OF HERBERT BLUMER

edited by

Tamotsu Shibutani

University of California
at Santa Barbara

BEE COUNTY COLLEGE LIBRARY
3800 CHARCO ROAD
BEEVILLE, TEXAS 78102
(512) 354 - 2740

PRENTICE-HALL, INC., Englewood Cliffs, N.J.

15211

LIBRARY
BEE COUNTY
COLLEGE

HUMAN NATURE AND COLLECTIVE BEHAVIOR
PAPERS IN HONOR OF HERBERT BLUMER

Tamotsu Shibutani, Editor

© 1970 by PRENTICE-HALL, INC.
Englewood Cliffs, New Jersey

All rights reserved. No part of this book
may be reproduced in any form without
permission in writing from the publisher.

Library of Congress Card No. 79–121070
Printed in the United States of America
13–445197-X

Reproduced by special permission from *The Journal of
Applied Behavioral Science,* "The Academy and the Polity:
On Social Scientists and Federal Administrators" by
Irving Louis Horowitz, pp. 309-35, copyright 1969,
NTL Institute for Applied Behavioral Science.

PRENTICE-HALL INTERNATIONAL, INC., London
PRENTICE-HALL OF AUSTRALIA, PTY. LTD., Sydney
PRENTICE-HALL OF CANADA, LTD., Toronto
PRENTICE-HALL OF INDIA PRIVATE LIMITED, New Delhi
PRENTICE-HALL OF JAPAN, INC., Tokyo

FOREWORD

Among sociologists Herbert Blumer is known primarily as an expositor of George H. Mead's social psychology and as a formidable critic. Over several decades he has repeatedly challenged some of the basic assumptions underlying sociological research, and on frequent occasions he has found himself involved in vitriolic controversies. To many of his colleagues, friends, and students, however, his efforts have come to have a significance that extends far beyond his reputation.

Without question one of his major contributions to modern thought is his part in getting Mead's seminal ideas into the mainstream of social psychology. This has not been a simple task; even Mead's most enthusiastic admirers admit that deciphering his prose is an arduous undertaking. Although Blumer has drawn heavily on Mead—along with Charles H. Cooley, John Dewey, and W. I. Thomas—he has gone far beyond, stating explicitly matters that are only implied in the work of his mentors. He has worked out some of the implications of Thomas' contention that what men do rests upon their *definition of the situation*. Like other pragmatists, Blumer has insisted that the meanings of objects are primarily a property of behavior and depend only secondarily upon the intrinsic character of the objects themselves. Meanings, furthermore, are constructed and reaffirmed in social interaction; they are shaped largely by the actual and anticipated responses of others. Human beings are neither creatures of impulse nor heedless victims of external stimulation; they are active organisms who guide and construct their line of action while continuously coming to terms with the demands of an ever-changing world as they interpret it. Of particular import is the object each person forms of himself, for the capacity of man to interact with himself makes some measure of self-control possible. From this foundation Blumer has gone on to an analysis of concerted action, insisting that each transaction is built up in communication, as the participants mesh together their respective contributions; repetition sometimes results in the formation of habitual modes of cooperation—social institutions. His forceful presentation of this point of view has affected the thinking of several generations of graduate students, many of whom have gone on to develop the position further. With mounting concern over problems such as communication and personal identity a resurgence of interest in Mead's work seems inevitable, and it appears that Blumer's clarifications will be increasingly appreciated.

Blumer's methodological orientation follows from his social psychology. His approach is more comprehensive than most, covering the entire investigative process: confronting the empirical world, raising questions in abstract terms, gathering data through disciplined observation, discovering relationships between categories and formulating generalizations, and testing them through renewed observation. Because sociologists are human beings, research is a form of activity that is subject to social control. Because all human beings perceive in terms of hypotheses that are products of social interaction, the adoption of a realistic conceptual scheme is of particular importance. Initial assumptions concerning subject matter are decisive, for the formulation of problems, the types of data sought, and the logical form of propositions all depend on them. Repeatedly Blumer has remonstrated against the uncritical use of procedures that have proved successful in the physical sciences, such as operational definitions, measurement, and experimentation. He has not opposed such techniques in and of themselves; any procedure could be useful, depending upon what is being studied. What he has been emphasizing is that merely *posing* as scientists does not automatically result in the production of scientific knowledge. Since sociology is still a poorly developed discipline, his stance has been that of a pioneer—stressing the importance of inductive, exploratory inquiries. To understand what people do one must get at the manner in which they define the situations in which they are involved. This requires an intimate familiarity with the sector of life being studied—whether it be decision making by corporation executives, experimenting with drugs by Hippies, or the development of an urban riot. Without close acquaintance sociologists run the risk of working with oversimplified, stereotyped conceptions and of missing much of what is happening. Although Blumer has stressed the importance of conceptualization, his approach is not solipsistic; he has always pointed to the necessity of continual reality-testing—against the recalcitrant features of the empirical world. His position has been interpreted in many ways, but for the most part he has been calling for a more direct examination of human life.

Blumer has also made substantial contributions to the study of collective behavior, carrying on the work of Robert E. Park. We live in a rapidly changing society, and much would be missed by working with conceptual schemes designed to analyze static structures. Although many transactions seemingly recur in institutional form, novelties are constantly arising, necessitating collective adjustments of one sort or another to problematic situations. Blumer's most original work is in the study of fashions. True to his dictum on the necessity of making firsthand observations, he went to Paris in 1932 as a fellow of the Social Science Research Council. He contends that fashion is to modern mass societies what custom is to static societies; it makes possible some measure of uniformity and is a mechanism of social control. Although collective behavior has long been a neglected speciality in sociology, the urban disorders of the 1960s and the preoccupation of many of the younger generation with revolutionary changes have once again called attention to the importance of these phenomena. First published in 1939, his statement outlining collective behavior as a field of inquiry now seems destined to become a classic.

A man of exceptional ability—probing scholar, respected teacher, astute administrator, gifted athlete—Herbert Blumer has given generously of his time and effort both to his profession and to the larger public. He was secretary-treasurer of the American Sociological Association from 1930 to 1935, then served in numerous positions and committees, and was elected president in 1956. From 1941 to 1952 he was editor of the *American Journal of Sociology,* and since 1934 he has been editor of the Prentice-Hall sociology series. Although he has not been a political activist, Blumer has long been concerned with human welfare and with the possibility of using sociological knowledge in the solution of social problems. He has supported a variety of causes, and his career has included many periods of public service. During World War II he served as liaison officer between the Office of War Information and the Bureau of Economic Warfare and as public panel chairman of the War Labor Board. He was also successful as a labor arbitrator, and from 1945 to 1947 he served as chairman of the board of arbitration for U.S. Steel.

Both at the University of Chicago, where he taught from 1925 to 1952, and on the Berkeley campus of the University of California, where he has been since then, Professor Blumer has been most effective as a teacher. Several generations of students have found themselves and their careers while sitting in his classes. Some have been impressed by the elegance and vigor of his presentation; others have been shaken by the penetrating questions he raised; still others have found themselves introduced to a new outlook in which previously unconnected observations suddenly fell into place. Even those who disagree with him have found themselves forced to consider questions that cannot be avoided. Many have continued to disagree, but this has not affected their personal relationship with him. Although his own position has long been clear, he has never insisted upon conformity by his students. The diversity of views represented in this book as well as the critical tone of several of the papers reveal the candor with which his friends and students are accustomed to addressing him.

His warmth as a person is remembered by those who have worked with him. During office hours he has received his students cordially and has made them feel that he is interested in their welfare and in what they are doing. Students have not hesitated to unburden their problems to him, for he has always been ready to listen, courteously and sympathetically, and to advise and assist those in need. For decades students have gossiped about his athletic prowess and about the manner in which he had managed his own graduate studies while playing professional football. In encounters following graduation they have found themselves once again greeted cordially by name, with inquiries about their well being, their families, and their work. Even sociologists who quarrel with his position and have recoiled from the sting of his critiques acknowledge liking him as a person.

The impact that Herbert Blumer has had on American sociology has been substantial, and it appears likely that his influence will grow because in many ways he has been a man ahead of his time. Many of the ideas he expounded early in his career in the face of vigorous opposition have since become generally accepted. His impact outside the profession is difficult to estimate. This volume is presented to Professor Blumer, affectionately and respectfully, in full realization that no set of papers, regardless of merit, can serve as a fully adequate tribute to a man who has contributed so much to the lives of those who have had the good fortune of coming into contact with him.

CONTENTS

I THEORY AND METHODOLOGY

III SOCIAL PSYCHOLOGY

IV SOCIOLOGY AND SOCIAL POLICY

I

THEORY AND METHODOLOGY

I

Bernard N. Meltzer
and John W. Petras

THE CHICAGO AND IOWA
SCHOOLS OF SYMBOLIC
INTERACTIONISM

Although the nature of symbolic interaction theory has been explored
and analyzed as a substantive school in itself, there have been no
analyses of the variations that exist within the approach. Our purpose
in this paper is to explore the differences between two major variations within the interactionist orientation: the Chicago school and the
Iowa school. Although the major theoretical issues dividing these
two orientations have been the subject of debate since the dissemination of the ideas of George Herbert Mead into the general population
of American sociologists, it is only within the last fifteen to twenty
years that these differences have crystallized into two distinctive
approaches.

If Charles H. Cooley, John Dewey, George Herbert Mead,

and William I. Thomas are considered to be the most influential of the early interactionists, one can single out several shared characteristics within their works. All conceptualized the individual and society as inseparable and interdependent units. Individuals, living together in society, were viewed as reflective and interacting beings possessing selves. In the words of Herbert Blumer, it was taken as a point of logical necessity that the study of human behavior begin with the fact of human association.[1] While common today, this position represented a departure from the tradition of Lester Ward and the mainstream of early American sociology, in which the individual and society were viewed as discrete and, therefore, separable units. It was as a reaction against this orientation in American sociology that the early interactionists developed the notion of interaction and unity between the individual and society. In response to individualistic perspectives on motivation, they often emphasized the positive role of the social group in its influence upon behavior. The nature of this reaction leads directly into the second characteristic of the early interactionists: a concern with the social development of the self and personality, coupled, however, with the recognition that such a theory had to account adequately for the role of biological factors in human behavior.[2]

Lester Ward and the early American sociologists had pictured the individual as the ultimate source of behavior, e.g., Ward traced motivation to innate tendencies that were manifested in fear of pain and desire for pleasure. The resulting social psychology stressed an inherent dualism in the individual and society relationship. The early interactionists, however, used the term "impulse" to refer to innate biological tendencies that could be satisfied only *within* the social group. Impulse, as opposed to instinct, entailed undifferentiated tension-states. The end result of this approach was a unique combination of the biological and social natures of man in which innate tendencies, in the form of diffuse tensions, had the ends of satisfaction defined by the social order. Group membership was a prerequisite for individual satisfaction, for only through group membership did the ends of satisfaction become defined for the individual members.[3]

The third characteristic of early interactionism concerns the meaning of symbolic behavior. Today, there is a tendency to equate language with the symbolic component. In actuality, the early interactionists utilized language as the principal symbolic form only in certain specific aspects of their theories,

---

[1] Herbert Blumer, "Psychological Import of the Human Group," *Group Relations at the Crossroads,* ed. Muzafer Sherif and M. O. Wilson (New York: Harper & Row, Publishers, 1953), p. 193.

[2] Cf. Roscoe C. Hinkle, "Antecedents of the Action Orientaton in American Sociology Before 1935," *American Sociological Review,* XXVIII (1963), 712.

[3] Cf. Kimball Young and Linton Freeman, "Social Psychology and Sociology," *Modern Sociological Theory,* ed. Howard Becker and A. Boskoff (New York: The Dryden Press, 1957), p. 564.

e.g., Mead's discussion of self-reflexiveness. As far as the early interactionists were concerned, the point to be emphasized was not *how* men communicated, but the fact that they were influenced *by* their communications in interaction. The fabric of society developed out of shared meanings, and it was here that the significance of the symbolic element rested.

As a final characteristic of early interactionism, one can point to the nature of the research that it generated in American sociology. The guiding methodological principle of the early interactionists was that individuals could never be understood apart from the social situations in which they were participating selves. The basic assumption was not that situational characteristics explain all behavior, but that knowing the individual's own interpretation of those situational characteristics was indispensable for understanding his behavior. The influence of this assumption was to lead to a reevaluation of an established methodological technique, interviewing, and to aid in the establishment of a developing technique, case histories. Information gathered in the interview was no longer seen as merely data for reconstructing the individual's situation, but also as a reflection of behavioral processes leading up to the interpretation he communicated in the interview. What had once been the simple recording of behavior as recounted to the interviewer was now seen as a microcosm of the processes characteristic of society as a whole. Implicit was the idea, especially associated with Mead, of taking the role of the other, along with its complementary notion of mutual influence between the self and the other. While not expanded upon within the interview context, interaction along the lines of the self-other relationship was explored in several early research studies.

It was not until much later in the development of American sociology that the original assumptions of the early interactionists began to be tested empirically. The vast majority of these later studies was directed at the particular concepts of identity, role, and self. The Iowa school was formed out of these later studies, aided by the convergence of three developments in American sociology: the rise of social psychology, the growth of role theory, and the introduction of the concept *reference group* with its associated empirical research.

The Two Schools

The Progenitors

During the past generation, the two foremost exponents of the symbolic interactionist orientation have been Herbert Blumer and the late Manford H. Kuhn. At the University of Chicago and, later, at the University of California at Berkeley, Blumer has led some of his students in what can properly be called the "Chicago school" of interactionism, which continues the classical Meadian tradition. Kuhn's Self-Theory, based at the State University of Iowa, constitutes a major variant of this tradition, which we shall call the "Iowa school." This latter school is sustained almost exclusively by Kuhn's students, largely through articles published in *The Sociological Quarterly*. Important substantive and methodological differences distinguish these schools. An examination of the writings of the chief protagonist of each school enables a delineation and illustration of these differences.

A few words about Kuhn's intellectual background may be helpful in understanding his modifications of symbolic interactionism. In the course of earning both his master's and doctor's degrees at the University of Wisconsin (in 1934 and 1941, respectively), Kuhn was introduced to the Meadian perspective by Kimball Young, an eclectic proponent of that perspective. After brief stints of teaching at the University of Wisconsin (1937–42), Whittier College (1942–43), and Mount Holyoke College (1943–46), in 1946 Kuhn settled down at the State University of Iowa, where he remained until his death in 1963. While holding this post, he encountered graduate students who were being exposed to Gustav Bergman's logical positivism and to Kenneth Spence's positivistic contributions to the disciplines of psychology and the philosophy of science. The impact of the influences so briefly sketched here is readily apparent in Kuhn's works.

Methodological Differences

The most fundamental point of divergence between the Chicago and Iowa schools of symbolic interactionism is, probably, that of methodology. Just as in the various disciplines concerned with human behavior, we find here the interminable opposition between humanistic and scientific viewpoints. Blumer tends to argue the case for a distinctive methodology in the study of man, while Kuhn stresses the commonality of method in all scientific disciplines. As in the nineteenth-century *Geisteswissenschaften—Naturwissenschaften* debate, one position implies an idiographic (or nongeneralizing) function of the behavior disciplines, and the other a nomothetic (or generalizing) function. Thus, Blumer seeks simply "to make modern society intelligible," while Kuhn seeks universal predictions of social conduct. The specific features of this methodological divergence can be presented in terms of three intimately related topics: (1) the relative merits of phenomenological and operational approaches, (2) the appropriate techniques of observation, and (3) the nature of the concepts to be used in the analysis of human behavior.

Blumer's demand for a special methodology lays stress upon the need for "feeling one's way inside the experience of the actor." The student of human behavior, he holds, must get inside the actor's world and must see the world as the actor sees it, for the actor's behavior takes place on the basis of his own particular meanings. Through sympathetic introspection, the student takes the standpoint of the acting unit whose behavior he is studying and attempts to use each actor's own categories in capturing his world of meaning. This intuitive, *verstehende* approach seeks intimate understanding rather than intersubjective agreement among investigators.

In a posthumously published article, Kuhn describes as "perhaps the most significant contribution of the Iowa research" its demonstration "that the key ideas of symbolic interactionism could be operationalized and utilized successfully in empirical research."[4] In the same article, he refers to self theory as an effort to develop a set of generalizations tested by empirical research—in contrast with the earlier "body of conjectural and deductive orientations" constituting symbolic interactionism. With this effort in mind, Kuhn sought to "empiricize" Mead's ideas by reconceptualizing or abandoning those he deemed "nonempirical" and by developing techniques of observation that were consistent with this aim. Repeatedly, his writings called for the operational definition of concepts, for methods that would meet "the usual scientific criteria," and for a "standardized, objective, and dependable process of measurement...of significant variables."[5] It should be understood, however, that Kuhn and the Iowa school do not reject the study of the covert aspects of the act. Rather, they urge the use of objective overt-behavioral indices (chiefly verbalizations by the actor) of the covert aspects.

Given Blumer's insistence upon sympathetic introspection, it is not surprising to find him advocating the use of such techniques of observation as life histories, autobiographies, case studies, diaries, letters, interviews (especially of the nondirective type), and, most important, participant observation. Only through close association with those who are being studied, he maintains, can the investigator come to know their inner world. His basic criticism of the experimental, instrumental, and quantitative approach, in the form of questionnaires, schedules, tests, and detached observation "from the outside," is that it fails to catch the "meanings" which crucially mediate and determine the ways in which individuals respond to objects and situations. He appears to be troubled but little by critics of the "soft science" techniques. Among the strictures most frequently directed at such techniques are the following: These techniques are subjective and, hence, unsuited to the development of scientific knowledge; information gathered through their use is too variable and unique for comparison and generalization; they tend to be too time-consuming for convenient use; it is not known how we can teach the skills required in their use; and they do not, typically, receive use in the testing of explicitly formulated theories by procedures subject to independent validation.

One would almost be justified in equating Kuhn's methodology with

---

4 Manford H. Kuhn, "Major Trends in Symbolic Interaction Theory in the Past Twenty-five Years," *The Sociological Quarterly*, V (1964), 61–84.

5 C. Addison Hickman and Manford H. Kuhn, *Individuals, Groups, and Economic Behavior* (New York: Dryden Press, 1956), pp. 224–25.

the technique of the Twenty Statements Test (TST), as Tucker does.[6] This test, known also as the "Who Am I" Test, was developed by Kuhn in 1950 as part of his effort to transform the concepts of symbolic interactionism into variables that might be employed to test empirical propositions. Concerned with the construction of an instrument for eliciting self-attitudes, Kuhn explicitly rejected as unfeasible all attempts to "get inside the individual and observe these interior plans of action directly" or to infer them from overt behavior. He concluded, rather, that such procedures as questionnaires and attitude scales could be adapted to identify and measure self-attitudes. The resultant TST, based upon an open-response model, requires a content analysis of the responses and lends itself to Guttman-scale analysis. Today, the TST is the most widely used instrument in the study of self-conceptions. A section (entitled "Iowa Studies of Self-Attitudes") of the 1958 meetings of the American Sociological Association was devoted to it. The TST has been involved in over 100 reported researches, and it achieved a degree of national popular attention when it was administered to the early astronauts.

In studying "the natural social world of our experience"—a phrase that recurs in Blumer's writings—he urges the employment of "sensitizing concepts." As Gideon Sjoberg and Roger Nett point out, "That Blumer objects to operational definitions of concepts and advocates the use of 'sensitizing concepts' is consistent with his image of social reality."[7] This image includes both societal fluidity and the actor's ability to reshape his environment. Contrasting conventional scientific concepts ("definitive concepts") with sensitizing concepts, Blumer maintains that the former provide prescriptions of what to see, while the latter merely suggest directions along which to look. The concept should, he adds, sensitize one to the task of "working with and through the distinctive nature of the empirical instance, instead of casting this unique nature aside. . . ."[8] In Blumer's view, the student of human conduct moves from the concept to the concrete distinctiveness of the instance, for he has to use the distinctive expression in order to detect the common. Putting it more fully:

> *Because of the varying nature of the concrete expression from instance to instance we have to rely, apparently, on general guides and not on fixed objective traits or modes of expression. To invert the matter, since what we infer does not express itself in the same fixed way, we are not able to rely on fixed objective expressions to make the inference.*[9]

---

6 Charles W. Tucker, "Some Methodological Problems of Kuhn's Self Theory," *The Sociological Quarterly*, VII (1966), 345–58.

7 Gideon Sjoberg and Roger Nett, *A Methodology for Social Research* (New York: Harper & Row, 1968), p. 59.

8 Herbert Blumer, "What Is Wrong with Social Theory?" *American Sociological Review*, XIX (1954), 8.

9 *Ibid.*

We can be quite brief in presenting the viewpoint of Kuhn and the Iowa school on the nature and function of concepts. In his endeavor to convert imprecise Meadian concepts into research variables, Kuhn formulated explicitly operational definitions of "self," "social act," "social object," "reference group," and other concepts. One instructive example is the following portion of his discussion of the self: "Operationally the self may be defined...as answers which an individual gives to the question which he directs to himself, 'Who am I?' or to the question another directs to him, such as 'What kind of a person are you?', 'Who are you?', etc."[10] The first of these proposed questions, of course, is the basis of the TST.

A final comment on the methodological divergences between the two schools relates to Blumer's well-known attack on the utilization in social inquiry of variables—with their implications of a static, stimulus-response image of human behavior. Despite Kuhn's rejection of psychological behaviorism, his quest for variables commits him to some of its favored methodological orientations. Thus, it is clear that our two protagonists assign different priorities to relevance and precision of understanding, as well as to the discovery and the testing of ideas. One could plausibly argue, moreover, that, while Blumer's image of man led him to a particular methodology, Kuhn's methodological predilections led him to a particular image of man. To these somewhat contrasting images we now turn.

Indeterminacy or Determinacy

A second salient difference between the two schools raises the ancient question of the degree to which man's behavior is free or determined. Viewing human behavior in terms of the interplay between the spontaneous and the socially-determined aspects of the self, Blumer builds into such behavior an unpredictable, indeterminate dimension. For him, this interplay is the fundamental source of innovation in society. Proponents of the Iowa school, by contrast, reject both indeterminism in human conduct and the explanation of social innovation based on the emergent, creative element in human action. The place of impulse in conduct constitutes the key issue.

In order to facilitate understanding of this issue, it may be useful to review certain widely known ideas. Following Mead's treatment quite closely, Blumer sees the self as involving two analytically distinguishable phases, the I and the Me. The first of these, the I, is the impulsive tendency of the individual. It is the initial, spontaneous, unorganized aspect of human experience. Thus, it represents the undisciplined, unrestrained, and undirected tendencies of the individual, which usually take the form of diffuse and undifferentiated activity. The Me, on the other hand, represents the incor-

---

10 "From Lectures on the Self by Manford Kuhn," mimeographed, n.d., p. 4.

porated other within the individual. Hence, it comprises the organized set of attitudes and definitions common to the group. In any given situation, the Me comprises the generalized other and, often, some particular other. Every act begins in the form of an I and, generally, ends in the form of a Me. The I represents the initiation of the act prior to its coming under the control of the definitions or expectations of others (the Me). The I thus gives *propulsion,* while the Me gives *direction* to the act. Human behavior, then, is viewed as an ongoing series of initiations by impulses (the I) and of guidance of the act by the Me. The act is a result of this interplay and "cannot be accounted for by factors which precede the act."[11]

It is not entirely clear from Blumer's work whether the indeterminacy that marks human conduct is merely the product of the exploratory, improvising, and impulsive I or is an emergent from the interaction between the I and the Me. Contrasting the symbolic-interactionist view with stimulus-response approaches and other conventional views, he points out that the former is interested in *action,* and the latter in *reaction.* More specifically, he indicates that activity begins with an inner impulse rather than with an external stimulus, and that this activity may undergo a significant course of development before coming to overt expression. This development may bring the emergence of new definitions and new arrangements of definitions. In any case, Blumer exhibits skepticism of social science theories purporting to present determinate, precisely predictive propositions.

Kuhn's self theory takes no explicit cognizance of either impulses or the I-Me components of the self. For him, behavior is determined—as in conventional role theory—by the actor's definitions, including self-definitions. Thus, the self becomes solely a Me, and conduct is held to be wholly predictable (in principle) on the basis of internalized expectations. If we know the actor's reference groups, according to Kuhn, we can predict his self-attitudes; and, if we know his self-attitudes, we can predict his behavior. In short, antecedent conditions determine the person's self; and the self determines his conduct. This view, of course, conveniently disposes of such nonempirical conceptions as the I and impulses. At the same time, it preserves a premise that many deem essential to the scientific enterprise, that of determinism. In so doing, however, it ignores the processual character of the self, a point to which we shall devote a part of the next section.

If the foregoing discussion were exhaustive of the determinacy-indeterminacy controversy as it is manifested in the two schools, the controversy might be relatively easy to resolve. Either or both standpoints might

---

11 Herbert Blumer, "Society as Symbolic Interaction," *Human Behavior and Social Processes,* ed. Arnold M. Rose (Boston: Houghton Mifflin Company, 1962), p. 183.

compromise simply by operating within a *probabilistic* frame of reference for human behavior. As the next section will show, however, the controversy has important implications for other substantive elements in the viewpoints of the two schools.

Process versus Structure

In the course of the preceding discussion, passing reference was made to related fundamental divergences in imagery. We now turn our attention to a more explicit and fuller presentation of these divergences, placing them in the context of a process-structure distinction. The Chicagoans have tended to conceive of both self and society in processual terms, while the Iowans have stressed structural conceptions of both phenomena. These divergent views are more clearly discernible in two very closely related topics: (1) images of behavior as "constructed" or "released", and (2) images of role performance as "role-making" or "role-playing."

Blumer states his predilection for a processual image of human conduct and his repudiation of the structuralist image in the following terms:

> ...*the likening of human group life to the operation of a mechanical structure, or to the functioning of an organism, or to a system seeking equilibrium, seems to me to face grave difficulties in view of the formative and explorative character of interaction as the participants judge each other and guide their own acts by that judgment.*[12]

Similarly, as previously noted, he refers to the self as a process of interaction between the I and the Me, and not merely a summation of the two aspects nor an organization of attitudes. This reflexive process is one in which the actor makes indications to himself, that is to say, notes things and determines their import for his line of action. Thus, action is seen to be built up, or constructed, in the course of its execution, rather than "merely being released from a preexisting psychological structure by factors playing on the structure."[13] The conditions that account for the action are not present at its beginning—"with the mechanism of self-interaction the human being ceases to be a responding organism whose behavior is a product of what plays upon him from the outside, the inside, or both."[14] Rather, he rehearses his behavior, summoning up plans of action, assessing them, changing them, and forming new ones, while indicating to himself what

---

12 Blumer, "Psychological Import of the Human Group," *op. cit.*, p. 199.
13 Herbert Blumer, "Sociological Implications of the Thought of George Herbert Mead," *American Journal of Sociology*, LXXI (1966), 536.
14 *Ibid.*, p. 535.

his action will be. This tentative, exploratory process gives rise, we have seen, to the possibility of novelty in behavior.

Kuhn has maintained that "the individual is not merely a passive agent automatically responding to the group-assigned meanings of objects."[15] Nevertheless, he and his adherents are led by their methodological and deterministic commitments slightly away from this disavowal. They view the self as a structure of attitudes derived from the individual's internalized statuses and roles and assign causal significance in behavior to these somewhat fixed characteristics. That these elements are considered stable "traits" during a given time period is reflected in the use of the TST as a predictor of behavior without specification of the situation in which the test is administered or to which the predictions will be applied.[16] This same assumption of relative stability is found in Kuhn's implied notion of a "core" self, as expressed in his view that "Central to an individual's conception of himself is his identity, that is, his generalized position in society...."[17] By omitting the I, impulses, or the spontaneous component of the self from consideration, Kuhn is constrained to ignore the process of interplay between the different aspects of the self.

Implied in the foregoing discussion are divergent conceptions of the nature of role-behavior. These conceptions can be summarized as "role-making," which designates a tentative, dynamic, and creative process, and "role-playing" (sometimes termed "role-taking" by some writers), which designates responses to the role-expectations of others. Both Dennis Wrong and Ralph Turner have referred to the changing character of role theory. Originally such theory depicted an exploratory and creative interaction process, one marked by fluidity and, often, by some measure of innovation. This theory, however, has increasingly come to be employed as a refinement of conformity, or social control, theory. Resisting this trend toward a collective determinism, Blumer describes human group life as a process of formative transaction. He sees cultural norms, status positions, and role relationships as merely the frameworks within which social action takes place and not as the crucial determinants of that action. Together with other members of the Chicago school, he conceives of man as creating or remarking his environment, as "carving out" his world of objects in the course of action—rather than simply responding to normative prescriptions.

In sharp contrast, Kuhn, as we have seen, conceives of personality as an organization of attitudes which are, in effect, the internalization of the individual's role recipes. The individual's roles are described as the norms

---

15 Hickman and Kuhn, *op. cit.,* p. 26.

16 Cf. Tucker, *op. cit.,* pp. 354–55. Tucker also points out that the TST requires the investigator to impose his own meanings on the subjects' responses, which contradicts the purported theoretical assumptions of the test.

17 "From Lectures on the Self by Manford Kuhn," *op. cit.,* p. 6.

by which he structures objects and situations. Putting the matter quite clearly, Kuhn writes:

> As self theory views the individual, he derives his plans of action from the roles he plays and the statuses he occupies in the groups with which he feels identified—his reference groups. His attitudes toward himself as an object are the best indexes to these plans of action, and hence to the action itself, in that they are the anchoring points from which self-evaluations and other-evaluations are made.[18]

To anyone familiar with the TST, in which the conformity assumption is implicit, the above explicit statement comes as no surprise. This assumption is foreshadowed, also, in an early (pre-TST) essay by Kuhn in which he writes, "Social and cultural factors become determinants of personality factors only as the individual comes to internalize the roles he plays and the statuses he occupies. He asks 'Who am I?' and can answer this question of identity only in terms of his social position...."[19] For Kuhn, even idiosyncratic elements in role-performance are fully explainable in terms of the role-expectations held by the actor's reference groups.

We see, then, that Blumer and Kuhn ascribe different qualities to the self. Blumer contends that the self is a process of internal conversation, in the course of which the actor can come to view himself in a new way, thereby bringing about changes in himself. Moreover, in his transactions with others, there occurs a flowing sequence of interpretation of the conduct of others, during which the actor may subject his attributes to highly variable use—or disuse. As Blumer writes, "The vital dependency of the attitude on the nature of the ongoing interaction suggests how fallacious it is to use the attitude to construct the scheme of that interaction."[20] Kuhn, on the other hand, describes both the self and human interaction as structures. The organized set of self-attitudes serves as a system of preestablished plans of action. And human association takes the form of fairly stable, ready-made patterns of role and counter-role prescriptions. Thus, for him behavior-prescriptions and behavior-predictions tend to coincide.

One or Two Levels of Interaction

The two schools also differ on many relatively minor points. In this brief section we shall deal only with one of these points, one we consider more noteworthy than the rest.

---

[18] Hickman and Kuhn, *op. cit.,* p. 45.
[19] Manford H. Kuhn, "Factors in Personality: Socio-Cultural Determinants As Seen Through the Amish," *Aspects of Culture and Personality,* ed. Francis L. K. Hsu (New York: Abelard-Schuman Limited, 1954), p. 60.
[20] Blumer, "Psychological Import of the Human Group," *op. cit.,* p. 199.

Following Mead, Blumer refers to two kinds, or levels, of human interaction: symbolic interaction (which is uniquely human), and non-symbolic interaction (which is shared with infrahumans). The latter is a conversation of gestures, essentially of a stimulus-response character, in which each organism responds to the perceived actions, or gestures, of the other and makes no effort to ascertain the viewpoint of the other. An example is the vague feelings of uneasiness two persons may experience in one another's presence, a feeling that may spiral in intensity even in the absence of symbolic behavior. Such interaction may involve either unwitting and unintended responses or responses to unindicated aspects of the other.

True, this level of interaction has received little theoretical attention and even less research attention from members of the Chicago school. But it appears to have been ignored completely by the Iowa school. Focusing its concern upon the interaction of socialized persons and viewing such interaction as responsive only to internalized meanings, the latter school leaves no room for nonsymbolic behavior. This omission is to be expected, of course, in view of this school's negation of the I concept. What emerges, then, is a conception of human interaction as a highly cognitive, non-affective phenomenon.

A Summary of the Differences

A close examination of the foregoing differentiation between the Chicago and Iowa schools of symbolic interactionism reveals the indicated differences to have an organic, systematic character. It is useful, in making this point, to recall an argument presented earlier: While Blumer's image of man dictates his methodology, Kuhn's methodology dictates his image of man. Thus, Blumer begins with a depiction of man's behavior as entailing a dialogue between impulses and social definitions, in the course of which acts are constructed. He proceeds to recognize a level of interaction devoid of social definitions and reflecting sheerly spontaneous behavior. Holding the two preceding ideas, he questions the extent to which human behavior is predictable. And finally, in the light of all of the foregoing imagery components, he must urge a methodology that combines scientific and humanistic elements.

Oppositely, Kuhn starts from a scientistic concern. This, although joined with his symbolic-interactionist orientation, brings him to an acceptance of a basically deterministic image of behavior. In the service of both scientism and determinism, he denies to the I any role in conduct, thereby dismissing the possibilities of both emergence and nonsymbolic interaction. Recognizing the magnitude of these modifications of symbolic interactionism, he relinquishes the conventional name of that orientation in favor of "self theory."

Prospects for Reconvergence

While our primary task in this paper has been to demonstrate major differences between the Chicago and Iowa schools of symbolic interaction theory, we shall conclude by examining the possibilities for reconvergence of the two approaches. Although it may be too early to state whether or not symbolic interaction theory will experience a reconciliation of the two schools, the likelihood that this will occur can be examined within the context of trends in American sociology as a whole.

One of the most notable developments in American sociology during the past several years has been the continually increasing interest in a sociology of sociology, reflected in the number of articles published on this subject, as well as in the time and space, both official and unofficial, allotted the subject at recent meetings of state, regional, and national sociological associations. As a consequence of this interest there has been a reconsideration of the origins of many of the established schools within sociology. We can expect that, as individuals involved in the various aspects of symbolic interaction theory experience a revived interest in their own intellectual antecedents, the differences among them will lessen, bringing a greater appreciation of the similarities due to a common intellectual heritage.

A second trend within American sociology that could prove influential in effecting a reconvergence of the Chicago and Iowa schools is the growth of interest in studies of adult socialization. Corresponding to this growth is the rapid increase of studies interested in the concepts of identity and self at the adult level. The very notion of "adult socialization" serves to incorporate work from both schools. The "adult" aspect is generally measured through some form of self test, and the TST is the most widely used self-inventory test. On the other hand, the "socialization" element has led to a renewed interest in and usage of some of the basic principles that were developed by members of the Chicago school.

Perhaps the most widespread development in American sociology, and one which involves the contributions of both the Chicago and Iowa schools, has been in the interrelated areas of reference group theory and role theory. Recent publications that question the various definitions of reference group, as well as the applicability of the concept to various types of research situations, have forced a reexamination of some of the basic principles underlying this approach.[21] Also, attempts that have been made

---

[21] Cf. Maureen E. Cain, "Suggested Developments for Role and Reference Group Analysis," *British Journal of Sociology,* XIX (1968), 191–205; Nicholas P. Pollis, "Reference Group Re-Examined," *British Journal of Sociology,* XIX (1968), 300–307; and Herbert Hyman and Eleanor Singer, eds., *Readings in Reference Group Theory and Research* (New York: The Free Press of Glencoe, Inc., 1968).

to delineate clearly what is meant by role theory and the wealth of studies classifying themselves by this label have drawn attention to the major conceptualizations of role, as used in both the Chicago and Iowa schools.[22]

A fourth development concerns the revitalization of an interest in the biological elements in behavior. Recent interest in this area differs from earlier interest in the following manner: In their earliest sociological application, biological factors were often treated as the most fundamental determinants of action. After the decline of instinct theories of motivation in American sociology there ensued a long period during which sociological explanations incorporating biological factors were regarded as unfashionable or unscientific. However, recent sociological works involving genetic factors in behavior give considerable weight to the social factor, so that biological and social elements are seen as co-determinants. The work in this area is presently restricted to a small minority of sociologists. A widening of interest, however, would very likely begin in symbolic interaction theory, which, as pointed out earlier in this paper, has been one of the few schools of thought to retain the notion that biological factors must be considered in any complete explanation of behavior.[23]

Finally, we might look at a matter which, paradoxically, members of the Iowa school took as their major point of departure from the Chicago tradition: the interest in, and emphasis upon, the operationalization of the key concepts of symbolic interaction theory. Blumer has consistently emphasized the need for conceptual clarity as a prerequisite to operationalization. It seems that the major differences on this point center less on the problem of operationalization itself than on the type of operationalization that is possible, given a particular definition of the key concepts, e.g., "self." As in the Blumer-Bales debate, the real issue involves such matters as the twofold, processual conceptualization of the self.

Of course, there are other avenues open to the two schools for a possible reconvergence. In our limited amount of space, we have presented what we consider to be the most important ones. We should also like to point out that several developments can work in the opposite direction, i.e., against a reconvergence. For example, we may soon see the specification of role theory as something independent of the two schools of symbolic interaction theory rather than as a subspecialty within the general area. In effect, this has already occurred with the dramaturgical school, which,

---

22 Cf. Bruce J. Biddle and Edwin J. Thomas, eds., *Role Theory: Concepts and Research* (New York: John Wiley & Sons, Inc., 1966) ; Theodore R. Sarbin and Vernon L. Allen, "Role Theory," *The Handbook of Social Psychology,* ed. Gardner Lindzey and Eliot Aronson (Cambridge: Addison-Wesley Publishing Co., Inc., 1968), Vol. I, pp. 488–567.
    23 Cf. Bruce K. Eckland, "Genetics and Sociology: A Reconsideration," *American Sociological Review,* XXXII (1967), 173–94.

as popularized through the works of Erving Goffman, was originally closely related to the Chicago school. However, Hugh D. Duncan recently has developed the idea that the advancement of sociology is in part dependent upon the creation of a sociological model of communication to be tested in propositional form.[24] Thus a reconvergence could take the form of many of the original differences between the two schools becoming assimilated into the mainstream of American sociology, dulling the distinctiveness of each.

There remains, of course, still another possibility. As in the past and present, the two schools may continue the pattern of taking little cognizance of one another and of going their separate ways. This pattern is evidenced by the fact that representatives of each school rarely cite the works of the other school. This type of parochialism is fostered by the fundamental and perhaps irreconcilable divergence of schools on the methodological level.

---

[24] Hugh D. Duncan, *Symbols in Society* (New York: Oxford University Press, Inc., 1968).

2

H. Warren Dunham

SOCIOLOGY: NATURAL SCIENCE OR INTELLECTUAL COMMITMENT?

In this paper, I have two general purposes: (1) to analyze the significance of the present and constant concern for methodology in sociology, and (2) to examine whether this continuing concern advances sociology as a scientific discipline.

Perhaps it might be helpful, in organizing one's thinking about this matter, to break up the historical period covering the rise and development of the sociological enterprise into three appropriate units. First, there was the period beginning about 1800 and encompassing almost the entire nineteenth century. This period was characterized by the rise of the so-called grand style theory in sociology, with its various attempts to develop a conceptual system which would provide a suitable explanation for human behavior and/or social organization.

Second, there was the period, beginning about 1890 and ending with the beginning of World War II, which might be described as one dominated by crude empiricism. In this period sociologists turned their attention mainly to the collection of various kinds of observations about the world of human experience, and they attempted to organize these discrete and diverse bits of data into generalizations that would help to explain human behavior and social organization. In this period, sociologists were less concerned with procedural matters, were less concerned with ties for binding the empirical world with theory, and were satisfied with the collection of an unusual amont of factual information about their own societies. There was a certain naïveté in this period because it was frequently thought that if one could just get at the facts concerning a social problem, issue, or institution, the facts would speak for themselves by providing generalizations that would be useful for guiding social policies. Further, it was a period of uncritical enthusiasm in the development of the new science. Workers within it began to amass mountains of data on IBM cards, hoping that the relationships they expected would emerge and provide clues to the nature of social organization and the factors that lie behind human behavior, both conforming and nonconforming.

The third period can be described as one that has been and is preoccupied with the methodological concern to an extreme degree. This period, beginning with World War II and continuing to the present, can be characterized by the annual avalanche of monographs, books, and symposiums devoted generally to the same methodological concerns. For the most part, all are devoted to an examination of the central methodological issues in sociology, in the faith that such explicit awareness and clarification will establish more firmly the claims of sociology to scientific status.

While I make no claims to having proven the case, I suspect that the evidence would sustain the general proposition that international events —such as the Russian Revolution of 1918 and the coming to power of a government dominated by communistic ideology, the rise and success of national socialism in Germany in the 1930s, the collapse of the League of Nations in 1936, the world-wide depression of the 1930s, and particularly the persecution of the Jews under Hitler in Germany—had tremendous impact upon the thinking of sociologists, as well as other social scientists, and caused them to turn their attention to a more systematic inquiry into the assumptions, procedures, and values behind their daily work. By focusing upon the methodological concern, sociologists intended to make their discipline more socially relevant and at the same time to iron out the difficulties in the way of achieving solid scientific status.

It should be perfectly clear that the three historical divisions that I have described as characterizing our discipline are somewhat arbitrary. But they do serve to point out that the increasing sophistication of sociologists required them to examine critically and carefully the assumptions upon which their discipline was to rest. In particular they were compelled to inquire whether the nature of these assumptions made it possible for the discipline to develop as a scientific enterprise of the same character as the natural sciences. It is not that the concerns of the second period—such as the rise of quantification, the concern with operational definitions, the conflict between statistical and case study methods, or the problems as to what constituted a social fact—have disappeared. Rather it is that the sociologist now approaches his task and his problems with a deeper degree of awareness and understanding of the procedures, assumptions, and values that were always present at the onset of all of his inquiries.

These historical periods gain their significance from the assumption that sociology was developing as a full-scale, natural science. When I first began my university teaching of sociology, I was vaguely aware that two intellectual positions in the field were struggling for recognition. One position characterized the field as containing a body of information encompassing various kinds of observations, analytical schemes, descriptive accounts, and attempts to depict the evolution of our society and other societies. These empirical and intellectual structures resulted in a plausible picture of contemporary social institutions and their interrelationships, of shifting and competing value systems, and of the behavior of man in various types of situations—all adding up to what might constitute a social philosophy rather than a social science. In other words, it seemed that these disparate materials aimed toward constructing a philosophical position about the nature and function of society at a particular time and place.

This naturally led to the position that perhaps sociology actually was merely a point of view, an intellectual position about our contemporary world at a given time in history. This position naturally suggested the possibility that each age and each generation tended to develop its own sociology or its own intellectual position about the world. This position was supported and manifested in the latter part of the nineteenth and early twentieth century by those persons in our field who appeared to be interested in the utilization of sociology primarily as a basis for various kinds of social action programs aimed at achieving social reform. This position is also present in our field today, although the manner in which it is stated is often more pretentious in raising the issue of how sociology can serve as a basis for effecting, determining, or influencing social policies. In other words, how is sociological knowledge to be utilized?

The other position conceived sociology to be a science in the accepted sense of the word. As a science, it would be expected to have a body of theory that would direct social inquiry by providing hypotheses that could be tested by various observations which, in turn, would be utilized to reformulate the body of theory. Of course, the possibility of the development of sociology as an empirical science has been present from its beginnings. There would seem to be no doubt that if the utilization of the empirical method is sufficient for the making of a science, then sociology should qualify. This is so because from classical times there has been a long line of investigators who have emphasized the necessity of building a social science upon observations of human behavior and human collectivities. The methodological problems arise, of course, in determining how to make these observations, and then in determining how reliable and valid they are as expressions of the empirical world.

When one examines the literature of sociology, one is struck with the fact that there seems to be no one valid body of theory. Rather there is a multiplicity of theories, of views of the world, of systems of concepts, that have been regarded by some people as constituting the theory of the field. For many years sociological theory in universities was taught as an historical subject, concerned primarily with the history of ideas. Thus, the current situation in theory seems a long way from the formulation of a systematic body of theory from which testable hypotheses can be deduced.

In the examination of the sociological literature one is also struck by the fact that there were numerous positions or patterns of thought about making sociology into a science.[1] These disparate schemes for making sociology into a science can be identified by the basic social unit that a given investigator feels is necessary for the development of his system of sociology. For example, one might speak of Leslie White's conception of the science of culture as an illustration of an attempt to build a scientific sociology.[2] On the other hand, Radcliffe-Brown places his emphasis on society as the basic unit and visualizes the possibility of the development of a comparative study of human societies.[3] Thus, the sociological enterprise from this perspective consists of an attempt to develop a series of generalizations that are derived from the empirical observations of the ways different social systems function. Or, one could take the sociological enterprise and consider it primarily from a sociopsychological perspective, where the emphasis is placed upon finding societal explanations for various kinds of human behavior. This view points to analytic schemes for explaining the development of the self. Here the unit of analysis consists of the interactions that take place between two or more persons. One finds the theoretical underpinnings for this position

---

[1] Helmut R. Wagner, "Types of Sociological Theory: Toward a System of Classification," *American Sociological Review*, XXVIII (1963), 735–42.

[2] Leslie White, *The Science of Culture* (New York: Farrar, Straus & Co. Inc., 1949).

[3] A. Radcliffe-Brown, *A Natural Science of Society* (New York: The Free Press of Glencoe, Inc., 1957).

in the social psychology of George Herbert Mead, Charles H. Cooley, and James M. Baldwin.[4] Several other possible positions might be examined here. The main point to be made, of course, is not that any one of them represents the flowering of sociology as a science, but rather that each one of them represents an intellectual commitment of the person who has initiated the specific system of ideas and of his students and followers who have adopted it.

Thus, when I began to teach, I found these two positions very prominent within sociology. By far the most prominent was the second position which held out the hope, and existed on faith, that sociology through its empirical examination of the social world might eventually discover the means by which it could become truly a science on a par with the natural sciences. This perspective has undergone a gradual change during the last half century, from the notion that a science is a deterministic and closed system to the notion that a science is always in the process of becoming. Sociologists took hope from this perspective and thus did not seek a closed deterministic system so much as a series of valid propositions that might constitute its theory and direct its further inquiry into the social world.

Thus, we have come to the central question of this paper: Can sociology develop as a deductive, theoretical social science supported by empirical findings that will provide explanations for the interrelationships of social behavior, organization, and change? Or is this a hopeless quest in that the very nature of the social world will prevent sociology from rising above the level of a social philosophy that might provide guidance for social action within a particular generation?

Methodological Issues Involved

In this section I wish to consider those methodological issues which seem to me to be crucial for obtaining an answer to the question I have just raised. As I will attempt to show, it is the inability to come to any widespread agreement about these issues that is so upsetting in efforts to make sociology into a science. Consequently, in their research endeavors individual sociologists make different intellectual commitments, generally implicit in their work, with respect to these issues. Such differences make it well nigh impossible for research to be cumulative.

---

[4] George Herbert Mead, *Mind, Self and Society* (Chicago: The University of Chicago Press, 1934); Charles H. Cooley, *Human Nature and the Social Order* (New York: Charles Scribner's Sons, 1922); and James M. Baldwin, *Social and Ethical Interpretations of Mental Development: A Study in Social Psychology* (3rd ed., New York: The Macmillan Company, Publishers, 1903).

Images of Man

First, let us consider the issue that centers around man's nature. This issue has been given diverse answers throughout history. The problem, of course, is that none of these answers are definitive in any sense. Rather, they represent different types of intellectual commitment that a given social scientist may adopt with respect to his approach to the empirical world. However, the point is that he makes an intellectual commitment. He does not adopt a position about the nature of man because of its empirical content or because it represents a scientific body of knowledge about man's nature. The notion that man is born good and then corrupted by society, the notion that he is born evil and hence his nature tends to corrupt society, and finally, the Lockian notion that man at birth is a *tabula rasa,* neither good nor bad, and is shaped in his mental life and personality by the nature of his experiences in social life—these conceptions of the nature of man are traditional and all too familiar to the student of social thought.

However, there is another body of thought that attempts to answer this question. It can be labeled as scientific, and it relates to the findings of biologists, psychologists, and sociologists with respect to man's nature. But here again, the findings are difficult to assess. This is so because the problems as defined by any given discipline generally refer to a minutiae of human behavior, and there is the final problem of effecting the synthesis of this knowledge to come to some general propositions about the nature of man. Up to this point, this has not been done. Whether one turns to the genetic studies of the biologist, to the learning experiments by the psychologist, to those disparate analyses of human experience and psychic content that have been the work of the social psychologists and sociologists, or to an examination of the impact of culture upon man's nature, one realizes that the findings in all of these areas are interesting and relevant to the problem but to date have failed to show how they may be interrelated in order that certain valid propositions about man's nature can be stated.

I might illustrate this matter by reference to the popularity and interest that a recent book by Konrad Lorenz has engendered in certain quarters.[5] Here it is interesting to note that we have a return to the instinct theory which both sociologists and social psychologists thought was dead a long time ago. But the popularity of the Lorenz book does suggest that the issue has by no means been closed, and in fact his book is reminiscent of William Trotter's volume in 1920.[6]

---

[5] Konrad Lorenz, *On Agression,* trans. Marjorie Kerr Wilson (New York: Harcourt, Brace and World, Inc., 1966).

[6] William Trotter, *Instincts of the Herd in Peace and War* (London: T. F. Unwin, Ltd., 1920).

The fact that a social scientist takes for his image of man that aspect of a body of thought that is most congenial to his general perspective is well illustrated by a recent discussion in *Commentary*. Both writers referred to Lorenz' work, one accepting and one rejecting Lorenz, and portrayed his thought in the manner that was congenial to each writer's already-developed perspective about man's nature. Perhaps these remarks should be enough to bring the reader to a realization that what a given social scientist holds or has to say about the nature of man will determine the character of the sociology that he tends to develop.[7]

The tendency among sociologists is to slide easily, and perhaps glibly, over the necessity for making an explicit statement about the nature of man. Rather are they more likely to make a conception of man's nature implicit in their work, because there is a strong resistance among them to taking account of the place and significance of psychological factors in social life. For this they would have to do if they made their image of man explicit. Thus, sociologists who keep their conception of man implicit do so with the authority of Emile Durkheim behind them. He had shown with his great example of empirical work emerging from theory that suicide rates could not be explained by resort to individual psychology but must be explained exclusively by those social conditions that characterize a given society.[8] However, today's student must recognize the time in which Durkheim worked and the task he set for himself, which was to oppose a one-sided psychology in order to show the significance of the solid cutting edge of societal factors. The student has Durkheim's accomplishment as background and is freer to take a clear look at how different conceptions about the nature of man condition and influence the definition and selection of problems for research.

Perhaps the most prevalent sociological conception of man is that which views him as primarily a product of socialization in every society. Man's original nature is thus seen as neither good nor evil, social nor unsocial, but rather as representing the potential that can be molded and shaped to several societal requirements and given various types of content. Dennis Wrong has labelled this view as the oversocialized conception of man.[9]

---

[7] Cf. Selma Fraiberg, "Of Human Bonds," *Commentary*, December 1967, pp. 47–57; and Herbert J. Gans' review of *Report from Iron Mountain on Possibility and Desirability of Peace,* in *Commentary*, February 1968, pp. 83–86.

[8] Emile Durkheim, *Suicide,* trans. J. Spaulding and G. Simpson (New York: The Free Press of Glencoe, Inc., 1951).

[9] Dennis Wrong, "The Oversocialized Conception of Man in Modern Sociology," *American Sociological Review,* XXVI (1961), 183–93.

Models of Society

Let me turn now to a second issue that influences and conditions the type of sociology that will be developed. Here I am referring to the image of society that a given sociologist utilizes implicitly as a guide to his research and to his selection of problems. The various conceptions that different social thinkers have held about the nature of society can be regarded as models of society, although sometimes they have been viewed as theories of society and have been the basis for the development of competing schools of sociology. However, there is a significant distinction between theories and models. A theory, in the final analysis, must fall or stand on the basis of evidence; a model can only be judged by whether it clarifies some aspect of the problem under study.

Sociologists have in general been clearer about the conceptions they hold of society than about the conceptions that they hold of man. Since sociologists have conceived of their subject matter as encompassing human society, it has been incumbent upon them, in order more satisfactorily to direct their empirical inquiries, to make explicit some conception of the nature of society.

Two difficulties are presented by the adoption of any model of society, and both are relevant to an attempt to answer the question I have posed. The first of these difficulties is that the construction of a model prevents one from seeing some facts and conditions that may develop. A second difficulty is the tendency for models of society to have political and moral implications. These implications tend to become ideological positions for conflicting political forces within a given society. This difficulty is not likely to develop in the physical sciences, for disagreements are more easily resolved by applying the rules of evidence to conflicting sets of facts. But in the social sciences there are often marked disagreements about what the facts are as well as about their interpretation. Then, too, the social sciences have not been able to develop and use the crucial experiment to the same extent as has been possible in the natural sciences. Consequently, it is difficult to determine which of two contending positions is valid.

Currently there are five models of society in use, and each enjoys a certain prestige within sociology. These different models of society are not so much contradictory to one another as they are supplementary, and any given sociologist who is empirically-minded may find himself utilizing more than one model in the course of his research. The differences among the models are frequently a matter of emphasis. The difficulty, of course, is that there is no means of determining whether one model is superior to another model. This means that the true nature of society, if there is such a thing, continues to elude us and thus heightens our inability to answer the question with which we began. Further, there does not seem to be the possibility of developing a more valid conception of the nature of society from the empirical work that is the outgrowth of each model.

For example, if one holds in mind an equilibrium model concerning the nature of society, one tends to focus upon the problems associated with the interrelationships, adjustments, and accommodations of the various institutions within the society as they move through a cycle of organization, disorganization, and reorganization. Here the focus of attention is much more on the structure and interrelationships of institutions. In sharp contrast, if one adheres to a conflict model of society, one calls attention to the perpetual conflict, disagreement, and dissension that characterizes persons and groups within the society as they struggle and contend for the scarce goods of wealth, power, and prestige. The focus of attention is less upon the structure of these groups than on the processes of competition and conflict between them. Thus, some problems would be defined in terms of the analysis of these processes and of the procedures used by the contending forces that find themselves in conflict. If one looks at both of these models and at what one is able to demonstrate empirically, one is forced to conclude that there is both accommodation and conflict present in any social structure.

In like manner one can contrast the evolutionary model of society with the organismic model. If one holds to the evolutionary model, one focuses upon the attempt to discover the natural laws that govern the social changes that take place within society. Those who hold to an evolutionary model see society passing through inevitable stages, sometimes from lower to higher, sometimes from one type of social organization to another. Or the process of change may be characterized in a cyclical fashion, in terms of action and reaction, or in terms of the birth, life, and death of a given social order. This model has often been a favorite of historically-minded sociologists as they have attempted to examine the process of change in social structure.

In contrast, those who hold to an organismic model view society as an organism, analogous to the individual human organism on the biological level. This structural-functional model, so widely used by contemporary sociologists, emphasizes the interrelationship between the structure of an institution, group, or norm and its function; the model also shows that function tends to affect the structure of the institution, group, or norm within a given society. From this perspective, activities and institutions can be identified that serve as an integrating force within the society, while others can be identified that might be regarded as dysfunctional with respect to the maintenance and continuation of the society. Here the final test is the survival of society.

Again, there is no way of determining which of these two models is more valid; rather one can only say that each serves a different purpose, for each calls attention to a different type of problem. The evolutionary model emphasizes and attempts to demonstrate how the institutions of society at any given stage determine the character of the institutions at a later stage. The organismic model merely attempts to demonstrate how the various institutions within society function advantageously or disadvantageously with respect to the maintenance and continuation of that society.

Finally, the physical science model, which is a very old one, views society as governed by laws that are comparable to those that operate in the physical world. Thus, sociology is thought to be on a par with the science of physics, utilizing the same techniques of measurement, experiment, and laboratory investigations that have proved so fruitful in the physical sciences. This model portrays the social world in mechanical terms and resembles closely a stimulus-response behaviorism. The model points to the necessity of developing various operational definitions that eventually will come closer and closer to the nature of the object or force that is to be depicted. With valid operational definitions, the investigator who holds this particular model of society attempts to examine the interrelationship of various social elements in the hope that this will provide increasingly better explanations of human behavior. As I have indicated, this model of society rests on a behavioristic psychology and contrasts rather sharply with the other models which have been mentioned. Each of the other models attempts to formulate some realistic conception of the nature of society, while this particular model presents a nominalistic view of society. That is, society can only be seen in terms of the responses of the individuals that compose it and thus cannot take on a realistic quality. From the perspective of this model, human behavior is the primary emphasis, in contrast to the nature and function of social organizations, which characterize the other models. Thus, there is a view of society that develops from these other models that is independent of the responses of the persons who compose it.

The Problem of Concepts

There is a third, unsettled, and vacillating methodological issue that also accounts for the difficulty in asserting that sociology constitutes a science in the usual, accepted sense of the term. The concept issue is most unsettling not only because it raises a question as to whether sociology has developed a set of concepts that has utility in advancing our analysis of social realities, but also because it throws in question the nature of existing concepts themselves—that is, whether or not any given concept actually is specific enough to delineate a segment of reality to which it is supposed to refer. Herbert Blumer has noted this issue by referring to the concepts that do exist in sociology as sensitizing concepts, as against definitive concepts which would have an empirical content and deal specifically with some aspect of a given class of objects.[10]

This issue is often put in terms of the distinction between nominal and real definitions. It has been held by numerous critics of sociology that most of the concepts that are present in the field are primarily nominal in character—that is, they are terms which are used in place of other terms.[11] Thus, "culture is custom" would be a nominal definition. In contrast, real definitions of concepts encompass a certain aspect of empirical reality and designate a relationship. For example, Robert Redfield has defined culture as "an organized body of conventional understandings, manifest in art and artefact, which, persisting through tradition, characterizes a human group."[12] This definition of culture comes much closer to being a real definition than does the previous one.

The vacillating and changing character of sociological concepts makes it extremely difficult to say whether sociology comes to grips with a specific type of social reality. The definitions of a given concept may vary markedly within the field. In general these contrasting definitions embody similar ideas, but different words and different emphases are given to denote these similar ideas. It has long been held in some quarters that the looseness of verbal definitions can be avoided by the development of operational definitions. An operational definition primarily utilizes measurement and permits the concept to be derived from a series of operations which are used to discover it. Such operational definitions can usually be stated in the language of mathematics, which is regarded as exact. Consequently, it is held that operational definitions lead to a series of concepts about social reality that have a definitive and precise character about them. The difficulty, however, is that whole segments of social reality may be avoided, because it is impossible to develop an operational concept which delineates them. From this perspective sociology would tend to become a kind of social physics, relating a series of operational concepts with one another, or at least those particular operational concepts which can be developed. In the final analysis, then, it can be said that sociology lacks a series of concepts which are definitive in character and which designate specific types of

---

[10] Herbert Blumer, "What Is Wrong with Social Theory?" *American Sociological Review,* XIX (1954), 3–10. In citing Professor Blumer, I should point out that he refers to the either/or issue that I have raised as two types of social theory. Thus, in his criticism of sociological theory it is difficult to determine if he thinks the deficiencies of sociological theory can be surmounted so that sociology can become a science or if he thinks this is an impossible quest.

[11] Robert Bierstedt, "Nominal and Real Definitions in Sociological Theory," in *Symposium on Sociological Theory,* ed. Llewellyn Gross (New York: Row, Peterson and Company, 1959).

[12] Quoted from William F. Ogburn and Meyer Nimkoff, *Sociology* (4th ed., Boston: Houghton Mifflin Company, 1964), p. 48.

reality. Thus, it is well-nigh impossible to develop a science in the accepted meaning of this term.

The Problem of Locus

The locus problem in social science is the attempt to specify the basic unit of observation and analysis that is to serve as a focus for inquiry. Here there are several possibilities, and each one of them at one time or another has been selected as a unit of inquiry for a particular problem. Such basic subject matter units that have been used include acts, roles, persons, personalities, processes, interpersonal relations, groups, social classes, social institutions, societies, and cultures. In the selection of any one of these units two associated problems arise: (1) What constitutes the identity of the element that is selected? (2) How can its meaning be specified on the basis of what can be observed? The first problem calls attention to the criteria essential for identification of the element, and the second problem points to the requirements essential for specifying the meaning of what is observed. While the type of behavior studied in the physical, biological, and social sciences may be different, the fact that unites all science, as Abraham Kaplan has pointed out, is the study itself—that is, the fact that it is an empirical inquiry.[13]

The locus problem is particularly acute among those sociologists who have devoted themselves almost entirely to theory construction. They have had to face this problem in an acute form and have become aware of the underlying philosophical premises. This was particularly true of theory which lacked an empirical foundation or had very limited foundation. Thus, Leopold von Wiese took process as the basic unit of social life and attempted to develop a typology of processes.[14] Max Weber took as his unit of analysis the meaningful act.[15] Durkheim took collective representations—social facts are things; Albion W. Small focused upon the group.[16] These examples only illustrate differences among sociologists as to what is considered the basic unit of social reality. Thus, it should be clear that the selection of one basic

---

13 Abraham Kaplan, *The Conduct of Inquiry* (San Francisco: Chandler Publishing Co., 1964), p. 79. Cf. Otakar Machotka, "Is Sociology a Natural Science?" *American Journal of Sociology,* LV (1949), 10–17.

14 Howard Becker, *Systematic Sociology,* adapted from *Beziehungslehre und Gebeldelehre* by Leopold von Wiese (New York: John Wiley & Sons, Inc., 1932).

15 Max Weber, *The Theory of Social and Economic Organization,* trans. A. M. Henderson and Talcott Parsons (New York: The Free Press of Glencoe, Inc., 1964), pp. 87–123.

16 Emile Durkheim, *The Rules of Sociological Method* (Chicago: The University of Chicago Press, 1938); and Albion W. Small, *The Meaning of Social Science* (Chicago: The University of Chicago Press, 1910).

unit rather than another will affect the type of sociological theory that will evolve.

The locus problem is dealt with much more adequately in the research. Here, a careful statement of the problem to be investigated and the development of an appropriate research design will decide the locus. The statement of the problem will determine the segment of social life that is to be studied, and the investigator only has to determine what observations he must make to illuminate a given aspect of social reality. The locus problem is resolved only within the research itself and not on the basis of arbitrary philosophical assumptions. The investigator in his research can use any concepts that he finds useful, as long as he is clear about the reality for which they stand. The only restriction upon him is that what he says can be checked by experience. It is, of course, preferable that others will be able to duplicate the experience in order to check on his work.

However, while the locus problem may be resolved for any specific piece of research in sociology, the variety of the resolutions found for the locus problem in different pieces of research merely highlights the difficulty. The difficulty is only resolved temporarily, but is not resolved for sociology in general; the consequence is that research results are not additive or cumulative from one research to another. Thus, the unsettled character of the locus problem makes it impossible for sociology to claim that it is a science comparable to a natural science.

The Dual Aspect of Social Reality

It has been conventional to assert that one of the reasons for the slowness in the scientific development of the social sciences, as compared to the physical sciences, is the greater complexity of that reality which is their focus of attention. One aspect of this reality with which sociology is concerned is noted in the fact that its data have both an objective and subjective character. Now it is no doubt true (and few sociologists are likely to deny it) that such phenomena as feelings, beliefs, attitudes, memory, private thoughts, and the like are subjective. But they are also a part of human experience and as such must be taken account of in the observations that sociologists make in their various studies. Questions, naturally, arise as to how this can best be done, and how this can be done to meet the rigorous specifications of scientific procedure.

There have been numerous attempts to bridge this gap between subjective and objective reality. So far none of these attempts have been completely satisfactory, if it is desired that sociology measure up to accepted scientific requirements. One attempt is seen in the distinction that the Germans have made between the natural and the social sciences. In this distinction they have used the natural sciences as being fully equipped to offer causal explanations for the phenomena which are observed, while the social sciences can only bring about an understanding, an increased awareness of the significance of what is being observed and of the relationships among the observations. This is reflected in Weber's postulation of the meaningful act as the central unit for sociological analysis, for Weber wants to understand and to get at the meaning behind the action.

A second device for bridging this gap is seen in the development of disciplines that are exclusively preoccupied with the mental. Such examples might include phenomenology and psychoanalysis. Phenomenology in a philosophical sense denies all knowledge and existence beyond phenomena. Thus, it leads to a study of the mind, where all phenomena are experienced. Through an intellectual process it attempts to isolate the various essences that represent the structure of the mind. Psychoanalysis, on the other hand, explores the complexity of mental life, particularly the unconscious part, in an attempt to account for man's behavior in the social world. That is, behavior is an outcome of repressed thoughts and feelings resulting from experiences in the real world which take place during the unfolding of one's sexual nature in the developing years. Experience is always taking place on top of previous experiences and at a certain period in the years of development. In its extreme form psychoanalytic theory has attempted to provide an explanation and determination for collective and institutional life at the level of culture.

One final attempt is seen in the efforts to develop operational definitions in order to define more carefully and to objectify subjective phenomena. This is reflected in the attempt noted among psychologists to develop instruments that supposedly will measure such phenomena as intelligence, attitudes, beliefs, values, self-interests, and memory and to view these entities as measurable characteristics of individuals being observed. Although each one of these attempts has its defenders and its critics, none of them provides a completely satisfactory solution which would enable sociology to move ahead as a strictly scientific enterprise. The distinction between objective and subjective reality is likely to be a false one for the sociologist. The problem is how to take account of it to assure validity, for it should be clear that those realities provide data that are a part of human experience. Data are not data because they can be observed through the five senses; they are data because they are part of the human experience, and as such can be described verbally and often in mathematical terms. For example, when a historian calls on a man's memory for a past event, he is using a subjective phenomenon as a datum, but as the man tells it to the historian, it becomes a datum for him, and he must still evaluate it and check on its reliability. But, as a datum it is also part of the new experience of the historian. Blumer saw this problem clearly when he described what he considered to be the dilemma of social research, which was not only the necessity of taking account of the subjective quality of social life in order to make any significant generalization about society, but also the inability to do so in a manner that would satisfy the canons of scientific procedure.[17]

As in the case of the other methodological issues that have been considered, the inability to resolve this issue in any final and definitive manner that is acceptable and valid to all sociologists naturally places a blight upon the dreams of those sociologists who would make of sociology a science on a par with the natural sciences. What happens, as in the other issues, is that individual sociologists make one type of intellectual commitment or another; namely, they take a position with respect to this issue, and this position governs the kind of sociology they develop and the kind of research they pursue.

Conflict of Orientation

While I have examined those methodological issues that must be resolved if sociology is to emerge as a natural science, I would note also that there is a conflict of orientation among sociologists as they go about their task of studying society in its varied and numerous aspects. This conflict of orientation can be described by asking if a sociologist is making his observations with an attitude that places him outside society or an attitude that places him inside of society. In the former instance he will attempt to make those observations that, when organized, will provide generalizations that will explain the structures, functions, and changes of a total society. Perhaps in demonstrating how a social order works he is hopeful that he will provide some substantive knowledge that will be useful in regulating and controlling social change. From this vantage point the sociologist is also in a position to examine critically and to question the myths upon which a given social order rests.

However, if the sociologist adopts the latter orientation, he is compelled to take a piecemeal view of his society, and thus his observations will be made on some limited aspect of or obstacle to the harmonious functioning of his society. Further, from this orientation he is less likely to examine the myths of his society but rather will tend to accept them.

In describing this conflict of orientation I am well aware that I have not touched on the several methodological issues involved. But, as in the case of the previous discussion of unresolved issues, I have only tried to indicate that each position points to the possibility of a different type of sociology. From the outside orientation the sociologist must face the question of

---

[17] Herbert Blumer, *An Appraisal of Thomas and Znaniecki's the Polish Peasant in Europe and America* (New York: Social Science Research Council, 1939).

whether he can make significant observations if he is not intimately involved in the society. And from the inside position he is constantly confronting the question, "Whose side are you on?...those who have the power or those who don't?...those who are top dogs or those who are underdogs?" Thus from both orientations not only is his capacity for objectivity challenged but also his ability to make significant observations of society that will provide the empirical basis for sociology to develop as a natural science.

These methodological issues and this conflict of orientation that I have examined in this paper are by no means the only philosophical problems which plague the sociological field. However, it is my contention that the failure to come to some valid resolution of them has stymied all the efforts that have been expended in the attempt to develop sociology as a natural science. This does not mean that sociology is destined to become an empty shell, but rather that it must develop methods of observation and analysis that are appropriate to its subject matter. When it does this, these particular methodological issues will cease to plague it. Rather, they will become problems in their own right for sociological investigation.

Thus, I return to the two questions that introduced this paper. With respect to the first question I think it is fair to say that the significance of this constant concern for methodology in sociology arises from the fact that these issues have not been resolved satisfactorily. The failure to resolve them restricts sociology in its attempt to become a science of the same type as a natural science. The second question, whether the commitment to this concern has advanced sociology as a scientific discipline, it seems to me must be answered in the negative, for here the assumption is present that a valid resolution of these issues would make it possible for sociology to develop as a natural science.

I would also call attention to a frequently overlooked matter with respect to various kinds of sociological research. While sociological research may not lead to or support a general theory, it does, with the accumulation of various kinds of researches in specific areas of social life, provide substantive information concerning numerous societal situations. These studies provide insight, understanding, qualified explanation, sophistication, and education about one's society that tends to increase our social and self-awareness about man in his relations to others and to the institutions of which he is a product. This is no mean accomplishment, and one might point out that today our knowledge about all social institutions is much greater than it has been in the past; our understanding will no doubt continue to grow from further accumulation of social research.

The problem as to whether sociology can become a science in the true sense of the word or must be content to remain a point of view and an approach to social life may not be an important issue, in the long run. What is important is that we should continue to add to our information and knowledge about the structure and function of societies throughout the world. Perhaps the man hours that have gone into an attempt to construct sociology as one of the natural sciences represents a certain kind of futility and loses sight of the main thrust of the sociological enterprise, which is to create for man a sophisticated awareness of the history, nature, and consequence of his involvement and identification with the social life of his times.

The whole concern over the scientific status of sociology may be irrelevant. Progress in the field does not depend upon its validation and acceptance as a natural science but rather depends upon the accumulation of specific, empirical studies in various areas of social life. Such research, *in toto,* will contribute to man's understanding of his place in society and will add to his social and cultural awareness concerning his relationships with his fellows and his role in the social system. But this is, of course, on the subjective and educational side. In addition such research, regardless of whether it supports, clarifies, or modifies theory, should and can provide substantive knowledge that should prove useful in coping with environmental obstacles and in formulating social policies that more satisfactorily balance the needs of man with those of his society. From this latter perspective it is the substantive aspect of research that becomes more important than the theoretical aspect, for it will be the substantive aspect of research that will prove useful in our social planning and in guiding social policies, irrespective of existing theory.

3

John Lofland

INTERACTIONIST IMAGERY
AND ANALYTIC INTERRUPTUS

What I want to say may first be said in summary. I am going to suggest that in many instances we interactionists have been too "hung up" on our general imagery and have not seriously gotten on to the main work that we have set for ourselves. As a result, at least one variety of interactionism is conceptually impoverished. One way in which this impoverishment might be corrected is for those of us who use an implicit paradigm of *strategic analysis* to stop engaging in what I shall call "analytic interruptus" and get on with the hard work.

Let me be clear that the friendly flagellation to follow is also self-flagellation. I feel free to throw stones because I live in an identical glass house.

Interactionist Imagery and Work

One orientation within the interactionist perspective is particularly enamored of what is seen as the moving, ever changing, processual, constructive character of social life. Herbert Blumer has perhaps been foremost in championing this imagery of ordered flux. Again and again, in a variety of contexts and on a variety of topics, he has pounded home the image and the vision.

> *Action is built up in coping with the world instead of merely being released from a preexisting psychological structure by factors playing upon that structure. By making indications to himself and by interpreting what he indicates, the human being has to forge or piece together a line of action*[1]
>
> *   ＊   ＊   ＊*
>
> *Under the perspective of symbolic interaction, social action is lodged in acting individuals who fit their respective lines of action to one another through a process of interpretation; group action is the collective action of such individuals.... Human society is to be seen as consisting of acting people, and the life of the society is to be seen as consisting of their actions.*[2]
>
> *   ＊   ＊   ＊*
>
> *A consciously directed and organized movement cannot be explained merely in terms of the psychological disposition or motivation of people, or in terms of the diffusion of an ideology. Explanations of this sort have a deceptive plausibility, but overlook the fact that* a movement has to be constructed *and has to carve out a career in what is practically always an opposed, resistant, or at least indifferent world.*[3]

And there have been large numbers of scholars who believe that he and others were correct in this emphasis. Inspired by the abstract and charismatic imagery sponsored by figures such as Blumer—along with his predecessors such as George Herbert Mead, William I. Thomas and Robert E. Park and his contemporaries such as Everett C. Hughes—the descendants have wanted to translate such imagery into more concrete accomplishments.

Such a mission of translation has moved in at least three directions

---

[1] Herbert Blumer, "Sociological Implications of the Thought of George Herbert Mead," *American Journal of Sociology,* LXXI (1966), 536.

[2] Herbert Blumer, "Society as Symbolic Interaction," in *Human Behavior and Social Process: An Interactionist Approach,* ed. Arnold Rose (Boston: Houghton Mifflin Company, 1962), p. 186.

[3] Herbert Blumer. "Collective Behavior," in *Review of Sociology,* ed. Joseph B. Gittler (New York: John Wiley & Sons, Inc., 1957), p. 147. Italics in the original.

that are of interest here. First, some descendants have been overwhelmed by the task and have taken to a doctrinaire reiteration of the masters' teachings, writing very little beyond a doctoral dissertation. Although rarely mentioned in print, the research and writing "hang-ups" of many imbued with the interactionist vision are well known in the oral tradition of sociology. Second, the mission of translation has resulted in a body of general books and essays which attempt to make slightly more specific the general imagery and to apply it loosely to more specific substantive topics. Contributors to this line of work have included, aside from Blumer and Hughes themselves, Anselm Strauss, Howard S. Becker, Alfred Lindesmith, Tamotsu Shibutani, Gregory Stone and even C. Wright Mills in his early social psychological phase.[4] In remaining quite general, such books and essays function to "put one on top" of a topic, but they have fallen short in the task of detailed translation. Third, there has emerged an affinity between descriptive case studies and interactionism. Indeed, the qualitative case study has become identified as *the* research method of that variety of interactionism that here concerns us. However, because the interactionist perspective has remained so abstract, the empirical case studies flowing out of it have often seemed little better than the kind of descriptions that can be produced by conscientious journalists or literate laymen.

Conceptual Poverty

In viewing this accumulated material, a peculiar feature begins to stand out, at least for me. That feature is the degree to which this material seems conceptually impoverished. It is characterized by (1) a general stance toward social life and (2) detailed descriptive information about this or that social location. But it seems sadly lacking in what one might call "mini-concepts" which are developed and treated with some care. There occur, certainly, encompassing conceptions such as "perspective," "negotiated social order," "impression management," and classic conceptions of the "act," the "self," "interaction," and the like, but there is very little attempt to develop limited and precise notions of microscopic social processes. It is instructive, indeed, to peruse what are currently perhaps the two leading texts of the tradition—Lindesmith and Strauss, and Shibutani—in terms of the proportion of sensitizing rhetoric they contain in relation to the number of carefully explicated and articulated concepts of social process that are

---

4 Cf. the interactionist anthologies by Arnold Rose, *op. cit.*; and Jerome G. Manis and Bernard N. Meltzer, eds., *Symbolic Interaction: A Reader in Social Psychology* (Boston: Allyn and Bacon, Inc., 1967).

conveyed.[5] (It is also instructive to contemplate how few distinctively interactionist textbooks have even been produced.) Recent anthologies of interactionist writings seem to display a similar problem of surplus sensitizing rhetoric as distinct from clear conceptual construction.

It is against this background of conceptual impoverishment that I think we can best understand two recent developments within interactionism. The first is the occurrence of, and attention to, the phenomenon that is Erving Goffman. I think that it is of more than casual interest to know that at least part of his intellectual development occurred in the context of the conceptually impoverished social psychological tradition at the University of Chicago in the late forties and early fifties. Goffman's subsequent emergence as the champion inventor of the mini-concept seems, at least in part, explicable as a response to the barrenness of the conceptual landscape of interactionist sociology. There is a sense in which Goffman has been to Chicago interactionism what Robert K. Merton was to Harvard functionialism. The latter made a loud call for "middle-range theory" in a similarly impoverished context, and propounded a few such theories. The former made hardly any call at all and propounded many "middle-range" concepts. Indeed, as one scholar has half-humorously commented, Goffman has more concepts than there are referents. On the consumer side, the attentiveness of interactionists to Goffman has, in part, to do with their lack of very much else to which to attend. Rather than having to make his way in the midst of intense competition among an outpuring of mini-concepts of an interactionist cast, Goffman has filled a virtual void.

A second development within interactionism that seems symptomatic of conceptual poverty is the occurrence of, and attention given to, the volume called *The Discovery of Grounded Theory* by Barney Glaser and Strauss.[6] Non-interactionists have tended to read this book as a license for subjectivism and a relinquishing of proper scientific procedure. Such a view seems to me not only to be erroneous but to miss what I take to be the more general and underlying thrust: a plea for the development of mini-concepts. The book is about procedures by means of which such concepts can be invented, or, as the authors put it, discovered. The procedure, called "constant comparative analysis," is the means by which they apparently hope the conceptual landscape of interactionism (and sociology more generally) can be made more lush. They attempt to provide us with something like a manual for the germination and care of concepts in our intellectual garden.

---

[5] Alfred R. Lindesmith and Anselm L. Strauss, *Social Psychology* (New York: Holt, Rinehart & Winston, Inc., 1968); Tamotsu Shibutani, *Society and Personality: An Interactionist Approach to Social Psychology* (Englewood Cliffs, N.J.: Prentice-Hall, Inc., 1961).

[6] Barney Glaser and Anselm Strauss, *The Discovery of Grounded Theory* (Chicago: Aldine Publishing Company, 1967).

They are, in a sense, agricultural extension agents bringing help to us interactionist farmers. The important point is that agricultural extension services—literal or methaphorical—get invented only because a need for them is felt. The need felt by Glaser and Strauss apparently arose in the context of a specific research project on dying. The *Discovery* volume is, rather incongruously, one of a four volume series, the other three of which deal with social aspects of dying.

This allegation of conceptual poverty might be taken as grounds for despair—as past defectors have so construed it—but I think there remain ample grounds for hope. It is not my intention here, however, to explore these in a general explication. I want now, rather, to narrow the focus quite drastically and to make some suggestions for the improvement of a single line of hopeful endeavor within the interactionist tradition.[7]

Strategic Analysis

In many interactionist case studies a simple but powerful paradigm of sorts has begun to crystallize. With varying degrees of explicitness, interactionists use an operating orientation toward their materials that seems to offer at least one way in which social life can be analyzed while (1) still being faithful to the general imagery we seek to sponsor and (2) also being more articulate in analysis by means of explicitly developed mini-concepts.

Attuned as interactionists are to social life as a *constructed* product of *active* humans, a number of similar terms and styles that refer to a single stance have begun to creep into their studies and essays. Terms that denote this stance have included the following: management, strategies, tactics, devices, mechanisms, maneuvers, strategems, practices. These terms are used vis à vis those aspects of social locations, more or less amenable to control, that are acted upon or toward by persons so as to effect some desired outcome. In other words, there is here a stripped down and modest version of game theory. However, it is a game theory that is not carried away by its internal logic into the mystic regions of hypothetical possibilities, but one that is attentive to the *in situ* details of social life. Following Schelling, such a modest and substantively oriented version might be called simply "strategic analysis."[8]

At least from the heyday of Park, there appears in interactionist

---

7 Among many hopeful lines of endeavor I will not here discuss, particular mention should be made of interactionist analyses of becoming, careers, and phase models of interaction.

8 Thomas C. Schelling, "Strategic Analysis and Social Problems," *Social Problems,* XII (1965), 367–79.

case studies a persistent concern with ways in which people *qua* interactants actually put together their lives. In the early twenties, observers such as Nels Anderson were already orienting themselves to an analysis of means of coping with social locations. Thus, in *The Hobo,* Anderson is partly concerned with "How The Hobo Meets His Problem" and " 'Getting by' in Hobohemia," the latter being a classification and description of "the various devices that are employed in accomplishing" more than a "coffee-an" level of living.[9] In the flowering of occupational case studies among Chicago interactionists in the fifties, there appears a repeated concern with ways in which that which is phenomenologically problematic is managed. So, for example, we find the janitor written about partly in terms of "the various means by which he 'trains' tenants..." and four "...method[s] of overt cutthroating" among janitors.[10]

More recently, such an orientation to ongoing strategic adaptation to, or management of, problematic circumstances has become a virtually rampant paradigm in interactionist case studies. Almost regardless of the overt and central themes, at the section and paragraph levels, a more or less explicit strategic analysis is the operating principle of organization. Here are a few examples.

Simmons, "On Maintaining Deviant Belief Systems": Five "processes or 'mechanisms' facilitate the maintenance of divergent beliefs: 1. Selective attention.... 2. Active structuring.... 3. [Confirming] interpretation. ... 4. Differential association.... 5. Ambivalence of the divergent larger culture...."[11]

Scott, The Racing Game: *"Whatever the order, the jockey must at least* appear *to be riding energetically and cleanly. To bring off these appearances the jockey has developed certain communication strategies—* dramatic accentuation *and* concealment *or a combination of both."*[12]

Dalton, Men Who Manage: *"Staff Counter Tactics." "Actual or probable rejection of their ideas provokes staff groups to (1) strengthen ties with top line; (2) adhere to the staff role, but 'lean over backward' to avoid troubles down the line that can reverberate to the top; and (3) compromise with the line below the top levels."*[13]

---

[9] Nels Anderson, *The Hobo* (Chicago: The University of Chicago Press, 1923), Part IV and Chap. iv.

[10] Raymond L. Gold, "In the Basement—The Apartment-Building Janitor," in *The Human Shape of Work,* ed. Peter L. Berger (New York: The Macmillan Company, Publishers, 1964), pp. 20–26, 34–36.

[11] J. L. Simmons, "On Maintaining Deviant Belief Systems," *Social Problems,* XI (1964) 250–56.

[12] Marvin B. Scott, *The Racing Game* (Chicago: Aldine Publishing Company, 1968), p. 43.

[13] Melville Dalton, *Men Who Manage* (New York: John Wiley & Sons, Inc., 1959), p. 101.

Bittner, "Police Discretion in Emergency Apprehension of Mentally Ill Persons": "In this paper we have tried to describe briefly certain practices of dealing with mentally ill persons." These include a set of "nonofficial ways of dealing with mentally ill persons" under the headings "restitution of control," "psychiatric first aid," and "continuing care."[14]

Roth, Timetables: Strategies used by patients to "move along faster through the hospital": have pressures applied by influentials outside the hospital; threaten to leave the hospital; threaten or undertake a "medication strike."[15]

Sudnow, Passing On: The morgue attendant's "...chief and daily problem was going about the hospital without, wherever he went, appearing to others to be working." His problem "...generally, [was] how to enter into any form of ordinary discourse without his affiliation with dead bodies intruding as a prominent way others attended to him." In response, "he attempted to convey a sense of not being at work by developnig clear styles...." "...one way...." "A general strategy...."[16]

Glaser and Strauss, Awareness of Dying: In order to sustain a closed awareness context, "...the staff members...use tactics intended to encourage the patient to make his own interpretations inaccurately optimistic."[17]

Becker, Geer and Hughes, Making the Grade: "In this chapter [number 6], we observe students as they go about the task of finding out what the rules are and where they stand with respect to them." "If the problems [of students] are similar..., students can develop a generalized set of actions...to which their own particular actions can be referred. It is this sort of individual action based on group perspectives that we discuss in the first section of this chapter [number 7]."[18]

Aside from case study efforts, the general frameworks spawned by interaction theorists such as Goffman have rested heavily upon a strategic imagery. *Presentation of Self in Everyway Life* is thus largely oriented to specifying the sources of discredited impressions and "common techniques that persons employ to sustain...impressions." His essay "On Cooling the

---

[14] Egon Bittner, "Police Discretion in Emergency Apprehension of Mentally Ill Persons," *Social Problems,* XIV (1967), 292, 285–90.

[15] Julius A. Roth, *Timetables: Structuring the Passage of Time in Hospital Treatment and Other Careers* (Indianapolis: The Bobbs-Merrill Company, Inc., 1963), pp. 48–54.

[16] David Sudnow, *Passing On: The Social Organization of Dying* (Englewood Cliffs, N.J.: Prentice-Hall, Inc., 1967), pp. 54ff.

[17] Barney G. Glaser and Anselm L. Strauss, *Awareness of Dying* (Chicago: Aldine Publishing Company, 1964), pp. 36ff.

[18] Howard S. Becker, Blanche Geer, and Everett C. Hughes, *Making the Grade: The Academic Side of College Life* (New York: John Wiley & Sons, Inc., 1968), pp. 80, 93.

Mark Out" seeks to specify six strategies for "cooling out" people who have failed, combined with four strategic responses possibly available to "marks" who refuse to be cooled. And *Stigma* is even subtitled "Notes on the Management of Spoiled Identity."[19] Other more or less general frameworks have likewise been so attuned, as in Glaser and Strauss' awareness paradigm where "the tactics of various interactants as they attempt to manage changes of awareness context" ranks as one of six major elements.[20] Weinstein's important essay is explicitly entitled, "Toward a Theory of Interpersonal Tactics."[21]

This kind of orientation appears to me to make a promising start toward the work of translating interactionist imagery, such as that promoted by Blumer, into an actuality in depicting and understanding the social order. An important source of conceptual impoverishment has resided, however, in the fact that although there are many studies with a strategic orientation, not many have proceeded to truly strategic analysis.

Analytic Interruptus

Interactionists of a strategic bent have been prone, rather, to what might be called "analytic interruptus." This label is intended to denote the practice of starting out to perform a certain task but failing to follow through to the implied, logical, or entailed conclusion. The label connotes the failure to reach an initially implied climax. Many of the studies cited above, and many others, suffer from analytic interruptus because they imply an analysis of mechanisms, devices, strategies, and the like but they neglect actually to do it. The presentations remain unsystematic, elusive, and simply suggestive of what given sets of such mechanisms, etc. might be as they have evolved in some concrete social location. In short, there is too frequently a failure to follow through. By actually following through I mean more specifically that the investigator goes to the time and trouble (1) to assemble self-consciously all his materials on how a given phenomenologically problematic topic is dealt with by the persons under study, (2) to tease out the variations among his assembled range of instance of strategies, (3) to classify them into an articulate set of what appear to him to be generic

---

[19] Erving Goffman, *The Presentation of Self in Everyday Life* (Garden City, New York: Doubleday & Company, Inc., 1959), p. 15; "On Cooling the Mark Out: Some Aspects of Adaptation to Failure," *Psychiatry,* XV (1952), 451–63; and *Stigma* (Englewood Cliffs, N.J.: Prentice-Hall, Inc., 1963).

[20] Barney G. Glaser and Anselm I. Strauss, "Awareness Contexts and Social Interaction," *American Sociological Review,* XXIX (1964), 671.

[21] Eugene A. Weinstein, "Toward a Theory of Interpersonal Tactics," in *Problems in Social Psychology,* eds. Carl W. Backman and Paul F. Secord (New York: McGraw-Hill Book Company, 1966), pp. 394–98.

or phenomenological types of strategies, and (4) to present them to the reader in some orderly and preferably named and numbered manner. The result of such careful work can be a set of mini-concepts relating to the construction of social life and social order. Such exercises would be, at minimum, articulate depictions of little rivulets of constancy in the flux of social life.

For a concrete sense of varying degrees of analytic interruptus, the reader may review the little capsule pieces of the eight studies given above, which are ranked, roughly, in terms of the degree to which analytic interruptus is present. (Let me be clear. This ranking is in terms of the degree of analytic interruptus indicated in the capsule only. No judgment of any study in its entirety or of the substantive merit or empirical viability of the content is intended.) Among them, the one by Becker, Geer and Hughes is of particular note. The emerging but implict paradigm of strategic analysis is apparently reaching the point where at least footnote reference must be made of the fact that investigators are not fully engaging in it.

> *It would be possible to study the kinds of actions students devise in response to particular problems of academic work, in the same way that one might, as we have already suggested, study the kind of information-seeking students devise in response to particuler faculty practices, using the model of a game of strategy. We have not undertaken such a detailed analysis and confine ourselves to the generalized set of actions, developed in response to the generalized problems the college creates for all students, of which the particular actions developed for particular circumstances are special cases.*[22]

As I said at the outset, I too live in a glass house and the same kinds of rocks can and should be thrown in my direction. Thus, in a work on a religious group, I blithely oriented the reader to a strategic analysis but throughout engaged merely a vague strategic orientation, constantly drawing back from the implications of the task set. Indeed, at one point I announced the intention to analyze "the devices adopted [by members] to manage [the] misinvolvement" of outsiders with the group, but then ignored the task altogether.[23]

Out of this discussion there arises, of course, the question of why there is a relatively high frequency of analytic interruptus. My own surmise about myself and others is a simple one. It is easier and takes less time to be vague than to be articulate. Strategic *analysis* prolongs the gap between research and publication. If it is possible to achieve a reasonable sense of

---

[22] Becker, Geer and Hughes, *op. cit.*, p. 93, footnote 1.

[23] John Lofland, *Doomsday Cult* (Englewood Cliffs, N.J.: Prentice-Hall, Inc., 1966), Chap. i and p. 143.

completion and to put the material in print without going very far, then there is a propensity to do so. Detailed analysis of qualitative material is tedious and difficult, and promises no sure result. Little patches of articulate statements of strategy and management may appear in studies, but a thoroughgoing pursuit of them throughout can appear a less than inviting task. And, too, the unsystematic materials assembled in qualitative studies may reveal, at the time of analysis, enormous gaps. It is easier to slough over such gaps by means of a random assortment of examples than to go back into the field with an eye to intensive observation on a topic that may constitute but a few pages in the published report.

Moreover, given the virtual lack of codified concepts to draw upon, strategic analysis requires from the analyst considerable effort at creative discernment. It requires that he pour over his materials with great intensity, very much on the model of procedure outlined by Glaser and Strauss. And it requires that he take the risk of inventing names for strategies, etc., opening himself to the charge of "needless jargon." Unfortunately, analytic interruptus is faster and easier.

In terms of the view taken here, however, it is also considerably less informative. Case studies of an analytic interruptus sort give us a "feel" for some sector of social life and they provide us with a "sense" of "what it is like." But we surely want more than feelings and senses, even though these qualities are not in themselves to be disparaged. We want in addition explicit—named, codified, documented—rendering of the little practices that make up that diffuse thing we call social life or interaction. It is to this task that we slovenly interactionists have barely begun to address ourselves, even though many of us have flirted with the possibility.

The Larger Vision

The admonition that interactionist case studies follow through on what they are already doing in a halfhearted way is, in effect, a request for a multitude of little lists of named strategies growing out of and attached to a likewise large number of case studies of particular social locations and situations. What can conceivably be accomplished through the creation of such a body of mini-concepts and empirical documentation? In longest and broadest terms one looks forward to a time when we will have carefully built back up to the large, abstract and magnificent imageries provided by people such as Blumer. The "building back up" can begin to occur when it is possible to engage in comparative analysis of interaction strategies as they evolve in various settings, being attuned to how the construction of superficially quite different social worlds can be, in terms of strategic con-stitution, quite similar. Thus, when we begin to see the possibility that strategies employed by Army Reserve enlisted men to avoid and decline the assignment of tasks by superiors have a resemblance to those used by children in avoiding or declining the assignment of tasks by parents, we begin to get on the track of generic features of social locations in terms of similarities and differences in their strategic constitution. We begin to get on the track of locating and codifying translocational interaction strategies and enter upon the task of discerning various *sets* of strategies vis à vis generically delineated features of types of social locations.

The strain toward such generic and comparative theories of strategic constitution is already manifest in works which proceed directly to construct such frameworks. The most conspicuous instance of this is, again, the work of Erving Goffman. He and others have proceeded, however, in the absence of a solid body of studies and concepts of the kind I here counsel. They have made up the conceptual substance as they have gone along, rather than being able to collate and carefully build upon a wide range of delimited analyses. In having to short circuit the process of theory building they create magnificent structures that lack solid foundations, deal with a narrow range of possible concerns, and likely strike very wide of the long term target. It is ironic and a bit sad that the same theorist who at one point tweaks other theorists for failure to treat sociological concepts "with affection," comes himself to participate in the same fate:

> I think that at present, if sociological concepts are to be treated with affection, each must be traced back to where it best applies, followed from there wherever it seems to lead, and pressed to disclose the rest of its family. Better, perhaps, different coats to clothe the children well than a single splendid tent in which they all shiver.[24]

By proceeding carefully and in small ways with affectionate concern for the development of mini-concepts in strategic analysis, it will hopefully become possible to have *both* splendid tents and well-clothed children.

---

[24] Erving Goffman, *Asylums: Essays on the Social Situation of Mental Patients and Other Inmates* (New York: Doubleday & Company Inc., 1961), p. xiv.

4

Anselm Strauss

DISCOVERING NEW THEORY
FROM PREVIOUS THEORY

Recommended by my undergraduate teacher Floyd House, I went eagerly to see Herbert Blumer in his office one hot September afternoon. It was one of the fateful encounters of my life. I found him in his shirt sleeves, feet resting easily on his desk, reading *Life* magazine (for data, no doubt!), and receptive to serious talk about serious issues in sociology. The conversation made of me, already partly won over by reading Dewey, a quick convert to sociological pragmatism. Before many weeks Blumer had won my admiration for his critical mind and tenacious grasp of truly relevant issues in social science. The paper below is addressed to one he raised on that same day—how to close the devastating gap between speculative theory and descriptive empiricism.

Perhaps most readers of this paper will be familiar with *The Discovery of Grounded Theory,* in which Barney Glaser and I discussed strategies designed to further the discovery and formulation of theory.[1] One strategy was the calculated use of theoretical sampling, a process of data collection which is controlled by emerging theory. (In theoretical sampling, the basic question is: What groups or subgroups does one turn to next in data collection? And for what theoretical purpose? Since possibilities of choice are infinite, choice is made according to theoretical criteria.)[2] We emphasized also the need for theory which is dense in conceptual detail, noting that much of sociological theory is thin—a collection of loosely integrated categories, none deeply developed. (As we remarked, "stable integration of the theory requires dense property development of at least some categories," and in thin theory it is "difficult to say which of the array are the core categories, that is, those most relevant for prediction and explanation.")[3] Because the *Discovery* book is spiced with an attack upon speculative theory, some readers have assumed we advocate abandoning all previous writing, whether theoretical or empirical, in favor of using only one's intelligence.

In this paper, I shall address two questions relevant to discovering and formulating effective theory when there is already extant grounded theory on which to build. We need not ignore the latter merely to show ourselves master of our own data or to parade our originality! First, how can we use previous theory to discover and formulate more extensive theory? Second, how can we render previous theory more dense, making certain that the final product is also well integrated? The key to both questions is a systematic use of theoretical sampling. This strategy eventually leads, if one goes far enough with the research, to verification and expansion of the theory through actual collection of data. (I shall not focus here on how to verify theory, although how this is done in connection with discovering theory should be clear enough.) I address the above questions because very little grounded theory, even when it is well integrated, is either extensive in scope or very dense in conceptual detail (at all levels of abstraction).

In his article on "Deviance Disavowal," Fred Davis has offered a useful, grounded theory about (as his subtitle reads) "The Management of Strained Interaction by the Visibly Handicapped."[4] Because this excellent paper is so widely known, there is no need to do more than highlight certain aspects of his carefully presented theory. By way of preface, I should note

---

[1] Barney Glaser and Anselm Strauss, *The Discovery of Grounded Theory* (Chicago: Aldine Publishing Company, 1967).

[2] *Ibid.,* Chapter 3.

[3] *Ibid.,* p. 71.

[4] Fred Davis, "Deviance Disavowal," *Social Problems,* IX (1961), 120–132.

that this presentation is exceptional because its author tells us exactly what his theory applies to, alerting us to what phenomena it does not apply and to matters over which it glosses. (Thus: "Because of the paper's focus on the visibly handicapped person...his interactional work is highlighted to the relative glossing over of that of the normal" person.) One of the most valuable features of this paper is that it stimulates us to think of variables which Davis does not discuss fully or omits entirely, including those quite outside of Davis' focus when he developed his theory. Indeed, when rereading the article I have often found myself aching to know more about all those untreated matters. The reader bears the responsibility to carry on this unfinished business, of course, if the author does not elect to do so.

Davis' theory is about (1) *strained* (2) *sociable interaction* (3) in *face-to-face* contact between (4) *two persons,* one of whom has a (5) *visible handicap* and the other of whom is (6) *normal* (no visible handicap). The theory includes propositions about tactics, especially those of the visibly handicapped person. But the central focus is upon *stages of management,* notably (a) fictional acceptance, (b) the facilitation of reciprocal role-taking around a normalized projection of self, and (c) the institutionalization in the relationship of a definition of self that is normal in its moral dimension. Emphasis on stages makes this a distinctly processual theory.

The italicized terms in the above sentences begin to suggest what is explicitly or implicitly omitted from Davis' theoretical formulation. The theory is concerned with the visibly (physically) handicapped, not with people whose handicaps are not immediately visible, if at all, to other interactants. The theory is concerned with interaction between two people (not with more than two), or with combinations of normal and handicapped persons (one interacting with two, two with one, two with two). The interaction occurs in situations termed "sociable"; that is, the relations between interactants are neither impersonal nor intimate. Sociable also means interaction prolonged enough to permit more than a fleeting exchange but no so prolonged that close familiarity ensues. Sociable interaction does not encompass ritualized interaction.

But the interaction is not merely sociable, it is face to face—not, for instance, carried out by telephone or through correspondence. This interaction represents the first meeting between the interactants, not a later meeting or one based on an interpersonal tradition. This meeting is only the first of a series of episodes that may lead to a more intimate relationship, and is so recognized by the handicapped person. Throughout this interaction the handicapped person attempts to minimize his handicap, rather than to highlight or to capitalize on it. The normal person also attempts to minimize the handicap, rather than favorably or unfavorably maximizing it. Also, control of the interaction is vested in the handicapped person, who has a willing accomplice in the normal. Moreover, the normal must agree to the game of normalization rather than resisting or being indifferent or even failing to recognize it. In addition, we should note especially that the interaction is strained—that is, the visible handicap tends to intrude into the interaction, posing a threat to sociability, tending to strain the framework of normative rules and assumptions in which sociability develops.

Visible handicaps which pose no particular threat to sociable interaction are not within the province of this theory. Also, because emphasis is on the handicapped person's management of interaction, the theory covers quite thoroughly the tactics and reactions of the handicapped, although it says relatively little about those of the normal. And finally, the theory pertains to a handicapped person who is already quite experienced in managing strained interaction with a normal—who by contrast is relatively inexperienced in interacting with handicapped persons. If we imagine a simple fourfold table, we can quickly supply three contrasting situations involving such experience.

This filling in of what has been left out of the extant theory is a useful first step toward extending its scope. We have supplemented the original theory. (Supplementation does *not* mean remedying defects of a theory.) Supplementation has led to the generation of additional categories, which in turn leads us—unless we cut short our endeavor—to think about those new categories. Thinking about those categories amounts to building hypotheses which involve them, quite as Davis built hypotheses around the categories generated from his data. We can think about those new categories, one at a time: for instance, the nonvisible handicap. We can do this much more efficiently, however, by comparing the new category with others, whether those are newly generated or inherited from Davis.

Imagine what happens in the first episode of face to face, sociable interaction when (1) a person with a relatively invisible (although potentially visible) handicap meets a normal person as against (2) when Davis' visibly handicapped meets a normal. The former situation is not too difficult to imagine, even if we have never been in that situation. Unlike the latter situation, one of its properties may be "secrecy," because the invisibly handicapped, if he is experienced, probably will be much concerned with keeping his handicap thoroughly hidden. If he is more experienced, he will probably be less anxious about betraying his secret. But immediately it must strike us that this person will indeed be experienced unless his handicap is of recent occurrence; as for instance, a woman recently operated on for mastectomy (cancer of the breast) who now appears in public with a breast prosthesis hidden beneath her dress.

By reaching out for this case as an example, we have begun (in imagination) to sample theoretically; we could, in fact, now either interview or seek existing data not only about such patients but about others who had newly acquired various nonvisible, but potentially visible, handicaps.

We can ask, what other kinds of persons (i.e., comparison groups) might those be? Clearly not included are persons who have just suffered strokes or irradicable facial burns or been through not entirely satisfactory facial operations after bad auto accidents. On the other hand, the other groups of nonvisibly handicapped persons whom we seek might include those born with stigmata which can be readily covered with clothes, and those with deforming arthritis of the shoulder which is not yet severe enough to show through clothing.

A moment's reflection about those comparison groups of handicapped —visibly or invisibly—tells us that we have generated additional categories. Possibly some may become core categories, among the many being built into our extension of Davis' original theory. Thus, there are invisible handicaps which have been present from birth, others which have been acquired whether recently or some time ago or long ago. There are some, whether visible or invisible, which never grow worse, and others which may grow much worse. Some may be temporary, disappearing over varying amounts of time. Some handicaps are seen by most people as stigmatizing, while other handicaps bring compassion or pity or indifference. They may also cause fear (leprosy) or revulsion (syphilitic noses).

If we pursue this analysis (resisting all temptation to shrug away the new categories, saying "oh that's all quite obvious"), we can eventually develop testable hypotheses about each class of handicapped person as these people interact in sociable or other situations with normal or other handicapped people. The hypotheses are designed not merely to illustrate what happens to this class of handicapped but to add density of conceptual detail to our evolving theory of interaction engaged in by handicapped persons generally.

Think again about women operated on for mastectomy, with their invisible defects. What is likely to be a dominant consideration for them in sociable interaction? Must they guard their secret because the loss of a breast is stigmatizing if it is known? Is the loss more likely to be a dread and guarded secret for unmarried young women than for young mothers? For young mothers than for elderly mothers? (We shall not even bother here with other obvious comparisons such as what happens in encounters with normal men versus normal women.) It should be easy enough to imagine the kinds of hypotheses that might be generated about each of those situations, including those involving tactics to keep secret the loss of a breast. For instance, we can hypothesize that a woman who has been operated on recently will be fantastically concerned with the selection and arrangement of her clothing and with her appearance when she leaves the house, and that she will pay close, if surreptitious, attention to her bosom during the ensuing sociable interactions. If we turn to the experienced women, who have worn their substitute breasts for many years, we can hypothesize that there will be less concern about betraying the secret—so that their social interactions are more like those between two normals. Under what conditions will anxiety, about accidental revelation, make the secret salient again for these more experienced women?

Our selection of secrecy as an important probable feature of the above interactions suggests that it is a core category, standing somewhat or exactly in the same relation to the nonvisibly handicapped as does "normalization" to the visibly handicapped. Using the terminology developed in *Awareness of Dying,* we may say that the nonvisibly handicapped attempt to keep the context "closed" while the visibly handicapped attempt—with the tacit cooperation of the normal—to maintain a context of "mutual pretense."[5] Secrets and the possibility of disclosure are characteristic properties of closed contexts, not to mention certain tacitly agreed upon matters characteristic of mutual pretense contexts. Note, however, that in our theoretical sampling we have built considerable variation into the probable management of secret handicaps, just as one might for the management of strained interaction by visibly handicapped persons under similar varied conditions.

At this point in his analysis, the theorist has various options. He can pursue further the case of the patient operated on for mastectomy, turning her around as if she were a complexly cut diamond and examining her many facets. The cues for that analysis have been adumbrated. How do these women act in various types of nonsociable interaction? How do they perform in the successive episodes of social interaction, rather than just in the first episode? What happens when women, each of whom has been operated on for mastectomy, meet each other in various kinds of interactional situations? What occurs in intimate interaction when the woman regards her striken bosom as ugly but her husband does not? Suppose she regards herself as victimized by fate, but he regards her with compassion? As the theorist answers these questions (in imagination or later with data), he builds hypotheses of varying scope and different degrees of abstraction, with his variables crosscutting again and again in his analysis. Thus he continues to build conceptual density into his theory and simultaneously to integrate it.

Instead of continuing to analyze the same comparison group (women operated on for mastectomy), the analyst has the option of examining other groups, especially those that will maximize the power of his comparative analysis because of the great differences among them. Suppose, for instance, he begins to think about the interactional situation in which Davis' visibly handicapped person is inexperienced while the normal person is exceedingly

---

5 Barney Glaser and Anselm Strauss, *Awareness of Dying* (Chicago: Aldine Publishing Company, 1965).

experienced in handling, say, stigmatized handicaps. Physical therapists are not only experienced—as professionals they are much involved in treating and giving "psychological support" to handicapped clients. We can now hypothesize, either from the professional's or the handicapped person's viewpoint, in sociable, nonprofessional encounters. We might even in imagination (and later, in fact) interview physical therapists about their reactions when they encounter different classes of handicapped. How do they react to those who have handicaps identical with or similar to those of their patients, as against those with dissimilar handicaps (the deaf, the astigmatic, the blind).

If the theorist wishes to build into his theory the phenomenon of handicapped patients interacting with professionals (normals), he can concentrate on comparisons of that type of interaction with the sociable type. His comparisons can include not only the case of the physical therapist managing his varied classes of handicapped clients (stroke, polio, arthritic, auto accident cases), but can include those comparisons with the professionalized interaction of physician and his mastectomy (and other physically handicapped) patients.

The theorist can, of course, decide to delimit his theory—indeed he must draw limits somewhere, restricting it even to as narrow a scope as sociable interaction. Then he will not focus on the nonsociable encounters (except secondarily, to stimulate his thinking about sociable encounters), but will focus steadily on comparisons that will yield him more and more hypotheses about this central phenomenon. Again, he will seek to make comparisons among groups that seem quite dissimilar and among those that seem relatively similar. In each comparison he will look for similarities as well as differences. These comparison groups will, as before, be suggested to him by his emerging theory. There is no end to the groups he will think of as long as his theory proves stimulating.

When does one stop this process, so fertile that it seems to have run riot? This issue was addressed in *The Discovery of Grounded Theory,* and I shall not repeat our discussion here. In brief, however, the directed collection of data through theoretical sampling leads eventually to a sense of closure. Core and subsidiary categories emerge. Through data collection there is a "saturation" of those categories. Hypotheses at varying levels of abstraction are developed (they embrace the categories). Those hypotheses are validated or qualified through directed collection of data. Additional categories and hypotheses which arise later in the research will be linked with the theory. If they are only "nice ideas" but link with the theory only distantly or not at all, they must be pruned away lest they distract from the main job of developing and publishing the theory.

Once we have developed this theory (whether or not we have jumped off from someone else's theory), there is no reason not to link other grounded theory with ours, providing this extant theory fits well and makes sense of our data. The one example given above was the linkage of "awareness theory" with our emergent theory. Useful linkages with other grounded theories may occur to other readers. In turn, our own theory is subject to extension, best done through theoretical sampling and the associated comparative analysis. This extension, perhaps it needs to be said, represents a specifying of the limits of our theory and thus a qualification of it.

Turning again to the main strategy illustrated by this paper, I wish to add three further points in conclusion. If we do not practice such modes of extending grounded theories, then we relegate them, as now, mainly to the status of respected little islands of knowledge, separated from others, each visited from time to time by inveterate footnoters, by assemblers of readings and of periodic bibliographical reviews, and by graduate students assigned to read the better literature. While the owners of these islands understandably are pleased to be visited, in time they will fall out of fashion and be bypassed. This is no way to build a cumulative body of theory. (We may even discover eventually that one bit of theory never really was theory, a discovery made about Robert Merton's famous anomie paper.) As the Merton example illustrates, another consequence of failing to delimit, extend, and diversify extant grounded theory is that sociologists continue to develop both speculative theory and general theoretical frameworks without recognizing the great difference between those formulations and theory which is genuinely grounded in data. However useful the former may be as rhetoric or for orientation, taken as theory they simply help to stall another generation in its discovery and formulation of testable theory. Speculative theory and theoretical frameworks have also turned away many of our generation from theorizing (because this is the only theory they recognize) in favor of publishing low-level description. Such description is a necessary sociological task, but it is comparable to the collection of specimens and the making of primitive classification by zoologists—a far cry from the creation of effective theory. Until we develop good methods for and the habit of building on extant theory—this paper represents one modest attempt—it will be easy to continue confusing excellent theoretical papers such as Davis' with others that are merely descriptive.

5

Nathan Keyfitz

EVALUATING PREDICTIONS IN SOCIAL SCIENCE: AN EXAMPLE FROM DEMOGRAPHY

Prediction has an insecure place in science. On the one hand the experimenter makes hypotheses, which are predictions, as to how an experiment will come out, each such hypothesis being tentative and its application confined to a specified class of situations. On the other hand, soothsayers and forecasters of all epochs have made predictions, acceptance of which most of us call superstition. Our feeling that the method of the soothsayer is wrong is so strong that we are not impressed by the instances in which the prophecy happened to be fulfilled. Our support of science is unshaken by any number of instances in which the scientific forecast failed. When the soothsayer is right we say he was lucky. When the scientist is wrong we say that some outside element intervened, and this may even be a happy circumstance, since the temporary error can be fruitful of further knowledge in discovering the outside element.

Closed Systems and Evaluations

What is it, then, in the method of science that retains our confidence even when the result is wrong, which distinguishes it from soothsaying that cannot interest us even by being right? Behind all scientific prediction is a theory, a rational model or mechanism, a representation of reality as a closed system containing symbolic elements that function in deterministic fashion. Constructing symbolic systems is a part of science; the other part is ascertaining their congruence with the real world. General systems analysis has increased our awareness of such models.

A laboratory facilitates arranging the closed systems known as experiments. Laboratory technique consists of protecting closure by whatever artificial means may be necessary; the bacteriologist wants his dishes and tubes to be clean. Louis Pasteur excluded the bacteria in the air by heating it for the control case to disprove the doctrine of spontaneous generation.[1]

Laboratory experiments are not the only way of securing effective closure of a system. Sciences unable to do experiments, including astronomy and demography, select the elements for their systems out of nature and attempt to obtain closure within selected sets of data. For example, certain moving lights in the sky are assembled into the solar system.

The other feature of prediction in science is the central place of evaluation. Prediction as such has little interest; what makes it interesting is comparison with the actual event. Unambiguousness in the initial statement is desired, so that one may be able to tell after the event whether it accorded with the prediction. Skill of the kind exercised by the Delphic oracle, whereby an apparently specific statement contained enough ambiguity to be consistent with various outcomes, is not highly prized in science. When the prediction specified exactly in advance is later compared with the event, then agreement or disagreement can feed back to reinforce or modify the theory on which the prediction was based. Prior to its evaluation the prediction is not part of science.

Predictions of Population Growth

The question of prediction has been especially acute in the study of human populations. Here is a discipline in which time's arrow points

---

[1] W. C. Dampier and M. Dampier, *Readings in the Literature of Science* (New York: Harper & Row, Publishers, 1959), p. 217.

sharply and moves rapidly. During the two or three centuries in which we are located the successive billions of mankind have been arriving more and more rapidly. Once forested areas of countryside in Europe and Asia have been intensively exploited to maintain massive populations. Continuance of present trends will mean exhaustion of resources, increasing disparity of living standards, and political tensions across national, regional, and racial boundaries. With higher densities will come changes in the value system; individual human lives can hardly continue to seem precious when we stand elbow to elbow. Widespread concern has been provoked by the population issue, repeatedly described as second in ominousness only to the nuclear arsenal. Just what numbers will be attained in the next century is important to everyone; this is patently a public matter, not private like most laboratory experiments which—happily for the independence of scientists—seem trivial to those outside the discipline concerned.

Since its inception the study of population has been concerned with the concrete future. H. Dorn, J. Hajnal, and J. S. Davis review many examples of this orientation of demographers.[2] Not only professional demographers, but a biologist like P. B. Medawar and a sociologist like Daniel Bell, think first of population when they start to talk about prediction.[3] Demography shares with few other disciplines so direct an orientation to what lies ahead in the continuum known since the advent of computers as real time.

It was exactly the prediction of matters of public concern in real time that was the field of soothsaying. The question for demography is how to deal with the future by scientific methods, to which theory and evaluation are central.

Past Successes and Failures in Forecasting

The record of population prediction is not encouraging. To develop a criterion by which we can judge the success of a forecast will be the main interest of this paper. But no subtle analysis is required for an estimate, published by Francis Bonynge in 1852, of 703 million for the United States in the year 2000.[4] Yet Bonynge's forecasts fell within about 3 per cent for

---

2 H. Dorn, "Pitfalls in Population Forecasts and Projections," *Journal of the American Statistical Association,* XLV (1950), 311–34; J. Hajnal, "The Prospects for Population Forecasts," *Journal of the American Statistical Association,* L (1955), 309–322; and J. S. Davis, *The Population Upsurge in the United States,* War-Peace Pamphlets, No. 12, Food Research Institute (Stanford: Stanford University Press, 1949).

3 P. B. Medawar, *The Future of Man* (New York: Mentor Books, 1959), p. 18; and Daniel Bell, "Twelve Modes of Prediction," in *Penguin Survey of the Social Sciences 1965,* ed. J. Gould (Baltimore: Penguin Books, Inc., 1965), p. 101.

4 Dorn, *op. cit.,* p. 316.

the five subsequent censuses through 1900, an accuracy of prediction over fifty years that later students have not equaled. He met at least one of the criteria of science: having a model. His model was the geometric progression, which did happen to apply to the United States for the half century after he made his statement but evidently has not applied since about 1900.

Other demographers were more immediately confounded by events. The distinguished Enid Charles wrote a book entitled *The Twilight of Parenthood,* published only a year or two before the birth rates of western countries started turning upward after a half century of decline.[5] Warren S. Thompson, who was sure that the direct and indirect effects of World War II would be to check population, made his statement on the eve of the baby boom.[6]

We would like to be able to say at least that wrong methods produce wrong results. But this is not so for Bonynge's successful use of the geometric progression, nor for the logistic curve of Raymond Pearl and L. J. Reed.[7] The latter, generally considered now to be based on a wrong principle, did not produce results which compared with the future less closely than the components method which superseded it. The components method using period cross sections is now in its turn superseded by cohorts, on whose use we do not yet have enough experience to make a statement.

It would, moreover, be nice to be able to say of a given method that with experience it comes to be more effectively used, so that predictions based on it become better and better. But the components method seems to have given its best results in its very first application, that by E. Cannan in 1895. Comparison of Cannan's predictions with subsequent performance for England and Wales is summarized in Table 1. Cannan finds a maximum of 37,376,000 by 1995, so his results beyond 1941 are low. (Those up to 1941 I have read from the chart in his article).[8]

May we not at least say that short-term forecasts are safer than long-term ones? Even this innocent assertion is not verified by past experience. Some estimates were contradicted by the census immediately following, but a later census agreed with them. Cannan's estimate was better for 1941 than it was for 1911. For Pearl and Reed's logistic the census first agreed in 1930, fell below in 1940, then agreed again in 1950. Far from being able to say that short-term estimates are correct and long-term ones wrong, we

---

5 Enid Charles, *The Twilight of Parenthood* (New York: W. W. Norton & Company, Inc., 1934).

6 Warren S. Thompson, *Plenty of People: The World's Population Pressures, Problems and Policies and How They Concern Us* (New York: Ronald Press Co., 1948).

7 Raymond Pearl, and L. J. Reed, "On the Rate of Growth of the Population of the United States Since 1790 and Its Mathematical Representation," *Proceedings, National Academy of Science,* VI (1920), 275–88.

8 E. Cannan, "The Probability of a Cessation of the Growth of Population in England and Wales During the Next Century," *Economic Journal,* V (1895), 505–515.

TABLE 1

POPULATION OF ENGLAND AND WALES,
AS PREDICTED BY CANNAN AND AS COUNTED IN SUBSEQUENT CENSUSES

Year	Cannan 1895	Census count
1891	29,091,000	29,091,000
1901	31,600,000	32,600,000
1911	33,600,000	36,100,000
1921	35,800,000	37,900,000
1931	36,500,000	40,000,000
1941	37,000,000	38,700,000

can almost say the opposite: An estimate may disagree with the performance at first, but sooner or later the line of estimation and the line of performance will cross. (This fails to apply principally where the predictor was unfortunate enough to specify an upper limit to population that is now bypassed.)

Timelessness of the Model

The model implicit in the successful predictions of Cannan is a simple one, consisting of the single proposition that the birth rate is falling in accord with the trend apparent in 1895. But the simplicity of a model is no objection to it. What is an objection is its time-dependent character. The model of the falling birth rate is useful for prediction as long as the birth rate continues to fall, and beyond that it will fail, as in fact happened. This suggests that the chief requirement of a model is not that it be simple or complex, commonsense or recondite, but that it be relatively timeless. Timelessness of the model permits cumulation of relevant observations. To the degree that the model continues to be applicable over time, and therefore used and subjected to modification and improvement on comparison of its predictions with the actuality, the science that uses it will be cumulative. The falling birth rate of Europe and America is now seen to be an historically bounded event that occurred mostly in the fifty years ending in 1935.

Evaluation of Population Forecasts

This paper does not pretend to help make better predictions. If anything it adds a whole new dimension to the difficulties. It deals with the problem of evaluating a prediction, after the time of the prediction has come around, and finds even this by no means easy.

A population prediction has the merit of being completely specified—it states the number of breathing human beings expected to be found in a certain area at a certain moment. A census taken at that moment counts the number of breathing human beings.

Using data up to 1957, the Organization for European Economic Cooperation, on the basis of a questionnaire filled in by member countries, asked a group headed by Louis Henry to estimate future populations.[9] The group predicted for January 1, 1966 (after my adjustment of 1,000,000 for Alaska and Hawaii, omitted in the publication) 196.0 million, against the estimate of the Bureau of the Census after the event, an estimate which we can take as the equivalent of a census, of 195.8 million.

Such virtual coincidence is rare enough that we can neglect it. To confine evaluation to those cases in which a discrepancy appears between prediction and performance does not exclude many instances. We will assume that a discrepancy occurs, and our problem will be to decide whether it is large or small.

One mode of evaluation is to compare two simultaneous predictions with the subsequent performance and say which was closer. But this is straightforward only when the two predictions concern the same event and were both made at the same time. Very few such pairs appear in the record.

A more typical comparison involves different time intervals. In 1931, the Scripps Foundation calculated a 1960 population for the United States of 144 million.[10] In 1949, the Bureau of the Census calculated 160 million for 1960.[11] The count for 1960 was 179 million. The Bureau of the Census calculation was considerably closer to the count, but it was made only eleven years ahead, while the Scripps estimate was made twenty-nine years ahead. The simplest form of the question I am asking is whether an error of 35 million made twenty-nine years before the census beats an error of 19 million made eleven years before the date. (That P. K. Whelpton was the moving spirit of both estimates does not affect my illustration.)

Some might answer that ignorance of the future is homogeneous, and therefore we should consider the cumulative error per year—that is, take 35/29 against 19/11. Aside from its absurdity even in a given country, this will not serve for comparison of predictions across countries. A forecast for England and Wales would be easier to make than one for the United States if fluctuations in the birth rate of the United States have been larger.

If method A and method B are used in the year X to estimate the

9 Organization for European Economic Co-operation, *Demographic Trends, 1956–1976, in Western Europe and in the United States* (Paris: OEEC, 1961), p. 22.

10 P. K. Whelpton, "The Future Growth of the Population of the United States," in *Problems of Population*, ed. G. H. L. F. Pitt-Rivers (London: A. Allen & Unwin, 1932), pp. 77–86.

11 U. S. Bureau of the Census. Series P-25, No. 18 (February, 1949).

population in the year Y, then the census of the year Y allows an immediate comparison of the forecasts. The problem was as difficult for the one as for the other because it was the same problem. We are interested in a more general comparison involving different countries and different time intervals, partly because this will throw some light on the nature of evaluation and indeed on the nature of prediction itself. We can always find whether runner A or runner B can do 100 yards faster if they are matched on the same track. To determine who can run 100 yards faster when they perform in different countries, we need instruments—specifically a measuring tape and a stop watch. Evaluation of runners by such instruments is familiar practice. Our question is whether corresponding instruments are available for evaluating demographic methods.

These issues may be illustrated with the weather. If we want to determine the success of a weather predicting operation, we cannot simply note what proportion of the times rain was forecast for the following day and it actually rained, or shine was forecast and it actually shone. In central Australia one could be 99 per cent correct without this testifying to much skill. On the eastern seaboard of the United States, on the other hand, 99 per cent correctness on the day-ahead forecast for rain or shine is beyond present human skill and knowledge. How can we compare the quality of forecasting in the two situations?

The answer is some kind of *benchmark*. If we can specify a method of forecasting that requires no skill, no instruments, and no expenditure, then superiority in relation to this might provide the desired comparison. Such a method is persistence, which is to say using the rule "Tomorrow will be like today." If a professional does not do better than this, the expense of his training and of gathering observations is wasted.[12]

Benchmarks for Population Estimates

For the analogous point in respect of population, consider another calculation of the 1960 United States total, made by Whelpton in 1935.[13] His estimates ranged from 137 to 159 million, and the central one among them was 149 million; Whelpton elaborated it in some detail. Let us try to evaluate this statement as though it had been a forecast. When 1960 came around the census counted 179,323,000. Can we say that 149 million is $149/179 = 0.83$ or 83 per cent of the true number and call this Whelpton's score? (In fairness, let it be said that Whelpton might not have cared for the game in which the present illustration enters him.)

---

12 F. Mosteller, et al., *The Pre-election Polls of 1948* (New York: Social Science Research Council, 1949).

13 P. K. Whelpton, "An Empirical Method of Calculating Future Population," *Journal of the American Statistical Association*, XXXI (1936), 457–73.

The purpose of assigning a score is to compare what Whelpton did on this occasion with what he or someone else did on another occasion. The most ignorant person forecasting 1960 population in 1955 or 1959 could do better than the most skilled demographer of the time did in 1935. It must be relevant that Whelpton's projection was made fully twenty-five years ahead of the date referred to.

One way of taking this into account is to say that the subject of the projection is not the 1960 population but rather the increase of population up to 1960. Since the 1935 population was about 127 million, the true increase was 52 million, and of this Whelpton estimated 22 million, or 42 per cent. Evidently the device of treating the estimate as one of increase rather than of absolute numbers helps towards putting on the same footing estimates over different time spans and in different countries.

But of two countries, one may have a very steady increase and the other may be quite erratic. On this test the man predicting in the country of steady increase would have an advantage. Pressing the above argument one step further handicaps suitably the predictor in the country of steady increase. We now take as the base or benchmark of the calculation not the total increase of 1960 over 1935 but the excess of 1960 over the projection from 1935 on 1935 age-specific birth and death rates and zero migration. This projection, as it happens, would give 141 million for the United States in 1960. The census figure of 179 million was in excess over this by 38 million. Of the 38 million we can say that Whelpton's calculation took in 149 minus 141 or eight million. His score on this benchmark would be 8/38 million or 21 per cent. (This measure would have to be modified if the prediction and the benchmark were on opposite sides of what turned out to be the true or census figure, though that difficulty is less fundamental. Moreover, the argument applies strictly not to one such calculation but to the average of a large number.)

Is an Objective Choice of Benchmark Possible?

We have now used three benchmarks for assessing the 1935 estimate of 1960: zero, the 1935 population, and the 1935 population projected to 1960 at 1935 birth and death rates. Each succeeding benchmark is a more realistic estimate of 1960 than the one before, and hence shows Whelpton's prediction in a poorer light. The scores were 83 per cent, 42 per cent, and 21 per cent. Where can we stop in the series of improvements in the benchmark and claim that the benchmark is in some sense the level of zero information?

Such a decision requires a judgment as to what we could reasonably expect the predictor to include within the range of *his* knowledge. Everyone knew that the United States population was about 127 million in 1935, and the birth and death statistics of the time were also readily available. Could one not expect a predictor in 1935 to work from the 1935 age-specific birth and death rates, and to make adjustments to these? But if we go that far, should we not take into account migration, and so make the benchmark more realistic and the assessment of the 1960 projection more severe yet?

No wholly objective answer to this question appears to exist. One can only say that Whelpton's expertness in choosing assumptions would be measured by setting his calculation for 1960 against some calculation that might have corresponded to the commonsense of 1935. Any evaluation seems to require us to put ourselves in the shoes of the predictor, and to exercise judgment from our superior position (superior only because later in time) about what he should have known.

The Benchmark for the United States

We have calculated the projections of the United States population to future periods from each point of time (1920, 1925, . . . , 1950), with the age-specific birth and death rates of that time, disregarding migration. The evaluation based on the work of those demographers who made judgments on the future can be summarized in the statement that, of the thirty forecasts that were compared with subsequent performance, some nineteen were closer than the benchmark, and eleven were in greater error. The nineteen to eleven score supports the view that the assumptions made by the demographer were on the whole superior to the benchmark that supposed fixed rates. More extensive evaluation of past efforts would seem useful to those making statements about the future. It would have the effect of inducing a seemly modesty without being as damning as was J. S. Davis, who rejected predictions out of hand on the ground that their results differed widely from the performance.[14]

A question still stands nonetheless. During much of the past century birth rates in Europe and America were falling. While this was so, the predictor could make relatively easy gains on the benchmark we have been using here. For the remainder of this century such easy improvements on our benchmark appear unlikely. The prospect could well be for simple ups and downs of births, with no fixed periodicity and no net trend, circumstances under which improvement on the benchmark is not simple.

Should we not admit that epochs may come in which no applicable theory provides reliable statements about the direction of future movements of births (or even deaths)? If we are in one such epoch now, then present birth and death rates (or else an average over the previous cycle) are the

---

14 Davis, *op. cit.*

best indication of the future. In such an epoch our benchmark (or a suitable modification of it expressed in cohort terms) becomes as good a prediction as can be made.

Other Methods of Evaluation

In presenting the benchmark method in some detail I do not pretend that it is the only one possible. Three other types of evaluation suggest themselves.

(1) A Probability Approach

By analogy to the use of probability in statistics, we could ask the predictor to provide us with a range rather than a single estimate and ask him also the probability with which he thinks his range will straddle the performance. We could perform a statistical test on a collection of such predictions. Past predictions often satisfy the first of these requirements— a range rather than a single figure—but the range is rarely accompanied by a probability. We note that the Whelpton calculation of 149 million in 1935 for 1960 was the middle one of calculations ranging from 137 to 159 million. Did Whelpton think that the probability of his upper and lower estimates straddling the 1960 census was 0.5, 0.95, or some other fraction? It would be gratuitous for us to go back after the event and impute a probability that the range would cover the performance. This approach then must be dropped for want of data, at least for past predictions, though future predictors might be urged to set probabilities on their ranges.

(2) Consistency

Evaluation may be easier when the forecaster estimates a whole scenario rather than a single parameter. We can then, without even waiting for the event, comment on the consistency of his scenario with itself, and can compare it with alternative scenarios. After the event we can tick off the points in which it agreed with the performance, of which population numbers would be one of many items. We could set up a system for scoring based on the proportion of points on which it agreed within a specified margin.

Consistency is no small virtue in many applications. A telephone company makes a plan, based on estimated future population, income, development of alternative means of communication, and other elements. Whether the scenario that it constructs corresponds to subsequent reality or not, it imposes consistency among various company activities: The manufacturing of hand instruments, the setting up of central office facilities, the construction of lines within and between cities—all will be coordinated by the agreed-on prediction. If the scenario turns out to be conservative these will all be low, but at least the company avoids the production of handsets for which central office facilities are unavailable.

(3) Relation to Use

In the real world predictions serve practical purposes, and for these purposes certain levels of accuracy are required. Not many practical uses of a forecast of the year 2000 would be jeopardized by an error of one per cent, or even five per cent. But an error of 50 per cent seems too much. Somewhere between five per cent and 50 per cent is presumably a point beyond which the error makes the forecast misleading or useless. Study of uses of forecasts could in principle show us which were wrong enough to do harm. And we might aspire to a statement that professional demographic forecasts have or have not been on the whole helpful for the purposes to which they were put. The difficulty is that population estimates are only one ingredient in the success of a government policy or a business operation. If a telephone company were to go bankrupt this could be due to errors other than its poor population forecasts. Though judgment in making forecasts is indeed an ingredient of market success, no one can disentangle it from other ingredients. That such predicting could ever be the main locus of interfirm competition is unlikely.

None of these approaches is as easily applied as the zero-information benchmark.

A Paradox

Science requires objectivity. No two words seem more opposed than "scientific" and "subjective." In arguing the importance of evaluation of predictions, if they are to be part of science, we suppose the evaluation itself to be objective. Yet the method of evaluation for which I have argued explicitly contains subjective elements; no one can say just how to construct a benchmark by which we can compare two predictions over different time periods or places. After searching for value-free evaluation I conclude that the subjective element is unavoidable, and the problem is to choose a method which makes it small.

Conclusion

The insecure place of prediction in science has been recognized and even overemphasized by sociologists. But in very recent years, perhaps pushed by natural scientists (who in turn may have been pushed by science fiction), sociologists have given thought to possible futures. Articles in

Bertrand de Jouvenel's *Futuribles,* and in an issue of *Daedalus* devoted to the year 2000, are signs of the times, as were Wilbert Moore's presidential address and a surprisingly long bibliography provided by H. Winthrop.[15] Richard L. Meier gives a serious course on the future in the School of Environmental Design at Berkeley. For me to interpret Whelpton's work as prediction is not as offensive as it would have been a few years ago.

I dedicate these remarks to Herbert Blumer because it was his lectures of thirty or so years ago that set me to worrying about prediction. In a time when social scientists sometimes gathered facts without being aware that they were guided by models, and when they even denied that models were necessary to scientific activity, Blumer incisively disentangled the logic implicit in their work. He was never taken in by the assertion that the scholar can observe society unprejudiced by theory. When theory was admitted it often was an importation from other fields and not necessarily appropriate to sociology. Blumer's wide knowledge made him sensitive to incongruities between the social phenomenon and a theory imported from physics or physiology.

Since that time, Thomas Kuhn and others have shown the pivotal role of models in scientific activity.[16] Could one say that scholars are likely to be unaware of the models they implicitly are following, when these are operating satisfactorily and therefore unchangingly over a period, to such an extent that they deny having a model at all, and that they first realize the importance of theory when their implicit models fail? Certainly in demography a crisis was brought on in the 1940s when people noted how inadequate population forecasts were getting to be. The crisis stimulated rethinking of underlying mechanisms, and a part of the response to it was the viewing of populations in terms of their constituent cohorts rather than in period cross sections.

The testing of models by their effectiveness in prediction suffers from the ambiguities noted at the beginning of this essay. Such tests may be too easy, in that the conformity of the performance with the prediction may be fortuituous due to a combination of offsetting errors. When apparently successful prediction leads to acceptance of a poor model, science receives a setback and suffers real damage. At least during the past quarter century demography has not been damaged by excessive accuracy of its predictions.

Most often the test of prediction is too severe. A concrete outcome, for example the birth rate of the year 1980, depends not only on the variables

---

15 Daniel Bell, "The Year 2000—The Trajectory of an Idea," *Daedalus,* Summer 1967, pp. 639–51; Wilbert Moore, "The Utility of Utopias," *American Sociological Review,* XXXI (1966), 765–72; and H. Winthrop, "The Sociologist and the Study of the Future," *The American Sociologist,* III (1968), 136–45.
16 Thomas Kuhn, *The Structure of Scientific Revolutions* (Chicago: University of Chicago Press, 1962).

isolated and dealt with in demographic theory, but also on variables in the political, economic, technological, social psychological, and other spheres. The ingression of these in real life is not inhibited by physical isolation such as experimenters manage. Impressed with the difficulties of predicting what will actually happen, demographers prefer to make at most conditional statements about the future, abstracting from changes in spheres outside their discipline. Evaluations of past predictions compel a respectfully modest attitude toward the future.

Briefly, when a current model is proving unsatisfactory and predictions fail conspicuously, one is forced to the degree of self-consciousness that Blumer was propagating. In many fields of social science, today seems such a time. If the necessity of models and of evaluation is now commonplace, this is a sign that social science is catching up with Blumer.[17]

[17] This research was supported by N.S.F. grant GZ995, by N.I.H. research contract 69–2200, and by teaching grants to the Department of Demography, University of California, Berkeley, from the National Center for Health Services Research and Development (8 T01 HS00059) and the Ford Foundation.

II

COLLECTIVE BEHAVIOR

6

Orrin E. Klapp

STYLE REBELLION AND IDENTITY CRISIS

Visiting Russia recently, I was interested to see a band of hippies—about ten long-haired, beard-wearing, unkempt young men and women—marching down the Moscow subway, strumming guitars, and singing "Flower Power Will Overcome." It was a jolly good tune and smart tempo. They seemed American and English. The Russians were amused and did not bother them. I asked a Russian if the USSR had any hippies of it's own. He said, "We had one, but they made him cut his hair." The wave had hit Russia, but it wasn't breaking very high.

Something odd is going on in the world—a rebellion which doesn't fit into the usual categories of political protest. There is a wide range of upheaval in styles of clothing, art, music, tastes, morals, and ways of living. Strange slogans like "flower power" and "turn on, tune in, drop out" don't really explain what people are doing; the slogans are as puzzling as the behavior itself. We should not, however, think only of hippies. There is a panorama of rebellion in style in all classes and most of the arts.

We see examples in the mod fashions of Carnaby Street; mini-skirts, mini-miniskirts, and nuns wearing minihabits; bikinis, nokinis, topless and peekaboo dresses; Castro-style beards on university students; fezzes, Moslem and tribal African garb on American Negroes; and black leather jackets, chains, knives, swastikas, and death's head insignia on boys riding motorcycles.

In entertainment, too, something odd is happening: beat music, loud, strident catawalling, shocking in themes and lyrics, shattering the ears and producing deafness in some. Folksingers like Joan Baez and Bob Dylan are not celebrating the days of "Tom Dooley" nostalgically. They are bitterly protesting what's happening now. A Broadway play *Hair* features nude people cavorting while facing the audience.

Art is producing incomprehensible products, neither meaningful nor pretty: op and pop styles; put ons like Robert Rauschenberg's famous goat—stuffed, with an automobile tire about its middle; underground movies on such interesting subjects as a patch of human skin; multimedia happenings such as men breaking up an automobile with axes. Everybody seems to be trying to be more sensational or incomprehensible, to shock and outshock, in escalation.

In the midst of this seeming pandemonium Bob Dylan plunks on his guitar and sings, "Something is happening, and you don't know what it is, do you, Mr. Jones?" Who is Mr. Jones? He is ordinary like you and me—the conventional person who works regular hours, dresses conserva-tively, doesn't spend his nights attending love-ins, be-ins, and happenings, and thinks a cigarette is something that gives you only lung cancer, not a trip to self-realization. Dylan implies there is a secret of some kind that Jones doesn't understand because he's square, straight—that is, accepts things as they are. Perhaps Dylan is right. We should examine this odd behavior carefully to see if it is saying anything to us.

It used to be that when a person disarranged his costume, let himself go, became dirty and unkempt, and made strange noises, he was locked up. Now he is a style leader or creative artist. The difference is that what would formerly have been regarded as sheer insanity is now being imitated widely and has authority for some. Why is this so? It seems to me that it is because more people now feel an urgent need for self-expression; so it is recognized as legitimate to "let go." A romantic right is growing to express oneself as one pleases.

With this new romanticism, we seem to be entering a new era, not just of science, technology and material progress, but of enlarged awareness, delighted acceptance and search for new experiences, seeing things and one-self in new ways by travel, scientific discovery, moon shots and undersea exploration, art, religion, sensitivity training, psychotherapy, and mind ex-pansion, even by drugs like LSD.

The most startling aspect of this search is style rebellion in the ways people dress and live. That rebellion is more than a mere expression of taste in new and creative ways. It is protest which opposes a style with a different style that attacks, rebukes, shocks—puts down—prevailing standards. It is aggressive; it makes people angry; it has a flaunting, flouting, defiant quality. It is not simply aesthetic; indeed, it may be shock-ingly ugly and in bad taste. Its shock value contrasts with smooth fashion in which good taste reflects conformity. Rudi Gernreich, the fashion designer, gives the secret away: "Clothes are not status symbols any longer. . . . Style today is a kind of flaunting of one's personality."

Style rebellion is essentially an attack not on style itself but on the underlying values of the status quo—middle class morality, the hard work ethic, the success image, and conventional religion. We can see this attack in hippie style. Their uncouthness offends middle class cleanliness and respectability. Their scrounging, carefree existence as free riders and parasites offends the belief that it is good to work hard for one's own living (an idea which kept their forefathers going). Flower power is a flippant rebuke to militarism and the authority of state. Free love is a threat to the monogamous ideal and parental responsibility. The use of drugs seems an unpardonable, selfish, sensual indulgence, threatening morality and perhaps the entire work structure of productive society. Finally, their hair is unkempt, dirty, long in males, indistinguishable from that of females. As much trouble today seems to be caused by hair as by politics and ideology. For some reason people get excited about too much or too little hair, hair in the wrong places, hair curled or straightened, dyed or natural. Psychologists and anthropolo-gists say hair is a sexual symbol; maybe that is why people get excited. Except on priests, long hair on males seems to be regarded as an attack on masculinity.

However, besides the attack on prevailing values, another feature of style rebellion should be noted. I call it ego screaming—behavior which says "look at me," "please pay attention to me." This shows the need for recognition. It indicates that such people feel ego deprivation, which is a significant symptom of modern times.

From this we can see that more is going on in fashion these days than the usual demand of people for something a little newer and better. Style rebellion is a protest of serious dimensions, not just a normal expression of freedom. It is a sign, I think, of social malaise. Something is wrong that people don't like and want changed. What, then, is wrong? What is the protest about?

When we ask what is wrong with the world, naturally we start looking for injustices, and we have no trouble finding them all over the world—displaced Arabs, starved Biafrans, suppressed Czechoslovakians, cheated sharecroppers, and crowded ghetto dwellers everywhere. But oddly this is not where style rebellion and protest are found. Style rebellion is characteristic of rather prosperous people, who enjoy freedom and have money for many indulgences. The middle class provides a large output of rebels; New Left activists, mods, beat musicians, folk singers, and hippies are well educated and have been raised with the "good" things of life. Only a fraction of the style rebels of today are poor and disprivileged. Nor is there among style rebels (as distinguished from the New Left) an ideology or radical program for remedying economic and civil injustice.

Style rebels appear on the same scene with New Left activists, and there is some collusion between them; but they are not identical and should be distinguished. The distinction seems to be as follows: members of the New Left are action oriented and concerned with public affairs, while style rebels are expression oriented and concerned with their own lives. The New Left attacks the Establishment and often attempts to seize power. Style rebels evade responsibility and drop out of the Establishment and its politics; they are not basically interested in politics. True, style rebellion sometimes verges on political protest when its activities clash with the police and regulations. Incidents such as the "filthy speech" rebellion at Berkeley or a man smoking marijuana cigarettes on the steps of a court building express disgust at laws which limit liberty. But, looking at activists of the extreme right and left, as one sees them in news photos or on television, one notes that most are conventionally dressed and do not fit the hippie or extreme mod or beat categories. What brings them together so often and confuses them in the public mind is their common antagonism to what they call the Establishment.

But we must ask what is this Establishment that they are protesting against? Is it capitalism? A certain government or party? Here we see that it is not so much protest against a political or economic system considered to be unfair as against such things as technology and bureaucracy in general, against standardization and impersonal treatment of human beings. The Establishment is not so much a class in Marxian terms as a way of life that restricts and denies full life for man, as Herbert Marcuse has pointed out. The Establishment is a set of middle class values that college students see in their own teachers and parents—in their own class, not an enemy class.

There is, then, a definite attack on the middle class these days, but the odd thing is that much of it is coming from the middle class itself. It is not a proletarian uprising. Two kinds of protest should be distinguished: Lower class protest reflects the feeling of being cut off from middle class values (as we see it when mobs drag television sets from stores). Middle class protest reflects alienation from such values already experienced or seen firsthand. The lower middle class stands appalled at middle class protest. What's the matter with them? How possibly can one not want to be a business executive or a highly paid white collar worker, have two cars, three television sets, and live in a nice suburban neighborhood with a patio, barbecue, and swimming pool? Yet, there it is; the prevailing image of success has been rejected by many educated young middle class intellectuals, especially university students, by the artistic and literary crowd (outside Madison Avenue), and by entertainers. The songs of the Beatles—"When I'm 64" and "She's Leaving Home," for example—are full of dismal pictures of middle class life. We have heard again and again the familiar charges against this way of life. It is described as being materialistic, hypocritical, immoral, square, dull, and lacking challenge. And there is also the constant complaint about neglect of the individual—"Don't fold, spindle, or mutilate."

What I am suggesting is that style rebels are protesting not against the injustices of the world but against the meaninglessness (to them) of a set of values and a style of life (identity) offered by "successful" people in current society. They want to strike out and forge a new identity for themselves. They experiment wildly, sometimes desperately, even pathetically, to find something new. In this reaction there is a swing away from the styles of the hard worker, the businessman, the white and blue collar workers, the bureaucrat toward a more expressive life—toward, in Marcuse's terms, not "one dimensional" but many dimensional man. It is a reaction of boredom against the prevailing image of success and the comfortable life of suburbia.

This, then, is what I would call a meaning problem, which, expressed in terms of the individual, is an identity problem. We have to ask why modern technological societies, which can distribute goods adequately, so often fail to give meaning and satisfactory identity to their members. In prosperous societies troubles seem to shift to the meaning (or, if you prefer, spiritual) sphere.

We are asking, then, why it is that identity problems break out in societies which are materially prosperous, highly modernized and technologized, many of which have philosophies emphasizing the importance of the individual. Unrest is understandable among Rhodesian blacks or overcrowded starving Indians. But it is a paradox that the have nations, such as England, France, the United States, Switzerland, Scandinavia, West Germany, and Japan should have abundant identity problems in the middle classes. These are countries with well developed economic and welfare systems, and many of them have constitutions emphasizing civil rights. The paradox seems to be that an individual can get what he wants in terms of material abundance and civil rights and still have a feeling that he doesn't count.

I can illustrate this with an anecdote about university graduation.

The senior class of a California university was rehearsing in the open air theatre for the graduation ceremony that afternoon. The sun was already high, and the prospect was that it would be warm that afternoon. A proposal was made to the class president to speed up the ceremony by dropping the calling of names, thus saving about forty minutes. After discussion the class voted to eliminate the calling of names. At this point a student in one of the upper rows rose and threw his folding chair down into the arena, narrowly missing the kettle drum of the orchestra. He said, "I have waited four years for this, and I am damned if I will graduate without having my name called." Then he walked out. There was a moment of stunned silence. Then came a new motion from a member of the class that names be called. The motion was passed unanimously.

Here we see how easy it is to forget, to lose the individual in the midst of a system designed to educate him for opportunities and give him the good things of life. What had they forgotten? They had forgotten that there is more to education than facts, skills, and a job. Being appreciated as a person by others is an essential experience. Every human being needs periodic recognition, to stand out from the mass as somebody who counts, to have people care emotionally, to know that one's friends and relatives are proud. College graduation is a ceremony that gives meaning to a person. It has a sentimental purpose, not a practical one. Abolish it and the individual loses meaning. There is no efficiency in education which ignores identity.

The meaning of an individual—his identity—can be analyzed into two parts: (1) his purpose, the significance of his work and goals; and (2) his self conception, his sense of his own importance, his feeling that he is somebody who counts and that people care about him. Lack of these things creates an identity problem.

The odd thing is that counting people does not make them count; votes and statistics have little value for identity. Identity is provided by certain kinds of experiences which others must give. An individual cannot invent or generate his own importance (unless, of course, he is insane).

We can here briefly indicates some kinds of things that give identity and the ways in which modern society often fails to provide these. I would like to point out briefly six sociological factors disturbing identity all over the world, more in some places than in others—hardly at all, for example, in a village in Crete or a kibbutz in Israel but very much in modern society characterized by advanced technology, urbanism, and mobility. All over the world disturbances of identity are beginning. But in advanced societies they are often farthest under way because of cumulative effects and rapid changes. These identity disturbances feed unrest; they add bitterness to the demands of the "have nots" and make middle class life seem unsatisfactory to many.

The most obviously technological disturbance to identity, perhaps, is *destruction of environment,* of places which constitute home. All over the world we hear the sound of bulldozers and jack hammers wiping away familiar landmarks and the homes of people. Symbolically, a home is a place where a child is raised, a place rich with childhood and ancestral memories. New housing usually does not replace home psychologically, for it has no memories. Sometimes the rich move in where the poor have lived and create an entirely new environment. New towns, suburban tracts, and old people's communities (with names like "Sun Villa") rarely create home psychologically. Likewise, social succession, i.e., turnover of people, in urban neighborhoods brings in waves of new dwellers even when the buildings remain the same. In five or ten years an entire population can change, as has happened in Knottinghill Gate, London. The English are appalled to see a village as they knew it destroyed by migrants from the West Indies and Pakistan.

It is becoming a universal phenomenon for people to find that they cannot go back where they were raised to renew themselves through familiar sights and the folks back home. Often a man returns to his old neighborhood to find a high rise building and a parking lot. Even landmarks may be gone —hills flattened, skylines altered, rivers filled. Strange faces look out from the windows of his old home. The neighbor's children—his former friends— are gone. Such a man, having lost his home, has lost one of the strands of his identity. He cannot meaningfully refer to himself the way a Greek does who says, "I'm a Cretan," and thinks of his village. So, symbolically, masses of modern people, however well housed in material terms, are a homeless generation psychologically. As the adage says, "A house is not a home."

A factor equally disturbing to identity is *loss of contact with the past and tradition.* People are forgetting what kind of people their ancestors were and are becoming people without a past. Ethnic and tribal identities are being abandoned; old customs and ceremonies are being forgotten (though people like Dora Stratou are trying to preserve them); and ancestors and genealogies are losing importance. Cleveland Amory's well-known story about the Bostonian who applied to a Chicago firm for a job illustrates this. The young man brought with him a letter of recommendation stressing the quality of his ancestry in Boston. But the Chicago office replied that, though they were very impressed with Mr. X's pedigree, they were not interested in using him for breeding purposes. This reply expresses the modern feeling of the practical irrelevance of the past. Old ways are viewed as obsolete, corny. Modernism is rampant. The motto is "away with the old and in with the new."

History is becoming abstract knowledge about the past rather than the story of our people and our heroes. There has been a loss of the heroic view of history and of the "chosen people" concept. The record of the past has become dead history rather than living tradition. Folklore, folk dance, and song, when revived, are not living tradition but quaint historical study, danced and sung by people who did not learn these from their grandmothers. Hence folk today is modern fad, not really living tradition. As the sense of continuity with the past is weakened, man loses another thread of identity. He cannot locate himself as a link in a chain of ancestors; he often doesn't even know who his people were. He is an ambiguous man who must be what he makes of himself and is dealt with not as a representative of his people but statistically in the mass.

But it is not just what a man does or makes of himself but how society recognizes him that creates identity. A third factor is *loss of identifying ceremony*. As already illustrated by the story about the college graduation, there is less emphasis today than in the past on ceremonies that recognize the individual—his status, achievements, importance as a person. A whole range of ceremonies do this: baptisms, birthdays, name days, religious confirmations, anniversaries, initiations, graduations, honors, retirements, funerals. Some families, institutions, and communities still do most of these things. But somehow—for reasons of efficiency or because there are too many people or we don't know people as individuals—we find less time for this sort of thing nowadays. Ceremonies of identity are becoming privatized— you do it on your own, the community rarely participates unless it is a man of distinction; each Joseph, George, and Peter is on his own. Or the ceremonies are so impersonal that the individual is lost. Even a funeral—that last of all recognitions—may be a quick and efficient disposal procedure with little satisfaction to the community (if they bother to come). Personal eulogies of the deceased are more and more rare. Today it is a fact that the average person doesn't have nearly enough ceremonies of recognition, and some don't have any at all. So it is not surprising to see a yearning for celebrities (who get what the average man doesn't), ego screaming in costume and faddism. Some people even commit crimes to get their name in the papers.

A fourth identity-disturbing factor, perhaps most important of all, is the relationship of mobility and numbers of people to *loss of social concern* in day-to-day relationships. We all know people are moving more and more these days, leaving their homes, crowding into cities, riding around in cars, airplanes, busses, vans, and scooters; homes are being built on wheels. The amount, speed, and radius of movement are increasing rapidly. Contacts with other people are increasing geometrically, accentuated by mass communication. We can easily see this means less time and attention for any *one* person, group, or locality. At the same time institutions are being redesigned for greater efficiency in handling masses of people. But that does not serve anybody in particular. It is not surprising, then, as sociologists have pointed out, that in the midst of social services people develop a sense of aloneness—the "lonely crowd" phenomenon, the feeling that nobody pays any attention to me. It is very hard to get anyone to take an interest in someone else, as is often seen in today's doctor-patient relationships. Old people, especially those whose children have moved away, feel neglected. Machinery and efficient services are used to replace social concern, but they fail. They arouse resentment by their red tape and cold professional manner. The production line, payroll number, and bureaucratic rubber stamps are all seen as enemies, as devices for denying identity.

Nor does increase of the number of friends with more contacts really remedy the problem. We know acquaintances cannot really take the place of friends, let alone kinfolk. Dale Carnegieism is a good political tactic but no substitute for concern. What I am saying is that, as mobility and number of contacts increase, life becomes more like a cocktail party and less like a birthday party; relationships shift toward the casual. This means that the chances become good that large numbers of people will suffer lack of social concern most of the time. As sociologists might say, there is an insufficient rate of meaningful interaction, man-to-man, day-to-day. The sheer amount of interaction is not the question. You can see a thousand people and not relate to anybody, but one phone call or letter can make your day complete. Most people, however, need more than a letter; most people require a matrix of frequent affection, support, emotional sharing, and genuine concern from a sufficient number of people outside their family, especially the approval of superiors and peers as confidants and buddies. The paradox, however, is that a buzzing extraverted society can suffer a lack of concern and not know it. This lack of concern is masked by what sociologists call false personalization or role-playing—for example, the pretense of concern by an insurance salesman. Associations and memberships may not mean anything beyond a membership card or being a member of an audience-crowd at meetings. How can one tell if there is genuine concern? Statistics of participation (for example, church attendance) are usually worthless. Some indices, however, can show it, such as the number of personal calls on a person who is sick. Few such calls invite the conclusion "I wasn't *that* important." Another sign of lack of concern is that people feel they can't get through to others, that they talk but nobody listens. There is a growth of psychotherapeutic programs devoted to breaking through emotional walls in modern society. This indicates inadequate feedback of emotional support, sincere affection, self-expression (to which others listen, as distinguished from ego screaming), and real information needed for personal guidance.

I have tried to explain how modern society can have a high level of involvement along with a low level of concern. Sociologists since Ferdinand Toennies and Emile Durkheim have pointed out that mass society suffers a chronically low level of social concern and that the break up of small groups which are the natural focus of concern (extended family, clan, tribe, village, parish) has not been replaced by associations of modern times like labor union, party, church, or social set. A vacuum persists. So rebels scream and say, "Look at me!", "Pay attention to me!"

It is not surprising that lack of concern goes with a fifth element in the context of modern identity problems: *shallowness of feeling,* inability to feel sentiments strongly or to sense that one is living fully. Many writers have noted various signs of emotional shallowness, such as violence and sensation in movies increasing without corresponding shock and depth of tragic feeling, and the passing away of romantic—strictly sentimental old-fashioned—love. Emotion is privatized. Everyone is trying to be cool; it is becoming embarrassing to express feelings openly, "wave the flag," be homesick, "wear one's heart on one's sleeve." Perhaps a reason is lack of emotional support; one sees evidence that others do not really feel what they say; and some say nothing at all—play it cool. In the background is the fact that our modern society continually overstresses reason, facts, and machinery at the expense of feeling, impulse, and intuition—the entire inner life. Objectivity is a fetish of science. One is apologetic for poetry, religious faith, artistic sensibility, premonitions, dreams, scruples, and prejudices of all kinds. I do not know all the reasons, but I think that the whole feedback network of emotion has become unplugged. So the batteries of sentiment do not get charged often enough. If this is so, then it is not surprising to see style rebellion and activism offsetting emotional shallowness with flamboyance, irrational extremes, search for intense experience even through drugs, a wish to feel oneself deeply, genuinely, even painfully.

Finally, we must consider the effect of entertainers, stars, recordings, films, and television on the success image. What does the current worship of celebrities do for identity? It seems plain that mass communication has a strong but confusing impact. It is confusing aspiration among the young by putting up dubious and unworthy ideals in place of the standard success image which has deteriorated. We can easily see that young people have been offered a variety of models in mass communication today which their parents never heard of and are very doubtful about approving. Some are downright alarming—rock musicians and their birds, playboys and playgirls, etc. Many are glamorous successes, such as the four unwashed boys who with one recording made a million dollars in a week.

Contrasting with such exciting possibilities is the standard success image, which has become tarnished. I refer to the ideal of the hard working Horatio Alger hero. Two reasons for the drabness of the standard success image can be mentioned. One is that literature has dismally depicted the mediocrity of the organization man and the bureaucrat in writings like William F. Whyte's *The Organization Man,* C. Wright Mills' *White Collar,* Sloan Wilson's *Man in the Grey Flannel Suit.* James Thurber's *Secret Life of Walter Mitty* and films like *The Graduate* present a similar picture. The white-collar worker's career is thus seen as unheroic, boring, restricted, a dreary shuttling between the rat race of business and the tame existence of suburbia. Material possessions do not compensate for such restriction; advertisements say "happy life" but that is not what the young see. The other reason for drabness of the standard success image is that the pileup of irrelevant information in a technological-scientific society has become an overload in education—boring and irrelevant school studies which discourage students and kill interest. One can almost hear a student say, "Look what you have to go through to get a job in bureaucracy and a fifty-foot lot in suburbia!" The college student feels acutely that he has to memorize and regurgitate at examination time (the phrase speaks of his attitude) the enormous pile of facts that he feels have no relation to his own life. But if he leaves the lecture hall and goes to the rest of life—television, community affairs, and all that—he finds the same irrelevance unless he restricts his attention to a narrow band of stimuli, such as rock and roll music, skin diving, or some other sport or hobby which for him means intense and meaningful life—"where the action is," "What's happening *now*, baby."

So, putting all this together, we see young people caught in a dilemma between a rather drab career outlook and unrealistic, inappropriate, sometimes demoralizing career goals offered by celebrities as models in mass communication. This I call the Mitty Syndrome, dreaming of being glamorous TV stars or jet setters but unable to attain this in fact, wanting to be what one cannot be and not wanting to be what one is and has a realistic expectation of being. When such an explosion of wishes stimulated by mass communication is not met by realistic career opportunities, frustration follows. It is a formula for unhappiness, for dissatisfaction with oneself.

These six factors—destruction of the home environment, loss of contact with tradition, lack of ceremonies recognizing the individual, lack of social concern, weakening sentiments, and confusion of aspiration—add up to identity frustrations of the middle class in mass society. They are symbolic disturbances, breakdowns in the meaning of various symbols of the environment and in the meaning of success. No amount of pile up of wealth and welfare services is going to solve these problems unless focused on improving meaningful relationships of people to each other and to their home environments, thus reducing psychological and spiritual frustrations.

Once the problem is seen in these terms, the natural question is: What can be done to provide more identifying experiences in a mass society? I teach at a university of 23,000 students, of which I face 200 every week. It is a challenge to me to think of how to focus more on the student's identity as a person—not on new facts in the curriculum but on how to make them more relevant to his life. Not by non academic substitutes, such as football games and riots, but by something going on in the curriculum which the student will regard as too important to be disturbed by football games and riots. If he lets his hair grow long, I hope it will be because he is so interested in his studies that he hasn't time for a haircut, not because he wishes to defy society.

But how to produce such an academic miracle? It is the duty of educators to find out what techniques will do this. There is a clear difference between devices that increase efficiency of education (defined as number of students reached times amount of information transmitted) and devices that will identify students as persons and help them find what they need to grow as persons. Many highly efficient methods—large lecture halls, computerized learning, TV courses, films, machine scored examinations which call for no more achievement than a check in the right place—do practically nothing for identity. On the other hand, many methods accentuate identity. These include debate, creative writing and art, producing and acting dramas, solo performances and competitions, first name relationships, frank and open discussions, the cluster principle of living together in small groups, self-directed groups not dominated by the authority of instructors, and cathartic group sessions and other kinds of group therapy.

I trust that many will be studying the same problem in the factory, bureaucracy, community, church, hospital, welfare agency, and psychotherapy. Sensitivity training today is seeking a kind of interaction that will help people get through to others, solve emotional problems, and find themselves. New things are being discovered every day. There is reason to hope that we are on the verge of discoveries about how to make the individual important again even in a mass society. Already new forms of welfare are appearing whose motto is, significantly, not material benefit but pride. And we must get over the idea that the focus of social welfare is entirely in the lower classes. In my opinion, universities are just as much in need of identity programs as slums.

We need to develop youth programs which will put back into growing up, family life, and school experience as many as possible of the identity-giving features which have been lost by the mass society. These features include a home environment, contact with tradition and pride in the past and ancestors, ceremonies of recognition, genuine social concern, strong sentiments, and clear and satisfying models of aspiration. The difficulty of this need not discourage us from searching for levers of constructive change.

If we can do this with any real success, in my opinion, style rebellion and hippieism will disappear.

7

Alan C. Kerckhoff

A THEORY OF
HYSTERICAL CONTAGION

>   ...*Group life consists of acting units developing acts to meet the situations in which they are placed.*
>   ...*Through previous interaction they develop and acquire common understandings of definitions of how to act in this or that situation. These common definitions enable people to act alike.... Since ready-made and commonly accepted definitions are at hand, little strain is placed on people in guiding and organizing their acts. However, many other situations may not be defined in a single way by the participating people. In this event, their lines of action do not fit together readily and collective action is blocked. Interpretations have to be developed and effective accommodation of the participants to one another has to be worked out.*[1]

---

[1] Herbert Blumer, "Society as Symbolic Interaction," in *Human Behavior and Social Processes,* ed. Arnold M. Rose (Boston: Houghton Mifflin Company, 1962), pp. 187–88.

The sociologist usually is concerned with the more orderly, culturally defined, and socially sanctioned forms of behavior. He is thus attracted to such conceptual tools as social system, social role, stratification, and normative expectation. As the statement quoted above indicates, this is a useful approach to the study of much of social life. As the statement also indicates, however, not all that is social is so orderly, and when one attempts an analysis of situations in which "ready-made and commonly accepted definitions" are not available, new analytic problems are faced. The field of collective behavior has developed in response to a recognition of the importance of such situations in social life.

The student of collective behavior is necessarily faced with the problem of understanding process. He cannot simply deduce the observed behavior from prior knowledge of the structured aspects of the situation. As Kurt and Gladys Lang have so rightly emphasized, the study of collective behavior is the study of "collective dynamics" and "collective processes."[2] But the field of collective behavior deals with many different kinds of phenomena. Crowds, crazes, panics, and social movements are all examples of collective behavior, and as such they have much in common, not the least of which is their deviation from the established forms of social behavior. But they are also different from each other, and one major dimension of differences is the degree to which they lead to an alteration of those orderly and structured features of society to which the sociologist usually directs his attention. The successful social movement brings about a change in the society in which it occurs. Many crowds lead to a response from the agencies of control which has lasting effects, such as new legislation or administrative reorganization. One concern of the student of collective behavior, therefore, is to chart the process of structural change which evolves from these phenomena.

A more fundamental concern of the student of collective behavior, however, is to examine the common features of all of these various phenomena. The very fact that they are all *collective* actions which involve deviations from the established forms of social behavior indicates that some new basis of concerted action must be evolved. Whatever the degree of lasting impact on the society in which they occur, therefore, all of these forms of collective behavior involve the development of new collective interpretations of a set of experiences. For the sociologist interested in collective behavior, therefore, the problem shifts from one of charting how preestablished definitions are put into action to one of charting how new definitions are evolved. As Blumer goes on to say in the source quoted above, "In the case of such 'undefined' situations, it is necessary to trace and study the emerging process of definition which is brought into play."

---

[2] Kurt and Gladys Lang, *Collective Dynamics* (New York: Thomas Y. Crowell Co., 1961).

The emphasis on definition and meaning is found in all works which emanate from the so-called symbolic interactionist tradition in sociology, the writing of George H. Mead forming the cornerstone of the tradition. This tradition emphasizes the importance of the attribution of meaning to all social behavior, and the situation in which that behavior occurs is also viewed as a socially defined entity rather than something that is "given." The famous statement of W. I. Thomas reflects both this conceptualization and the importance attributed to it by those who write in this tradition: "If men define situations as real, they are real in their consequences."

Such an emphasis on meaning and on the evolution of new definitions of the situation is found in all contemporary discussions of collective behavior. Neil Smelser, in his ambitious attempt to organize the field, notes the significance of what he calls "generalized beliefs" as a basis of all collective behavior.[3] Such beliefs provide the basis of action by making the resulting action a reasonable response to the situation, once the belief is accepted. The Langs recognize "collective definition" as one of five basic processes found in the various forms of collective behavior. Since collective behavior is an attempt at collective problem solving, definition of the problem is a basic prerequisite of action. Shibutani has examined the rumor process as one in which "improvised news" evolves to fill a gap in a collectivity's understanding of a problematic situation. Rumors are found in situations in which the need for understanding exceeds the available information, and rumors are thus attempts at collective definition.[4]

The process of collective definition in cases of collective behavior, however, takes place under special circumstances. There is a shared sense of arousal due to the lack or inadequacy of preestablished definitions of the situation. There is a sense of problem and a need to do something about it. Under such conditions, there is a heightened sensitivity to interstimulation, an openness to suggestion. Blumer uses the term "circular reaction" to refer to the process of interstimulation in such situations.[5] He emphasizes the emotional nature of the process and notes that social unrest (as distinct from individual neurosis) involves heightened arousal and excitement, erratic behavior, and increased suggestibility. It is within such a context that new collective definitions are particularly likely to evolve. This is true both because the pre-existent definitions are inadequate (and thus a need exists) and because processes of interstimulation are set in motion (thus providing a means of evolving a collective definition).

It would misrepresent the dynamics of such situations, however, if

---

[3] Neil J. Smelser, *Theory of Collective Behavior* (New York: The Free Press of Glencoe, Inc., 1963).

[4] Tamotsu Shibutani, *Improvised News: A Sociological Study of Rumor* (Indianapolis: The Bobbs-Merrill Co., Inc., 1966).

[5] Herbert Blumer, "Collective Behavior," in *Principles of Sociology,* ed. Alfred McClung Lee (New York: Barnes & Noble, Inc., 1951), pp. 170 ff.

only the lack of cultural definitions were stressed. Certainly such inadequacies (which the Langs call "gaps in the social structure") are crucial as a basis for the evolution of new definitions. But it is important to recognize that the redefinition occurs within a preestablished social setting, whatever its particular inadequacies. The evolution of a new definition, therefore, is influenced by pre-existent cultural definitions to the extent that basic values and images of reality will limit the degrees of freedom of innovation. Although some emergent definitions may be quite revolutionary, it is seldom, if ever, the case that they will be inconsistent with all that preceded them. Similarly, although most forms of collective behavior occur in what are relatively unstructured social contexts, it is only a most extreme, limiting case in which prior structuring of social relations plays no part in the interaction that occurs. Those persons most aroused by the inadequacies of the social structure are those most implicated in a particular kind of situation, and thus they are likely to have had shared experiences prior to the collective response being studied. Those differentially placed in the social situation both respond differently to the problem and vary in the likelihood of their interacting with particular other kinds of persons. Even given a shared sense of problem, the search for meaning, though often wide-ranging, must begin somewhere, and it is not completely free from the spatial and social limitations of the setting.

In short, collective behavior reflects inadequacies of social definition and involves the disruption and reinterpretation of social situations. But it also occurs within a larger social context, not all of which is amenable to restructuring—even in the eyes of those most sorely troubled. The above suggests that if we are to increase our understanding of collective behavior, we must at least concern ourselves with the dynamics of the process of redefinition. It also suggests that the process of redefinition can seldom be understood without reference to both the inadequacies of the social setting which lead to a need for redefinition and of the characteristics of that setting which place limits on the kind of new definition which can evolve.

In what follows, I have taken a very limited subcategory of collective behavior as the subject matter of close scrutiny from the perspective outlined above. The delimitation is based on the need to restrict the range of phenomena considered, due to the variability of forms of collective behavior, even though common processes may be involved in all forms.[6] The choice of this particular form is the result of a recent attempt to organize the empirical phenomena of a case of hysterical contagion under

---

6 A discussion of such variability, even in the dynamics of a basic process found in all collective behavior, may be found in Alan C. Kerckhoff, "Social Contagion," in *Social Psychology: An Introduction,* ed. Kurt W. Back (New York: John Wiley & Sons, Inc., forthcoming).

some kind of theoretical formulation.[7] That attempt profited from the use of the general perspective expressed above and led to the theory which follows.

The General Process

We have all seen such headlines as the following: "Mysterious Malady Sends Sixty-Three Students to Infirmary," "Plant Closes as Workers Overcome by Gas—No Gas Found," "Elusive Insect Puts Fifty Women in Hospital." Such headlines are usually followed by stories which include at least two salient facts: First, the "real cause" of the difficulty has not been found. Second, various kinds of experts have been summoned to investigate the case. Follow-up stories generally report that the experts were unable to locate any cause of the illness, and they at least hint that the difficulty was "nothing but hysteria."

Such cases are the subject of this discussion. I will call hysterical contagion any such case in which physiological symptoms for which no satisfactory physical explanation can be found spread through a collectivity. The central issue in this section will be to describe the kinds of factors which bring about such an event. The basic question will thus be: What general explanation can be suggested for the occurrence of such events and the pattern of development they follow?

To begin with, it is proposed that hysterical contagion occurs in situations that have characteristics in common with those in which all other forms of collective behavior occur. As stated earlier, these are situations of inadequate social definitions in which a general sense of dissatisfaction or discomfort is experienced by members of a collectivity. A problem is shared by a number of people, but there is no clearly defined institutionalized means of coping with the problem. There is, of course, a wide range of possible outcomes from such tension-filled collective situations, and hysterical contagion is only one of them. In fact, it is in some respects a limiting case. Such other forms of collective behavior as crowd action, social movements, and expressive outbursts all, in one way or another, channel the energies of the individuals involved in ways that reduce the sense of tension—although they vary in the degree to which they actually serve to alleviate the tension-producing situation. In all such cases, the salient feature is an activity—the participants do something. In hysterical contagion, the observable salient feature is an experience—something evidently happens to the participants. Rather than actors, they are viewed as victims. The first major definitive

---

7 Alan C. Kerckhoff and Kurt W. Back, *The June Bug: A Study of Hysterical Contagion* (New York: Appleton-Century-Crofts, 1968).

characteristic of hysterical contagion, therefore, is that it occurs where the actors, faced with a collective problem, fail to take active steps toward reducing the shared experience of tension.

There seems to be no easy or general answer to the question of why active problem-solving steps are not taken. As with all forms of collective behavior, there is no preestablished and socially prescribed action to be taken. But in cases of hysterical contagion there seems to be an uneasy balance between the need to do something about the problem that is faced and the need to avoid the kinds of action which seem most suitable for coping with the problem. In all of the hypothetical cases reflected in the headlines presented above, the outbreak of symptoms occurred in a circumscribed setting such as a school or a factory. This is the usual kind of setting for such events. The circumscribed setting provides the commonality of experience which sets the conditions of the collective problem. Such a setting is also likely to provide structural limitations on the kinds of solutions which can safely be adopted. If the basic problem is strained labor-management relations, for instance, any action which might tend to relieve the individual worker's sense of tension is also likely to worsen relations with management. If the problem is the restrictive atmosphere of a boarding school, any action to relieve the strain of that restriction would be likely to violate the very rules that are the source of the tension.

The source of the tension may not, however, be clearly understood by the members of the collectivity. Especially in well-established, structured settings, the pattern of expectations and proscriptions may seem so natural and appropriate to the situation that it is not even clear to the members of the collectivity just what their problem is. There is often a pervading sense of tension but difficulty in specifying its source—which, of course, makes it doubly difficult to define suitable means of coping with it. It is in this kind of situation that Smelser's reference to the "generalized belief" is appropriate. The generalized belief, in this case a "hysterical belief," comes to be associated with the sense of tension and gives tangible meaning to that tension.[8] Within such a situation some credible external threatening agent comes to be associated with the sense of tension. The invention of such an agent is evidently a random event, although cultural factors certainly limit what will be generally viewed as credible. Rather than amorphous anxiety, therefore, the members come to experience fear of this threatening agent. The belief serves to objectify the sense of strain and provides a point of reference for any action that is taken.

In many cases such a belief undoubtedly enters the scene before the first cases of illness are reported, and when they occur they are easily

---

[8] "We define a hysterical belief as a belief empowering an ambiguous element in the environment with a generalized power to threaten or destroy." Smelser, *op. cit.,* p. 84.

associated with the threatening agent. In our hypothetical headlines two such sources were a poisonous insect and an asphyxiating gas. It may often happen, therefore, that the order of factors is: tension, generalized belief about a threatening agent, illness. However, as our other headline suggested, a generalized belief may not precede the illness. There may be an outbreak of illness which can only be referred to after it occurs and even then in only vague terms such as "mysterious malady." In such cases, of course, the occurrence of the illness provides the basis for creating a belief in some agent which might be the source of symptoms, but the belief involved may still be no more specific than that there is an unknown source of threat "out there."

But whichever order occurs, the outcome involves a number of people who exhibit symptoms for which no tangible source can be located—even though a belief may have evolved to suggest what kind of source should be observable. Thus, the next question is: If there is no tangible source of symptoms, why do people get sick—why do they behave as if they had been the victim of some external source of poisoning? The general answer seems to be that their physiological responses to unresolved tension are often superficially quite similar to those associated with such toxic agents as gas, food poisoning, poisonous insect bites, and so on. The familiar symptoms are nausea, vomiting, headache, chills, and fever, and general aching.[9] They are sufficiently disturbing symptoms that they cannot be ignored (by the victim or by others), but they are sufficiently vague so that it is very difficult to specify what their cause might be.

The original tension, however, is likely to be increased as it becomes generally believed that there is a threatening agent in the situation. Although the generalized belief may operate to objectify the source of discomfort, it also operates to add to the situation another source of tension. To the extent that experts of various types are brought into the case and act as if there might very well be such an agent present, the fear becomes more reasonable. Whether or not there is a belief in a specific threatening agent, the increasing number of sick persons, together with the legitimating action of experts, adds more strain to an already tense situation. This increases both the likelihood that any given individual will experience symptoms and the likelihood that any symptoms he experiences will be attributed to "it"—whatever it is.

Our general view of hysterical contagion, therefore, may be sum-

---

9 Engel refers to a "psychologically decompensated state" in which intrapsychic coping breaks down, and "psychological stress acts to mobilize biological systems for the defense and protection of the body." G. L. Engel, *Psychological Development in Heath and Disease* (Philadelphia: W. B. Saunders Company, 1962), p. 367. Under such conditions there is the experience of tension, anxiety, and so on, and also "the awareness of physiological changes such as palpitation, sweating, flushing, muscle tension, or 'butterflies in the stomach'." (page 384).

marized briefly as follows: A number of people are exposed to common sources of strain from which no very attractive means of escape are present, although it may be known that acts which have negative consequences might serve to reduce the tension. The combination of the original strain and the impossibility of using any known solution brings about a general state of tension whose intensity is probably increased by interstimulation among the people so situated. The state of unresolved tension leads to the experience of physiological symptoms. These symptoms become associated in the minds of the distressed people with some credible (though factually incorrect) "cause" in the situation, the connection deriving from what are probably random events that become interpreted in the context of the experienced discomfort. This external cause both objectifies the source of the discomfort and adds a further source of strain to the situation: fear of a threatening agent. The belief in the threatening agent, the rising number of victims, and the legitimating actions of outside experts all increase the sense of tension and the probability of experiencing symptoms which may be defined as relevant to the presumed source of the spreading sickness.

Variations Within the Collectivity

It is necessary to go beyond this general conceptualization, however. Very rarely, if ever, do such illnesses spread throughout the entire collectivity in which they are found. Ususally only a relatively small proportion of the people in the situation become medically recorded cases. We must take this fact into account if we are to present even a roughly adequate theory. To do so, we must look within the collectivity and find means of differentiating between those who become cases and those who do not. In doing this, it will be important to remain consistent with the general conceptualization just discussed. In that conceptualization, the critical factors were: sources of strain in the situation, difficulties of coping with that strain directly, the experience of symptoms, a belief in the external source of those symptoms, the public enactment of illness behavior, and an increase in tension due to the behavior of others. These same factors will constitute the basis for the analysis of variations within the collectivity. Although each of these factors may be seen as attributes of the collectivity, they may also be viewed as variables, and individuals may vary in their positions on each of them.

There are presumed to be general sources of strain in such situations, but individuals will vary not only in the degree to which they are exposed to these general sources of strain but also in the degree to which they are exposed to other, more idiosyncratic, sources of strain. That with which each individual must cope, therefore, is not fully determinable from the general characteristics of the situation. The same may be said, of course, with respect to the resources available to each member of the collectivity for coping with the strain he experiences. In the general case, the difficulties in coping will usually involve some normative or structural barrier to the actor's carrying out appropriate coping action, but the relevant norms may not be fully accepted by some members, and/or their variable position in the collectivity may present them with different structural barriers. Personality characteristics are likely to be relevant here, because individuals will vary in the degree to which they will be willing to deviate from norms or will dare to take independent action. In fact, they will vary in the degree to which they are able to acknowledge that they have a problem that necessitates action. These comments about variation in strain and means of coping with strain also suggest that the individuals will vary in the degree to which their tension will be great enough to lead to physiological arousal which would be uncomfortable.

All of these sources of variation, however, are a function of qualities of individuals which exist before the contagion begins. Other sources of variation are probably equally important and more directly relevant to the earlier discussion. A generalized belief, which may serve as an explanation of symptoms, evolves in the collectivity, and its credibility will determine to some extent the degree to which an individual will have an increased sense of strain. Since this belief is a collective invention, an emergent, it will evolve within a network of communication links among the members. The belief may thus be adopted more rapidly by some sociometric clusters than others. In fact, interpersonal communication networks must also be assumed to be important in the original development of a sense of strain in the situation. Therefore, persons differentially situated in these networks would be expected both to have evolved different levels of tension and to have different probabilities of acceptance of the generalized belief.

The same factor of intracollectivity structure would lead us to expect that, given the public enactment of illness behavior on the part of some members, this behavior would be more salient in the experience of some observers than others. Those who are closer to the original victims, both socially and spatially, would be more likely than others to be impressed with the seriousness of the problem and would find it more difficult to "explain it away." If the occurrence of new cases continues over a period of time, however, we would expect that the significance of the illness would become increasingly accepted throughout the collectivity as well as by those outside it. Both the spread of reported symptoms and the mobilization of therapeutic and investigative agencies would make it increasingly difficult to deny the significance of the problem. The need for some explanation would also presumably increase, thus increasing the likelihood that whatever generalized belief had evolved would be widely disseminated.

An important factor in this later development is the action of outsiders, especially those defined as experts. If they take the problem seriously, it should increase the likelihood of belief within the collectivity, the incidence of symptoms within the collectivity, and the ease with which members of the collectivity define symptoms as warranting official attention. Thus, we might expect that the longer the process continues to be defined as a legitimate epidemic, the more cases will come to the attention of the authorities and the more likely these cases will exhibit mild rather than severe symptoms. The important point here is that the process of dissemination within the collectivity is a very complex and multifaceted one. The manifest element is the spread of reported symptoms, but there are at least two other processes going on which are closely associated with this manifest process. The first is the spread of the generalized belief in a threatening agent; the second is the spread of the definition of a legitimate means of coping with the experience of symptoms—reporting them to the experts. These three processes are closely related to each other, but they are not identical in content or form.

But the complexity is even greater than this would suggest. In such cases as those which become newsworthy, the focus of attention is on those factors I have just discussed. The fact that the whole collectivity is seldom affected, however, suggests that other processes are occurring at the same time. Due to variations in situational, personal, and sociometric characteristics within the collectivity, it is likely that some members will remain rather aloof from the processes I have described. It is also probable that others will experience tension but will evolve other less indirect definitions of it and take other less newsworthy action to cope with it. Even among those who become quite upset and who believe in the external source of threat there may evolve methods of coping with symptoms that do not bring the victims to the attention of the authorities. Thus, within any such collectivity we should expect that multiple processes will occur simultaneously and that one of the outcomes of this fact will be the eventual intersection of these processes. One of the reasons for a less than complete spread of the most salient process, therefore, will be the availability of alternative sources of influence in the situation. This should have a dampening effect on the most disruptive outcomes.

Hysterical Contagion as Collective Behavior

This view of hysterical contagion puts it clearly within the field of collective behavior. It also provides a basis for differentiating it from other forms of collective behavior. The discussion has emphasized the importance of the shared nature of the tension which results from inadequacies in the social structure. It also has stressed the importance of interstimulation among the members of the collectivity and the function of this circular response in heightening the tension and increasing the probability of experiencing symptoms. Finally, it has been central to the whole discussion that a new definition evolves and is disseminated in the collectivity, and that this new definition provides the basis for some kind of action.

However, this is the point at which the special nature of hysterical contagion becomes salient. The new definition is only indirectly related to the original tension and its cause. It is not a new definition of the tension-producing situation but a definition of the symptoms which result from a failure to cope with that situation. The action that the new definition legitimates provides a means of coping with the tension and the symptoms it produces, but it does not provide a means of coping with the social setting which produces the tension.[10]

The view provided here, therefore, places hysterical contagion within the general field of collective behavior, but it also defines it as a kind of limiting case. The distinction was made earlier between those forms of collective behavior which have a lasting effect on the social structure and those which do not. One of the difficulties with that distinction is that almost any kind of collective behavior *may* have a lasting effect, and it is necessary to wait some unspecified period of time to see if it does. The present discussion suggests a somewhat different distinction, that between forms of collective behavior which do and do not cope directly with the source of tension and dissatisfaction. If we accept the view that collective behavior occurs where there are "gaps in the social structure" and an "undefined situation," it is possible to distinguish between those forms which constitute attempts to alter the situation and those which are expressions of the tension experienced but are not attempts to cope with the source of the problem. Hysterical contagion appears to be an example, par excellence, of the latter.

There are undoubtedly other kinds of cases which are closely allied to the type discussed above and which could be subsumed under the heading of hysterical contagion. These would include the sighting of flying saucers, the sometimes bizarre explanations of natural phenomena, and all kinds of popular delusions.[11] There are two significant differences between the kind of

---

10 It may, of course, have some effect on that social setting which may reduce the strain causing the tension. If nothing else, it removes the victims from the tension-producing situation and disrupts that situation. But this is a highly indirect means of "coping."

11 A number of writers have discussed such phenomena. For example, see E. J. Ruppelt, *The Report on Unidentified Flying Objects* (New York: Doubleday & Company, Inc., 1956); D. M. Johnson, "The 'Phantom Anesthetist' of Mattoon: A Field Study of Mass Hysteria," *Journal of Abnormal and Social Psychology*, XL (1945), 175–86; N. Z. Medalia and O. N. Larsen, "Diffusion and Belief in a Collective Delusion: The Seattle Windshield Pitting Epidemic," *American Sociological Review*, XXIII (1958), 180–86; A. M. Meerloo, *Delusion and Mass-Delusion* (New York: Nervous and Mental Disease Monographs, 1949).

phenomenon discussed above and these kinds of phenomena. First, the latter occur in a more diffuse collectivity rather than in an institutional setting, which is the usual setting of the kind of case I have discussed. Second, these other cases generally involve experiences other than those defined as illness. These two differences pose problems in the application of the proposed theory to such cases. It is more difficult in such cases to assume a single source of tension which is shared by those who become participants in the contagion, and even more difficult to specify what that source might be. Also, we often cannot make reference to patterns of interstimulation with any confidence in such cases and must introduce the effects of mass media into the discussion. Even more troublesome is the problem of attempting to link the experience of tension with the particular content of the contagion. (Why should tension lead one to see flying saucers rather than to have some other experience as a result of his arousal?) However, in spite of these difficulties, the theory offered here is consistent with the known facts in such cases, and it provides a basis for their further explication. It suggests that sensory experience can be "explained" in several ways and that one person's report of a kind of experience may sensitize another both to "become aware" of an experience and to explain it in the same way. It suggests, further, that in the course of the contagion less extreme experiences will suffice to bring about a report. And it suggests that both the cultural definition of the explanation and the response of outsiders, especially experts, will influence the extent and pattern of contagion. All of these suggestions are subject to empirical investigation. It is such investigation, in fact, that is the most pressing need in the whole field of collective behavior.

Finally, the view of collective behavior presented here calls for a greater concern with the dynamic interplay between the collectivity and other social elements. This is a perspective which has been emphasized in the literature on social movements for many years, because the success of a social movement is a function of the response to its actions made by outside agencies.[12] Students of crowd behavior, especially those concerned with the control of crowds, have also noted the importance of interaction between the crowd and other social elements.[13] As with these other forms

---

[12] Ralph Turner and Lewis M. Killian suggest a typology of social movements which is based on the relationship between the public definition of the movement and the kinds of action open to the movement. See their *Collective Behavior* (Englewood Cliffs, N. J.: Prentice-Hall, Inc., 1957), p. 329. James W. Vander Zanden in "Resistance and Social Movements," *Social Forces,* XXXVII (1959), 312–15, stresses the importance of countermovements which sometimes evolve in opposition to a social movement. A recent discussion of the shifting tactics of the civil rights movement notes not only the importance of the response of outsiders but also the evident anticipation of this response in the planning by the leaders of the movement. See Howard Hubbard, "Five Long Hot Summers and How They Grew," *The Public Interest,* No 12 (1968), 3–24.

[13] Cf. W. A. Westley, "The Formation, Nature, and Control of Crowds," Report to the Defense Research Board of Canada, April, 1956; and Smelser, *op. cit.,* pp. 261–69.

of collective behavior, I have suggested that the social and cultural context is a most significant factor in the course of hysterical contagion. The explanation of the symptoms, the generalized belief, must be credible in light of the basic values and beliefs of the social groups involved. Not only must the participants find it credible, but those outsiders who are directly relevant must do so as well. Especially if various officials and experts behave as if the threat were a legitimate source of concern, the evolving definition will be strengthened, and others will be encouraged to define their discomfort in those terms. This will encourage a greater number of victims to acknowledge their symptoms and thereby increase the credibility of the threat. Thus, the position taken here suggests that such an interactive view might profitably be used in the analysis of all forms of collective behavior, even those which seem to be directed "inward" and which do not move toward an alteration of the social structure. It also suggests that such a view would illuminate not only the action of the collectivity but also its ideology. In short, even though collective behavior results from "gaps in the social structure," it is not simply a lack of structure that affects its course. We must also take into account both the behavioral and ideological responses of outsiders if we are to understand what occurs within the collectivity.

8

Kurt Lang
and Gladys Engel Lang

COLLECTIVE BEHAVIOR THEORY AND THE ESCALATED RIOTS OF THE SIXTIES

Despite the important place the crowd has occupied in sociological theory as the prototype of elementary collective behavior, neither the internal dynamics of crowds nor their role as vehicles of social change is too well understood. This remains true despite the new interest in riots and the spurt of research that followed the escalated riots of the mid-sixties.

These widespread disturbances offer an opportunity to refine concepts by which we differentiate among various kinds of collective behavior and, in particular, to clarify the relation of crowds to social movements. In what follows we present a brief outline of what we see as the underlying dynamics of the disturbances. This includes: first, the face-to-face confrontations that precipitate polarization to a point where violence develops as a solidary response; second, the epidemic spread of disruptive behavior to nearby areas and mutations in the pattern of rioting; and third, the way in which direct action and other kinds of "illegality" became accepted forms of protest, so that the pattern repeats itself, undergoes conventionalization, and culminates in the myth of the violent uprising. The implication for collective behavior theory will be stressed throughout the discussion.

The Precipitating Event:
Violence As Spontaneously Shared Defense

Elementary collective behavior emerges in problematic situations.[1] A situation is problematic when the norms toward which conduct is ordinarily oriented are for one reason or another inoperative, in doubt, or in dispute. The resultant patterns of interaction are elementary in the sense that they are spontaneous and unstable. Behavior in these circumstances is greatly influenced by what those involved feel and experience at any given moment. Thus, violence becomes collective if such behavior is defined as a justified and acceptable response under the circumstances.

All social conduct rests on a fabric of common meanings, on an imagery shared by relevant persons. This is what makes the behavior of individuals predictable and gives society at least a semblance of stability. Violence is not always disruptive but often serves a consensually legitimate purpose—as in warfare, in supportive protests, or in dealing with offenders. Although such purpose seems lacking in the free-for-all brawl or in indiscriminate competitive looting, completely privatized license is rarely encountered in even the wildest kind of disorder. There is usually some coalescence of individual reactions. In our view, violent outbursts like riots can best be understood as a spontaneously shared collective defense. This collective defense counteracts demoralizing tendencies which, unless checked, would atomize the collectivity and privatize the individual members. A group demoralized beyond a certain point becomes unable to pursue any socially legitimate objective. In this context, the violence and destructiveness, the willful violation of laws, and the occasional savage acts of intimidation encountered on the streets constitute a method of social control, albeit a very unconventional method. They are the acts of an aggrieved population, whose members coercively assert certain norms against established authority and

---

[1] For a typology of problematic situations, see Kurt and Gladys Lang, "Collective Behavior," *International Encyclopedia of the Social Sciences* (The Macmillan Company, Publishers, 1968) II, 556–65.

who impose their own conceptions of justice against opponents or deviants whom they define as a threat.

This treatment of violence as a form of collective defense is based on several postulates. The first of these holds that group consensus is always to some extent tenuous and a matter of negotiation. This is clearly evident when one considers the nature of morale. The level of morale is subject to much change, and demoralization refers specifically to the process by which morale is undermined. High morale is manifest in the willingness of the members of a group to cooperate in the solution of a problem that confronts them collectively or individually. Thus, every problematic situation puts morale to the test. A crisis occurs when there is no adequate response to a new problem confronting the group. Similarly, prolonged stress and deprivation may have a demoralizing influence. These lead to changes in the perceived balance of rewards, so that cooperation no longer seems attractive or worth the effort. While competition favors an individual solution, conflict tends to bipolarize a group. However, the spontaneous reintegration of a group around an emotional impulse may raise morale—at least for a time.

A second postulate holds that all societies and groups develop practices to counter demoralization, practices that are in some sense analogous to the characterological defenses of individual persons. They bind anxiety and channel sentiments to support and maintain social solidarity in the presence of all kinds of stress. These collective defenses vary in the degree to which they are structured and conventionalized. The element of structure is especially evident in ceremonies that provide group-sanctioned occasions for collective license. As Max Gluckman's anthropological work on Africa indicates, feuds and rituals of rebellions help support order.[2] People may transgress against moral norms without invalidating them—as on New Year's Eve, at Leap Year celebrations, at mask-and-wig shows, and, more recently, in the "feelie-therapy" movement. On other occasions sentiments are mobilized for the purpose of repressing heresy, as in loyalty parades, propaganda rallies, etc. Indeed, certain aspects of law enforcement and of foreign policy involve violence that is explicitly sanctioned.

Third, collective violence as a means of conflict always contains a mixture of "realistic" and "unrealistic" components.[3] To be sure, it is as difficult to determine on substantive grounds what is and what is not realistic as it is to separate issue from methods; yet few conflicts ever reach a level of absolute force, where the goal is complete annihilation. They are

---

[2] Max Gluckman, *Order and Rebellion in Tribal Africa* (New York: The Free Press of Glencoe, Inc., 1963).
[3] Lewis Coser, *The Functions of Social Conflict* (New York: The Free Press of Glencoe, Inc., 1956).

almost always tempered by some tacit understandings about the ends toward which force or violence may be used. In treating rioting as a form of collective defense, we mean to draw attention to the presence of conventional elements in these outbursts. Although the sometimes subtle understandings on which public order rests are seriously disturbed, this does not transform the riot into a blind expression of impulse. Rioters have their own notions of order. The residues of conventionality to be found in most of these acts is what makes the violence acceptable to the participants. Just as the rioters in the first year of the French Revolution hoped to bring the King to Paris, where he could see the sufferings of his people, reports to the Kerner Commission contain observations that many rioters expressed the demand that the Mayor and/or other public officials appear on the scene. This appeal to higher authority shows the degree to which rioters continue to act within some normative framework.

The probability that a population will be susceptible to rioting as a spontaneously sanctioned form of collective defense depends on three factors: (1) the existence of a threat, particularly when it touches closely on matters related to a person's self-esteem and arouses common moral sentiments; (2) the degree to which persons feel entrapped and cannot escape as individuals (i.e., they share a common fate); and (3) the effectiveness of conventionalized and institutionalized means for achieving redress. With this in mind, let us turn to the "precipitating incident."

In almost every instance of full-fledged riotous activity in northern cities during the sixties—St. Louis (1964), Harlem (1964), Rochester (1964), Philadelphia (1964), Watts (1965), Newark (1967), Detroit (1967), etc.—the riot was precipitated by an incident between police who were trying to make an arrest (often but not always of a more or less routine nature) and spectators who were on the scene or immediately drawn to it.[4] In and of themselves these were not racial incidents. But wherever the arresting officer is white and the person charged is black, racial overtones are implicitly present from the very beginning. Moreover, some ambiguity is inherent in any arrest situation, even where policeman and suspect are of the same race. As a representative of the law, the officer is entitled to use whatever force is necessary to ensure the apprehension of a suspect. What "necessary force" means in any specific situation is left to the judgment of the police officer acting on his own. Force that appears necessary from

---

[4] This pattern is gradually beginning to change, but a confrontation with a police officer still has a strong potential for escalating a relatively minor disturbance into a full-scale riot. There is also a spillover effect. During August 1964, rioting that had begun in Jersey City the week before spread to Paterson and Elizabeth. Incidents of rock throwing and looting multiplied without any apparent local provocation. Similar satellite disturbances in several surrounding cities followed the Newark riot (1967) and the Detroit riot (1967).

his perspective but appears excessive to onlookers is particularly apt to stir up resentment when it occurs within a context of racial apprehensiveness. Wherein lies the special potential of such situations to evoke sentiments of moral outrage which then culminate spontaneously into a common hostile reaction that polarizes bystanders against the police?

First of all, there is a disposition common to all segments of the population to view the use of force by police as provocative and offensive. The police do not enjoy unlimited authority and are frequently suspected of being high-handed. Thus, any arrest is apt to elicit spontaneous sympathy from those bystanders who identify themselves with the victim of the action. This is especially true when the reasons for arrest are obscure while the arrestee's protests and the policeman's reactions are highly visible. Yet the less restrained the use of force, the more will bystanders feel themselves threatened, and the greater, as a consequence, will be the impetus to take some action, verbal or physical, to allay the sense of outrage.

Second, this reaction is all the more likely among a population where many persons have suffered severe damage to their sense of self-esteem at the hands of impersonal authorities. Charges of police brutality in Negro areas are, indeed, difficult to prove. The behavior that arouses the strongest resentment is more psychologically than physically damaging.[5] The most pervasive abuse is verbal, including stopping persons to "check up" on them, calling detainees by first names or addressing them as "boy," and using harsh, insulting language. Much of this is directed against the young, who suffer most from unemployment and are, for many other reasons, most vulnerable. Police behavior is indeed cited by many Negroes as one of the main grievances that lead to rioting, and self-styled participants in the riot tend to be vociferous in their criticisms of the police.

Third, the residents of Negro ghettoes constitute in a very special sense an isolated mass, segregated together by color and with little sense of participation in the larger community. This facilitates the generalization of sentiment even if the grievance is, to begin with, minor. The increased contact of police with ghetto inhabitants has turned these areas in many respects into "occupied territory." This implies not only the ready use of armed force with relatively little inhibition; it also implies the usual corruption of the occupying force by opportunities for gain. Thus police do not enforce all laws indiscriminately. Many criminals are permitted to "escape" into the racial ghettoes where their activities are often tolerated. As a result,

---

[5] See, for instance, the study jointly sponsored by the Detroit Urban League and the *Detroit Free Press, The People Beyond 12th Street: A Survey of Attitudes of Detroit Negroes After the Riot of 1967,* and the survey after the Watts riot by R. J. Murphy and J. Watson, *The Structure of Discontent* (Los Angeles: U.C.L.A. Institute of Government and Public Affairs, 1967).

force, even when it is used against persons who have clearly committed an offense, ceases to be a proper exercise of police power, and policemen become readily available targets of hostility even when they are carrying out their duties.

Finally, civil disobedience as a political tactic to force compliance with nationally proclaimed policies for eliminating discriminatory practices also contributes indirectly to the hostility. Often such action has run up against one-sided law enforcement in which demonstrators were clearly victimized. Publicity has centered as much on police against demonstrator as on the policy against which he demonstrates. Without doubt, the true meaning of civil disobedience as a tactic meant to force attention to griev-ances has not always been fully understood. But the image of the struggle for equality disseminated by the news media into the Negro community can be invoked to justify acts of overt resistance even to legitimate arrests.

The disposition of groups of slum dwellers to view the use of force by the police as threatening accounts for the frequency with which it elicits a hostile response from spectators. Yet, no matter how much all may be disposed to view the situation in the same way, far from all are ready to react with overt violence. *For a polarization with the victim against the police to take place, there must also be a critical mass of susceptible individuals ready to go into action at any type of provocation.* How many susceptible people must be on the scene for a collective outburst to occur probably varies with the amount of counterforce at hand. To defy a single policeman in a dark corner takes no more than half a dozen determined young men. However, the scene in which these incidents have typically erupted ensured that people ready to act against police authority would be present in sufficiently large numbers. An incident is more likely to trigger violence: (a) when it occurs at a busy intersection or some other locality where many people are present; (b) when the weather is unusually hot and sidewalks are packed with people sitting and standing around—especially the young and idle—so that the sound of sirens quickly brings a throng of onlookers; (c) at a dance, at a public facility, or on a holiday (like Halloween)—all of them occasions of legitimate license; (d) at a demonstra-tion when participants are stirred up as, for example, in a protest over segregated schools (as in Oakland in 1966) or against an act of police violence (as in Harlem during the summer of 1964); (e) when an extra-ordinary event, such as the assassination of Martin Luther King, stirs widespread indignation (as in Washington, D. C. in 1968).

These crowds will contain some highly susceptible and volatile individuals ready to engage the police (or anyone else) should there be a likely opportunity. Because such a crowd has no initial organization nor any agreed upon policy on demands it will back by demonstrating, the initiative readily passes to those conspicuous by their action. They are the visible representatives of the crowd; their actions speak for it. The mass of passive bystanders—perhaps themselves immune to violence—lend tacit support merely by their presence. Lacking a representative leader, a crowd can only act, and once it gets going very few within its ranks will dare intervene, except by word, to preserve law and order. Despite the appearance of psychological unity, the commitment of many persons to the violence remains tenuous, critical, and even hostile.

The frequency with which certain kinds of incidents have, in the 1960s, triggered violence points to a partial breakdown in the etiquette by which relations between police and ghetto dwellers have been governed in the past. The present is obviously a period of transition, until the limits of what either police or public will tolerate have been collectively redefined and new forms of accommodation worked out. Yet police action cannot in itself eliminate the riot potential. It can only influence its forms.[6] The real issue is the hypocrisy—actual or imaginary—of the power structure. Violence redresses past wrongs or at least gives the appearance of doing so. It also tends to leave the participants with a feeling of power. Whether or not it is effective in bringing about social reforms, violence in this situation is a collective defense that resolves inner tension.

It is important to separate the action that triggers an outburst from the process by which a larger conflagration is kindled. Escalated riots pass through several phases.

In the initial phase, the confrontation is between police and others near the scene of the original incident. We are, of course, aware that in some of the recent riots attacks on property and looting preceded the arrival of police. Indeed, as "rioting" begins to take on the character of a social movement, the range of events with the capacity to trigger a major disturbance widens. So far, however, the largest number of outbursts have arisen from some local incident.

In the second phase, what was a confrontation between police and a specific crowd of people becomes a general confrontation between two groups of which the individual persons are only representatives. Thus, police reinforcements brought to the scene of an original disturbance may, in dispersing that crowd, be inviting other confrontations with persons with no connection or direct knowledge of the precipitating event. Once order breaks down the whole situation changes.

In the third phase, people begin to feel that there is general immunity from punishment. Any visible representatives of what is considered

---

6 Cf. Morris Janowitz, *Social Control of Escalated Riots* (Chicago: University of Chicago Center for Policy Study, 1968).

the power structure—including press, autoists, curiosity seekers—become potential targets of attack. During this phase destructiveness also becomes more wanton and looting for personal gain begins to proliferate. Idlers and brawlers coalesce with political groups.

Those who never get close to the action may gain the impression that the whole ghetto "blows up" during a major riot, an impression often promoted by picture-oriented news coverage that concentrates on the more dramatic events. Closer observation contradicts this impression. No more than a small percentage of adult residents in any riot torn area have participated in any way. In a study of riots in six cities in 1967, Fogelson and Hill estimate that "about 18 per cent of the riot area residents, on the average, took part in the disorders."[7]

Epidemiology of Disruptive Behavior

The epidemic spread of rioting throughout the community does not primarily hinge on close physical contact with others who are engaged in this kind of activity. Only a small proportion of the residents in the ghetto initially become aware of a riot by what they see or hear firsthand. Although being on the scene no doubt draws some people into activities they would otherwise avoid, there is considerable evidence that many near the scene remain passive bystanders, that others hide indoors to avoid danger, and that some try to intervene to stop or contain the disorder.

The issue of how rioting spreads can be translated into one of identifying leaders, carriers, and susceptibles. Not only are such identifications difficult to make, but the categories themselves are somewhat nebulous. Consider for a moment the matter of "leadership." In one sense, the person who first resists arrest is the real leader—the "cause" of the whole thing— but he often plays that role unwittingly and his influence soon recedes into the background. Other "leaders" are instigators who deliberately stand back and incite others to take the lead in activities in which they themselves do not openly participate. The active participant who, for one reason or another, "casts the first stone" or acts in ways that serve as a model for others to follow represents quite a different kind of leader (or carrier). Yet not all activists are leaders in the sense of initiating action that others follow. There can be "leaders" without followers, i.e., persons carried away by their own excitement, sense of mission, or feelings of self-importance. They "lead" as long as they occupy the center of the stage, and their behavior is condoned by others who cheer them on or passively approve. Some acts

---

[7] R. M. Fogelson and R. B. Hill, *Who Riots? A Study of Participation in the 1967 Riots* (New York: Bureau of Applied Social Research, Columbia University, 1968).

are merely for the benefit of an unseen mass media audience. Finally, there are the leaders of small groups who act in concert. The importance of these groups increases as rioting spreads. Their activities have the appearance of spontaneity inasmuch as they tend to seize opportunities rather than follow any preconceived plan. In this way they certainly contribute to keeping the riot going.

It is highly unlikely that an incident can expand into large-scale rioting without the prior existence of groups that become the nuclei of trouble from which other incidents develop. These groups are of two kinds: (1) politically oriented associations whose activities sometimes lead to confrontations but who are ready to seize on any sign of trouble in order to agitate for their goals, and (2) groups who normally engage in various sorts of illegal activity and who therefore take advantage of any disorder as a cover for such pursuits. That militant cells have played some part in many of the riots is undeniable, but the extent of their responsibility for keeping the rioting going is difficult to fix. In addition, there are indications that, despite the presence among the rioters of many persons with "major" criminal records, most of those picked up did not have "a record as serious as that generally present in many nonriot felony bookings usually handled by urban police and courts."[8]

Surveys of attitudes among Negroes concerning rioting as a means of protest provide little ground for the belief that the majority will in the reasonable future become sufficiently infected by the contagious appeal of violence to participate, even though many are apt to justify the riot after it has occurred. The overwhelming majority do not approve violence as a tactic for redressing grievances, and a large proportion assess negatively the utility of the riot. After the Detroit riot (1967), only 24 per cent of the black residents interviewed believed Negroes had more to gain than lose by resorting to violence, and very few wanted another riot. In Miami (1968) just before riots began during the Republican convention, some 10 per cent of the black residents said they were themselves prepared to riot; more than half expressed unqualified disapproval of violence as a philosophy.

As regards the social characteristics of rioters, the statistics available from police blotters, postriot surveys, and interviews with prisoners fail to substantiate some press reports that point to the unemployed teenagers as the prime movers behind the activity. All indications are that those most active in the riots of the 1960s approximated in certain respects a cross section of the younger male population in the ghetto areas. Thus, the typical (modal) male rioter arrested in Rochester (1964) and in Watts (1965) was in his upper twenties—only one-fourth were under twenty-one. Likewise, the majority

8 Statistical report on the Watts riot by the California Bureau of Criminal Identification and Investigation, distributed by the California Department of Justice, 1966.

were employed—albeit usually in an unskilled job.[9] Among a group of men arrested (mainly for crimes against property) on the first day of the massive 1967 Detroit riot, 84 per cent were employed, students, or trainees; their median age was between 24 and 25.[10]

The various studies of rioters show them to be as well educated on the average as nonrioters. In Detroit, what seems to have distinguished the young rioters, however, was a "distinctive set of attitudes suggesting aliena-tion." They were said to have "little concern for their fellow men and a frus-tration in meeting near-term goals—people susceptible to the black nationalist philosophy that the law and order of a white-built society is not worth pre-serving." The greatest support for violence as a political tactic was found neither among those least educated nor among those best educated (beyond high school) but among those in the middle—the "in-between group who have an idea of the better life that education brings but have a low sense of efficacy —that is, they believe that they have little influence on the political scene . . . and are wondering whether anything is worthwhile anymore."[11]

These general statistics notwithstanding, we will be able to explain fully the epidemiology of any riot—or to arrive at less time-and-place bound generalizations about the epidemiology of violence—only when we have better information on the types of participation by different types of people in various phases of riot development. Systematic observations and analysis are needed, but police records and self-reports (mainly based on survery data on the social characteristics of rioters) remain the most available and cited source of evidence on the escalated riots of the 1960s. Everyone working with these statistics is aware of the caveats of the inherent biases in these data.

Those arrested during a riot are often picked up on the merest sus-picion and booked afterwards on charges of loitering, refusing to obey a police order, or curfew violation. The same booking charge may be made whenever an arresting officer fails to provide a detailed account of what led to the arrest. The young, just because they are young, may be more vulnerable to arrest, but more of them are able to escape because the old move more slowly. Both experienced criminals and political agitators have some motive to cover their activity. Indeed, as long as police attention is focused on those who stand out because of their visibility (because of beards, insignia, clothing, etc.), it is conceivable that the more naive are the ones most likely to face arrest.

---

[9] The statistics on Rochester are from P. W. Homer, *Riots of July 1964: Report to the Council* (Rochester: Office of the City Manager, 1965) ; those on Watts are from the source cited in the preceding footnote.

[10] J. E. Brent, *et al.*, *A Study of Selected Characteristics of a Sample of Detroit Rioters*, Michigan Department of Justice, Bureau of Prisons (draft, August 9, 1967).

[11] Detroit Urban League, *op. cit.*

There are similar difficulties with self-reports obtained in a postriot survey. Response errors are not always distributed randomly, and the young and the transients are frequently excluded by the procedures used to construct a sample. Still, the implication is, as pointed out, that those who were most active in the rioting represented a reasonable cross section of the young adult male population in the ghettoes where riots occurred. What we still have to pin down is: Who are the core persons who initiate and sustain the activity that others imitate and take up? How does their behavior—illegitimate and disjunctive as it may be—gather the force to carry away so many people? What contributes to the rapid expansion of "rioting" once order breaks down is the congruence of such activities with many favored forms of gang violence—throwing rocks, breaking windows, setting fires, ganging up on victims, vandalizing and other crimes against property. These are relatively normal for a large number of boys—white as well as black—growing up in disorganized slum areas. As rioting spreads these acts increase in frequency; in some blocks of some cities they obviously reached rather unprecedented proportions. There are also fewer inhibitions against engaging in acts of a more serious nature. Vandalism, which is ordinarily confined to breaking windows and defacing property, comes to include the use of Molotov cocktails. Finally, the visibility of such activity increases, and persons ordinarily not prone to this kind of behavior become involved.

To recognize that much of the behavior observed in a riot has antecedents in the delinquent acts characteristic of members of the lower class subculture of the United States is not to adopt the hoodlumism theory of riots. That theory, emphasizing the search for troublemakers, is far too simpleminded to merit the attention of social scientists, except perhaps to refute it conclusively. The point is that on riotous occasions more people engage in more violent acts. Some mutations in behavior do occur, and, what is more, they encounter far less than the expected amount of disapproval from ghetto residents, who are also the major victims in any disturbance. Many who disapproved of the rioters were less ready to condemn their violence or lack of temperance; the rioting appeared to some extent justified by circumstances.[12]

An individual may turn violent simply because he is frustrated and becomes enraged. However, the escalation and spread of violence can occur only when such behavior appears to be somehow sanctioned, at least tacitly, as an appropriate and justifiable response to a problematic situation. Acts of violence differ by their very nature from legitimate demands; compliance

---

12 See, for instance, Joe R. Feagin and P. B. Sheatsley, "Ghetto Resident Appraisals of a Riot," *Public Opinion Quarterly,* XXXII (1968), 352–62, concerning the Bedford-Stuyvesant riot in 1964. Though most residents of the riot area were negative toward the persons involved, a majority saw them as protesting against discrimination and deprivation in its various forms.

with the latter derives from beliefs in the sanctity of the authority behind them in a way that acquiescence to brute force does not. This does not preclude that violence may be excused, condoned, or even praised. Knowledge of how behavior during a riot is sanctioned and justified contributes to our understanding of its epidemiology.

The self-justifications of rioters who continue to pay lip service to a necessity for self-restraint usually involve a denial or displacement of personal responsibility. A situation that makes it possible to say to oneself, and to others, that "someone else started it," that one "was doing only what everyone was doing already," that one's "own action was clearly provoked," or that those victimized "deserved what they got" helps to reduce misgivings and still the voice of conscience. The subjective freedom, the euphoria, and the carnival atmosphere so frequently encountered on the riot scene exemplify the momentary sense of power that persons who normally feel oppressed, threatened, and insecure experience when they can cast off restraints with apparent impunity. Aggrieved people want to see results, and they derive considerable satisfaction from revenge against those responsible for past wrongs, real or imagined. These self-justifications, on the part of persons whose living conditions have caused them to suffer considerable psychological damage, contain an important irrational component. Their actions are often directed at substitute objects, provided they are readily available as targets (as, for instance, firemen). Since internalized controls are to some extent neutralized, long-range implications are rarely considered. It is in this respect, then, that behavior during a riot represents a spontaneous collective defense. The participants collectively seize the opportunity for acting out their whims and impulses; their behavior appears to be sanctioned by default.

In addition, the reactions of outsiders may give tacit sanction to the riotous activities.[13] Thus, inaction by law enforcement officials, who deliberately look the other way or simply appear to condone the violence by their reluctance to intervene decisively, provide sanction and contribute to the climate of tolerance which surrounds the riot. This definition of the situation can result from a whole range of actions, from mere indecisiveness, at some strategic moment before public order has broken down, to a promise of full amnesty for all violators. Moreover, people may simply expect no interference because policemen are from the same ethnic group as they, or because they suspect governing officials would find an open confrontation too politically unrewarding, or because the courts are known to be lenient. In part, the continued rioting itself helps define the situation as sanctioned, but

---

[13] Illustrative of riots with tacit sanction are the eighteenth century mobs that ransacked the homes of political radicals and dissenters in the name of the King and Church, or the language riots in Hyderabad in 1956. Others that come to mind are southern lynch mobs, not to speak of some more recent attacks on civil rights and peace demonstrators.

a general tolerance of violence as justified, understandable, and even unavoidable, though unfortunate, invites disruption as a method of protest, to gain revenge, or as means for personal enrichment.

It does not follow, however, that riots can be easily suppressed by a simple display of force. On the contrary, force used arbitrarily disrupts even the tenuous consensus on which the restoration of order must rest. Authority that is defined as totally unresponsive to the needs of its subjects loses all claim to legitimacy and, as a consequence, may increasingly resort to tyrannical rule. Violence and terror thus gain justification among the subjects. Those who employ these tactics set themselves up in deliberate opposition to the dominant order, whose morality and laws they no longer accept as binding and against which they assert their own conception of justice. The deviant behavior is accepted as an appropriate form of conduct—it is a sanctioned counternorm. However, violence against an enemy who is seen as the personification of all evil ceases to be rational. It tends to become absolute. One occasionally encounters this excess of violence in communal rioting, where the society has literally split apart.

It need hardly be argued that the black ghetto, whatever its potential promise, represents a highly pathological segment of American society. Violence is always close to the surface because much of it receives tacit toleration from police and some of it appears justified by the continuing victimization of ghetto inhabitants. A riot offers new justifications, though these are not the same for all participants. In the first place, it offers new opportunities to evade personal responsibility for many delinquent and illegal acts. Second, to the extent that law enforcement breaks down, many rioters do indeed become relatively immune from punishment for acts perpetrated during the riot. Finally, any clearly unreasonable or indiscriminate use of force against rioters and, more particularly, bystanders, elicits an inevitable counterreaction. The polarization becomes inevitably racial. An image of black solidarity helps redefine and so justify disruptive acts. The riot mentality is fed by images and justifications, and, as these are accepted, the riot diffuses to become a communal uprising. It begins to subside when the sanctions that have given it the appearance of an appropriate collective response are replaced by others, including shock at the consequences, fear of reprisals, and the gradual reemergence of counterrioters as leaders whose voices are heard. In no sense can one view the entire ghetto as arising in a single spontaneous act all at the same time.

Replication of a Pattern:
Rioting as an Anomic Movement

It is usually considered axiomatic that racial outbreaks of the kind that have rocked our major cities can be prevented by dealing with basic structural deficiencies that undermine morale and cause unrest in the slums. Accordingly, even those who condemn violence after it occurs frequently speak beforehand of its inevitability. By such prediction they seek to dramatize the need for structural reforms. Regardless of where the "basic causes" of these racial disturbances lie, one cannot treat rioting as simply a response to cumulative frustration. Rather we must look at it within the context of political negotiations, where many different groups are actively engaged in presenting the interests of the poor and the oppressed as they perceive them.

What Almond and Coleman have called the "anomic interest group" is characteristic of many underdeveloped countries.[14] It is a more or less spontaneous (unorganized) breakthrough into the political system. Direct action on the streets has typically been the avenue by which a suppressed group gains recognition and lends force to its demands. In the United States, for example, violence in the labor field has generally occurred more frequently in disputes in which management refused to treat the union as a responsible bargaining agent than in disputes in which management recognized the union. The machine-wrecking actions of Luddites had elements of what Hobsbawn has called "collective bargaining by riot."[15] Historical research has shown that attacks on mills and places of storage likewise served to reduce prices and exact money from the wealthy. These outbursts were hardly direct or primitive responses to frustration—some of the most politically conscious citizenry joined the action. In fact, anomic movements are more likely to occur not when frustrating circumstances seem unchangeable but when change is expected, yet there seems to be no other way to assure it or speed it up.

To what extent, then, were we dealing in these riots with an anomic interest group that employs violence as an instrument of politics? The evidence bearing on this question is to be found largely in the pattern of replication throughout the country. That there should have been so many similar incidents of large-scale rioting within a short time span indicates that, however spontaneous the elements that underlay any incident and its particular pattern of expansion, the rioting reflected at the same time the stirrings of a major social movement.

Two observations seem at first glance to contradict this contention. First, most of these outbreaks coincided with unusually hot weather rather than with politically significant events. This was especially true during the long hot summer of 1967, the year rioting in urban centers appears to have reached its peak. Also, the diffuse nature of most of these outbursts points to their function as an occasion for collective license, i.e., as an occasion where

---

[14] G. A. Almond and J. S. Coleman, eds., *The Politics of the Developing Areas* (Princeton: Princeton University Press, 1960).

[15] E. J. Hobsbawn, *Social Bandits and Primitive Rebels* (New York: The Free Press of Glencoe, Inc., 1959).

many of those present can readily cast off normal restraints. Yet the present political climate lends implicit sanction to this disposition and tends to channel it into intergroup conflict. According to many reports, Negro rioters, far from going on a binge, were in fact highly discriminating with regard to their targets, venting their destructiveness primarily on stores of white property owners, while Negro owners of stores were able to secure some measure of protection by displaying "soul brother" signs. The impression left may nevertheless be misleading. Supermarkets, drug chain outlets, appliance, clothing, and liquor stores were among the favored targets of rioters. Most such stores, even in Negro areas, are owned by whites, and when a Negro owned store was burned and ransacked, as happened on occasion, no sign remained to indicate the owner's race. Nor did the selection of stores correspond to the pattern of Negro grievances. For example, liquor stores, which rarely went unscathed, were judged by Negroes in Detroit to be far more fair in their dealings with customers than most other business establishments, such as loan offices and real estate agencies.[16] Yet attacks on property usually are attacks on white property, and general resentment can always be linked to some grievance.

Our second observation refers to the militant rank and file of the civil rights movement. Except for a relatively small but nevertheless significant minority on its extreme wing, they have dissociated themselves from the violence. Nevertheless, increasing militancy reflects the growing expectation among Negroes of all walks of life that they should be enjoying full equality and their fear that even legitimate claims are being denied. The appeal of mass civil disobedience was certainly the product of such a pairing of frustration with hope. Yet, sit-ins and passive resistance were not only tactics for dramatizing especially irritating Negro grievances. Mass civil disobedience carried with it the mystique of direct action and thus often attracted recruits who caught its spirit without grasping the uses and limitations of the new tactic. This then set the context within which collective protest could spill over and become collective license.

In other words, the looting, vandalization, or destruction in riots hardly represent a deliberately planned tactic meant to secure specific goals. These actions satisfied some feelings of revenge and brought some personal gain, but by their destruction of many Negro homes and of businesses where Negroes held jobs, they also brought much suffering. Even where they closed down white businesses, they did not automatically make it possible for blacks to come in. They brought about neither an extension of credit nor a reduction in retail prices. The protest was primitive and anomic (not a solidary form of action) because most participants lacked any clear perception of interests of the black community.

The real political significance of the riots lies in the new political

---

16 Detroit Urban League, *op. cit.*

leadership they bring to the fore and in the way the white power structure reacts. The latter has in the past been inclined to respond to outbursts, or threats of violence, by focusing on troublemakers while avoiding serious negotiations over issues that touch the entire Negro community. Black accommodationist leaders are then caught on the horns of a clear-cut dilemma. On the one side, they need dramatic successes in order to maintain even a tenuous hold over their following. On the other side, their ability to gain a hearing within the power structure depends on their ability to restrain their constituencies. The prospect of violence gives leverage to their demand that legitimate Negro claims be met. But the rules of the political game have clearly been changing. The game is in some ways played more effectively by those who do not shrink back from the consequences of direct action in the streets.

The ambivalence of many Negro leaders about civil disobedience and extremes of militancy as tactics is aggravated by a tendency on the part of the mass media to give a disproportionate amount of attention to some would-be leaders without a large following, whose status is enhanced by—indeed, may be the creation of—the publicity given some of their statements advocating violence or predicting that it will come. It lends to violence a degree of legitimacy as a conflict tactic beyond what it would otherwise have. Not only does it gain attention—sometimes it even leads to results. This does not imply that the media are the "cause" of the riot; only that they are intricately involved in the process by which a movement raises demands.

A society with a mature civic culture is disinclined to react to violence with physical repression. In such societies the use of force to suppress a disorder is apt to arouse strong criticism. The forces of law and order are committed only with the utmost hesitancy, and any excesses on their part diminish the legitimacy of their authority to restore order without resort to force. This is well-known to the opponents. The same motor vehicles, two-way walkie-talkies, and other devices relied on by the police for maintaining control during a riot are also available (though on a more restricted basis) to those bent on exploiting the potential for disorder which is always so close to the surface in depressed communities. The movement constitutes a partly political reaction against structural maladjustments within the society at large. It will remain anomic until new forms of interest articulation are evolved. These forms are already in the making. Violence has become more discriminating, but there is some danger that counterviolence on the grass-roots level will increase the potential for communal rioting.

Implications for Collective Behavior Theory

Collective violence among residents of Negro ghettoes in the urban centers of America challenge the student of collective behavior to put his theories to some test. Our own reading of the escalated riots in the sixties strengthens a conviction that the theory of the psychological crowd—the cornerstone of many generalizations about collective violence—sheds little light on either the causes behind the riots or on their internal dynamics, and ought finally to be relegated to history. Whatever the specific version of the theory, its explanatory value is limited. It tends to exaggerate the degree of mental unity among the participants and points to that unanimity to account for the impulsivity and irrationality that one encounters in such disturbances.

Disturbances of this type are complex social phenomena that involve many different kinds of behavior and different kinds of participants. The widespread disorders did not develop as a direct response to frustration but must be viewed as an element in a new pattern of Negro militancy as it has developed among the depressed people of the ghetto. The pattern of rioting may have varied from time to time or place to place. But it has its sociological roots in an isolated mass, where the level of political organization is still low, though rapidly rising, and where an effective political leadership is in the process of developing. To understand rioting as collective protest, it is important to study carefully what happens in each particular riot. One has, especially, to avoid a perspective that emphasizes the disruptive elements in a riot to the exclusion of its problem-solving aspects. Otherwise all riots appear alike—as simple disturbances of public order. The question is how we can arrive at a level of explanation that goes beyond the idiosyncratic elements of any particular riot situation.

All crowd behavior has to be studied as collective problem-solving activity within the larger context of social and organizational breakdown and change. Rioting, in this context, evolves as a form of collective pressure or protest where large numbers of people are crowded and alienated together, sharing a common fate that they no longer accept as necessary, though to them it may seem inevitable. Even small incidents are likely to precipitate large disturbances. Whatever the underlying cause of riots, civil society cannot tolerate physical violence and destruction (or the threat of it) as a means of pressure without changing its character, but neither can it suppress them by force alone. Conflict needs to be rechanneled into more effective day-to-day negotiations with visible results. The main result of efforts toward the political organization of slum dwellers is to provide organizational alternatives to collective bargaining by riot. Until this happens, the isolated mass within the black community is apt to continue to produce its own forms of anomic protest, forms that can at best be contained.

9

Enrico L. Quarantelli

EMERGENT ACCOMMODATION GROUPS: BEYOND CURRENT COLLECTIVE BEHAVIOR TYPOLOGIES

Collective behavior as a field of inquiry has traditionally been interested in the emergence of new social groups. In this connection, the focus has primarily, although not exclusively, been on such phenomena as the coming into being of lynch mobs, rioting crowds, religious sects, deviant cults, disputing factions of publics, revolutionary uprisings, reform movements, etc. One aspect that characterizes such groups is that they are conflict groups. That is, the new or emerging groups are typically at odds or engaged in some kind of social struggle with other groups and/or the contemporary social order.

      Sometimes the explicit focus in collective behavior has been less on conflict per se, and more on the emergence of a new social order. However, this is merely a difference in emphasis and does not constitute a different kind of approach. Instead of looking at the nature of the group relationship itself—conflict, the concern is with the end product—the replacement or displacement of aspects of the old social order. This is noticeable in Blumer's classic statement which delineated the field of collective behavior and represented the dominant formulation about the field for the decades of the 1940s and 1950s. He notes that the study of collective behavior traces

> ...the way in which the elementary and spontaneous forms develop into organized forms.... The appearance of elementary collective groups is indicative of a process of social change. They have the dual character of implying the disintegration of the old and the appearance of the new. They play an important part in the development of new collective behavior and of new forms of social life.[1]

Such a focus on conflict and on groups attempting to build a new social order was especially noteworthy when sociology was dominated by notions of integration and the use of equilibrium models. If heed had been paid to this focus, it would have served as a salutary corrective to theoretical developments and empirical research in a number of areas of sociological concern. The field of collective behavior under Blumer's guidance, while unable to shift the dominant orientation, helped keep alive in American sociology at least the notions of conflict and of emergence.

Much remains to be done yet to develop the conflict strand in the collective behavior approach. For example, as Blumer noted just a few years ago, and as is very aptly documented in the work by scholars and researchers attempting to categorize the recent racial and student disturbances in American society, there as yet does not exist a workable typology of "riots."[2] Likewise, for instance, little is understood of the factors which enable functioning entities to develop in the form of conflict groups despite the fact that many of them are frequently marked by considerable internal division into factions and strife among their members. Thus, the development of a typology of conflict groups and the determination of the conditions leading to their emergence and of what aspects of them, if any, get institutionalized still remains a major task of collective behavior analysis.

However, even less well studied has been another kind of emergent group—what might be called the *accommodative* type. (To avoid a neologism we have resurrected an old Park and Burgess term, one they specifically use to contrast with their concept of conflict groups, but a somewhat more melo-

---

[1] Herbert Blumer, "Collective Behavior," in *New Outline of the Principles of Sociology,* ed. Alfred M. Lee (New York: Barnes & Noble, Inc., 1946), pp. 168 and 196.
[2] Herbert Blumer, "The Justice of the Crowd," review of *The Crowd in History* by George Rude, *Trans-action,* II (Sept./Oct., 1965), 44.

dious sounding label than "accommodation groups" might be desirable.)[3] These groups are characterized by the fact that their internal activities are highly cooperative in nature and their external behavior aims at or results in action of an integrative sort. As we shall show, these groups may and sometimes do arise in a discordant context, but in themselves they are not conflict groups at odds with other groups or the larger society. We would suggest that the study and understanding of such kinds of emergent behavior is a second major task of collective behavior analysis, for such groups also contribute to the development of new social orders, some of a temporary, others of a more permanent nature.

In this paper we propose to develop a typology of and to illustrate accommodative types of groups. Of more crucial importance, of course, would be the detailed setting forth of the specific conditions associated with the emergence, development, and establishment of these kinds of social groups. However, such a task cannot be undertaken unless it is first recognized that this particular kind of social phenomena does exist and assumes different forms. Thus, this paper, although it does indicate at least two general situational contexts from which nonconflict groups emerge, focuses primarily on the different types of accommodation groups that can develop in crisis situations.

The data used to illustrate our ideas are drawn from a variety of sources, but the greatest bulk of them have been derived from the early work of the Ohio State University Disaster Research Center, especially its initial field studies of natural disasters and civil disturbances.[4] However, no claim to definitiveness or closure is made. Even though grounded in empirical observations, the typology set forth and the general conditions discussed are to be treated as rather tentative and subject to considerable revision on the basis of later more systematic data analysis. The presentation in this paper is an illustration of the kind of direction towards which this kind of collective behavior analysis should go, rather than a setting forth of established findings.

Situational Contexts

There are different situational contexts in which new groups arise. A general context which often leads to emergent phenomena is a crisis situation. However, in ideal terms at least, such a situation can be either of a consensus or of a dissensus nature.

---

[3] Robert E. Park and Ernest Burgess, *Introductoin to the Science of Sociology* (Chicago: University of Chicago Press, 1924), p. 722.

[4] This study was partly supported by PHS Research Grant Number 1 RO1 MH 15399–01 from the Center for Studies of Mental Health and Social Problems, Applied Research Branch, National Institute of Mental Health.

A consensus crisis situation is one in which there is general overall agreement about goals and about what should be done. It is one in which there is little dispute about the assignment of priorities, about what legal constraints can be ignored during the emergency, etc. This kind of situation is well exemplified by what can be found in most communities after a major natural disaster. Typically, there is very widespread agreement about the saving of lives, and about the need to put all resources—including normally private property—at the disposal of the community until the major emergency needs are met.

The potential in such kinds of situations for behavior that differs considerably from the normal has generally been recognized. However, the prevalence of a series of myths has obscured an understanding of what occurs and has deflected attention away from important social phenomena that comes into being. These myths, believed by scholars as well as others, tend to lead to a search for deviant behavior, primarily for such phenomena as looting, panic, and other antisocial activities. Actually these kinds of behaviors in consensus kinds of crises are extremely rare. The Jekyll and Hyde conception of social behavior, on which these myths rest, incorrectly leads researchers to anticipate or project certain kinds of misbehavior. The myths also help to hide, in descriptions and analyses, the great amount of cooperative and integrative behavior that actually emerges in such situations, especially the collective and group efforts to cope with the emergency. These range from informal search and rescue teams combing a stricken neighborhood to overall community coordinating committees directing mass assaults upon the new and pressing problems generated by major catastrophes.

To be sure, groups do occasionally emerge even in overall consensus situations that are at odds with other groups or the larger society. Thus, several coordinating committees at different levels of operation may develop and compete if they do not clash with one another. However, this is a rare happening in overall consensus situations; the overwhelming emergent pattern is accommodative types of groups.

In contrast to consensus kinds of crises are dissensus ones. The very essence of such situations are basic differences about overall goals and means to meet the emergency, whatever it may be (in fact, part of the controversy may be on the very issue of the existence of an emergency). The participants, often aligned in sharply contending factions and groups, are divided about what priorities to assign, whether certain laws are to be obeyed, etc. This kind of crisis is well illustrated by what could be observed in disturbances in American racial ghettos during the last few years, and in the even more recent university student disorders around the world. In general, these dissensus situations are marked by extensive disagreements about allocation of resources and the assignment of priorities in dealing with the perceived emergency, for example. This is the exact reverse of what is found in a consensus kind of crisis.

Because of the dramatic nature of such situations, with their confrontations of opposing forces, there has been a very strong tendency to look only at the conflicting groups involved. Yet even in such crises there often emerges solidaristic and integrating behavior that is new to the situation. In fact, the conflict groups themselves frequently spawn subgroups and new groupings which are primarily of an accommodative nature and have little to do directly with an attack upon other groups or the larger society. For example, informal "Black Cross" groups, visualized as similar to neutral Red Cross teams, are being developed in some urban ghetto areas in anticipation of casualties following possible racial clashes. And in these kinds of crises there also frequently emerge accommodative types of groups made up of persons not principally parties in the dissensus situation itself. These groups— for example, the *ad hoc* faculty committees that attempt to act as mediators between dissident American college students and embattled administrators in campus disturbances—often attempt to act as a third force between antagonists.

When groups emerge, they may be manifestations only of a temporary, situational adjustment in the social structure involved, or they may be the forerunners of social change. In other words, some emergent groups cease to exist when the immediate crisis is over, whereas others become part of a new social order. An example of the former is the informal coordinating group—composed of the city engineer, the county sheriff, the city planning director, state and local civil defense officials, and allied personnel—that came into being in the face of the threat of a major flood in the vicinity of a major community in Montana. This group unofficially organized warning and evacuation efforts and the systematic integration of various emergency measures by different agencies and organizations. Shortly after the danger was over, the group dissolved. It represented only a short-run or situational adjustment in the existing social organization that had been faced with a crisis.

On the other hand, recently, in many American cities conflict groups on the same side of an issue have banded together in a new group form in order to exert more pressure on the community power structure. For example, in 1968 in Buffalo, New York, an overall coordinating group called BUILD emerged to integrate the efforts of 165 different black organizations. The particular crisis which generated it passed, but the new social form in existence represents more than just a situational adjustment. The emergent group became part of the new social order in the city. Its relative permanency was an indication of social change.

The General Framework

Thus, the general elements of our framework are as follows. Situational contexts such as crises may be of a *consensus* or *dissensus* nature. Either

TABLE 1

TYPES OF COLLECTIVE ADJUSTMENT

	Situational context	Emergent group	Consequences for social structure
Crises	Consensus	Conflict	Change / Adjustment
		Accommodation	Change / Adjustment
	Dissensus	Conflict	Change / Adjustment
		Accommodation	Change / Adjustment

may allow the emergence of *conflict* and/or *accommodation* groups. Any of the four possible kinds of groups may contribute to *situational adjustment* and/or social *change*. In more graphic terms the framework may be depicted as in Table 1. However, for reasons indicated earlier, this paper will confine itself to an examination of accommodative types of groups in both consensus and dissensus situational contexts. Conflict groups will not be discussed further.

Involvement in Crises

In any crisis situation, persons may be involved in a primary or in a secondary way. That is, they may be parties initially and directly involved in the crisis situation, or they may participate only at a later stage and indirectly. Time and degree of involvement are only partly correlated. But in general, the later in the crisis period such involvement occurs, the more indirect or secondary in nature the participation will be. Thus, individuals who move into a disaster location after the initial impact is over are normally less directly involved in the emergency than the permanent inhabitants of the area. Similarly, the involvement of students engaged in direct physical confrontations with administrators or security forces is primary relative to that of a new faculty committee that later attempts to compromise the dispute between the two contending forces. In one sense, primary participants are necessary for the crisis itself to exist; the absence of secondary participants, although a condition that might alter the development of a crisis, would not make it disappear. For example, if an earthquake hits an uninhabited area there are obviously no primary participants; if the area is inhabited, however, there is a crisis to which the victim population has to repond whether or not groups from outside the stricken zone form to come to its assistance.

In many instances—in fact probably the majority—the members of new accommodation groups are drawn in the main from persons and groupings already primary participants in the crisis. In some relatively rare circumstances the membership may come exclusively from such a source.

A good illustration of this is the instance described by Charles E. Fritz of the unified group that developed in a small turnpike restaurant out of an aggregate of about 800 strangers isolated for several days from outside contact by a massive snowstorm. Despite the great heterogeneity in personal and social background of the participants, an overall social organization quickly developed to handle the problems stemming from physical crowding, scarce facilities, short supplies, and uncertainty over when the emergency period would end. Informal leaders, a fairly elaborate division of labor, space allocation for different functions, and new roles, norms, and sanctions appropriate to the emergency all appeared. In one sense, a quasi-new little society composed of the trapped motorists alone came into being.[5]

In other crisis situations the members of the new accommodation groups may come from secondary participants in the initial emergency situation. A recent example of this was the banding together of parents with friends and some school personnel in an attempt to maintain some sort of educational program for their children during the 1968 strike of New York City teachers. These persons were not at all involved in the original Ocean Hill-Brownsville dispute among the local governing board, the United Federation of Teachers, and other interested parties in the population. However, when almost all of the schools in the city were closed, a number of groups began to emerge in neighborhoods far distant from the original source of dispute. These groups were concerned with somehow continuing the educational process of the children in their own neighborhoods. In some instances, parents successfully took over schools, called in sympathetic teachers, ran essential services, provided makeshift educational materials, and hauled in school lunch milk supplies. These groups, which provided the new social organization in the informally reopened schools, were composed of secondary participants. The persons involved were not parties to the original crisis and never really got directly involved in the basic antagonisms which closed the schools in the first place.

It should be noted that it is not the nature of the crisis itself that determines primary or secondary participation. Search and rescue teams in a disaster, for example, may involve persons from both sources. Thus, in the

---

[5] Charles E. Fritz, Jeannette F. Rayner, and S. L. Guskin, *Behavior in an Emergency Shelter: A Field Study* (Washington: Disaster Research Group, National Academy of Sciences-National Research Council, 1958).

Anchorage, Alaska, earthquake, the first informal groups that searched for victims developed out of the coming together of local residents of stricken neighborhoods; later rescue teams that came into these localities were composed of persons from communities not directly hit in the catastrophe. In our terminology, the latter were secondary participants. The distinction between primary and secondary participation is consequently not one of activity per se, but of the timing and degree of involvement in the crisis, as indicated earlier.

In any given situation there may be only primary participants, only secondary participants, or a mixture of primary and secondary participants. This observation in itself, of course, is not very illuminating. The composition of the emergent group is important from an analytical viewpoint only to the extent that it affects either the development or establishment of emerging phenomena, a point that shall be discussed later.

Types of Emergent Accommodation Groups

If crisis contexts—as to consensus or dissensus, and involvement in crises—as to primary or secondary—are cross classified, it is possible to arrive at a four fold ideal typology of accommodation groups as shown in Table 2.

TABLE 2

TYPES OF ACCOMMODATIVE GROUPS

	INVOLVEMENT IN CRISES	
SITUATIONAL CONTEXTS	*Primary participants*	*Secondary participants*
Consensus	Type I	Type III
Dissensus	Type II	Type IV

Type I

These groups involve primary participants in a consensus situation. Without question, these are the most prevalent of all accommodative type emergent groups in emergencies. It is the rare crisis that does not generate them; in fact, multiple versions of them are likely to develop in crises of any magnitude. They also seem to be the emergent accommodation groups that most quickly come to the fore.

An example of this kind of group would be one of the groups that emerged in Anchorage, Alaska, after the 1964 earthquake. It was of a totally unplanned and unofficial nature and was headed by a lower echelon official from the public works department, the manager of an office supply company, and a union business agent—who at the time of impact happened to be in one of the hardest hit areas of the city. At first the group primarily engaged in search and rescue efforts but then expanded into damage assessment and other information seeking activities. It used several designations during its existence, such as the Damage Control Committee and the Disaster Desk. Although it was never formalized, it was responded to as an operating emergency group by other community organizations.

Type II

These groups involve primary participants in a dissensus situation and appear to be the rarest of the emergent type of accommodation groups. Even when they develop, Type II groups are furthest from the ideal type form. This is hardly surprising. Primary participants in an antagonistic relationship are not likely to turn to clear cut integrative efforts. However, there are some circumstances under which this occurs.

In at least twenty American cities "White Hat" patrol groups emerged in 1967 and 1968 during the course of racial disturbances.[6] Sometimes they were composed of youths who had participated in the initial stages of a disorder, but in all cases they involved young black people. Operating within their own neighborhoods, these groups worked in association with or had official support of the civil authorities. In general, they acted as mediators or buffers between the ghetto areas and the police. Their primary function was to aid in the maintenance of security or the restoration of order in their community, and they performed such tasks as calming crowds and observing and monitoring incidents. In a few instances these groups actually policed their neighborhoods. While the formation of such groups has now become partly institutionalized, their first appearances were quite unplanned and unofficial.

Type III

These groups involve secondary participants in a consensus situation. These appear relatively frequently, more so than other emergent type accommodation groups; they often have members from official organizations in them. That is, the participants seem to be disproportionately drawn

---

6 Terry Ann Knopf, *Youth Patrols: An Experiment in Community Participation* (Waltham, Mass.: Lemberg Center for the Study of Violence, Brandeis University, 1969).

from personnel who occupied formal positions in associations and groupings prior to the crisis. In general, Type III groups tend to be small in size and frequently dissolve relatively soon after the immediate emergency.

For example, this type of accommodation group appeared after the Indianapolis Coliseum explosion where eighty-one persons were killed and over four hundred were injured. Because of inconsistent codes, each of three different governmental agencies had the legal responsibility to assume overall control in the emergency. In the face of this and other emergency conditions an informal and *ad hoc* coordinating group emerged instead. It consisted of unofficial representatives of city, county, and state organizations and for about eight hours fairly well exercised overall control at the disaster site and on the community level over almost all organizations involved in responding to the disaster.

Type IV

These groups involve secondary participants in a dissensus situation, and they tend to be more varied in the forms and functions they assume than other emergent type accommodation groups. They also seem to appear mostly in relatively large scale crises and frequently remain in existence past the crisis that generated them. Not unexpectedly, there is somewhat of a tendency for Type IV accommodation groups eventually to get involved in the conflict themselves and to lose their integrative function.

An example of this type of accommodation group is the following. In the 1967 civil disturbance in Detroit, ghetto dwellers came to have several emergency needs. The food supply of many ran low because neighborhood groceries and supermarkets were closed by the strife, and other residents found themselves suddenly in the need of shelter as they were displaced from their homes by the widespread fires. In the face of this a number of ministers, church laymen, and other nonparticipants in the disturbance banded together to form the Interfaith Emergency Center. The core of this was composed of about a half a dozen leaders helped by a number of full-time volunteers who coordinated the work of hundreds of part-time volunteers at twenty-five collection points and twenty-one distribution points as well as at a central headquarters. A complex division of labor emerged in the Center including four separate departments (e.g., a staff of volunteer social workers operated a needs department). The Center was an around-the-clock operation which helped any victim of the disturbance who asked for assistance. In its initial form the Center lasted for about ten days. During that time it not only acquired a name, personnel, resources, facilities, and a table of organization but also formal and informal recognition from Detroit officials and other community associations, although at one point there was some verbal conflict with a few other organizations. In general, the Center in its core constituted a new group made up of secondary participants in the dissensus situation. In many respects the Center served as an integrating force in a very divisive community crisis.

The examples above have been taken from American society. However, emergent type accommodation groups appear in other societies also, although it is to be supposed some social structures are more conducive to their development than others. (For example, probably because of detailed and extensive advance emergency planning in Japan, emergent groups of any kind appear to be relatively rare in natural disasters there.) Nevertheless, as the following illustrations show, a wide variety of societies may give rise to emergent type accommodation groups.

During the Florence floods of 1966, nearly 350 displaced families unofficially occupied an empty but recently constructed housing project. A Type I group of seventeen persons emerged that informally organized what essentially was a new small community. During the French student occupation of the Sorbonne and other universities in May 1968, the presence of numerous conflict groups was well publicized. Less noticed were the accommodation groups (Type II in our category) that appeared. There emerged a great range of informal councils, assemblies, and commissions that took on the functions of infirmaries, nurseries, welfare and sanitation services, cafeterias, etc., as well as action committees that were primarily concerned with integrating the various activities that were going on. The participants of the action committees stayed apart from the direct conflict that was raging. When much of Chile was hit by an earthquake in 1965, a national coordination committee was established. This did not follow from any prior disaster plans, but was a Type III accommodation group composed of representatives from several national ministeries and a community action group. Finally, in the wake of the civil war in Biafra, international relief teams emerged apart from the usual church and Red Cross groups that operate in such situations. These teams were Type IV groups.

General and Specific Conditions for Emergence

A crisis is obviously a basic general condition necessary for the emergence of new groups. However, while this is a necessary condition, it is not a sufficient one. It is easy to find crises in which no groups emerge, and also crises in which such groups develop but show no staying power even of a limited nature.

Further, crises may bring out accommodation or conflict groups. In fact, both kinds of groups may simultaneously appear in the same situation, as indicated in some of the examples given earlier. Likewise, as previously discussed, the particular kind of emergent group is not directly dependent on the nature of the crisis context, although there is some degree of correlation present. That is, accommodation groups are more likely to appear in consensus situations, whereas conflict groups develop more frequently in dissensus contexts. But both kinds of groups may appear in each kind of situation. Whether they do or do not is dependent on something other than these general crisis conditions.

Thus, groups of the accommodative type do not simply spontaneously appear. Nor does the appearance of such groups bring automatic acceptance of them. There are specific conditions which facilitate the emergence of accommodation groups, and there are specific conditions which encourage the establishment of such groups—in the extreme case, to the point where they become institutionalized. This last point is an important one, because even accommodation groups need to be recognized, legitimated, and integrated into the ongoing social order if they are to have any duration whatsoever.

While it is not the purpose of this paper to detail the specific facilitating and establishing conditions, a few factors which seem to be of some importance may be mentioned. In every crisis situation there are persons who seek to interpret events and find consensual validation among their friends and acquaintances. Whether anything of a collective nature emerges from such interaction appears to be faciliated by a precrisis pattern of interaction among the potential participants, and by individuals who act as keynoters, defining the situation so that other persons can relate to the crisis and articulate a possible group role for themselves in it. But it also appears that consensus on appropriate action is not enough. Actions must be taken, whether intended or not, that commit the actors in a collective fashion. Given these and other conditions, an accommodation group is likely to crystallize. It does not last, however, unless there are conditions that help it to establish itself. Among the factors important in this connection are those that bring the newly emergent group to the awareness of others (e.g., a collective name often serves this function). Perhaps most crucial of all is the legitimation of the new accommodation group. In general, this seems to rest on the new group being defined as one that carries out necessary tasks or activities not the traditional responsibility of already established groups or organizations.

In this paper we have stressed the need to look at accommodative type emergent groups. In no way does this diminish either the importance of or the absolute necessity for study of emergent conflict groups. What is suggested is that a more balanced view be taken, that collective behavior as a field of study attempt to understand the nature of both types of groups as well as the conditions responsible for their emergence. As Blumer once noted, the field of collective behavior has not been effectively charted, and there is no generic classification of unstructured groups.[7] Our intent in this paper has been to help in this mapping, to indicate the need for recognition and conceptual clarification of emergent accommodation groups, phenomena that are outside of current collective behavior typologies.

---

[7] Herbert Blumer, "Collective Behavior," in *Review of Sociology*, ed. Joseph Gittler (New York: John Wiley & Sons, Inc., 1957), pp. 130–31.

IO

Guy E. Swanson

TOWARD CORPORATE ACTION: A RECONSTRUCTION OF ELEMENTARY COLLECTIVE PROCESSES

The study of collective behavior has always had two major parts. The first has consisted of an explanation of the forms and careers of certain spontaneous but transient groups—of panics, for example, of riotous or revelous crowds, of mass movements, social movements, reforms, revivals, or revolutions. The second major topic under collective behavior has had less attention and will be my special concern. This is the area of investigation which has focused upon those processes in which a body of people, not already organized for that purpose, moves from a state of social unrest toward a state of concerted action, such action becoming possible because these people evolve an organization through which they can work. The study of these processes has come to be coupled with research on crowds, social movements, and the like because both lines of inquiry are concerned with the appearance and consequences of social unrest. It is crucial, however, to keep them separate. The elementary collective processes may sometimes be inconspicuous, but they are always in operation in every organization. Crowds, revolutions, and similar movements are not.

It is Herbert Blumer who, in writing of these collective processes, refers to them as elementary.[1] So they are, if we think of them not as the simplest relations that can exist among people but as conditions that are required for the appearance of any organization—whether it be large or small, short-lived or enduring—and as conditions that must continuously be fulfilled if any organization is to persist for any length of time whatever.

We assign to elementary collective behavior those developments in interaction that specifically mark, and embody, a people's movement from the rise of social unrest to the creation, or recreation, of a social order. This criterion eliminates from consideration what might otherwise seem to be plausible candidates. For example, it eliminates the processes in interaction that Robert Bales considers to be elementary.[2] Bales is interested in processes that lead specifically from people's confronting of a collective problem to their deciding upon a solution. The sequence he has in mind recurs constantly in the life of every group. The participants become oriented to their problem; they assemble the information relevant for a solution, evaluate that information, draw conclusions, make a final choice, and assess their group's solidarity in the light of the choice they have made and of the events that led up to it. These steps do lead to collective action, but they need not be intiated in any important sense by social unrest. Moreover, the action taken need not entail the emergence, or the examination and reaffirmation, of a social organization.

It may help to clarify the point involved if we make it again, this time in connection with the relations involved in psychotherapy. The sequence important for Bales will be repeated again and again in the shifting relations between patient and therapist; but it does not, of itself, mark or embody the movement from mental disorder to mental health. In order to catch that movement, we would need to focus upon a sequence of processes that would include transference, resistance, and the like.[3]

The processes of social behavior that George C. Homans terms "the

---

[1] Herbert Blumer, "Collective Behavior," in *New Outlines of the Principles of Sociology,* ed. Alfred M. Lee (New York: Barnes and Noble, Inc., 1946), pp. 163–222.

[2] Robert F. Bales, *Interaction Process Analysis* (Cambridge: Addison-Wesley Publishing Co., Inc., 1950).

[3] Cf. Talcott Parsons, *The Social System* (Glencoe. Ill.: The Free Press, 1951), pp. 297–325; Chapter 10.

elementary forms" are not suited for our purpose on these same grounds.[4] What Homans has in mind are processes that lead specifically from two or more people being in a state of need to the development, between them, of the special kind of interpersonal relationship that he chooses to call "exchange"—a relationship in which each person gets as much as possible of whatever he requires from the others and gets it at the lowest possible cost.

Among the salient processes that serve to connect these two points will be: a search by individuals for potential resources and facilities, their encounters with others who may serve them in return for their services, the possible formation of partnerships or other coalitions among participants in this "market," and a sequence of bargaining in which it is determined who will provide what, to whom, and at what price. Such processes are elementary for Homans' analysis, given his objectives. They are not elementary if what we seek is an explanation of movement from social unrest to concerted action —to the emergence or reemergence of a social organization.

The Occasion for a New Look at Elementary Collective Processes

If we take a fresh look at our understanding of the elementary collective processes, we find that many of our assumptions have altered and that many of our expectations have changed. The research of the last twenty years has had its effect.

We have discarded the older idea that people in a state of unrest are like children who—being thrown together in some isolated spot and having never experienced human association—are building up society from their immediate experience. Such an assumption was always incompatible with our understanding of social unrest, but it took continued work based upon that concept to undermine a romantic imagery. Social unrest does not mean simply that individuals are discontented or unsettled or that unrest is widespread. It means that people want a new or renewed social order to replace one that they find unjust or ineffective, and it means that they believe that such an order will evolve if they work together. It has gradually become clear that, in this meaning, participants in social unrest will already be skilled in conducting social relations and in interacting with others to form organizations. Their diagnoses and prognoses may be hasty, erroneous, or unwitting; but people could not make them at all were they unaware of the relevance of social organizations for coping with certain classes of problems, or were they inexperienced in generating organizations or in using them.

---

[4] George C. Homans, *Social Behavior, Its Elementary Forms* (New York: Harcourt, Brace, and World, Inc., 1961).

Continued work has also made us aware that social unrest is ubiquitous and so, therefore, are the collective processes built upon it. The spectacular outbursts associated with great public issues are only a tiny fraction of the instances available for study. The career of every organization, large or small, includes frequent, perhaps regular, periods of renewal, revival, or reaffirmation. Each period springs from a weakening of collective solidarity, actual or foreseen. There is no organization in which the participants are fully content. Some measure of injustice and of ineffectiveness is endemic in groups. No participant is unalterably committed to any organization or to a particular role within it.[5]

Much of this everyday social unrest is expressed in conversations among kinsmen, friends, and co-workers. As recent research has shown, riots, revels, or repentance are often but the final products of countless sober conversations in which difficulties and opportunities were defined, commitments formed, and directions set. Indeed, so great is the evidence that people work through their collective problems before they act and the evidence that they often work in a purposeful, self-conscious fashion, that we are now in danger of forgetting, and of not explaining, the passion, the determination, and the speed with which that action can sometimes occur.

Great advantages accrue from our seeing that social unrest is ubiquitous, that it need not involve a sudden, inarticulate pouring out of social discontent, and that it involves people in the making of socially informed choices. Our opportunities to study social unrest, and the collective processes resulting from it, are vastly expanded. We can see the possibility of bringing these phenomena into the laboratory for controlled observation. And we are alerted to the further possibility that much that is relevant for the subject is already known but is hidden from us by our focus upon exceptional rather than everyday events. It seems, for example, that the recent work by Richard Mann, Theodore Mills, and Philip Slater on the natural history of training and therapy groups has had the elementary collective processes as its focus.[6] Since these investigators have looked at ranges of elementary phenomena not previously understood as a part of the emergence of an organization, an immediate need is for the integration of their work with that of others. The result, I hope to show, is more than a broadening of our knowledge. This integration gives a rather different meaning to many of our old

---

[5] Cf. Herbert Blumer, "Sociological Implications of the Thought of George Herbert Mead," *The American Journal of Sociology,* LXXI (1966), 535–44, 547–48.

[6] Richard D. Mann, et al., *Interpersonal Styles and Group Development* (New York: John Wiley and Sons, Inc., 1967); Theodore M. Mills, *Group Transformation, An Analysis of a Learning Group* (Englewood Cliffs: Prentice-Hall, Inc., 1964), and *The Sociology of Small Groups* (Englewood Cliffs: Prentice-Hall, Inc., 1967); and Philip E. Slater, *Microcosm: Structural, Psychological and Religious Evolution in Groups* (New York: John Wiley and Sons, Inc., 1966).

observations and enables us for the first time to understand certain of the others.

The training groups from which much of the data have come are formally structured as university courses. Enrollment is kept small. Students sit around an oval table. Here is Theodore Mills at the first meeting of such a course:

> *My name is Mills and this course is Social Relations 120. Its aim is to develop our skills in observing and understanding more fully concrete instances of human behavior. My role is to assist in this process.*
>
> *The materials we will deal with are of three sorts: first, the cases which are instances occurring in real life and written up by persons who were directly involved. Some of them, a good proportion of them, are written by former students in this course, for one of our assignments in the spring is to write up a case from our own experience and to present an analysis of it.*
>
> *I suggest for Wednesday and Friday of this week we discuss the first case, called "The Michaelson Family." I suggest that we raise the questions of what is happening and why persons are behaving as they are.*
>
> *The second set of materials is the readings. You will see that the first part contains selections from Fromm, from Piaget, from Freud, and from Schachtel. I suggest that we leave Monday, October 19, open so that we can raise questions in the group here about special problems you have encountered in the readings. From the list you will see that later on we will have selections from Leary, Hayakawa, Bateson, Baruch, Malinowski, and other selections from Freud.*
>
> *The third set of materials consists of events which take place here in our group. What we do here can be seen in itself as a case. Part of our task will be to understand what we find ourselves doing as a group, to understand why we do it as we do. I suggest that after we discuss the Michaelsons and the second case, called "The Seitons," we leave a session free to go back over what has happened in our own group.*
>
> *There will be an hour exam on November 9 and an examination covering cases, readings, and our own processes as a group at midyear. There is a spring paper—the personal case I mentioned earlier—and a final examination covering the entire year.*[7]

And then, except for his brief answers to questions concerning assignments, his presentation of further assignments, and his occasional Socratic questions directing the students' attention to a further examination of their own group, the instructor falls silent for the remainder of the academic year.

---

[7] Mills, *Group Transformation, op. cit.,* pp. 11–12.

Elementary Collective Processes: A Reconstruction

In the most extreme cases, elementary collective processes begin when people discover that they must do something together but do not know exactly what it is that they must do and are not organized to do it. That situation often arises naturally in the course of social life. It is purposely created for the students in training groups. In both natural and created situations people are accustomed, if they are interdependent, to employ an existing organization in defining and carrying out the action they must undertake together. Now they are interdependent but lack organization.

In training groups interdependence is created by students' enrollment in a formal course, by their desire to get for themselves what that course has to offer, and by all of the customary pressures in universities against dropping any course. Interdependence is strengthened by the requirements that they reflect upon their own collective life as a case for study, that they learn from one another, and, implicitly, that they develop an agenda and a set of procedures that will lead to their success in understanding social processes and in writing acceptable examinations and course papers. The instructor, present and attentive but usually silent, is the living embodiment of all these forces.

It is not uncommon in training groups, or in other extreme situations, that people try at first to employ accustomed forms of organization to get on with their task. It is a sign of the nature of their problem that these efforts fail. The critical indicator is that they are unable to talk relevantly to one another. Their words and sentences are uttered in conventional form, but are irrelevant for this situation. Lacking a proximate objective, and a procedure for reaching it, participants cannot assess the meaning of one another's words for actions that they might collectively undertake. Their utterances are just words—standardized cues to standardized referents but otherwise of no immediate help.

In training groups, there may at first be an effort to operate in the fashion of a conventional university class. This effort collapses because that form of organization presumes an active instructor, and none is present. Or, perhaps, the students adopt a loose parliamentary system for the conduct of business. But a parliamentary system has little correspondence to the relations among these people. Such a system is designed for work on a formal agenda under a legitimate chairman, with participants who have definite and divergent positions regarding some issues. These students lack that agenda. They have no chairman, and, at this stage in their affairs, no one is legitimated so to serve. Above all, they do not know what issues there are and so have no positions to advocate or oppose.

Another common tactic is to operate immediately as a direct democracy. But even that proves difficult. To what end will they work? By what rule will they make decisions? By unanimity? Tacit agreement? Majority vote? And who has a right to speak? How often? A right to summarize? How will they know what to discuss? How will they judge whether they are making progress or just talking? And what precautions must be taken so they will not have wasted their time, or be caught with troublesome commitments to one another, should the instructor reenter their affairs in the role conventional to a professor in the classroom?

The struggles to overcome these problems, and the failures, document for participants their interdependence and the inability of the existing organization of the classroom to enable them directly to do the work for which the course is designed. Certain participants lead in criticizing the existing organization. Others take a more positive role.[8] The latter, the "independent enactors" as Mann calls them, want to get on with the job. They waste little time on regrets, recriminations, or visions of an easy solution. Things are as they are, they say, and the members must work with the situation as it is, however far beyond it they may eventually go.

When the independent enactors' view has come at least tacitly to be accepted, there is at last a collective focus for energies and unrest. People stop hoping that they will find a solution ready at hand. They are freed from the old order of things and ready to move together toward something new, something they must jointly create. They are for the first time in their group's history, in a state of social unrest.

As people subsequently interact, they make a discovery. They find that one another's utterances are meaningful for collective action in a sense that they were not before.[9] People must know the sources, or referents, of one another's behavior if they are to judge its meaning. Social unrest embodies such sources and referents. Once it exists, participants can understand one another as exploring the possibilities for collective action that will transform the social order. Their words and deeds now have the status of gestures and not merely of cues. A cue is a stimulus that is found regularly to precede or accompany the occurrence of a certain other stimulus. Gestures are cues to the minds of others, to their knowledge, their feelings, their

---

[8] The rise and the powers of the independent enactors should probably be understood as that of the only "winning coalition" that is possible under these conditions. For a review of coalition theory, see William A. Gamson, "Experimental Studies of Coalition Formation," in *Advances in Experimental Social Psychology,* ed. Leonard Berkowitz (New York: Academic Press, Inc., 1964), I, 82–110.

[9] Cf. Peter McHugh, *Defining the Situation, The Organization of Meaning in Social Interaction* (Indianapolis: The Bobbs-Merrill Co., Inc., 1968). See also Table 1, Column A, below. I have discussed the phenomena in Column A in an article, "On Explanations of Social Interaction," *Sociometry,* XXVIII (1965), 101–23.

beliefs, and the like. In a situation of social unrest people pay close attention to one another's behavior—interpreting it, when possible, as a cue to the possibilities and alternatives for collective action that are sensed by others, to the implicit choices that others are making, and to their willingness or unwillingness to risk the undertaking of any particular course of joint activity.

The transformation of cues into gestures, and the conditions that bring it about, now enable and require more purposeful, more concentrated, interaction. Participants do a great deal of talking, and they talk in an almost random way to many people, trying to discover where others stand and to sense what they might or might not be willing to do. We know from studies of rumor that this period of milling about may be brief or prolonged and that it enables people both to explore the relative merits of collective, as contrasted with individual, action and to evaluate various proposals for action that are being offered.

Milling stops when some proposal is winnowed out from the others as having sufficient support and as being workable. Were milling devoted to the working out of all the relative merits and deficiencies of all the things proposed or sensed, the process of winnowing might go on indefinitely. In training groups something else occurs. The independent enactors take informal initiatives to select a likely course of action. If they coalesce around a proposal, encouraging the person who sponsors it to elaborate on its potentialities—thereby making him and his ideas into the focus of attention, other proposals quickly drop away. In doing this the enactors make that person into a hero and make his proposal the basis for collective action—a charismatic center. In every case, the hero's proposal is double-edged: a definitive attack on the existing organization that breaks all bonds with it (the hero-as-critic) and a definition of a new course of positive action (the hero-as-leader).

By this stage, our understanding lags behind the progress of collective action. How can we explain the course of the events already sketched and of those yet to come? I have built a possible interpretation into Table 1. The first two rows contain the story to this point. Consider the rows in the table and then the columns.

The rows represent main stages in the formation of a new social order. The process begins with the participants' discovery that an existing order has broken down, this being objectively apparent to them in the fact that, despite their seeming interdependence, they can provide one another only with cues and are unable to take collective action. A new social order is achieved when roles have been defined through which collective purposes can be implemented, when people have been assigned to those roles, when they have accepted their assignments, and when they have been empowered to do what is collectively approved. That is the emergence of agency as specified in the first column of the last row. With the emergence of agency

TABLE 1

The Sequence of Elementary Collective Processes

Stage	A. Collectively relevant information that each participant's behavior provides to the others:	B. Distinctive form of collective action that can be undertaken:	C. Specification of inadequacies of the existing collective structure:	D. Proposals for alternative structures:	E. Commitment to a new structure consisting of:	F. Collective definition of the current state of interdependence:
I	Cues	Communication of unrest	Critics of the old organization	Independent enactors	Independent enactors and peripheral participants	Social unrest
II	Gestures	Milling	Hero-critic: rejection of the old organization	Independent enactors and hero-leader: proposes new social order	Hero, independent enactors, and peripheral participants	Existence of a charismatic center
III	Signs	Collective excitement	Resisters: moralistic and paranoid	Independent enactors and hero	Hero, independent enactors, members performing task or social-emotional roles, and peripheral participants	Existence of a work group
IV	Self	Social contagion	Sexual scapegoat	Hero-member	Charismatic idea and procedures; members performing task or social-emotional roles	A constitutional order
V	Identity	(Morale building)	(Critics of implementation)	(Statesmen)	(Charismatic idea and procedures and a system of offices)	(An administrative system)
VI	Agency					

there exists a corporate structure—a social organization—through which participants can act collectively.

For one reason or another we may want more or fewer steps in our explanation. The only claims I make for the steps represented by these rows are that they (a) contain the points in change observed independently by students of crowds, social movements, and training groups (and of psychotherapy) and that (b) each step seems naturally to supply conditions necessary for the appearance of the next. I note that these six rows correspond closely in number and purpose (but not in contents) to the "levels of specification" that Talcott Parsons and Neil Smelser first suggested in describing the socialization of the individual from birth to his assumption of adult employment and that Smelser later employed in placing various kinds of transient organizations according to their role in a process of social change.[10] This similarity is understandable because all three schemes are constructed to describe what Smelser calls a "progressive restriction" of a generalized orientation of relationship "which makes it more nearly applicable to concrete action." Because each of the steps in Table 1 seems necessarily to lead to the next, we have some confidence that six steps are required in this case to encompass a full course of specification.

The course of collective action is sustained and propelled by everything in the situation that presses people unremittingly toward effective corporate action, these forces being augmented by the progression of the participants' successes, by their enlarged commitments to one another, and by their discarding of alternative courses of action. That sequence of collective action is shaped, in this interpretation, by what is conceived to be the objective character of the final step—of agency—required for corporate undertakings. It is also shaped by the specific opportunities in the situation for movement toward that step and by the constraints entailed in each preceding stage.

The opportunities at any given stage are contained in the legitimized collective apparatus available from the preceding stages (Column E), in the current commitment that people have toward one another (Column F), and in the tools for further interaction (Column A) that these make possible. If we assume that people will persist in trying to effect corporate action, the

---

[10] Talcott Parsons and Neil J. Smelser, *Economy and Society, A Study in the Integration of Economic and Social Theory* (Glencoe, Ill.: The Free Press, 1956), p. 139; and Neil J. Smelser, *Theory of Collective Behavior* (New York: The Free Press of Glencoe, Inc., 1963), pp. 34–42. The number of rows in Table 1 would be seven, and identical with that used by Parsons and Smelser, were we to include a stage earlier than any in this figure. The first column of that new row would read "Stimulus", and events pictured in succeeding columns would lead in Column F to widespread but uncommunicated unrest among people who are interdependent. That row is not relevant here since we begin with conditions directly responsible for social unrest.

use of these new tools will create among them relationships that lead to further commitments, further tools, and so on to the end. Thus the rise in Stage I of independent enactors (the collective apparatus) and the general acceptance of their analysis of the situation (the current commitment) involve participants in a relationship of social unrest. This is not a matter of cause and effect but a definition of their collective situation, a description of their existential condition. If they continue toward corporate action and conduct themselves in terms of that collective definition, their behaviors will have the meaning of gestures rather than cues. That too is inherent in the definition of the existential relations already present. In this way, as a result not of contingent cause but of formal necessity, Stage I in Table 1 leads to a new stage. That is the kind of link we shall find between each pair of adjacent rows in the figure.

The columns of Table 1 represent steps in the solution of the problem peculiar to a given row. As we can see, these steps are a collective form of the phases of interaction first systematized by Bales (or of the stages of thinking as sketched by John Dewey).[11] To see the correspondence with Bales, begin at Column C and work to the right. We seem to have, in order but at the collective level of analysis, what Bales referred to as the steps of orientation to the group's problem (Column C), evaluation of alternatives (Column D), control by some members over the choice that will be made (Column E), and a collective decision (Column F). Then to Columns A and B, these corresponding to Bales' steps of tension management—of people's relating in terms of their new situation and of the reintegration of the group following the participants' mastering of their new relationships. We are probably correct in believing that Bales' rationale for his sequence of steps applies here also.

To summarize, the figure depicts a series of six stages, each conceived as a collective act and containing the phases customary to any act, each stage constructing a situation in terms of which further action will be structured. The over-all sequence moves from left to right along each row and from the first row to the last. This movement embodies the greatest gain that I have found from combining observations of training groups with observations of crowds, social movements, and the like. Each set of observations is so fragmentary that one gets no picture of the flow of social development. Brought together, these observations provide a plausible picture of the whole process.

I recognize that contingencies can deflect or modify the sequence presented in Table 1, but I must simplify and shall write as though people desire and are able to move unswervingly until the emergence of a new social order and its empowerment of agents. As we resume our examination of

---

11 John Dewey, *How We Think* (Boston: D. C. Heath and Company, 1910).

collective development, Table 1 can serve as a convenient summary-record of the events that occur.

The situation at the end of the second stage is this. The participants have developed a simple collective apparatus—the hero, the independent enactors, and the remaining members of the group. Most participants are committed to work together in the directions that the hero set and that the independent enactors supported. The implementation of that commitment lies before them.

As participants continue to work they find that their acts again have a new relevance for one another. This time they have a framework of organization and purpose that enables them to classify what others say and do in terms of the relevance of that behavior for some broad categories of collective advance. Some suggestions, they can now recognize, have bearing upon implementation, some upon the clarification of the principles in terms of which implementation will be designed, some upon the rights and duties of people in the central apparatus as contrasted with those of other members. This is what I mean in Table 1 by saying that people find that one another's behavior serves them as signs—as cues referring to classes of gestures.

All observers report a fresh spurt in the rate, intensity, and directedness of interaction at this point, a phenomenon that Blumer calls "collective excitement." People feel appreciably more hopeful than before. The powers of their new collective arrangements are being demonstrated in the clarification and analysis of their immediate problems. Anticipations of final success are in the air.

But two problems are immediate and cannot be solved by mere analysis: the problems of distinguishing, in the hero's plan, between implementation and purpose, and of adjusting each part of the plan to the other without disrupting the members' support for both.

We know from observations of training groups that some participants now act as critics—what Mann calls "resisters," some "moralistic" and some "paranoid." They define whatever in the hero's analysis is not collectively appropriate and identify those features of his plan that are special pleading on behalf of concerns peculiar to the hero. They may also try to insert into the plan, or into its implementation, special concerns of their own, trying to obtain for them the status of having collective import. The independent enactors and hero are again important, this time in sorting out these criticisms, in accepting, refining, or modifying some of them, and in committing themselves to certain of them and not to others. By this means, and providing there is general assent to the enactors' and the hero's work, the group comes into a new situation. Plan and implementation are separated and are articulated with one another. This separation of plan from implementation embodies a clear difference in the roles that members may fill—if not in the members who fill them. It is the familiar difference between what Bales calls "task" and "social emotional" roles—between applying the group's purposes to the surrounding environment and conserving the plan and the collective apparatus in terms of which that application will be made.[12] Slater, Mann, and Mills say that a "work group" has now come into being.

The fourth stage opens, as did the others, as people find that they mean something different to one another than at the beginning of the preceding stage. They are now related as selves. The group has a scheme for implementation on which it is about to act. People must commit themselves, not merely to concur with that scheme but personally to do something in a collective effort. The group's purpose must in some measure become that of each participant, and his overt performance will provide a concrete test of his loyalty. Members are related as selves, because they now can take one another's behavior as an indicator of a personal commitment to a course of action.

There then ensues that rallying to the collective standard that Blumer refers to as "social contagion." Fence sitters, and those who have come this far just for the ride, now commit themselves or drop out. The collective micromechanisms involved seem to be those that Smelser employs to account for a craze—a panic of acquisition, in this case the acquisition of a firm position in the group.[13]

We know from training groups that other mechanisms are also involved. There typically appears what Mann calls the "sexual scapegoat." He is a member, previously rather silent, who now enters a moral plea on behalf of other silent, "sensitive" participants, asking not that the developing action be halted but that sensitivities be respected and that everyone, even the peripheral members, be admitted equally to the relations of respect and mutual support that exist among the more active members. His statement documents the weakness of his position—his impotence to change things or to force the issue—and the irresistability of the collective order. In training groups this spokesman is degraded for his impotence, considerable sexual imagery being employed. Nonetheless, the active members say that there is no need for his pleas, that all who care to join in are welcome as equals.

It is in this same period in training groups that another important event takes place. The hero withdraws and then, at the end, returns. His withdrawal may be physical or psychological or both—he is absent or indifferent. This is followed by his expression of feelings of helplessness and of dependence upon the group, and by his return, now as only one among others

[12] Robert F. Bales, "Task Roles and Social Roles in Problem-Solving Groups," in *Readings in Social Psychology,* ed. Eleanor E. Maccoby, *et al.* (New York: Holt, Rinehart and Winston, Inc., 1958), pp. 437–47.

[13] Smelser, *op. cit.,* chap. 7.

who serve the collective purpose. He thus accepts the transfer of his charisma to the group.

These two events, the incorporation of peripheral participants and the return of the hero, embody a new development. The group's purpose is now abstracted from the persons of its founder and of its developers and so also is the process for the implementation of that purpose. Both are now available to be internalized by anyone who will make them his own: who will commit himself to them and support them. The group may now be said to have a constitutional order.

The sure sign of this new state of affairs, and the one with which we begin the fifth stage, is that people relate to one another in terms of identities. Whatever special roles they may have in the life of this collectivity, they are equally under the collective purpose and prepared to serve it in whatever ways seem desirable rather than confining their commitment to the particular roles they presently fill. This takes us well beyond empirical observations now available (hence the parentheses around the entries in Row V of Table 1). It seems likely, however, that people begin to do things to encourage one another's confidence in the constitutional order and to develop an understanding of the requirements that it sets for them, both individually and collectively. That is what I have in mind by "morale-building" in Row V, Column B.

We can be certain that no group can function well until the generalized commitment entailed in an identity becomes specified. Until that is done members may, with the best will in the world, move pointlessly from one role to another, leave undone things that urgently need attention, or invest too much time in activities that do not require it. There soon appear critics of these difficulties in the group's operation, and, therefore, persons who perform the statesman-like role of developing means by which informal roles become stabilized as particular offices which can then be legitimately allocated to particular members. The offices, in turn, must be articulated in a systematic way. In these steps there appears an administrative order.

As the sixth stage begins, people now relate to one another in their status as authorized agents of the group. A social organization is fully present.

Nonsymbolic, Noninterpretative, and Circular Interaction

In reconstructing the elementary processes, I have by-passed most controversies, problems, and implications. Two of the problems get an exceptional amount of attention in discussions of collective behavior: the problem of the place, in elementary processes, of nonsymbolic, noninterpretative, and circular interaction, and the problem of the continuing role of the elementary processes in the life of stable organizations. The way we look at these two problems is due largely to formulations by Blumer.[14] A way to clarify these problems and to solve them seems opened by the reconstruction of the elementary processes just presented.

Blumer proposes that, in the earliest stages of elementary collective processes, people are involved in a form of interaction that he calls nonsymbolic or, by implication, noninterpretative, and he proposes that it is only later in collective development that interaction becomes symbolic or interpretative. The comparison of interpretative with noninterpretative interaction comes later in his work and represents a narrowing of what he originally had in mind in comparing symbolic and nonsymbolic interaction. I begin with these narrower conceptions.

Noninterpretative interation is described residually by contrasting it with interpretative interaction:

> *Ordinarily, human beings respond to one another...by interpreting one another's actions or remarks and then reacting on the basis of the interpretation. Responses, consequently, are not made directly to the stimulation, but follow rather upon interpretation....*[15]

In noninterpretative interaction, people respond directly to the behavior of others.

Blumer is led to this distinction by his assertion that, in the simplest stages of collective process, people, although interdependent, must conduct their relations with one another in the absence of "preestablished understandings or traditions."[16] He therefore concludes that there is a form of interaction that is possible under these conditions, and noninterpretative interaction is his candidate.

Many observers agree with Blumer's premise but are skeptical about his conclusion. Kurt and Gladys Lang are representative of those who take this position. They believe that all human interaction is interpretative:

> *Even though they appear automatic, responses to visible expressions of emotions, such as anger, fear, or hate, are nevertheless learned. Concerning the observation of signs of fear in others, Allport writes that we have learned to read them "as signs that there is really something to be afraid of."*[17]

---

14 Like his predecessors, Blumer intended by this thesis to explain observations assembled by McDougall. Cf. William McDougall, *The Group Mind* (New York: G. P. Putnam's Sons, 1920), chaps. 2, 4, and 5.

15 Blumer, "Collective Behavior," *op. cit.*, p. 170.

16 *Ibid.*, p. 168.

17 Kurt Lang and Gladys Lang, *Collective Dynamics* (New York: Thomas Y. Crowell Co., 1961), p. 217.

Their point is that all learning entails the acquisition of criteria by means of which later experiences are interpreted. And they say, "Even the response to social stimuli that are solely gestures entails some interpretation."[18] (In their discussion, "gestures" refers to nonverbal behavior.) They then give an illustration of what they have in mind:

> ...*an attack on a grain merchant or an ower of a bakery during a bread famine suggests to bystanders that a person responsible for the shortage has been found. His anger thus aroused, the bystander joins the others. Their unanimous action documents the guilt of the victim.*[19]

The Langs' point is well taken. Blumer is wrong in assuming that human adults are ever without some "preestablished understandings or traditions," however rudimentary these may be. But this criticism is important only if we ignore the objectives that Blumer sets for his understanding, and for ours, and the social context within which he believes his position to be valid. He proposes that people who are involved in a situation from which elementary collective processes spring will discover that they are talking past one another and that they no longer have a collective criterion that enables them to judge the relevance or irrelevance of one another's behavior with respect to at least one area of life in which they are interdependent. Therefore, with respect to that area, their behaviors have for one another the status only of stimuli or cues but not of gestures, signs, selves, or identities. In cognitive terms, it is so by definition that stimuli and cues, as such, carry less information then do gestures or signs. Correspondingly, they afford less room for interpretation, hence less room for considered choice. It is also true, by definition, that participants in the situation that Blumer describes cannot interpret the bearing of one another's behaviors upon some specific collective act to be undertaken in connection with their difficulties, because no such act is as yet in being or in view. Blumer does not imply, nor should he, that people who are caught up in elementary collective processes cannot concurrently interpret the relevance of each other's behavior for social relations other than the one that has collapsed, or that they cannot—within the affected area—interpret cues or stimuli as such. The reconstruction I have made of the elementary processes makes it possible for us to pinpoint these considerations entailed in his account, but it does not modify the central features of that account.

This brings us to his earlier formulation: the comparison between symbolic and nonsymbolic interaction. We find there that the ideas just discussed are joined to others that deserve separate attention.

At least some features of nonsymbolic interaction are conceived to

---

18 *Ibid.*, p. 218.
19 *Ibid.*, pp. 218–19.

be present in all social situations, whether transient or stable. All features of nonsymbolic interaction are believed to be more salient in the early stages of the elementary collective processes. Blumer writes:

> *While we have only limited knowledge of what occurs in the interaction between human beings, I think one can recognize that the process has at least two levels, levels which perhaps represent extremes, with different admixtures of the two in between. I prefer to call the two levels the symbolic and the nonsymbolic. Little need be said here of symbolic interaction.... Suffice it to say that on this level individuals respond to the meaning or significance of one another's actions. The gestures of the other is subject to interpretation which provides the basis for one's own response....*
>
> *Interaction on its nonsymbolic level operates...in an intrinsically different way. It is marked by spontaneous and direct response to the gestures of the other individual, without the intermediation of any interpretation.... People are unaware of this kind of response just because it occurs spontaneously, without a conscious or reflexive fixing of attention upon those gestures of the other to which one is responding.*
>
> *It is this nonsymbolic phase of interaction that should be considered with reference to the formation of the affective element of social attitudes. It is from this type of interaction chiefly that come the feelings that enter in social and collective attitudes.... It is a familiar experience in meeting people for the first time to discover in oneself immediate likes or dislikes, without any clear understanding of the basis of these feelings....*
>
> *...Such impressions, it should be remarked, are not trivial. That they provide the immediate bases for the direction of conduct is clear....*
>
> *...On its stimulus side nonsymbolic interaction is constituted, I believe, by expressive behavior; i.e., a release of feeling and tension, to be distinguished as different from indication of intellectual intention, which properly comes on the symbolic level. Expressive behavior is presented through such features as quality of the voice—tone, pitch, volume—in facial set and movement, in the look of the eyes, in the rhythm, vigor, agitation of muscular movements, and in posture.... It is through these that the individual...reveals himself as apart from what he says or does.*[20]

Two new themes are sounded in these paragraphs. First, noninterpretative, now nonsymbolic, interaction is said to consist on the stimulus side of the presentation of expressive behaviors. That is so by definition. In the collective context that Blumer has in mind, and that becomes explicit in our

---

[20] Herbert Blumer, "Social Attitudes and Nonsymbolic Interaction," *Journal of Educational Sociology,* IX (1936), 518–20.

reconstruction, these behaviors must be wholly or primarily expressive. A collective object or objective has yet to be developed, and without it, there can be no "indication of intellectual intention" that could link people's collective awareness of problems or opportunities to their holding of a collective cognition of means and ends. Their behaviors, in their collective reference, are therefore expressive.

Later in this same discussion he makes a second point: people engaged in nonsymbolic interaction necessarily pay close attention to one another and are certain to be affected, to be impressed, by what they perceive. The certainty of an effect has been challenged by other analysts. Why, they ask, is it not possible for people to be indifferent to their neighbors, to miss the affective quality of what is being presented, or to perceive that quality but be unstirred? These questions are sensible, but they again miss the collective context that Blumer has in mind when discussing elementary processes. In that context effects are certain.

When we say of a man that he is unusually objective, we mean that he has resolved to let his course of action be determined by information that is independent of his will or desire: the scientist who accepts or rejects a hypothesis depending upon the result of a statistical test, the administrator who activates or changes a program as indicated by the popular reception given to his present efforts, the lover who falls out of love if his overtures are rejected. In the examples of objectivity that I have just given, the actions are highly interpretative, symbolic. But objectivity is sometimes dictated by existential conditions rather than directly by choice. I think that the conditions from which the elementary processes emerge provide a case in point. When people are in fact interdependent, are unable to relate in a manner consonant with that fact, are hopeful that their difficulties may be overcome, and are paying close attention to one another, then the cues or gestures that they provide each other will necessarily determine whether their hope survives and whether they do, in fact, begin a collective effort. If those cues and gestures indicate that others are hopeful and that they are willing to make the necessary effort and to take the attendant risks, then action will proceed. Otherwise it will not. The dispositions represented by those cues and gestures objectively contain the potentialities for collective action in this situation. Each participant will, necessarily, let his choice be determined by the readings that these indicators provide without a further, intervening interpretation. When the reading is in hand, the matter is settled.

But will the reading, if favorable, make participants more alike? That is what Blumer suggests when he writes of noninterpretative, nonsymbolic interaction as "circular reaction":

> ...*circular reaction*...*refers to a type of interstimulation wherein the response of one individual reproduces the stimulation that has come*

from another individual and in being reflected back to this individual
reinforces the stimulation. . . .

In interpretative, symbolic interaction:

> *. . . Responses . . . are not made directly to the stimulation, but follow,*
> *rather, upon interpretation; further, they are likely to be different in*
> *nature from the stimulating acts, being essentially adjustments to these*
> *acts. It tends . . . to make people different; circular reaction tends to make*
> *people alike.*[21]

The Langs have a comment on this conception. "Bodily signs of emotion, of
euphoria or fear," they write, "do not invariably produce the same emotion
in an observer."[22] Of course not. But these signs are very likely to have that
effect when, as in the first stages of elementary collective process, all persons
concerned are as one in the problem and the prospects that they confront and
in their appreciation, however dim it may be, that the situation requires that
they try to act together in a way as yet unknown. In that situation people are
very likely to be expressing the same affects and dispositions and to be
strengthened in those tendencies as their appraisal of the situation is confirmed by others. That, is seems to me, is exactly what Blumer has in mind.

The Continuing Place of Elementary Collective Process in Organizations

In any process of behavioral or social development—and the career
of elementary collective behavior is one—abilities and structures acquired
in each earlier period persist in those that follow. They are reorganized
under new systems, yet each continues as a distinct and potent force.

Blumer points to the continuing presence of elementary process in
stable organizations by reminding us that such organizations persist as the
continuous mobilization of their participants—as the continuous reaffirmation of their interdependence and the continuous employment of the interpersonal and collective mechanisms that continually generate and energize the
social organization that originally emerged from them.[23] To put it differently,
any social organization is a constitutional order, and it persists only if its
constitutive processes—those that brought it into being or some equivalent
set—continue to operate.

One obvious form in which constitutive processes continue their role

---

[21] Blumer, "Collective Behavior," *op. cit.*, p. 170–71.

[22] Lang and Lang, *op. cit.*, p. 219.

[23] Blumer, "Sociological Implications of the Thought of George Herbert
Mead." *op. cit.*

in stable organizations is through the routinization and use of charisma.[24] In training groups, charisma first appears as the property of one or a few individuals. The hero, when recognized and accepted, is more than a person. He is a source of creative, formative power, power that is manifest in his ideas, conduct, and purposes, power that enables his fellows to overcome the chaos in which they find themselves and reestablish effective, meaningful relations both to one another and to their world. As we have seen, there typically arises in elementary collective process a point at which this power, this living purpose and premise, must be separated from its applications. That point is recorded in Stage III of Table 1. Still later, the power originally found in the hero comes to be vested in the collectivity itself. One of the striking events in Stage IV is the hero's withdrawal from the group, this being followed by his acknowledgment that he, too, is under the collectivity's power and by his return. In the same stage, a further development is the peripheral members' acknowledgment of the collectivity's power—of their being possessed by it. In Stage V, that power is employed to authorize agents to act for the group—to empower them.[25]

Mills and Slater give us an especially detailed picture of the earliest steps in the growth of charisma or power. The groups they study are, of course, peculiar in that they have a formal leader who is powerful yet usually silent and inactive. It seems probable, however, that in all collectivities in which people are able to act only in terms of cues there will occur events like the ones that Mills and Slater record. In all cases, people must rediscover that they are nonetheless interdependent, must withdraw their allegiance from an old organization that has failed, must vest it in a commitment to one another to work together to overcome their problems, and, when a suitably charismatic person or procedure appears, must transfer a part of their allegiance to that source of collective power. Slater, following a suggestion of Mills, and Mills recasting an insight in Freud's essay on group psychology, describes the growth of a deep ambivalence in training groups toward their formal leader.[26] On the one hand, the leader represents the members' interdependence and a set of conditions that serve as constraints on their actions. He embodies the creation and the continuous renewal of the situation with which they must deal. But beyond that, he is otiose. Therefore, say Slater and Mills, the group deifies him and then goes about its business.

But the formal leader has a further quality. He has authority to act,

---

[24] Cf. Schmuel N. Eisenstadt, ed., *Max Weber on Charisma and Institution Building* (Chicago: The University of Chicago Press, 1968), pp. ix-lvi.

[25] It is this occurrence of possession that has given rise to discussions of similarities between elementary collective processes and the induction of an hypnotic trance.

[26] Cf. Sigmund Freud, *Group Psychology and the Analysis of the Ego,* trans. John Strachey (London: Hogarth Press, 1922).

should he choose. Unless that authority can be disregarded, the group cannot move. Therefore, says Slater, it is inevitable that the group must attack the leader (the old order), must appropriate for itself his unused authority to act (in what Slater calls an orgy of a cannibalistic communion in which, having "killed" the leader, his active role is ingested by all the members). When the collectivity is thus vested with the leader's powers to act, the members find themselves momentarily in a state of equality, fraternity, and autonomy.

Again, as the academic year ends and the group faces dissolution, we find evidence of the presence of charisma. Slater, Mills, and Mann all record the members' expressions not only of regret, but of weakness—of being disempowered, of being subjected again to chaos.

Mann has unusually rich descriptions of the ambivalence with which the hero himself is viewed, at least until his charisma is transferred to the whole collectivity and the hero is brought to serve it. Up to that point, there is always the danger that these powers will be used to exploit or subjugate the weaker members of the group rather than to serve them, and the hero is viewed with fear as well as respect.

Once an organization is established, it both employs certain formative conceptions and procedures and it acts as their agent. They are mainsprings of social and cultural creativity. Their existence is demonstrated on every occasion when they enable the group to overcome a fresh difficulty. It is demonstrated in the group's successful empowerment of members through rites of passage and investiture, in rituals that symbolize the character and promise of the charismatic forces and that relate all participants to these roots of their collective life—relate them, perhaps, through myth and legend and through the induction of mystical or ecstatic or uncanny experiences.

As I have described the elementary collective processes, they are constitutive of organizations and are general in the formation of all organizations. If they run their full course, they eventuate in a constitutional and administrative order. If we follow Blumer's suggestion, we shall expect to see them within that order as processes that must persist if that order is to be sustained. One sign of their persistence, I suggest, is to be found in observations from training groups and others of the existence, and free movement, of the charismatic powers which first gave life and form to these collectivities.

II

Ralph H. Turner

DETERMINANTS OF SOCIAL MOVEMENT STRATEGIES

The theory of social movements, as it has evolved from the point of view of collective behavior, has dealt chiefly with the variables that help to account for the focusing of unrest into a movement and the mobilization of massive support for the movement. The classic statement on social unrest by Herbert Blumer can be used to form hypotheses to predict when there will and will not be a social movement,[1] and Neil Smelser's six necessary and sufficient conditions are designed to predict the incidence of a movement.[2] Other students

---

[1] Herbert Blumer, "Collective Behavior," in *New Outline of the Principles of Sociology,* ed. Alfred McClung Lee (New York: Barnes and Noble, Inc., 1946), pp. 170–77, 199–20.
[2] Neil Smelser, *Theory of Collective Behavior* (New York: The Free Press of Glencoe, 1963), pp. 270–381.

have been concerned about the success or failure of a movement, once it is launched, but have generally equated success with the acquisition of massive support. For example, Theodore Abel extracts several generalized conditions for a successful movement from the experience of Nazism in Germany.[3] The greatest body of empirical research has dealt with the differential appeal of social movements to different classes of individuals.[4]

Insofar as students have been interested in social movements beyond their formation and enlargement, the concern has been to describe some typical sequences during the life of a movement rather than to specify the variables that determine one course rather than another for the movement. There is considerable agreement on a generalized life cycle for a social movement, governed by a transformation from a spontaneous and loosely structured but intense group of people, in the pattern of the sect, to a highly organized and tradition-bound group of people who take their cause with reasonable detachment and humor, according to the pattern of a denomination.[5] The approach has not, however, provided the basis for predicting which movements will go one way rather than another.

The theory of social movements has been concerned primarily with predicting *support* for a movement, as if the most important consequences of a movement in society are adequately subsumed by the extent or limitations in support. The question of how a movement acts upon the larger society to promote the changes with which it is identified has received scant attention. This omission undoubtedly stems from the model of democratic process and the theory of a public in which issues are resolved when most of the public's members become convinced adherents to a particular point of view. The omission also probably stems from the model of a social movement as concerned primarily with overcoming inertia in support of a relatively consensual goal rather than representing deep-seated cleavages in society.

Transformations in the civil rights movement since World War II, the development of a violent and disruptive peace movement, the generalized culture of protest among youth, and the beginnings of rebellion among the Mexican-Americans have shaken us loose from the benign and consensual

---

[3] Theodore Abel, *The Nazi Movement* (New York: Atherton Press, 1966).

[4] These studies include investigations of voting behavior, such as Seymour M. Lipset's "The Sources of the Radical Right," in *The New American Right,* ed. Daniel Bell (New York: Criterion Books, Inc., 1955), pp. 166–233; and survey studies of movement adherents, such as Denton E. Morrison and Allan D. Steeves, "Deprivation, Discontent, and Social Movement Participation: Evidence on a Contemporary Farmers' Movement, the NFO," *Rural Sociology* XXXII (1967), 414–34.

[5] For a synthetic account of movement life cycles, see Rex D. Hopper, "The Revolutionary Process: A Frame of Reference for the Study of Revolutionary Movements," *Social Forces,* XXVIII (1950), 270–79. An early account of the sect-denomination cycle is found in John L. Gillin, "A Contribution to the Sociology of Sects," *American Journal of Sociology,* XVI (1910), 236–52.

model of a social movement. In the language of one approach to social movements, recent events demand more attention to the power orientations of developing movements.[6] The aim of this paper will be to specify in general terms some of the variables that seem to affect the choice by a movement of strategies for exercising power. We shall examine first a choice among three broad and inclusive strategies, and then examine a more specific and culturally concrete instance of one of the broad types, namely nonviolence.

The Strategies

By defining the problem as the choice among power strategies, we treat the question in collective behavior as an instance of the more general theory of power. In order to draw upon this broader theory of power, we shall begin by defining the alternative strategies in the most general terms, as *persuasion, bargaining,* and *coercion.* At any given time and in any given situation a movement may employ any one or a combination of these three strategies.

Before defining the three strategies, we must identify the term *target group.* Each strategy is an effort to provoke some change in the behavior of some group of people whose action can serve the movement's aims. The group whose behavior the movement is trying to influence will be called the target group. The target group is not fixed, but is intimately connected with the choice of strategies. For example, a movement to repeal the Oriental exclusion laws in the United States at the close of World War II could have chosen to launch a nationwide campaign to arouse public support for repeal. In this case the potentially sympathetic citizenry would have been the immediate target group. However, leaders of the movement chose to appeal directly and quietly to legislators, on the assumption that there was already sufficient support to repeal the laws. They hoped in this way to avoid a massive countermovement, which would have increased greatly the cost of the original campaign and perhaps have generated enough suspicion and fear to undermine support for liberalized immigration laws. The success of the movement seemed to confirm its wisdom in choosing the smaller but more crucial target group.[7]

Although we shall define three primary strategies, the strategies in practice are seldom entirely separate. One type of strategy will usually dominate the relationship between movement and target group, but many specific

---

[6] Ralph H. Turner and Lewis M. Killian, *Collective Behavior* (Englewood Cliffs: Prentice Hall, 1957), pp. 326–27, 361–84.

[7] Fred W. Riggs, *Pressures on Congress: A Study of the Repeal of Chinese Exclusion* (New York: King's Crown Press, 1950).

procedures depend upon a combination of two or all three primary strategies. It will be easiest to define bargaining first, and then to identify coercion and persuasion as alternatives to bargaining.

Bargaining takes place when the movement has control over some exchangeable value that the target group wants and offers some of that value in return for compliance with its demands.[8] One of the commonest forms of bargaining in a democratic society is the offer of votes or other support to the target group. The movement offers to deliver the votes of its constituency to a political party or candidate in return for support of the movement and its objectives. Or one movement offers to form a coalition with another movement in which each movement supports the aims of the other movement, in the manner of the abolition-woman suffrage coalition, or of the attempted labor-civil rights or labor-farmers coalitions. Bargaining is employed here in a restricted sense, close to popular usage, and not in the extended meaning employed by some exchange theorists who treat the giving of approval and similar unsubstantial acts as bargainable values.

Coercion is the manipulation of the target group's situation in such fashion that the pursuit of any course of action other than that sought by the movement will be met by considerable cost or punishment. The extreme form of coercion is the threat of total destruction, when it is in the power of the movement to determine whether the target group will or will not be destroyed. Lesser forms of coercion involve weakening or inconveniencing or embarrassing the target group. Terrorism is one of the most highly coercive strategies. A less intense form of coercive strategy is illustrated in organized civil disobedience when there is no obstructive activity. Authorities are embarrassed by having to arrest otherwise law-abiding persons and by giving them the dangerous publicity of public trials. Authorities run the alternative risks of arousing public sympathy for the offenders and loss of confidence because of their own ineptness, or of weakening the entire authority structure by overlooking the law violations.

Coercion can be viewed as negative bargaining. In the strict sense we employ here, the outcome of successful bargaining is that each party is identifiably better off than it would have been if the bargaining relationship had not commenced. In coercion, the coerced party's best hope is that they will be no worse off than they would have been had the coercive relationship never commenced. The coercing movement offers no value that will improve the target group's position, but threatens to worsen that condition unless compliance is granted.

The essence of coercion is usually the *threat* of harm. Whether

---

[8] For the best general discussion of bargaining, see Peter Blau, *Exchange and Power in Social Life* (New York: John Wiley & Sons, Inc., 1964).

actual harm is done or not is a tactical consideration, with the prospect of further or greater harm being the coercive element. Actual harm is employed tactically as a way of demonstrating that the movement truly *can* or *will* inflict harm or of indicating the *extent* of harm that is possible. Even if no harm is actually done, the strategy is genuinely coercive to the extent to which it is believed that harm will be done if compliance is not forthcoming.

The threat of harm gives way to actual harm as the essence of coercion in the extreme or limiting case of that coercive strategy in which the aim is to destroy the target group or so disrupt their activity as to render them completely powerless. Assassinations may be employed with the intention of frightening surviving members of the target group and strengthening the enthusiasm and resolve of the movement constituency, in which case the threat of further violence is the effective agent of coercion. But the classic coup d'etat, in which the top leaders of government are assassinated, imprisoned, or otherwise disabled so that key movement agents can immediately take over and exercise government power, bypasses threat and employs coercive force directly to accomplish its ends.

Persuasion is the use of strictly symbolic manipulation, without substantial rewards or punishments under the control of the movement. The basic procedure of persuasion is to identify the proposed course of action with values held by the target group. In a movement to recall a public official, the strategy is to arouse popular indignation by dramatizing how far the conduct of government has drifted from the pattern that is valued by the public. Persuasion may center about calling attention to rewards and penalties that will ensue for the target group on the basis of various courses of action. A major appeal of the Townsend movement for old age pensions during the 1930s was the contention that everyone would benefit when the economy was vitalized by the vast monthly reexpenditure of old age pension funds for consumer goods. But calling attention to potential rewards and penalties that are not manipulated by the movement distinguishes persuasion from bargaining or coercion.

Determinants of Strategy

Before outlining the determinants of strategy, we must complete our identification of the components of the situation in which strategy is applied. We have already identified the target group. Applying the strategy is the movement. But the nature of the movement is to have an indefinite membership. There are normally a well-defined inner core group and a few conspicuous leaders, often identified by some organizational membership. Movement boundaries are never coterminus with formal membership in any specific

organization, and a given organizational core often loses control of a movement it has once held. Instead of sharp boundaries there is always a wide
belt of potential or uncertain adherents. The outer limit of this belt shades
into the larger group or category of people for whom the movement presumes
to speak. Thus, in the labor movement there were specific leaders and organizations contending for control of the movement, a large group of sometimes
active and sometimes inactive adherents, and the still larger class of laboring
men which the movement attempts to claim.

A movement must be concerned not only with acting upon a target
group, but with winning and holding the support of these more loosely identified elements. We shall refer to the group or class of potential supporters
for whom the movement must be able to claim to speak as the *constituency*.
Characteristics of the constituency are one of the principal components of
the situation within which a movement makes its choice of strategy. Black
militants, for example, if they are to sustain a movement, must establish a
credible claim to speak for Blacks in general. Blacks as a whole are their
constituency.

Finally, there are various other groups who may, for one reason or
another, be concerned with the movement to the extent of supporting or under-
cutting movement efforts.[9] For convenience we shall call these *publics*. They
include interest groups, such as Mexican-Americans who come to fear that
concessions to Black leaders will be made at the expense of attention to their
own minority problems, the teachers' unions that see local community autonomy as undermining rights they have won only by hard-fought struggles
in the past, and groups such as liberal whites whose values are such that
their sympathy and support for Black demands can be aroused under favorable circumstances.

In summary, we have defined the components of the situation as the
movement, the movement constituency, the target groups, and publics. The
nature of each of these elements and their interrelationships will provide
several important clues to the choice of strategies by the movement.

The choice of strategies is determined by two major principles that
operate sometimes supportively and sometimes in opposition, and by three
sets of limiting factors. The two major principles are the *strategic* and the
expressive principles. The first is the rational principle of selecting strategies
according to their anticipated effectiveness. The second is the principle of
projecting an image through the movement, often an image of power that
the movement adherents can assimilate into their own self-conceptions.
Before discussing these two major principles, we shall review the three sets
of limiting factors.

---

[9] Michael Lipsky, "Protest as a Political Resource," *American Political Science
Review*, LXII (1968), 1144–58.

Limiting Factors

First, the *values* held by the movement constituency affect selection of strategy both directly and indirectly. Directly, some strategies are favored and others disfavored by various groups. Religious or humanistic values sometimes inhibit the use of coercion as an unacceptable strategy. Extreme democratic idealism may lead to excessive reliance on persuasion and to blindness to the possibilities of bargaining. Persuasion, regarded as a high accomplishment among groups who value highly the skills of verbal manipulation, is downgraded among other groups as unmasculine, as an indication of weakness, and as self-debasing pleading. Such groups are likely to resist the use of persuasive methods, regardless of whether these are likely to be most effective in the situation or not.

Values affect selection of strategy indirectly through awareness of the image of the movement formed by a larger public reacting to the strategies the movement employs. There is no one-to-one relationship between strategy and the definition that a public will place on the movement. But certain connections are frequently observed. Bargaining strategies incur the risk that a movement may be viewed as having sold out and the sincerity of its adherents held in doubt. Coercive strategies, when impressively effective, are likely to evoke admiration and respect. However, they are also conducive to fear. The categories of people who form constituencies for social movements differ in the extent to which they are pleased to be viewed with fear or concerned to avoid such reactions. Likewise they vary in sensitiveness to being thought unscrupulous and unprincipled in their dealings.

The second limiting factor includes the values and interests of publics that may intervene so as to affect the outcome of the movement's efforts. Potentially conflicting interest groups, such as the teachers' union in relation to Black civil rights activity in New York City, are the least important groups in determining selection of strategy, because the threat to their interests exists regardless of the strategy employed. Potentially cooptable groups, on the other hand, can have the greatest effect on movement strategy, since the relationship here resembles a coalition in which partners bargain over strategies as well as rewards.

Cooptable groups include those whose interests are different but compatible, so that two movements might benefit by pooling their strength, and those groups who may be expected to give support to the movement on the basis that the movement cause is a tangible expression of their values. Coalitions of the former type have often been attempted but have been notably unstable except when the coalition could be achieved through the medium of a broadly based and established political party. Coalitions are related to the use of a bargaining strategy, and their stability depends largely on the effectiveness of bargaining efforts. A coalition offers little to enhance persuasion strategy, and the use of coercive strategies tends to create distrust within the coalition.

Adjustment of strategy so as not to affront the values of large poten-
tially sympathetic groups has been a recurrent factor, limiting the use of coercive strategy and augmenting reliance on persuasive strategy, in the movements of various minority interests in the United States. The important thread of charitable and humanitarian values in middle and upper class society has supplied a constant flow of support for movements of many sorts. But these supporters are also firmly committed to the established order of things. They are more willing to lend their support when persuasion is the accepted strategy and increasingly reluctant when coercion becomes a conspicuous part of strategy. While it is true, as Seymour Lipset has effectively documented, that violence and coercion have been recurring features of social change in America,[10] it is probably also true that coercion and violence have relatively infrequently been openly adopted and presented as the major strategy of reform movements. The pressure of cooptable humanitarian elements in American society has probably been the major factor accounting for the degree to which movements have claimed to rely on persuasive strategies.

A bystander public often becomes a factor when coercive strategies are employed. A *bystander* public is one whose concern with the aims of the movement is minimal, but which reacts to the disruptions and inconveniences to which people who are not directly involved are subjected because of the struggle.[11] The first development of a bystander public usually involves pressure to give up coercive techniques—e.g., transport workers should call off their strike and go back to work and rely on persuasion to gain their ends. But as the disruption continues, growing concern for the restoration of peace and order finds expression in demands that concessions be made to bring the strike to an end. The ultimate attitude of the bystander public is "a plague on both your houses," accompanied by insistent demands that the more powerful group, to whom the relative cost will be least, make concessions to bring peace. Only a sophisticated movement leadership is likely to be guided by an understanding of this process from the start. But the effect is to reward and encourage the use of coercive strategy over an intermediate span of time.

It is characteristic of small, weak, and inexperienced movements that they are especially fearful of opposition from these publics and hopeful of support from a humanitarian public. Consequently there are strong inhibi-

---

10 Seymour M. Lipset, "On the Politics of Conscience and Extreme Commitment," *Encounter,* XXXI (August, 1968), 66–71.

11 Ralph H. Turner, "Collective Behavior and Conflict: New Theoretical Frameworks," *Sociological Quarterly,* V (1964), 127–28.

tions against the use of coercion and great reliance on persuasion. But there is also a tendency for these restraints to become less effectual as the movement progresses. Similarly, the weaker the tie between movement and constituency, the greater the tendency to rely upon support from other publics, and thus to have strategies limited by the conditions imposed from outside.

The third limiting factor is the nature of the relationship between the constituency and the target group. The way in which one group deals with another has an effect on the established relationship between the groups, and also signifies the way in which that group sees their relationship.

Generally speaking, persuasive strategies are least likely to undermine a positive relationship, while coercive efforts are most likely to provoke resentment and consequently damage a relationship. Bargaining is intermediate in its significance, being less threatening and unilateral than coercion but still indicating a manipulative rather than a consensual relationship. The stronger the bonds and the more personal or intimate the relationship between movement constituency and target group, the greater the tendency to favor persuasion and to minimize coercion as a movement strategy. Bargaining and coercion applied upwards are generally less tolerable in a markedly inequalitarian relationship than in a relationship between near equals. Hence, the more subordinate the general relationship of movement constituency to target group, the greater the tendency to favor persuasion and avoid coercion as a movement strategy.

Just because persuasion signifies a relationship of mutual confidence between constituency and target group, constituencies whose relationship to the target group is pervasively conflictual and marked by severe resentment will eschew persuasion and favor coercion, even when the use of coercion may be strategically unwise. In the civil rights movement in the United States, the shift away from an extended period of reliance on persuasion was marked by repeated declarations that Blacks had no desire for the good will or association of whites. Bargaining may be employed when there are some independent resources or power, but it may not be a viable device because the angry group sees adherence to the terms of the original bargain as a form of submission to the target group.

The two key variables in the constituency-target group relationship are dependency and interpenetrating relationships. The least restraint against the use of coercive and bargaining strategies applies to movements such as the cargo cults and other nationalistic developments in colonial countries. The presence of a relatively self-sufficient community, able to sustain its members along traditional lines regardless of the presence or absence of colonial rulers and having very few personal dealings with the ruling group, makes any fear of damaging relationships a trivial consideration. The increased use of bargaining and openly coercive strategies in youth movements in the United States is directly related to shifts in both of these variables, but especially to the reduction of interpenetration. The rise of the peer group and an elaborated youth society has increased the separation between youth and adults and permitted the growth of an autonomous community of youth. With this community at hand, it is less important than formerly if relationships between youth and their parents and other adults are badly strained. In the past, segregation of Blacks in American society has not freed them from restraints upon using bargaining and coercion, because they remained quite directly dependent upon the favor of specific whites for their employment and many other needs. The decline of special Negro forms of employment and the dispersion of Blacks into the larger impersonal labor force have undermined much of this longstanding sense of dependency.

Strategic and Expressive Principles

Within the limits imposed by constituency values, the pursuit of support from external publics, and concern for the constituency-target group relationship, selection of strategy is determined by a dynamic interplay between strategic and expressive principles. *Strategic* considerations are those having to do with the judgment of which strategy is likely to contribute toward the attainment of the movement goals. *Expressive* considerations are those involving the gratifications that come with the exercise and display of power. People gain satisfaction just from the act of wielding power, and conspicuous and dramatic displays of power give more personal satisfaction than behind-the-scenes or restrained maneuvering.

Two conditions are foremost in determining the relative strength of these two sets of considerations. First, the more sophisticated the leadership, and to a lesser extent the membership, of a social movement, the greater the tendency for the movement's power activities to be directed by strategic considerations rather than expressive considerations. Sophistication is not only a matter of general orientation: It is acquired through experience in social movements. Hence, the pursuit and exercise of power in a social movement tends to be less expressive and more strategic as the movement gains experience. Second, the more effectively disciplined the members, the more the movement will be directed by strategic considerations. The members, who are not closely in touch with the possible consequences of wrong moves and who do not operate under the same sense of responsibility, are more inclined to be governed by expressive considerations than are the leaders. Consequently, an undisciplined grass-roots movement is likely to follow power strategies that are determined largely by expressive considerations. The more that a movement can bring its membership under organizational discipline, the greater the chance of subordinating the expressive tendencies to strategic planning.

The major difference between expressive and strategic considerations is found in the tendency to use and display maximum or minimum power. Expressive tendencies mean a preference for coercion, rather than bargaining or persuasion, as part of a general principle of taking advantage of all opportunities to display power and to employ the more extreme and dramatic forms of power in preference to others. The chief circumstances determining how much of this power display will occur are the sense of confidence and *esprit de corps* in the movement. Any apparent successes build up self-confidence and tend toward escalation of strategies. On the other hand, lack of self-confidence in the constituency, disconcerting setbacks for the movement, and loss of fellow-feeling among members tend to weaken support for strong coercive and bargaining strategies.

The order of preference for strategies under the expressive principle is coercion, then persuasion, with bargaining last. Bargaining comes after persuasion for two reasons. First, in bargaining one must give something in exchange for whatever concessions are gained. To "talk the man out of it" is more impressive than to buy it! Second, bargaining subjects the bargainer to an agreement that he must honor, an agreement that later becomes a limitation on his own freedom of action. The offer of bargaining, then, tends to come at the lowest ebb of group self-confidence if expressive considerations are paramount.

The first strategic principle is to exercise the minimum power needed to attain the goal at hand. Strategically it is better to win by persuasion, if possible, than to employ bargaining or coercion. With persuasion, less must be paid for the results attained, and the resentment often evoked by coercion can be minimized. Furthermore, by not revealing the extent of power at its disposal the movement retains an ambiguity that complicates the target group's efforts to combat the movement. Strategically it is also important not to reveal unmistakable clues to the rise and fall of self-confidence and *esprit de corps* by corresponding changes of strategy. Coercion may be cheaper than bargaining in the short run, but is usually more costly in arousing suspicion and resistance in the long run.

The strategy selected is dependent, secondly, upon the resources at the disposal of the movement. The resources vary in both quantity and kind, and the requirements of the three strategies are to some degree qualitatively distinct. Coercion requires resources that will enable the movement to punish the target group; bargaining depends upon resources that the target group desires and which can be exchanged for something of benefit to the movement; persuasion requires little in the way of power in the usual sense, but it does depend upon skills in communication and access to communication media. Strategically, terroristic coercion may be the only potentially effective strategy available to a relatively impoverished, disenfranchised group.

A third strategic consideration is that bargaining and coercion, when applied by movements whose principal strength is in large numbers of supporters, depend upon a well-disciplined membership. Bargaining cannot take place unless agents of the target group are convinced that movement spokesmen can deliver on their promise of block voting. When coercive strategies capitalize on disruptive and violent behavior among members of the constituency, there must be some assurance that disturbances can be turned off by movement spokesmen if the threat of future coercion is to be effective.

Fourth, the exercise of power is a reciprocal phenomenon. The application of power brings forth a response from the group toward which the efforts are directed. The anticipated response initially affects the choice of strategy, and the actual response leads to reinforcement or revision of the strategy. It is important to recognize that groups do not normally employ all of the power at their disposal. The most fundamental reason why a movement would not employ all the power at its disposal—apart from the strategic principle of using no more power than necessary to gain the immediate end— is fear of activating stronger retaliatory power on the part of the target group.

The circumstances that inhibit an established target group from exercising all of its latent power are several. (1) Routines must be disrupted in order to bring unused power into play. The inconvenience of putting aside established routines means that troublesome demands will often be tolerated without retaliation and propitiatory concessions made. (2) The costs and risks involved in fairly severe conflict are often great, even when the one-sidedness makes the outcome unquestionable. A large nation which could easily subdue a small one may be unwilling to accept the casualties and property losses involved in even a small war. Similarly, a corporation may prefer to grant concessions to a labor organization rather than accept an extended strike with the possibilities of violence and property damage. (3) There is a danger of alienating groups other than the movement constituency by an excessive display of force and of creating a united opposition where only disparate groups existed before. The uninhibited exercise of power—whether by the state with its monopoly of the legitimate use of violence, by a school or church with its power of expulsion, or by a corporation—is frightening. The resulting reaction may lead to steps that curtail the power of these groups in future. (4) The established group is often bound by rules and scruples of its own, which define only limited exercise of power as legitimate. Thus a modern state is restricted in the exercise of the real power at its disposal by its constitution and legal structure. (5) Finally, an established group is commonly inhibited in the exercise of power by ties to the movement constituency. In the case of youth movements and women's movements that cut across family lines, the interpersonal ties make it difficult to deal with these movements in any but the gentlest of ways. The ties may also arise out of sympathy for the movement cause. Ambivalence concerning the rights to national independence inhibited democratic nations from completely ruthless suppression of nationalistic movements in their colonies.

If the choice of bargaining is principally determined by whether the movement has resources with which to bargain, the choice between coercion and persuasion depends upon the effectiveness of those conditions inhibiting a strongly repressive response and upon the willingness and ability of the movement to undergo such a repressive response. (1) When the inhibiting conditions are strong and the movement is unwilling or unable to undergo strongly respressive retaliation, there will tend to be a tentative use of coercive procedures, within limits that will not provoke a full response. When the inhibiting conditions are weak, the movement will be largely limited to persuasive and bargaining strategies. (2) When the movement is willing to undergo repressions, not only will coercive strategies be readily employed, but coercion may be employed with the aim of provocation. By coercive efforts, the established group may be provoked into the intemperate exercise of repression, inspiring fear and resentment and uniting other groups in opposition. By acting ruthlessly, the established power may arouse indignation and weaken support within its own constituency. Or by exhibiting a drastic disproportion between the massive use of power and limited effectiveness, the established group may lose respect and weaken support from both its own constituency and other groups.

Coercive strategies ranging from harassment to systematic terrorism follow the pattern we have just described. They typically occur under conditions in which the movement has very little coercive power in comparison with the target group, and would be easily suppressed in an open, frontal, and uninhibited program of repression. The situation is typically one in which a protective cover for the movement is provided by a larger group whom the established power is unwilling to punish with the full force at its disposal. The group supplying cover may do so out of sympathy for the movement, fear of the movement, or combination of both. Terrorism as a strategy depends upon just such a combination. Underground resistance movements, such as those that developed in Europe during the German occupation of World War II, depend more on popular support and sympathy, but must still occasionally resort to direct action against the potential informer.

Nonviolence as a Strategy in Social Movements

Among many strategies that are more specific and delimited than the three broad types we have discussed is nonviolence. Nonviolence as a strategy attracted great attention in the United States during the period just before our direct involvement in World War II, with Gandhi's *satyagraha* as the model. Interest in nonviolence has been reawakened by the more recent civil rights leadership of Martin Luther King and by efforts to employ non-violence in the peace and draft resistance movements.

Nonviolence is not an elemental form of strategy, such as coercion, bargaining, and persuasion, but a self-consciously selected and collectively disciplined strategy applicable only in certain circumstances. Because it is a self-conscious and disciplined strategy, the strategy of nonviolence is insepa-rable from value orientation. That is, the strategy of nonviolence is a natural expression of certain kinds of pacifistic and religious values, and the strategy tends to be viewed as intrinsically good and right (apart from its conse-quences) because it embodies and expresses these values.[12]

Violence means a physical attack on persons or property, usually but not exclusively with the implication that the attack is illegal. Hence, nonviolence may or may not involve both legal and illegal actions and may involve harassment and harm to both person and property by such means as boycott and even mass assemblages and sit down tactics that effectively block the movement of people and machines. Nonviolence refers to studied avoidance of positive and direct physical attacks upon property and persons.[13]

The mere absence or avoidance of violence does not constitute non-violence as a strategy: the term only has meaning in a situation in which violence is the normal expectation. Nonviolence is a self-conscious and collectively disciplined avoidance of violence when the situation is strongly provocative of violence.

Nonviolence refers to positive action, not mere passivity. Mere failure to retaliate and acts of submission are not to be confused with non-violent strategy. Nonviolence is a positive effort to employ power so as to secure changes in situations in which the constituency find themselves.

Although individuals may employ nonviolence, as in the solitary civil disobedience of Thoreau, we have reference to a collective strategy in which the overwhelming majority of the representatives of the movement scrupulously avoid the use of violence. It is important to make this observa-tion, since the use of violence by only a small number of people is enough to make the problem of containing and coping with that violence a central concern of the community and of the opposition. When this happens, the movement ceases to be effectively nonviolent, even though the majority of

---

[12] For general discussions on nonviolence, see Joan V. Bondurant, *Conquest of Violence: The Gandhian Philosophy of Conflict* (Berkeley: University of California Press, 1957); Leo Kuper, *Passive Resistance in South Africa* (New Haven: Yale Uni-versity Press, 1957); William R. Miller, *Nonviolence: A Christian Interpretation* (New York: Schocken Books, Inc., 1966); and the issue of *Sociological Inquiry,* XXXVIII (Winter 1968), 1–93.

[13] Leo Kuper points out that some leaders of allegedly nonviolent movements have proscribed only attacks on persons, denying that attacks on property can be called violence.

its representatives and even its most widely accepted leaders (i.e., those accepted by the constituency) remain nonviolent.

Nonviolence is a special form of coercion, in the sense that we have treated coercion as a primary strategy.[14] Nonviolence always couples persuasive strategy to coercion, and in some respects this combination is its most distinctive feature. But the main and proximate aim of nonviolent strategy is to coerce a target group into some desired action. Both persuasion and bargaining are inherently nonviolent in the generic sense, and hence they cannot be nonviolent in the special sense implied by nonviolence as a distinctive strategy in social movements. The coercion is directed toward the proximate target group (e.g., King's original bus boycott coerced the bus company and municipal officials); the communication by way of exemplifying moral superiority is aimed primarily at larger publics of which the proximate target group must take account.

Nonviolence is not applied except by a group that is disadvantaged with respect to power, one that does not have access to the generally accepted means for effecting the changes it seeks.

There is a continuum, bounded by two polar types of nonviolent strategy that have been designated as *conscientious* and *pragmatic* nonviolence.[15] The types are normally mixed in practice, but they tend to arise and be supported by different circumstances. Conscientious nonviolence stresses the use of the strategy to exemplify the value of nonviolence. Hence it is conceived by its practitioners more as persuasion than as coercion and is less affected by the observable effectiveness of the coercive aspects of the strategy. In this sense idealistic nonviolence is a rather atypical instance of strategy determined by expressive rather than strategic considerations. Pragmatic nonviolence is value-neutral and employs nonviolence because it is the most prudent and feasible procedure that offers a strong chance to gain desired ends. The principal focus of attention is on the effect of the strategy, and the strategy will be reinforced or altered according to the observed effectiveness. In general, it is unlikely that conscientious nonviolence will remain the dominant force once a movement is vigorously involved in promoting its aims. The provocations to violence and commitment to the struggle rapidly neutralize the conscientious restraints and the movement remains nonviolent only if strategic considerations operate strongly to keep it so.[16]

---

[14] Clarence M. Case, *Nonviolent Coercion* (New York: Century Co., 1923).

[15] Judith Stiehm, "Nonviolence is Two," *Sociological Inquiry,* **XXXVIII** (Winter 1968), 23–29.

[16] Inge Powell Bell's study of CORE members indicates the weak commitment to nonviolence. Cf. "Status Discrepancy and the Radical Rejection of Nonviolence," *Sociological Inquiry,* **XXXVIII** (Winter 1968), 51–64. Gandhi's autobiographical writings indicate his own deep distress over the fickle dedication of his followers to the principle of nonviolence. Cf. Mohondas K. Gandhi, *Gandhi's Autobiography: The Story of My Experiments with Truth* (Washington, D. C.: Public Affairs Press, 1948).

Violence as an Issue

It is impossible to formulate simple propositions that relate conditions to the probability of nonviolent strategy, except when a separation is made between circumstances conducive to the essential precondition for nonviolence and circumstances conducive to nonviolence when the precondition exists.

The precondition to nonviolent strategy is that violence has become a vital issue in the selection of strategy, that violence is a normal and expected strategy so that an active choice between accepting or repudiating violence can be made. Given the precondition, the question then becomes that of identifying the circumstances that push a movement toward violence or toward the active avoidance of violence. The circumstances that determine the latter choice are largely different from those that determine whether the use of violence becomes a vital issue for the movement.

The two-dimensional model can be illustrated as in Figure 1.

Figure 1

Nonviolence in Relation to Alternatives

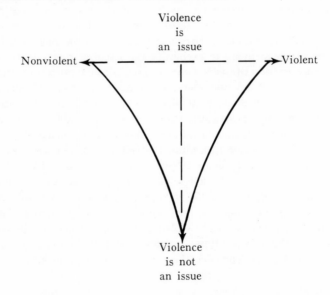

Violence is a normal (i.e., typical and understandable) response to violence, and violence is a legitimate (i.e., normatively sanctioned) response to violence. Hence, violence tends to be an issue in the selection of strategy to the degree to which the movement constituency is itself the victim of violence. The degree of moral indignation required to justify violence is greater than the degree of indignation required to justify the use of other means. Hence, violence tends to be an issue in the selection of strategy to the degree to which the constituency is or perceives itself to be the victim of intense injustice.

Violence among normally socialized human beings is something of a last resort strategy. Hence two hypotheses: (a) Violence tends to be an issue in the selection of strategy to the degree to which the movement constituency is subject to restrictive and comprehensive coercion. (b) Violence tends to be an issue in the selection of strategy to the degree to which the movement lacks or is denied access to other tactics for the promotion of its ends.

A corollary to the last pair of propositions, resting on the same assumption, is as follows: The tendency for the selection of violence as a strategy to become an issue is augmented by the dramatic frustration of other strategies, especially when that frustration can be attributed to an unwillingness by the target group to enter into "reasonable" discussion and negotiation.

Violence is inconsistent under most circumstances with bonds incorporating a common social identity; hence the tendency for the selection of violence as a strategy to become an issue is directly related to the degree to which the relationship between constituency and target group are in the nature of we-group they-group relations.

Finally, we should not overlook the most directly strategic consideration. Violence tends to be an issue in the selection of strategy to the degree to which there is a realistic prospect of employing violence effectively.

Choice of Nonviolence as a Strategy

Circumstances leading to the choice of nonviolent strategy can be divided to correspond with the two kinds of nonviolence, i.e., values and instrumental considerations. The relative importance of the two sets of conditions will vary according to the degree to which the movement approaches either pole of the continuum. To the degree to which the movement approaches the conscientious type of nonviolence, variation in the instrumental circumstances will make little difference, but variations in the values of the constituency will make a great deal of difference in the choice of strategy. To the degree to which the movement approaches the pragmatic type of nonviolence, variation in the values of the constituency will make little difference, but variations in the instrumental circumstances will make a great deal of difference in the choice of strategy. Two generalizations are applicable to value determinants of nonviolent strategy.

Violence tends to be rejected as movement strategy to the extent to which the movement's constituency shares religious or other traditional (i.e., cultural) values that incorporate disapproval of violence and specifically place positive evaluation on avoiding the use of violence. The Hindu religion of India and the special southern Negro form of Christianity were important preconditions to nonviolent strategy.

Nonviolence tends to be rejected as movement strategy to the extent to which the movement's constituency shares values that lead the avoidance of violence under provocation to be viewed as an indication of weakness, of deficient masculinity, or of other negatively valued qualities.

If movements first adopt nonviolent strategies because there is strong cultural support for idealistically based nonviolence, pragmatic considerations become more important as the movement engages in struggle to promote its aims. Consequently, the following propositions expressing instrumental considerations become increasingly crucial as the movement becomes active.

Nonviolence tends to be adopted as movement strategy when the target group has sufficient strength to make catastrophic retaliation but is unlikely to retaliate with full force unless there is great provocation.

Nonviolence tends to be adopted as a movement strategy when the target group shares religious or other traditional values that incorporate disapproval of violence and when it specifically places positive evaluation on the avoidance of the use violence. This proposition is really a special application of the former proposition, since the respect for nonviolence on the part of the target group inhibits it from retaliating violently or even with excessive coercion against a group employing conspicuously nonviolent strategy.

The assumption in the first proposition above, that nonviolence is a strategy to optimize the balance between effectiveness and the probability of retaliation, suggests a processual hypothesis, as follows: Successful use of nonviolent strategy tends to lead to the use of violent strategy, because the fear of retaliation is lessened by the experience with nonviolence.

Nonviolence tends to be adopted as movement strategy when adherence to nonviolence facilitates a coalition with a third group against the target group or facilitates a favorable view in a larger public to which the target group is responsive. The appeal of King's nonviolence to northern public opinion, which then brought pressure to bear on the southern political decision makers, illustrates this proposition.

Nonviolence tends to be abandoned as movement strategy when coherence and discipline within the movement are not high. Here we must remember that violence can break out but nonviolence cannot. A few dissident acts of violence make a nonviolent movement into an effectively violent movement, while a few dissident acts of nonviolence do not identify the nature of the movement as nonviolent. Hence nonviolence is only possible when there is a high degree of discipline, and sporadic violence is the normal consequence of weak discipline.

The special problem of coherence and discipline in nonviolent movements leads to another proposition. One of the most effective supports for group discipline is the achievement of some tangible end to reassure the group that more distant goals are genuinely attainable. Hence, nonviolence tends to be adopted as a movement strategy when there are proximate goals that can be rather directly achieved through nonviolent methods. For example, the immediate and tangible goal of forcing integrated bus seating facilitated the discipline of nonviolence, while broader and more remote goals such as changing the Negro's position in the United States would not have done so alone.

Finally, nonviolence tends to be adopted as movement strategy to the extent to which severing or weakening of the bonds between the constituency and the target group affords an intolerable prospect for the constituency.

Nonviolence as Marginally Coercive Strategy

Comparing the circumstances that are conducive to nonviolent strategy with those affecting the choice among primary types of strategy leads to the suggestion that nonviolent strategies are most likely to occur when the situation is in some respects conducive to coercive strategy and in other respects inhibits the use of coercion. The situation fosters coercion because of the lack of resources to make persuasive or bargaining strategies effective and because of the social cleavage between constituency and target group. However, the overwhelming retaliatory power of the target group and/or the symbiotic dependency of the constituency tend to inhibit the use of coercion. Under these circumstances the most common response is withdrawal from the struggle and inability to launch an effective movement. If other conditions are adequate to launch effective movement activity, the alternative tends to be either terrorism or nonviolence. Because of this basic constellation of factors, nonviolence is most commonly found in association with terrorism and not with the more conventional persuasive and bargaining strategies. Both require a well-disciplined group of participants; but nonviolence can prevail only when a large proportion of the constituency accept the general discipline of the movement, whereas terrorism can operate with only a small disciplined group. The two additional ingredients without which a nonviolent movement cannot be sustained are (1) a mobilizable amount of sympathy for the movement cause within the social circle of the target group, or other considerations that inhibit retaliation in full strength, and (2) the presence in the constituency of an ethos that makes both nonviolence and self-sacrifice for a worthy cause admirable experiences.

Conclusion

There are many forms of movement strategy. We have examined two types of choices. First is the choice among three primary and rather abstract forms of strategy, namely, persuasion, bargaining, and coercion. Second, we have looked at a more specific and culturally defined form of strategy known as nonviolence. In suggesting a basis for predicting the selection of strategy, we have proposed attention to a determining situation consisting of the movement and its constituency, a target group, and various potentially concerned publics. Analysis of these components in any situation provides the basis for an initial set of predictions regarding which strategies a movement will employ at a particular time and place.

12

Shu-Ching Lee

GROUP COHESION AND
THE HUTTERIAN COLONY

This paper is written to serve two related purposes: (1) It will attempt to define more explicitly the term *group cohesion*. In plain language, group cohesion simply means that the members of a group stick together to form a unified whole under any circumstances. In sociopsychological literature, however, the term is used to refer to a wide range of observed social phenomena that show any signs of attachment or solidarity. It has become a blanket term rather than a scientific concept. Unless its properties or attributes as defining qualities are distilled and spelled out in unequivocal terms, group cohesion as a concept is of little value in research. (2) By a thorough analysis of Hutterian colonies as a case study of a high degree of cohesiveness, it is hoped that the properties of group cohesion can be ascertained and identified. Among all those who have studied this religious sect in any capacity one point of agreement is unanimous and outstanding, i.e., that the colony is described as having a high degree of cohesiveness.[1] This writer's empirical study of the South Dakota colonies was carried out in 1965–66 for a period of 12 months. From the findings obtained in this study there seems to be little doubt that the Hutterian Brotherhood, though differences exist between one colony and another, manifests the highest quality of group cohesiveness. This research study was, in fact, focused on the issue of cohesiveness through an intensive investigation of their religious practices and community organization.[2]

The quality of cohesiveness in the Hutterian colony is achieved primarily through faith in Anabaptism or Hutterianism. One question naturally arises: If the properties or attributes of group cohesion are derived from an analysis of a single case, may they be taken as generic qualities commonly shared by all cohesive groups? The basic concern of this paper is the establishment of the loosely used blanket term, group cohesion, as a scientifically defined concept. Additional analyses of other cases may modify or reduce the number of defining qualities of this concept, but this should not impair in any way the validity of this endeavor.

In making an analysis of this kind, it is desirable to state unequivocally at the outset some of the basic propositions involved. In attempting to identify the properties of a scientific concept in the social sciences, one is not likely to arrive at such simple mathematical equations as $x = y$; what one does is more analogous to diagnosing the symptoms of a disease. Any property that is isolated is frequently only one of the many conditions which may lead to a certain approximation of a social or physical phenomenon (or a disease). Any single condition alone, though necessary, may be insufficient to account for the occurrence. Thus, any attempt to reverse this relationship by taking a single, identified condition to account for the whole phenomenon will lead to serious difficulties. For example, included in the symptoms of an attack by appendicitis are: (a) pain in the abdomen on the right side, (b)

---

[1] The literature in English of the Hutterian Brethren (or Brotherhood) is increasing. Recommended sources include the following publications: (1) the *Mennonite Encyclopedia* contains a rich mine of reliable information and is a major reference for all three Anabaptist sects; (2) John Horsch, *The Hutterian Brethren, 1528–1931* (Goshen, Ind.: Mennonite Historical Society, 1931); (3) Robert Friedmann, *Hutterite Studies* (Goshen, Ind.: Mennonite Historical Society, 1961); (4) Joseph W. Eaton and Robert J. Weil, *Culture and Mental Disorder* (New York: The Free Press of Glencoe, Inc., 1953); (5) Victor Peters, *All Things Common* (Minneapolis: University of Minnesota Press, 1965); (6) John A. Hostetler and Gertrude E. Huntington, *The Hutterites in North America* (New York: Holt, Rinehart and Winston, Inc., 1967); (7) Lee Emerson Deets, *The Hutterites: A Study in Social Cohesion* (Gettysburg, Pa.: Time and News Publishing Co., 1939); and (8) Paul S. Gross, *The Hutterite Way* (Saskatoon: Freeman Publishing Co., 1965).

[2] The investigation of the Hutterian colonies in South Dakota was supported by the National Institute of Mental Health under research grant MH10586–01.

nausea, (c) sometimes sweating and dizziness, (d) a high fever, and some others. No single symptom can be taken as an indication of appendicitis; only the presence of all these symptoms warrants a safe and sound identification of the disease.

Since the sticking together of group members is an observed property common to many groups, the quality of cohesiveness may thus be regarded as a continuum, with the most cohesive groups at one end and the least cohesive ones at the other. Given this situation, it is posited that the group that shows less cohesiveness may contain all the attributes to a lesser degree or may simply be devoid of some of the important attributes. On the other hand, only in the most cohesive group one can expect to find all of these properties. The Hutterian colony is taken for this reason to illustrate not only what these properties are but also to show how and why they contribute to such a quality. If this religious sect, though most cohesive in community organization and group life, still does not possess all the properties that lead to cohesiveness, the missing variables can only be sought in further analyses of other cases.

The endeavor to discover the properties of group cohesion is not new. Although many writers and researchers have tried to identify the characteristics of this sociopsychological concept, none of these attempts can be regarded as satisfactory. A well known experiment carried out by Kurt W. Back showed that highly cohesive groups, irrespective of the source of cohesiveness, tend to have the properties of personal attraction, task orientation, and group prestige, and to exert more influence on their members than less cohesive ones. The true significance of these findings lies in the implication that group cohesion has "similar properties and similar outcomes."[3]

Other equally well known experiments, devised as a measure of group cohesion by the use of sociometric diagrams, arrived at the conclusion that, among other things, members of a highly cohesive group tend to be associated with in-group members, while members of a less cohesive group make choices or references to outsiders.[4] Granting that members of cohesive groups show little tendency to befriend outsiders, one key difference arises when this isolation is self-imposed by the individual members or is adopted officially as a policy of the group. In both instances, the members know very little of

---

[3] Kurt W. Back, "Communication in Experimentally Created Hierarchies," in *Theory and Experiment in Social Communication,* ed. L. Festinger, *et al.* (Ann Arbor: Institute for Social Research, University of Michigan, 1950); also "Influence Through Social Communication," *Journal of Abnormal and Social Psychology,* XLVI (1951), 190–207.

[4] Cf. L. Festinger, S. Schachter, and K. W. Back, *Social Pressures in Informal Groups: A Study of Human Factors in Housing* (New York: Harper & Row, Publishers, 1950); and L. Libo, *Measuring Group Cohesiveness* (Ann Arbor: Institute for Social Research, University of Michigan, 1953).

the world about them, and any reference to or association with outsiders would be incidental and insignificant.

Another salient feature that is often singled out to indicate cohesiveness of a group is the sense of psychological unity, referred to by C. H. Cooley as "we-feeling" and by W. G. Sumner as "in-group feeling." To the extent that the personal pronoun "we" is used more frequently by group members than "I" in referring to themselves, it is posited that the degree of group cohesion can be gauged.[5] True, the members' mutual attraction or the feeling of "we-ness" undoubtedly constitutes a component of cohesiveness. What one is uncertain about is the context in which these personal pronouns are used, and the extent to which group sentiment is expressed by these pronouns. Such expressions as "We Americans" or "We Democrats" are quite different from the manner in which "we" is used to designate a smaller unit, say the family. And, unless the groups are artificially created as in laboratory experiments with children, the preference for one personal pronoun over another—we or I—generally is a matter of conventional usage and fixed by custom through the process of learning.

The instances mentioned above should suffice to indicate how unfruitful have been attempts made by the experimental method to tackle the problem of a group quality by taking only a single variable. The results of these experiments seem to raise more questions than they answer.

Background: The Hutterian Colonies

The Hutterian Brotherhood was founded by Jacob Hutter[6] as an offshoot of the Reformation in Central Europe during the early sixteenth century. It was one of the three Anabaptist sects—the Mennonite, the Amish, and the Hutterite—although the term Anabaptism is not accepted by them.[7] Similar to the other two, the Hutterian Brotherhood has advocated the practices of (a) acceptance of the Bible as containing all the wisdoms for

---

[5] Cf. R. Lippitt and R. K. White, "The 'Social Climate' of Children's Groups," in *Child Behavior and Development,* eds. R. G. Parker, J. Kounin, and H. Lorights (New York: McGraw-Hill Book Company, 1943).

[6] Although Jacob Hutter was not the original founder (prior to him there had been several others) and he served as leader for only two years (1533–35), it was he who actually laid firm foundations of a communal, evangelical community for the group and established a viable system to bind all the members together as a spiritual unit. "Hutter, himself a very strong prophetic and charismatic leader, had given to this group such definite foundations that it could survive and, in spite of many ups and downs, preserve its basic principles through more than four centuries." *Mennonite Encyclopedia,* eds. H. S. Bender and C. H. Smith (Scottdale, Pa.: Herald Press) II, 854–55.

[7] Anabaptism is a Greek word meaning "rebaptism." It was used by the enemy of the "Anabaptist" groups because of "the opprobrium and criminal character attached to this name." It was never used by the Anabaptists themselves but often vigorously objected to by them. . . ." *Mennonite Encyclopedia,* I, 113.

mankind, (b) membership consisting in unreserved lifelong commitment to the faith, (c) baptism only of adult conscientious believers, (d) complete separation of the church from the government, and (e) as a corollary, no participation in government service, particularly military service. Unlike the other two, however, this sect has, from the outset of its founding, lived communally in colonies, a form of life which is often referred to as "theocratic communism." Because of its strong faith and also its deviation from the main stream of Protestant movements, members of this sect have suffered the worst forms of political oppression and religious persecution and have left a total of more than two thousand martyrs, including the founder, Hutter, at the stakes. In the process of tribulation, the small band of Anabaptist believers was forced to migrate from one country to another, and they finally settled during the last quarter of the nineteenth century in the United States and Canada.[8]

Because of the manner in which they were grouped for migration in Russia and the leader who brought each unit over to the Western Hemisphere, the Hutterites are today divided into three branches: Schmiedenleut, Dariusleut, and Lehrerleut. They are living in some 170 colonies with a total population of more than 16,500 persons.[9] Although intermarriage among these three branches has virtually ceased, the community organization and mode of life prevailing in them are in fact so similar that any analysis and generalizations based on some of them can be safely applied to all other colonies. The data on which this paper is based have been collected by the author through his empirical study of all twenty-six Hutterian colonies in South Dakota, one in Minnesota, and two in Manitoba, Canada, during the year 1964–65 and thereafter.

Shared Consensus

Emile Durkheim, in his famous work on the elementary forms of religion, argues that one basic function of all the religious activities is the reaffirmation and refreshment of the collective sentiments which serve to bind the group together, regardless of whether it is a clan, a tribe, or a larger community. After a detailed analysis of the elementary beliefs (such as totemism) and the principal rituals and cults, he concludes that "this moral

---

[8] The account of the life of the Hutterite colonies in North America by John A. Hostetler and G. E. Huntington is based on three colonies, each taken from one branch. See Hostetler and Huntington, *op. cit.*

[9] These are approximations of the number of colonies and the size of population at about 1965. Because of the rapid increase in population and the branching off of new colonies, figures that may appear accurate at the moment will soon become outdated. Cf. Joseph W. Eaton and A. J. Mayer, *Man's Capacity to Reproduce* (New York: The Free Press of Glencoe, Inc., 1953); and Robert C. Cook, "The North American Hutterites," *Population Bulletin,* X (1954), 97–197.

remaking cannot be achieved except by the means of reunions, assemblies, and meetings where the individuals, being closely united to one another, reaffirm in public their common sentiments, . . ."[10] Thus, according to him, the promotion of group cohesion is the fundamental aim and purpose of religion and "the idea of Society is the soul of religion."[11]

If Durkheim's theory of religion cannot be applied categorically to modern mass society, its application to the Hutterian colony seems to be highly cogent and pertinent. The ethos of the religious sect is centered on its unshakable faith in the Bible and the unreserved commitment by its members to an ascetic, communal life. Ever since its founding this group of Anabaptist believers has demonstrated, time and again, its tenacity, fortitude, and high morale in sustaining tribulation and suffering. "These people," as stated in a letter by the government to King Ferdinand in Vienna in 1529, "not only have no horror of punishment, but even report themselves; rarely is one converted; nearly all only wish to die for their faith."[12] This spirit of sacrifice and conviction can still be observed in the colony today.

Religion, to a Hutterite, is not merely the worship of a deity or the reading of the holy scripture; it permeates every aspect of life. A parallel drawn by Victor Peters between life in the colony and outside is extremely relevant:

> *What is in our society a routine function, such as the gathering of a family around the dinner table, becomes to the Hutterites an expression of worship as the entire community assembles in the colony dining hall to partake of a meal in almost complete silence. The taking of nourishment to them is more than just that; it is a religious service, a tribute to the glory of the Provider of all.*[13]

Perhaps no word is more adequate to describe a life of complete devotion and undivided piety than the German term, *Gellassenheit* (self-surrender to the guidance of God), which the Hutterite accepts as his guiding principle. An illustration that fully reveals this principle is found in a recent publication by an anthropologist who himself has an Anabaptist background. The passage reads:

> *In their morning and evening prayers, children acknowledge an "eternal God who has wonderfully created all things in Heaven and on earth." In catechism at school they learn the difference between a "right faith" and a "false hope." A right faith is both "living" and a "gift from God," made possible by "believing in God's word," and demonstrated by*

---

[10] Emile Durkheim, *The Elementary Forms of the Religious Life* (New York: Collier Books, 1961), p. 475.

[11] *Ibid.,* p. 466.

[12] Cited in *The Mennonite Encyclopedia,* II, 751.

[13] Peters, *op. cit.,* p. 75.

"pious living" and suffering. When baptized at the age of about twenty, the young adults "establish a covenant with God and all his people" to "give self, soul, and body, with God and all possessions to the Lord in Heaven." In marriage a spouse is acknowledged as "a gift from God."[14]

From this fundamentalist, and nearly monastic, mode of life, it becomes apparent that religion to Hutterites is not only a focal object but a very inclusive value; out of this comes a monolithic value system. Since the Hutterian faith is placed above all other considerations and activities, there is uniformity of experience among all members and also similarity in attitudes, in a word, a strongly enforced *consensus*. More important, every member is brought up in the same mode of life, and his interactions are limited largely to the members of his colony. He is therefore fully aware of the consensus; there is a unanimous perception of consensus—*a second order consensus*.[15] Admitting that the source of consensus and of the sharing is peculiar to the colony, the collective *awareness* of consensus, or shared consensus, is a generic property of some groups. It is one of the conditions that is necessary to bring about the quality of cohesiveness.

Organized Attitudes

If the commonly shared consensus in Hutterian life is a group property contributing to cohesiveness, most of the activities carried on in the colony can be appropriately viewed as efforts to retain, if not strengthen, this property. The Hutterite knows too well that consensus can be readily shared only when there is uniformity of social norms, and norms are, of course, the derivatives of a value system. In order to ensure this uniformity the value system must remain monolithic and unadulterated so that all the objects, events, and situations in the physical and social surrounding can be defined according to the one and only source of authority, namely, the Hutterian faith. The mechanisms that the Brethren have been using to retain all these features are as follows:

(1) No alien ideas or unorthodox behavior patterns can be brought into the colony without contact and communication. The Hutterites, therefore, prefer to set up their colonies in the heart of rural areas and live virtually in isolation. When visitors, and sometimes customers or salesmen, occasionally come to the colony, contact is restricted to a few authorized officials. The minister, for instance, is the one to receive and entertain, if necessary, visiting guests; and the business manager is the one to do business

---

[14] From Hostetler and Huntington, *op. cit.*, p. 6.
[15] Cf. Theodore M. Newcomb, Ralph H. Turner, and Philip E. Converse, *Social Psychology: The Study of Human Interaction* (New York: Holt, Rinehart & Winston, Inc., 1965), pp. 222–28.

with the outside world. The media of mass communication are the sources through which influences of the outside world can be introduced; therefore, these channels are shunned. Subscription to local newspapers is strictly for business news, and reading them is limited to a few authorized officials in each colony. Furthermore, since the language that is used as a vehicle of communication by the Hutterites is still Tyrolean German, many Hutterite men and women are simply unable to express themselves in English; as a result, communication is going on continuously and extensively among members living within the same colony. Any deviating opinion, view, or interpretation of an object, event, or issue expressed by a dissenter tends to draw attention and remarks toward him until he repents and returns to the orthodox line.[16]

(2) Conformity to group norms is vigorously enforced to such an extent that it includes external appearances, such as the wearing of costumes, the growing of a beard for men after marriage, and even the physical layout of a colony. Thus, regardless of what colony a Hutterite is visiting, he feels completely at home. The effects of this external conformity are (a) a clear marking out of group boundaries between Hutterites and non-Hutterites, and (b) more important, perhaps, the creation of what is referred to by F. W. Allport as the "illusion of universality."

(3) In order to maintain the so-called narrow path in terms of the faith and the ascetic mode of life, education in public school is limited to the eighth grade. This limitation is deemed necessary, for higher level education is likely to broaden the intellectual horizon of the individual; this might eventually challenge and undermine practices based on traditionalism. The few well educated Hutterites in the field of medicine have left their colonies.

(4) Since converted adults may bring to the colony ideas and influences from "the world," the Hutterian Brethren prefer to rely primarily upon their own reproductive power rather than recruitment for growth. This does not mean that the door of conversion is closed altogether to outsiders who desire to join the colony. Few candidates have ever been accepted, and those who have have been required to go through careful screening and a period of probation to prove their complete break with the past.[17]

---

16 Cf. S. Schachter. "Deviation, Rejection, and Communication," *Journal of Abnormal and Social Psychology,* XLVI (1951), 190–207.

17 Among the 26 colonies in South Dakota the writer knows of only one adult convert who came from a farm family adjacent to a colony. He once lived in a trailer parked in the compound of that colony to practice the Hutterian way of life for several months and later requested to be taken in as a convert. He published a number of articles and pamphlets to explain the virtues of Hutterianism and its practices. The last the writer heard of him was in the summer of 1967; he had participated in the life of a North Dakota colony, and, for a short while, in a colony in South Dakota; he finally joined a colony in Manitoba, Canada, but had still not gone through his probationary status.

In reviewing the outcome of all these vigilant precautionary measures, one may conclude that they are justifiable and necessary. The fact is that while the Hutterian Brethren are still growing and thriving, virtually all other socialistic or communalistic experiments, religious or otherwise, have failed to persist.[18] To enforce a life of austerity, conformity, and simplicity with conviction, the Brethren have, in fact, succeeded in creating a community in which life is dominated and integrated by a single institution. The Hutterian colony is a religious cosmos characterized by internal harmony and consistency based on a religious faith.[19] "The institutions of society," says Mead, "are organized forms of group or social activity —forms so organized that the individual members of society can act adequately and socially by taking the attitudes of others toward these activities."[20] In this particular religious cosmos the values are centered on one faith, and the mother tongue, Tyrolean German, is preserved to preclude the entry of any possible deviant or dissenting definition of objects or situations. One may safely expect to find that not only is the consensus shared by all but the attitudes of an individual Hutterite are also organized. Organized attitudes, thus identified, constitutes another generic property and should be taken as a defining quality of group cohesiveness.

Structural Integration

A religious cosmos with all the characteristics mentioned above can be achieved only when the size of membership is kept small, so small that it can function as a primary group. No sociologist would deny the cohesive quality of a primary group; so is the same quality found in the Hutterian colony. The population figures of the Hutterian colonies in North America show a range roughly from fifty members in the newly branched-off colonies to one hundred and fifty persons in the well established ones, yielding an average of ninety-five persons.[21] This number of persons is a viable, if not optimum, size of group which can operate on the basis of intimate face-to-

---

[18] Cf. John H. Noyes, *History of American Socialisms* (New York: Dover Publications, Inc., 1966); Charles Nordhoff, *The Communistic Societies of the United States* (New York: Dover Publications, Inc., 1966); and William A. Hinds, *American Communities and Coorperative Colonies* (Chicago: Charles H. Kerr Co., 1908).

[19] "As is common with religious men in all cultures, the Hutterites desire to live in a pure and holy *cosmos*, as it was in the beginning, when it came fresh from the Creator's hand. They believe that this *cosmos* can be achieved only within a Hutterite colony, for only within a colony can man maintain God's order." Mircea Eliade, cited in Hostetler and Huntington, *op. cit.*, p. 18.

[20] George Herbert Mead, *Mind, Self and Society* (Chicago: University of Chicago Press, 1934), pp. 261–62.

[21] For a fuller discussion on this point, see S. C. Lee and Audrey Brattrud, "Marriage Under a Monastic Mode of Life: A Preliminary Report of the Hutterite Family in South Dakota," *Journal of Marriage and the Family*, XXIX (1967), 512–20.

face association, continuing communication among members, and a "fusion of individualities in a common whole."[22]

It must be remembered, however, that the Hutterian colony, though functioning as a primary group, still constitutes a community, even if it is an institutional community. This religious cosmos, unlike ordinary primary groups, is composed of both a church and a business corporation. In spite of its monastic mode, the colony after all is the center of production and consumption and has to feed, clothe, house, and find work for so many persons and to assign to them work according to the interest, training, and competency of each member. Thus, the colony structurally is confronted with problems much more complex than in any primary group. In order to carry on these many lines of activities with efficiency and profit, the operation of the colony calls for at least some division of labor; yet, the members must, as a religious principle, live and work in equality without feeling status differentiation.

Part of this dilemma is resolved through the practice of what is referred to by them as the "community of goods." All members of a colony eat the same food in public dining halls, get the same allotment of clothing, and receive the same amount as an allowance. Thus, in the matter of consumption, equality is observed without discrimination, except in accord with the primary factors, age and sex. This cannot be said with regard to production, however. A fully grown colony is a business corporation and has, aside from farming as a mechanized operation, many other sidelines—cattle and hog raising, dairy and bakery, poultry, truck gardening, shoe repairing, broom making, and the tending of bees. The structure of the corporation is diagrammed in Figure 1.

The number of tasks listed in this diagram is not exhaustive, but sufficient to show that Hutterian members may assume greater or lesser responsibilities according to the jobs they perform. The president, concurrently minister of the church, is, of course, the leader, and many important decisions are made by him, the board of directors, and his secretary (popularly known as the boss or business manager); the crucial decisions are made by the whole congregation. Other staff members are invited to participate in decision making only when their respective lines of business are at stake. The field man in charge of farm operations has the most hands under his supervision and appears to carry a burden more significant than the others. And, finally, the teacher of the German Biblical school is frequently bilingual and also in charge of the disciplinary measures against all children when they misbehave outside of home.

In spite of the differences in responsibility, in the relative difficulty of tasks, and in work load and skill, there is little or no status distinction and no sense of inequality and discrimination. This is achieved through an

---

[22] Charles H. Cooley, *Social Organization* (New York: Free Press of Glencoe, Inc., 1956), p. 23.

FIGURE 1

THE STRUCTURE OF THE HUTTERITE BUSINESS CORPORATION

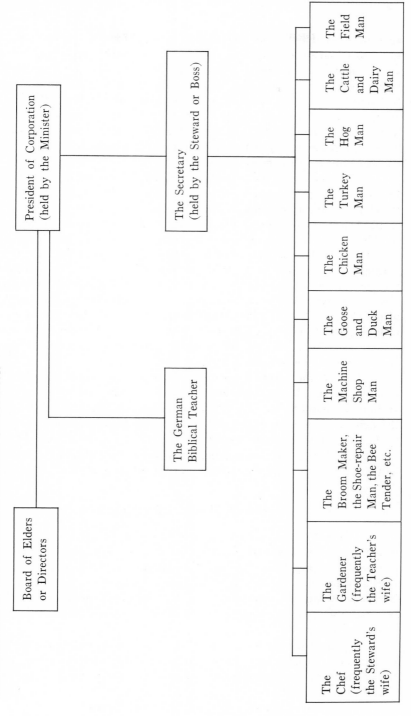

amazing *integration of the sacred and the secular aspects of life* in a colony so as to eliminate competition, rivalry, or any desire for prestige or power among individual members. A man may be doing one job or other in the secular part of the colony, the business corporation, and also be a member of the sacred institution, the church. In the mind of the Hutterite, the latter always takes precedence over the former. Work, to a Hutterite, is one way to fulfill the command of God. Any assignment, big or small, significant or insignificant, which may come to him in the corporation is gracefully accepted and performed with honesty and vigor.

In the church the minister, the leader of the colony who is elected to his post, enjoys no special privileges despite his total responsibility in both the church and the corporation. The board of elders of the church also serves as the board of directors of the business corporation. Even on lower levels, the kitchen chef—a job for a woman—often goes to the manager's wife, for the "boss" is the one who is to buy the necessary food for the cook. The teacher's wife, on the other hand, customarily serves as the gardener; in the summer, when vegetables in the field need the utmost attention and care, the labor supply is provided primarily by the children in upper grades of the German Biblical school. Her husband is thus at hand to discipline the children, when necessary. In both instances, the marital relationship is utilized to facilitate the functioning of the colony in at least some areas where such effects can be brought about.

When the foregoing features described are placed together, it becomes apparent that a condition conducive to cohesiveness emerges in the Hutterian group life, namely, structural integration. This condition—achieved through the imposition of the church on the business corporation, the fusion of the holy with the secular aspects of life, and the application of some social ties to ensure the effective functioning of other unrelated activities—should be taken as another defining property of the group quality of cohesiveness.

Sense of Group Identification

In ascertaining the properties of group cohesiveness, it would be incomplete if one aspect of group life is left untouched, namely, interpersonal relationships. The phrase "the members sticking together" necessarily implies mutual attraction. A high level of mutual attraction, as pointed out by Theodore Newcomb and others, means "not necessarily in the form of personal liking, but in the general sense that members attribute reward value to each other."[23]

Logically, cohesive groups should have little hostility and disagreement among the members. In our study of the Hutterian colony, however, the property of interpersonal attraction as a positive variable has failed to

---

[23] Newcomb, Turner, and Converse, *op. cit.*, p. 486.

stand up. True, it is conceivable that to some other groups manifesting a certain degree of cohesiveness, particularly the ones which have no historical or religious heritage, interpersonal attraction may play a foremost, decisive role in holding the members together. In the Hutterian colony, with its unique historical experience and its devoted religious commitment, it is the members' firm identification with the group and consequently their psychological gratification and exaltation which serves as the binding force, and, hence is an outstanding property.[24] Thus, emotional exaltation must be recognized as a defining quality of social cohesiveness concomitant with the other group properties mentioned above.

As it has been previously pointed out, the Hutterian colony is organized as a religious cosmos and an institutional community to practice the Biblical ideal of the community of goods or theocratic communism. The highest principle that the members set out to implement is mutual assistance and support through daily affirmation and reaffirmation to live together collectively a pure, faithful, and sinless Christian life. It is a life with a culturally prescribed and divinely sanctioned purpose. Ever since its founding, the sentiments of communion and the feelings of solidarity referred to generally in sociological literature as *esprit de corps* have been very strong, and they are still very strong. In a colony life is always carried on in a concerted and orderly fashion. One observation on colony life, which was made several centuries ago and is still valid today, has to do with a vivid simile declaring: "Where all the busy bees work together to a common end, the one doing this, the other that, not for their own need, but for the good of all."[25]

A life with such a high degree of emotional involvement creates not only a "universe of discourse" but also a situation of "team work." The most profound analysis of this is done by Mead who says:

> In the case of team work, there is an identification of the individual with the group; but in that case one is doing something different from the others, even though what the others do determines what he is to do. If things move smoothly enough, there may be something of the same exaltation as in the other situation. There is still the sense of

---

[24] At this point it may be pertinent to indicate a possible difference between the term "group cohesion" and that of "social solidarity," although these two are overlapping in many respects and used interchangeably by many writers. Group cohesion emphasizes the *nature of interpersonal association,* while social solidarity is often used (Emile Durkheim, for example) to refer to *the functional integration of society.* Although Durkheim admits there is psychic cohesion in the type of community like the Hutterian colony, he argues that there is another type of solidarity based on the recognition of individuality and division of labor. He designates the former as "mechanical solidarity," and the latter "organic solidarity." Mechanical in the sense, he explains, that "the social molecules which can be coherent in this way can act together only in the measure that they have no actions of their own, as the molecules of inorganic bodies." See his *The Division of Labor in Society,* trans. George Simpson (New York: The Free Press of Glencoe, Inc., 1933), pp. 129–32.

[25] Quoted from Friedmann, *op. cit.,* p. 79.

*directed control. It is where the "I" and the "Me" can in some sense
fuse that there arises the peculiar sense of exaltation which belongs to
the religious and patriotic attitudes in which the reaction which calls out
in others is the response which one is making himself.*[26]

From this passage, which is extremely informative and illuminating
in explaining the particular property of group cohesiveness, one is able to
review the ethos of Hutterian life with confidence and insight. It is their
practice of *Gelassenheit* as a religious principle that makes the I in the self
structure more accommodating and malleable. It is the fusion of the I and
the Me which engenders the sentiment of exaltation and which firmly binds
the membership together. In fact, because of the absence of this psychological
element in life outside of the colony, many a defector has been driven to
return to the colony shamefacedly and to confess his sins. Finally, their
strong group identification and deep emotional involvement in their concerted
efforts to achieve commonly shared goals enable the members to attribute
reward value to one another; their bonds go beyond mere reciprocal attraction. In organized team work a contribution toward progress attained by any
one member is viewed as a contribution by all. Looking from this angle, it is
easy for one to visualize the circular relationship and mutual reinforcement
between goal achievement and group cohesiveness.

On the basis of the foregoing generalization a further inference can
be made about the difference between the Hutterian colony and American
society at large. In an American community, especially one in an urban
setting, a number of competing institutions exist which are preaching different
ideals, advocating divergent values, and often even operating at cross purposes. The individual brought up in such circumstances is discouraged from
developing an integrated structure of the two selves, impeded from taking
effectively the role of the generalized other, and as a result is left with an
inadequately socialized I that surges ahead toward aggrandizement, aberra-
tion, or both at the same time. Group cohesion on a large scale has become a
phenomenon of rare occurrence. On the other hand, for the Hutterian
Brethren, a "blessed" community or religious cosmos with a sense of universal
neighborliness and helpfulness is thriving. It remains one of the few communities characterized by social solidarity and group cohesiveness.

In summary, group cohesion, as exemplified by the analysis of this
case, the Hutterian colony, can be defined as a useful, scientific concept. The
defining qualities so identified, though they may not be equally relevant to
other cases, are to consist of (a) shared consensus, (b) organized attitudes,
(c) structural integration, and finally (d) psychological exaltation (or group
identification). It may be further stated that these properties are concomitant
rather than independent—none alone is sufficient; all of them are necessary
to render this group quality known as cohesiveness.

---

[26] Mead, *op. cit.*, p. 273.

13

Lewis M. Killian

HERBERT BLUMER'S CONTRIBUTIONS TO RACE RELATIONS

If the average sociologist were asked to list the outstanding students of race relations, it is most unlikely that he would name Herbert Blumer. If Blumer were to be identified with the field, it would probably be in terms of his recent contribution to the language: "race prejudice as a sense of group position." This expressive concept is a valuable corrective to overly individualistic notions of prejudice. Yet it is only the words that are relatively new; Blumer has been examining race relations in terms of this concept since 1939.

Certainly race relations has not been one of Blumer's primary areas of interest over the years. He has loomed far larger as the chief inheritor of George Herbert Mead's approach to social psychology and Robert E. Park's interest in collective behavior. It is evident, however, that he was also strongly influenced by Park's interest in race relations, for he has included this aspect of human relations in his multi-faceted analysis of society. This inclusion of race relations as one of his areas of interest without making it paramount is consistent with Blumer's conception of the phenomenon, expressed in the words, "As far as I can see there is no evidence whatsoever for assuming that race relations are a special kind or class of social relations with a distinct generic character that sets them apart. . . ."[1]

Just as he has been an incisive critic of studies of industrial relations without becoming an industrial sociologist, he has been an acute observer of trends in race relations and a constant critic of emerging trends in theory without becoming a specialist in either field. Perhaps there is a lesson for other sociologists here. Blumer's very detachment from the main stream of race relations analysis gives his writings a freshness and depth which evoke the reaction, "Why didn't I think of that?" More significantly, the fact that he approaches race relations from the perspective of a broader theory of human behavior, rooted in his conception of the nature of social attitudes and the act, has given his analysis of race relations a timeless quality that is often prophetic. Always viewing race prejudice as a reflection of social structure, not of individual predispositions, Blumer has never been guilty of failing to see the forest for the trees. As the institutional nature of racism forces its way into the awareness of social scientists, the relevance and validity of his approach become increasingly evident.

Blumer's observation that "the study of race relations in the United States has sprung from, and has been sustained by, a melioristic interest in the improvement of the relations between racial groups" suggests one of the reasons why his professional detachment has enlightened his sociological observations.[2] This interest has led to preoccupation with a search for democratic solutions, as Blumer further observes, but the complex relationship between the democratic creed and pluralism has not been sufficiently explored. Furthermore, an unwarranted optimism has characterized the evaluation of changes and prospects for change in race relations, with social scientists magnifying any ray of hope that racial justice would be achieved, that the salience of race would even be wiped out, all through the full implementation of the democratic ethic of equal rights for individuals. Blumer's personal commitment to humanitarian ideals has been beyond challenge, but he has been singularly capable of describing in realistic, not wishful, terms the durability of a color line established through long, historic experience.

---

1 Herbert Blumer, "Reflections on Theory of Race Relations," in *Race Relations in World Perspective,* ed. Andrew W. Lind (Honolulu: University of Hawaii Press, 1955), p. 6.

2 Herbert Blumer. "Research on Racial Relations: The United States of America," *International Social Science Bulletin,* X (1958), 405.

His insight that a color line, where it arises, becomes part of the very warp and woof of the fabric of a society is reflected in his assertion that the theory of race relations must be "concerned with the *establishment and maintenance of a hierarchical racial order within a given society.*"[3]

This quality of realism and caution is seen in a unique confluence of Blumer's interests in industrial relations and race relations. In 1965 he contributed a chapter, "Industrialization and Race Relations," to a volume published under the same title by the Institute of Race Relations in London. After noting that industrialization is assigned a central role in the shaping of modern life, he observes that, despite a paucity of empirical evidence, "one can piece together from the literature a rather imposing body of theoretical conception of what industrialization is said to do to race relations."[4] Summarizing this conventional conception, he contends that it rests on the seemingly reasonable assumption that the introduction of an industrial system would undermine a racial order of the sort developed in a preindustrial society. According to this view, industrialization introduces a transitional stage into race relations—"a stage marked by unfamiliar association, competitive contact, and a challenge to previous social standing." The assumption of students of industrialization that an industrialized social order "is guided in its formation by a rational imperative of instrumental efficiency," plus the optimism of the scholar of race relations, leads to the conclusion that this is a transition to a beneficent new order.

> In the long run, race vanishes as a factor which structures social relations. Workers will compete with one another on the basis of industrial aptitude and not on the basis of racial makeup. Correspondingly, members of the managerial force will be chosen and placed on the basis of managerial competence and not of racial affiliation. Imagination, ingenuity, and energy and not racial membership will determine success in industrial entrepreneurship. Ascent on the social ladder will depend on the possession of necessary skills and ability, wealth or capital; racial make-up becomes extraneous. The premium placed on rational decisions will relegate racial prejudice and discrimination to the periphery.[5]

Blumer labels this picture "utopian" but charges that it is widely reflected in the literature. His critique of the utopian vision is informed by both his realism and his careful review of empirical studies. First, the assumption that rational decision making in industry will necessarily push managers to discount the racial factor rests on a narrow conception of the rational perspective. Particularly in the early stages of industrialization in a society

---

[3] Blumer, "Reflections on Theory of Race Relations," *op. cit.,* p. 14.

[4] Herbert Blumer, "Industrialization and Race Relations," in *Industrialization and Race Relations,* ed. Guy Hunter (London: Oxford University Press, 1965), p. 221.

[5] *Ibid.,* pp. 229–30.

with a strongly established racial system, managers may conclude that the resentment that nondiscriminatory employment practices arouses in other workers or in customers would disrupt efficient operations. Thus, *"rational operation of industrial enterprises which are introduced into a racially ordered society may call for a deferential respect for the canons and sensitivities of that racial order."*[6]

The moralistic argument that such decisions are not really rational, but are based on the personal prejudices, conscious or unconscious, of the decision maker, arbitrarily relegates the reality of the racial order to a position of minimal importance. That the melioristic bias of the social scientist leads him to postulate that the racial order is highly amenable to manipulation does not change the perceptions of the manager. To him, the need to avoid trouble and maximize efficiency by deferring to the canons of the racial order is phenomenologically real.

Central to Blumer's critique is his observation that industrialization does not automatically change the racial order; it may, instead, "reproduce and continue the social position of the races." His review of studies of the early stages of industrialization in the southern United States and in South Africa lead him to conclude:

> *Where a superordinate-subordinate racial arrangement was deeply entrenched, industrialization meant essentially a transfer of the framework of the established racial scheme to the new industrial setting. Members of the subordinate race were assigned to and essentially confined to the lower levels of the industrial occupational structure; no positions were opened to them inside of the managerial ranks of the industrial enterprises operated by members of the dominant race; doors were shut to their entrepreneurship in the operating world of the dominant racial group; and the traditional color line was firmly held.*[7]

Another sobering observation by Blumer is that the transitional racial tension and conflict postulated by the conventional theory of industrialization do not always arise between dominant and minority groups, but are more likely to arise between different subordinate racial groups. He cites outbreaks of friction between Negroes and Mexicans in the United States, Africans and Indians in South Africa, and different tribal groups in colonial Africa. He concludes:

> *Such competition and discord occurs at the lower levels of the industrial structure and does not touch the basic racial framework as constituted by the relations between the dominant and subordinate racial*

---

6 *Ibid.*, p. 233.
7 *Ibid.*, p. 235.

*groups. That framework shapes the reshuffling process under industrial-
ization rather than being shaped by it.*[8]

Blumer takes into account the argument that industrialization will
have the conventionally predicted effects in the long run but wryly comments, "We do not know how much time is needed to constitute the 'long
run'; certainly half a century of industrial experience in both South Africa
and the south in the United States brought no appreciable changes in the
position of the races in the industrial structure."[9]

This is not a simple argument that industrialization does not affect
the racial order. The call is for recognition that industrialization and racial
alignment act on each other. Where a racial order is weak and vague, industrialization is likely to produce greater and more rapid change than when
the racial order is clear-cut and firm. In addition, both industrial operations
and the racial order are affected by forces external to both. Thus, Blumer
argues, it was not industrialization per se but outside political pressures
which finally began to bring about changes in employment practices in the
American south. In concluding this little-known essay, he predicts that
throughout the world the importance of race as an issue in the new international world will cause such external forces to have increasingly greater
effects on the reordering of race relations in domestic settings. The effects of
industrialization will continue to be limited.

> *Industrialization will continue to be an incitant to change, with-
> out providing the definition of how the change is to be met. It will con-
> tribute to the reshuffling of people without determining the racial align-
> ments into which people will fall. Its own racial ordering, to the extent
> that it has any, will be set by that in its milieu or that forced on it by the
> authority of a superior control. In general, it will move along with,
> respond to, and reflect the current of racial transformation in which it
> happens to be caught.*[10]

In reading this paper, one can barely recognize the more familiar
Herbert Blumer who is the leading exponent of a particular school of social
psychology and has spent so much of his time calling for a reformulation of
the concept of "attitude." He is, rather, the sociologist par excellence writing
of racial orders, the structural imperatives of industrialization, and broad
social forces sweeping through national and international arenas. His analysis
is eminently on the macrosociological level.

This is a major component of the genius of Blumer's approach to

---

8 *Ibid.*, p. 236.
9 *Ibid.*, p. 238.
10 *Ibid.*, p. 253.

race relations. Though renowned as a social psychologist, he is fundamentally a sociologist, not a psychologist. During an era when a highly individualistic, psychologistic mode of analysis held sway in the study of race relations, he has maintained a consistently sociological approach. He has never lost sight of the profound significance of the fact that race relations are essentially relations between *groups,* arising out of a collective process in which one racial group defines another racial group and, by opposition, defines itself. Racial identification and race prejudice arise within this framework; they do not precede it. Thus, in his famous article, "Race Prejudice as a Sense of Group Position," Blumer proposed, "It is the *sense of social position* emerging from this collective process of characterization which provides the basis of race prejudice."[11] Reflecting his hypothesis that in the formation of public opinion not all attitudes are equal in importance, he also proposed that the collective process of definition "operates chiefly through the public media in which individuals who are accepted as the spokesmen of a racial group characterize publicly another racial group."

The emphasis on the sense of *group* position came as a clear reaction to the conception of race prejudice as an attitude lodged in individuals and arising from individual lines of experience, particularly lines of experience such as childhood disciplines which seemed to have little to do with the prevailing racial order. Blumer's foundation for this approach, obviously much influenced by Park, was first laid down in 1939 in "The Nature of Race Prejudice."[12] In this article he pointed to the rather obvious fact, not likely to be challenged by sociologists or psychologists, that racial contacts are not always accompanied by race prejudice. While biologists may divide mankind into a great variety of classifications, the "races" towards which the average man may be prejudiced are socially defined. It is for this reason that racial prejudice is so highly variable. The racial attitude itself is a product of collective experience and it is directed toward a conceptualized group.

It is evident that Blumer has always attached great importance to the historical dimension as essential to the understanding of any given instance of racial prejudice. He states that " . . . the content of collective experience of one group will determine what classifications they will make of other peoples and so what conceptualized objects they will build up." By way of illustration he observes:

> Southern whites with their experiences during slavery and fol-
> lowing the civil war formed a conception of the Negro which was neces-

---

11 Herbert Blumer, "Race Prejudice as a Sense of Group Position," *Pacific Sociological Review,* I (1958), 3.

12 Herbert Blumer, "The Nature of Race Prejudice," *Social Process in Hawaii,* V (1939), 11–20.

sarily different from that developed by the whites in Brazil, where the line of experience was significantly different.[13]

In this early article Blumer sees race prejudice as being related to a social fact so familiar to sociologists that they often seem to forget its significance—ethnocentrism. Feelings of antipathy towards other groups because of their strange and uncouth ways and a feeling of the inherent superiority of one's own group appear to be generic features of race prejudice. "There seems to be little doubt that ethnocentrism, in these two phases, is a primitive tendency of group life; as such it must be reckoned with as a nucleus around which an attitude of racial prejudice may develop."[14] Yet ethnocentrism is not the decisive factor in racial prejudice. At this point the influence of Robert E. Park becomes particularly evident. Park distinguished race prejudice from the enthnocentrism of relatively isolated groups in his statement, "It is obvious that race relations and all that they imply are generally, and on the whole, the products of migration and conquest." He saw race relations as one outcome of the competition for status between diverse peoples thrown together in a single, heterogeneous society.[15]

Similarly, Blumer proposed that racial prejudice would be most pronounced and serious in a social situation with three features: (1) two groups live together as parts of a unitary society; (2) the acceptance of the subordinate group is limited, and it is assigned to an inferior status; and (3) the dominant group fears that the subordinate group is not keeping to its place. Variations in the intensity of prejudice are to be explained primarily in terms of these social conditions, not of variations in individual life experiences—"the greater the threat which is *felt*, the greater is likely to be the prejudice."[16]

Twenty years later he characterized race prejudice as a "sense of group position" involving four basic feelings:

(1) a feeling of superiority;

(2) a feeling that the subordinate race is intrinsically different and alien;

(3) a feeling of proprietary claim to certain areas of privilege;

(4) a fear and suspicion that the subordinate race harbors designs on the prerogatives of the dominant race.[17]

All four of these feelings are held to be necessary for the existence

---

13 *Ibid.*, p. 13.

14 *Ibid.*, p. 15.

15 Robert E. Park, "The Nature of Race Relations," in *Race Relations and the Race Problem*. ed. Edgar T. Thompson (Durham: Duke University Press, 1939), p. 31.

16 Blumer, "The Nature of Race Prejudice," *op. cit.*, p. 16.

17 Blumer, "Race Prejudice as a Sense of Group Position," *op. cit.*, p. 3.

of race prejudice, according to this definition. The first two types of feelings may give rise to antipathy and aversion. The first three are present in certain forms of feudalism and in caste relations. In such situations, where a hierarchical structure is accepted by all, group prejudice is not present. Thus, it is the fourth element, the sense of threatened status, which gives rise to race prejudice. "The dominant group is not concerned with the subordinate group as such, but it is deeply concerned with its position vis-à-vis the subordinate group. This is epitomized in the key and universal expression that a given race is all right 'in its place.' "[18]

Those who have taken hope from Gunnar Myrdal's famous "principle of cumulation" might well have gained caution from Blumer's hypothesis. According to the former theory, low Negro standards and white prejudice are mutually supporting. A change in either will cause a change in the other. Thus, an improvement in the objective conditions of Negro living should lead to a reduction in white prejudice and set the system spiraling upward. It may be countered, however, that if the improvement in the Negro's conditions or the forces that lead to this improvement are interpreted as evidence that the subordinate group is "getting out of place," then an intensification of prejudice would follow. Thus, the intensification of racial tension in the United States at a time when the living conditions of a majority of Negroes were better than ever before may not be explicable simply on the basis of the revolution of rising expectations in the minority group. The aggressive actions required to produce these gains, as well as the gains themselves, may have produced a threat to the white man's sense of group position. The widespread assent to the proposition put by public opinion pollsters, "Negroes are trying to move ahead too fast," may be the modern, sophisticated version of the complaint, "They're getting out of place."

While the principal import of Blumer's writings has been that the analysis of prejudice must start with the empirical study of the historical process through which the sense of group position is formed, he has not analyzed actual instances of such a process himself. He has suggested that such analysis should take into account the conditions of initial contact and the subsequent experience of the peoples in the relationship, especially in the area of claims, opportunities, and advantages. An outstanding example of the sort of study he suggests is found in the work of his colleague, E. Franklin Frazier—*Race and Culture Contacts in the Modern World*.[19] Blumer himself has devoted more time to the role of critic of what he regards as the predominant theme in the social psychological analysis of race relations between 1930 and 1950. The trend which he discerned and so vigorously attacked implies

---

[18] *Ibid.,* p. 4.
[19] E. Franklin Frazier, *Race and Culture Contacts in the Modern World* (New York: Alfred A. Knopf, Inc., 1957).

that race relations arise out of individual feelings of prejudice and that these feelings reflect the personality structure and life experiences of individuals rather than the collectively defined orientation in the given social order. This attack was part of his broader critique of the preoccupation of sociologists and psychologists with attitude measurement. Thus he declares:

> *During the period from 1930 to 1950 American social psychology was in large measure preoccupied with the measurement of attitudes. A number of such measurement devices were developed and used extensively. To a preponderant extent the research work of social psychologists in race relations during this period consisted of making measurement studies of racial attitudes.*[20]

Anticipating by several years the declarations of the National Advisory Commission on Civil Disorders that "race prejudice has shaped our history decisively" and "white racism is essentially responsible for the explosive mixture which has been accumulating in our cities since the end of World War II," Blumer emphasized that it was not the specific feelings of hatred, hostility, or contempt revealed in the attitudes of bigots which lay at the heart of the problem of race prejudice.

> *These are only a few of many different patterns of feeling to be found among members of the dominant racial group. What gives a common dimension to them is a sense of the social position of their group. Whether the members be humane or callous, cultured or unlettered, liberal or reactionary, powerful or impotent, arrogant or humble, rich or poor, honorable or dishonorable—all are led by virtue of sharing the sense of group position to similar individual positions.*[21]

Blumer clearly and firmly adheres to what has been called the "group norm" theory of prejudice. The collective image and feelings which constitute race prejudice are forged in a long, complicated social process. This image is an abstract image, "a vast entity which spreads out far beyond...individuals [of the minority group] and transcends experience with such individuals."[22] This image building takes place primarily in the public arena, in the area of the remote and not of the immediate experiences between individual members of the two groups. The major influence "is exercised by individuals and groups who have the public ear and who are felt to have standing, prestige, authority, and power." Their formulations are extended and perpetuated, however, through gossip, anecdotes, jokes, and the like.

---

[20] Blumer, "Research on Racial Relations: The United States of America," *op. cit.*, p. 406.

[21] Blumer. "Race Prejudice as a Sense of Group Position," *op. cit.*, p. 4.

[22] *Ibid.*, p. 6.

Strong interest groups have an opportunity to direct the lines of discussion in a way which works to their advantage—witness the many instances in which interest groups have fostered anti-Semitism for extraneous purposes. Finally, Blumer points to the crucial role of the "big event" in developing a conception of the subordinate racial group. "The event that seems momentous, that touches deep sentiments, that seems to raise fundamental questions about relations, and that awakens strong feelings of identification with one's racial group is the kind of event that is central in the formation of the racial image."[23]

So a sharp contrast is drawn between the formation of individual attitudes through "the huge bulk of experiences coming from daily contact with individuals of the subordinate group" and the process of public definition of the minority group as a conceptualized object and of its proper "place." "It is the events seemingly loaded with great collective significance that are the focal points of the public discussion. The definition of these events is chiefly responsible for the development of a racial image and of the sense of group position."

The sense of group position is not, therefore, a reflection or summation of individual attitudes or personality traits but a matrix in which the individual himself is shaped and organized. Moreover, the sense of group position is not merely a reflection of individual predisposition but is a powerful norm which "guides, incites, cows, and coerces." It is more than a feeling of hatred, contempt or condescension—it involves "a fundamental kind of group affiliation for the members of the dominant racial group."[24] Personality components of racial prejudice should properly, therefore, be regarded as "mere individual variations inside a collectively defined orientation."[25]

In view of Blumer's conception of race prejudice as a central feature of the identification of self within a firmly established racial order, it is not surprising that he has viewed the prospects for rapid improvement of race relations in the United States with pessimism. Writing of "Social Science and the Desegregation Process" in 1956, he foresaw that efforts to bring about desegregation would lead to a tremendous power struggle, not to a gradual dimunition of racial prejudice. He observed:

> The carrying through as well as the blocking of deliberate desegregation depends on mobilizing and focusing influence and power on central functionaries. This calls, in the case of either side, for the development of organizational strength. The vehicle of procedure is strategical

---

23 *Ibid.*
24 *Ibid.*, p. 5.
25 Blumer, "Research on Racial Relations: The United States of America," *op. cit.*, p. 427.

maneuvering, designed to marshal and ultilize the potentials of power and prestige available in the given situation.[26]

Thus, again he saw the struggle to transform the racial order as taking place chiefly in the public arena, not in the hearts and minds of men. By the time of the publication of his article "The Future of the Color Line" in 1965, it appeared that great progress had been made toward destruction of the pattern of segregation in the south as result of the civil rights struggle. Blumer accurately predicted that this struggle to change the segregated position of Negroes in the public arena would prove to be only the prelude to a more intense struggle. To his oft-repeated propositions that the color line, or sense of group position, represents a definition of whites and Negroes as abstract groups with normatively defined positions in the social order, and that this color line is a collective definition of social position and not a mere expression of individual feelings, he added a third principle. This was that "the color line is not appropriately represented by a single, sharply drawn line but appears rather as a series of ramparts," of which outer portions may be given up while inner bastions are still steadfastly defended.[27] The area of civil rights—free access to public accommodation and voting rights—constituted only the outer citadel. As Blumer was writing this essay the battle was shifting to what he characterized as the next defense of the color line— the area of economic subordination. This he described as an area which would be "exceedingly tough because it is highly complicated by private and quasi-private property rights, managerial rights, and organizational rights." Remaining within this circle of resistance and yet to become the focal point of the struggle is the area of private associations. Falling outside of the formal controls of society, this area is peculiarly immune to assault.

Persuaded of the great tenacity of the color line, Blumer saw, even before Watts and the rise of the Black Power theme, indications of the shift of Negroes towards pluralism. He noted the intensification of racial consciousness among Negroes as a by-product of the bitter struggle for civil rights. He identified the formation of a large, urban, Negro proletariat as a new element in the positioning of the two races. He noted that certain conditions in the new urban Negro community, including increased bitterness toward whites and a stronger disposition to fight back, pointed to the probability that

---

[26] Herbert Blumer, "Social Science and the Desegregation Process," *Annals of the American Academy of Political and Social Science,* CCCIV (March 1956), 142.

[27] Herbert Blumer, "The Future of the Color Line," in *The South in Continuity and Change,* eds. John C. McKinney and Edgar T. Thompson (Durham: Duke University Press, 1965). p. 323.

The urban Negro proletariat, unlike Negroes at the bottom of the social and economic ladder in the past, will not humbly accept this position but be poised to protest and rebel in some fashion.[28]

If conditions among urban Negroes are not significantly improved, the prospects, he said, "are indeed high that discord and overt strife will be persistent marks of the color line." The major battlegrounds would be the large cities of the north and west, the headquarters of national organizations, and the seats of government.

Pessimistic about the chances for the reduction of tension and conflict during the struggle of Negroes for economic equality, Blumer sees the prospects for peaceful dissolution of the barriers to private association as even dimmer. He concludes with a tentative prediction of a form of Black pluralism:

It is entirely conceivable that even in a situation of equal social status the Negro group would accommodate to exclusion as a separate racial group—as, indeed, Jews have done in large measure. Such an accommodative relation is fully tenable without being a source of tension and discord in a social order.[29]

Blumer has been bold in his predictions of trends in race relations. These predictions have not been based on firsthand empirical research, particularly on attitude surveys. Instead they have been based on painstaking reviews of historical and comparative studies focused on the sociological level. Consistently Blumer has looked at racial groups as complex, highly structured, and differentiated entities, not as aggregates of discrete individuals possessed of attitudes and personality traits which add up to race prejudice. Prejudice, as a sense of group position, is eminently a group product and as such is a powerful force shaping the personalities, the attitudes, and the behavior of the group members. Sociological interest has belatedly turned from the prejudice and the discriminatory behavior of dominant groups to the collective definitions and the protest activities of minority groups. Blumer, in "The Future of the Color Line," was one of the first sociologists to take serious account of the new spirit of bitterness, hostility to whites, and Black self-consciousness arising among Negro Americans, particularly the urban proletariat. As sociologists turn to the analysis of this phase of the struggle for status they would do well to keep in mind his emphasis on the significance of leaders, of interest groups, and of "big events" in the emergence of the collective definitions which, he suggests, are at the core of race relations.

---

[28] *Ibid.*, p. 333.
[29] *Ibid.*, p. 336.

III

SOCIAL PSYCHOLOGY

I4

Thomas J. Scheff

ON THE CONCEPTS
OF IDENTITY AND
SOCIAL RELATIONSHIP

Like most concepts in sociology, the concept of a social relationship, though central to virtually any sociological analysis, is undeveloped. The concept is used today in much the same way as it was defined by Max Weber, as one of the key terms in his systematic sociology: "The term social relationship will be used to denote the behavior of a plurality of actors insofar as, in its meaningful content, the action of each takes account of that of the others and is oriented in these terms."[1] By the reference to the meaningfulness of the content, Weber intended that substantial attention be paid to the subjective

---

[1] Max Weber, *The Theory of Social and Economic Organization,* trans. T. Parsons (New York: The Free Press of Glencoe. Inc., 1947), p. 118.

state of the actor, in his orientation to the other actor. Thus, he goes on to say:

> The subjective meaning (of the act) need not necessarily be the same for all the parties who are mutually oriented in a given social relationship. ...It may nevertheless be a case of mutual orientation in so far as, even though partly or wholly erroneously, one party presumes a particular attitude toward him on the part of the other and orients his action to this expectation.[2]

Like Emile Durkheim and George Herbert Mead, Weber thus stresses the mutual subjective orientation of the participants in a social relationship.

Although Weber's usage has been accepted by sociologists, current discussions of social relationships remain at almost exactly the same point that Weber left them. Making the point that social relationships are subjectively meaningful, Weber and his subsequent followers did not pursue the implications of this definition. For example, in the above quotation it is implied that there are two dimensions along which relationships can vary. The first is the degree to which subjective meaning is imputed to the other actor. The second is the degree to which such subjective imputations are accurate. When these implications are not developed, the resulting definition is relatively gross and undifferentiated. It does not discriminate among the myriad kinds of human relationships that occur and is therefore of little use for theory or empirical studies.

In this paper, two recent articles which are relevant to the concept of social relationship will be used to expand and elaborate on Weber's fundamental notion. The first article, on shared awareness, explores in concrete instances some of the implications of the possibility that orientations toward the other may be incomplete, inaccurate, or equivocal.[3] The second article, on consensus, develops a formal conceptual and operational model of the degree of shared orientation.[4] This paper will seek to apply the procedures of the two earlier articles to the development of the concept of a social relationship and thus contribute to the usefulness of this basic sociological idea.

By establishing a precise definition of the degree of shared awareness, the proposed model of social relationship will seek to show the relationship between social structural concepts, such as social role, and processual

---

[2] *Ibid.*, p. 119.

[3] Barney Glaser and Anselm Strauss, "Awareness Contexts and Social Interaction," *American Sociological Review,* XXIX (1964), 669–79.

[4] Thomas J. Scheff, "Toward a Sociological Model of Consensus," *American Sociological Review,* XXXII (1967), 32–46. An application is found in his paper, "A Theory of Coordination Applicable to Mixed-Motive Games," *Sociometry,* XXX (1967), 215–34.

concepts, such as identity. The proposed definition of social relationship will be based on the process in which identities are established in social interaction, but will also articulate closely with role analysis.

The first article referred to above by Barney Glaser and Anselm Strauss, concerns awareness contexts. Their analysis makes the degree of shared awareness between the two parties in a transaction the key feature of the interaction. The awareness contexts they delineate concern the degree of shared awareness of each other's identity between the interactants in four contexts: open (both parties aware), closed (one party unaware), suspicion (one party suspicious), and pretense (both parties aware, but neither acknowledging their awareness). Glaser and Strauss suggest that analysis of interaction should determine the type of awareness context, the conditions that give rise to each type, the empirical sequence of contexts, and the tactics that interactants use to maintain or transform the context. Applied to the situation of the dying patient in the hospital, this paradigm leads toward an examination of the processes of information control, interpersonal power and tactics, impression management, and other crucial social psychological issues in the interaction between patients and staff.[5]

The awareness contexts outlined in the Glaser-Strauss paper are suggestive of a consistent way of analyzing many different kinds of social interaction. Before applying this approach, however, a number of ambiguities in their analysis must be clarified. Three problems concerning their concept of identity will first be discussed: the lack of a conceptual definition, the question of "true identity," and the narrowness of the range of interaction implied by their use of this concept.

In their discussion, Glaser and Strauss define an awareness context as "...the total combination of what each interactant in a situation knows about the identity of the other and his own identity in the eyes of the other." The key concept in this definition, identity, is never defined. Rather than defining identity, the article provides only an example of the way the concept is used. Two identities are implied in the discussion: a patient who is dying, and a patient who is not dying. Without an abstract definition, the kinds of situations to which the analysis is applicable and the way in which it is applicable are not clear.

The difficulty is further compounded by the phrase "true identity," which is used repeatedly in the article. This usage implies a subtle bias in the viewpoint of the investigators. They side with the staff's definition of the patient's identity, rather than the patient's. That is, there is the implica-

---

[5] The formulation of these issues as the central focus of the study of social interaction is due to Erving Goffman, *Presentation of Self in Everyday Life* (New York: Doubleday & Company, Inc., 1959); and *Behavior in Public Places* (New York: Free Press of Glencoe, Inc., 1963).

tion of a medical perspective in the discussion. It is the staff, not the patient, who actually knows whether the patient is dying. This bias has the unfortunate implication that the analysis should be limited to situations in which the investigator knows something that the interactant doesn't. The paradigm would seem to require that the investigator be more of an insider than at least some of the participants.

Finally, the concept of identity as used in the articles, and particularly in the dying patient example, implies a very narrow range of situations to which the paradigm might be applied, the kind of strategic bargaining situation in which one or both parties seek to maintain or dispel a deep secret about his or the other's identity.[6] Even within this narrow range, the Glaser and Strauss typology does not purport to exhaust all the possible types of shared awareness. This limitation is particularly crucial for the problem of relating the concept of awareness contexts to other sociological concepts and particularly to the concept of a social relationship. Before taking up this issue, let us first suggest how some of the ambiguities in the Glaser-Strauss paradigm may be clarified by using the Scheff model of the degree of consensus.

Shared awareness can be related straightforwardly to the concept of the degree of consensus. In the second article referred to above, it was proposed that consensus be viewed as an infinite series of reciprocating attributions of each interactant to the other: I know that you know that I know, etc.[7] As an operational definition of consensus, it was proposed that these reciprocating attributions be correct at the first three levels of coorientation, with respect to some statement. That is, there would be consensus between nurse and patient that the patient is dying, if each agreed, knew that the other agreed and knew that the other knew he agreed with the statement: "Mrs. Jones (the patient) is dying." If one or more of the attributions of both parties is inaccurate, the situation is called one of dissensus. As can be quickly seen, this model of consensus is closely related to the Glaser-Strauss paradigm of shared awareness.

Although the application of the awareness context paradigm by Glaser and Strauss is built upon the troublesome concept of identity, they do give a broader definition in a footnote: "A more general definition of awareness context is the total combination of what specific people, groups, organi-

---

6 This focus is also indicated in their final paragraph: "Certain types of social phenomena are probably strategic for extending our knowledge of awareness contexts: for example, research discoveries in science and in industry, spy systems, deviant communities whose actions may be visible to squares, types of bargaining before audiences, such as occurs in diplomatic negotiations, and unofficial reward systems...." Glaser and Strauss, *op. cit.,* p. 679.

7 Scheff, "Toward a Sociological Model of Consensus," *op. cit.*

zations, communities, or nations know what about a specific issue."[8] If we use their more general definition, then the subject of awareness becomes some *specific issue*. The definition then is quite similar to the model of the degree of consensus above. Taking the subject of awareness as a verbal statement facilitates the development of an operational definition. Any verbal statement can be taken as the subject of awareness. Ascertaining the degree of awareness becomes a matter of determining the extent to which the interactants subscribe to the statement, correctly attribute agreement with the statement to the other, the other's attribution to oneself, and so on.

In the Glaser and Strauss treatment, identity is a trichotomy: other's identity, own identity, and own identity in the eyes of the other. Substituting attribution concerning a given statement for identity, the three values of the variable become other's attribution, own attribution, and own attribution in the eyes of the other. These three values correspond to the three levels of coorientation in the model of consensus. The other's attribution is the first, or *understanding* level; own attribution is the zero, or *agreement* level; and own attribution in the eyes of the other corresponds to the second, or *realization* level of coorientation.

To illustrate the relationship between the two schemes, it is helpful to depict the different awareness contexts in terms of levels and types of coorientation. For the present, we will let the issue be the statement "Mrs. Jones is dying" and the situation be the interaction between Mrs. Jones (the patient) and a nurse. Later in this paper, in our discussion of identity, the meaning of such a statement will be specified.

Open awareness refers to a situation where both patient and nurse agree with the statement, and each is aware that the other agrees. Using the coorientation notation, the situation would be shown as follows:[9]

Context:		LEVEL OF COORIENTATION						
		3	2	1	1	2	3	
Open	Nurse	(R	U	A	A	U	R)	Patient
		+	+	+	+	+	+	

Each person agrees, understands that the other agrees, and realizes that he is understood.

---

8 Glaser and Strauss, *op. cit.*, p. 670, fn. 1.

9 In the following diagrams, pluses will be used to indicate agreement with the statement, minuses to indicate disagreement. The plus under the A on the nurse's side indicates that she agrees with the statement, the plus under the U indicates that she thinks that the patient agrees, and the plus under the R indicates that she thinks the patient thinks that she, the nurse, agrees. The pluses and minuses on the patient's side have corresponding meanings. This notation follows R. D. Laing, H. Phillipson, and A. R. Lee, *Interpersonal Perception* (London: Tavistock, 1966).

Closed awareness would be the situation where the nurse agrees that the patient is dying, and understands that the patient disagrees. The patient disagrees, and thinks that the nurse disagrees, i.e., she misunderstands the nurse's position on the issue. The nurse realizes that she (the nurse) is misunderstood, and the patient realizes that she (the patient) is understood, as follows:

Context: LEVEL OF COORIENTATION

		3	2	1	1	2	3	
Closed	Nurse	(R	U	A	D	M	R)	Patient
		—	—	+	—	—	—	

To this point, there is close correspondence between the Glaser and Strauss definitions and those used here. With the third category used by Glaser and Strauss, the suspicion awareness context, one can see some of the complexities in the analysis of shared awareness. Their definition of this context is quite casual, and leaves a number of ambiguities: "A suspicion awareness context is a modification of the closed one: one interactant suspects the true identity of the other or the other's view of his own identity, or both."[10] Applying this definition to the nurse-patient situation, one rendering would be:

Context: LEVEL OF COORIENTATION

		3	2	1	1	2	3	
Suspicion	Nurse	(F	U	A	D	U	R)	Patient
		—	—	+	—	+	—	

The nurse agrees, and understands that the patient disagrees. The patient understands that the nurse agrees, and realizes that she (the patient) is understood. The nurse, however, fails to realize that she (the nurse) is understood. RUA/DUR would be almost the same, except that the nurse would realize that she is understood.

If we are to use Glaser and Strauss' suggestion that awareness should be treated as a trichotomy, with aware, suspicion, and unaware as possible states, it becomes necessary to change the definition of suspicion to a situation where the patient suspects her own identity. This can be rendered by depicting the patient as both agreeing and disagreeing with the statement:

Context: LEVEL OF COORIENTATION

		3	2	1	1	2	3	
Suspicion	Nurse	(F	M	A	S	U	R)	Patient
		—	—	+	±	+	—	

---

10 Glaser and Strauss, *op. cit.*, p. 670.

The nurse agrees with the statement; the patient is suspicious, i.e., she both agrees and disagrees. The patient understands that the nurse agrees, the nurse misunderstands—she doesn't know that the patient is suspicious. Finally, the patient realizes that she (the patient) is misunderstood, but the nurse fails to realize that she (the nurse) is understood. Obviously, the profile could be permuted in a number of other ways at the first and second level and still be considered a suspicion context.

In order to relate the fourth context, pretense, to the model of consensus, a new dimension must be introduced, the relationship between gestures and attribution. An interactant acknowledges awareness by making gestures which are consonant with his attributions. Pretense involves making gestures which contradict one's attributions. For example, a nurse says to a patient she knows to be dying: "You are looking well this morning." To include the acknowledgment of awareness in the analysis, a second dimension of interaction, pertaining to gestures, will be added. A pretense awareness context involves both interactants being aware, but pretending not to be, i.e., making gestures as if they were unaware.

Context:			LEVEL OF COORIENTATION						
			3	2	1	1	2	3	
Pretense	Attributions		(R	U	A	A	U	R)	
		Nurse	+	+	+	+	+	+	Patient
	Gestures		(R	U	D	D	U	R)	
			−	−	−	−	−	−	

That is, both parties agree that the patient is dying, both understand that they agree, and each realizes that she is understood. Their gestures indicate, however, that each disagrees, thinks the other disagrees, and that the other thinks that she disagrees. (For simplicity, I am assuming agreement between the interactants on the meaning of the gestures. In a situation where the gestures are verbal and overt, this is not a highly restrictive assumption.)

In the other awareness contexts, acknowledgment or lack of acknowledgment is also implied. In an open context, the gestures would be the same as the attributions (all positive). In a closed context, the gestures of both parties would be all negative, making them congruent, except for the zero level for the nurse. (She agrees with the statement, but does not acknowledge her agreement.) This scheme obviously can lead a large number of permutations, each describing a complex awareness context.

Let us now recapitulate the criticism of the Glaser-Strauss paradigm, and the suggestions in this paper for improving it. Most of the criticism concerned their concept of identity, which, it was argued, was not defined, made further confusing by the notion of "true identity," and finally, implied a very restricted range of interaction to which it was applicable. In the proposal outlined above, these ambiguities were met by replacing the concept of identity with that of specific issue, a verbal statement. With this substitution, it becomes possible to state an analytic definition of shared awareness, based on a formal model of the degree of consensus. This definition avoids the problem of deciding on the "true" state of affairs, it being necessary only that the investigator ascertain the interactants' attributions and gestures, and compare them in the manner indicated. Defined in this way, the paradigm is no longer restricted to a narrow range or interaction.

If one takes the broad definition of awareness contexts in terms of specific issues, then this analysis becomes applicable to all types and levels of social behavior—that is, to what Weber called social action. At this most general level, attention can be given to such general phenomena as shared meanings, the concept of the "topic of conversation," consensus, and most broadly, to what Weber referred to as *verstehen*, or interpretive understanding.

The remainder of this discussion will be devoted to the narrower definition of awareness context, in terms of the identities of the interactants. By formulating an explicit definition of identity, this paper will seek to use the above model of the degree of shared awareness to give a conceptual and operational definition of a social relationship.

In order to develop a working definition of identity, a number of limitations will be imposed. The first step will be to limit our discussion to the concept of *situational* identity, in order to establish an elementary unit of social interaction. Given this limitation, we will define situational identity as the mutually recognized verbal statement of the projected sequence of behavior by and toward a participant in a transaction. The projected sequence of alter's behavior that is expected by ego may be contingent upon ego's response. Nevertheless, the verbal statement of the projected plan of action, including the contingent responses, is taken to be the specific issue for the model of shared awareness. Usually associated with this statement of projected acts is a summary label, which is taken to represent that sequence. Thus, the label "dying patient" is a label which can be taken to represent a whole sequence of acts by and toward the person so labeled.

Since the identity of a dying patient is rather complex and diffuse, let us use a situation with simpler identities in order to illustrate the proposed concept of identity. The Prisoner's Dilemma is a well-known experimental game based on a transaction in which there are only two interactants, each of whom has only two choices of behavior. The game derives from a situation in which the participants are two prisoners whom the police suspect of a crime. The police have separated the prisoners and made identical offers to each: If you will turn state's witness against the other, your punishment will be lenient. Not being able to communicate with the other prisoner, each fears that the other will betray him. The situation can be taken to represent a fundamental unit of social behavior, where there are restrictions on communication, mutual fate control, and a temptation to betray the other.[11]

At its very simplest, the Prisoner's Dilemma has three parameters: two participants, two choices for each participant (to trust or to betray), and only one trial (i.e., only one choice of action is made, to trust or to betray). In this simplest situation, there are only two identities, the prisoner who doesn't turn state's witness, whom we will call the "cooperator," and the one who does, whom we will call the "defector."

The situation in the experimental game of Prisoner's Dilemma is somewhat more complex, since there is a series of trials, with each participant making a new choice each time. Suppose, for example, that the number of trials in a sequence were two. A participant might then build up a series of contingent responses which he attributes to the other. "If I play C on the first trial, and he plays C, then he will probably play C on the second."

A player, may, in fact, formulate a generalized sequence of contingent plays for himself and the other player for any number of trials. One example of such a sequence is the following: Begin by playing C on the first play; on the second play, choose the same play as the other player chose on his last play; and continue this pattern until the end of the series. This sequence is called a matching strategy. It tends to encourage the other player to choose the cooperative play, since it begins with a C choice, and reciprocates the other's C choice on the following play. It also has the feature, however, of discouraging the other from exploiting one's own C choices, by reciprocating with a D choice of one's own, following a D choice by the other. A player following such a strategy might be given the summary label of a contingent cooperator.

A second example of a generalized sequence would be to always play C. Such a player might be called a "'constant cooperator," and the strategy "turn the other cheek." Another strategy might be to always play D. A summary label for such a player would be a "constant defector." Obviously, many other more complex strategies could be formulated.

As a final example, we will take one of the more complex sequences. A player might formulate the following strategy: Begin by playing C. On the second play, match the other's first play. If, however, the other's first play was D, on the third play, choose C (giving the sequence C, D, C for the first three plays.) The first two plays in this sequence represents an offer of the following kind: "I want to play cooperatively, if you will. If, however, you play D when I play C, I will respond, on the second play,

---

11 Anatol Rapoport and Albert M. Chammah, *Prisoner's Dilemma* (Ann Arbor: University of Michigan Press, 1965). Cf. Scheff, "A Theory of Coordination Applicable to Mixed–Motive Games," *op. cit.*

with a D." So far, the sequence is the same as the matching strategy. The third play, C, however, is a departure, representing the offer: "If you respond to my C with a D on the first play, and we have both played D on the second play, I will play C on the third play, giving you a chance to play cooperatively again." Such a sequence might be called a contingent cooperative strategy with a conciliatory feature.[12]

By the definition of identity given earlier, a strategy is only a component of an identity. A strategy becomes the basis for an identity when it is mutually recognized as applicable to one of the participants in a transaction. For example, two players, each coming to recognize that the other has begun to follow a matching strategy, may, after intitial variation in their choices, both settle down to playing C. This is to say that the identities had both been established as contingent cooperators, leading to a constant C choice. Notice that a constant C choice does not in itself demonstrate that these identities have been established. The players may both play C because they have established each other as constant cooperators, or both may play C only because neither understands the game, and neither makes any attribution at all to the other player. In order to determine whether identities have been established and if so what these identities are, the investigator needs to determine what attributions are being made by the interactants and, as we shall see below, what gestures are made avowing these attributions.

We have been discussing interaction in terms of identities. Now, having defined identities, we can state how this definition may be used to define a social relationship. We will employ the following terminology: the relationship between the participants in a transaction is social to the extent that they have established their identities. In this usage, identity and relationship are closely related concepts. Identity is the individual and relationship the collective term for the same underlying situation; parties to a transaction have mutually recognized parts to play in the transaction.

Having established this terminology, we may now return to the Glaser–Strauss typology of awareness contexts. It becomes clear from the discussion so far that the four awareness contexts they discuss are four different types of social relationships implicit in Weber's conception. Their scheme simply explores some of the variations in the completeness and accuracy of imputation of the other's orientation.

If we add two more contexts, we can complete the definition of types

---

12 For a still more complex set of contingent strategies, see the "solution" to Prisoner's Dilemma developed by the mathematician Nigel Howard, "The Theory of Metagames," *General Systems Yearbook,* XI (1966), 167–68. A less technical presentation can be found in Anatol Rapoport, "Escape from Paradox," *Scientific American* (July, 1967), pp. 50–56. This treatment is interesting in the present context because it develops strategies based on the first, second, and third level of attribution, suggesting a possible convergence with the model of identity proposed here.

of social relationships by setting up a continuum ranging from the absence of a social relationship, through relationships that are marginally social, to relationships that are social. The two new contexts are situations in which imputations are (1) not made to the other by either party, and (2) made by only one of the parties. The continuum of social relationships can then be represented in the following diagram:

SOCIAL RELATIONSHIPS	MARGINAL RELATIONSHIPS	NONSOCIAL RELATIONSHIPS
Open awareness context	Suspicion context	No imputations
Pretense context	Closed context	One-way imputations

We are proposing that relationships are social to the extent that both parties have mutually recognized identities. The most clearly social relationship is the open context, in which both parties mutually impute to the self and other sequences of forthcoming behavior. Where no imputations of projected behavior are made, or only one of the parties makes an imputation, there is no social relationship. In the suspicion context, where at least one of the parties is unsure about his own and/or the other's identity, the relationship is only marginally social. The same is true of the closed context, in which both parties make imputations to the other's orientation, but for at least one of the parties the imputation is incorrect.

The divisions set up in this typology between relationships that are social, marginal, and nonsocial are necessarily somewhat arbitrary. It might be argued, for example, that the pretense context could be classified as a marginally social relationship, along with suspicion and closed contexts. Nevertheless, the threefold division indicated in the diagram would seem to have some utility in discussion and research dealing with social relationships.

Note that the concept of the awareness context makes manifest the need for the determination of the gestures of the interactants that may convey the kinds of attributions they are making. In the pretense context, for example, there is mutual awareness of the correct identity of the dying patient, but both parties gesture as if they are making attributions that the patient is not dying. This analysis suggests, then, the need for a second level of measurement. Not only must one determine the attributions of the interactants, but also the gestures that are made to convey the kinds of attributions being made.

In the case of the dying patient, for example, in order to specify the kind of relationship which exists between the patient and the staff, it would be necessary to determine (1) the kinds of attributions that are made by the patient and the staff (i.e., a staff member is expected not to become involved in a discussion of the patient's future if he knows that the patient is dying), and (2) whether their gestures reveal the kind of attributions being made. This example suggests the need for an approach to the study of identity, and therefore of social relationships, somewhat different from current approaches. In order to talk about social identities and relationships in a precise and concrete way, one would need to catalog the distinctive features of the expected sequences of behavior that form the basis for an identity.

Before continuing the discussion further it is necessary to relate the proposed definition of social relationship to that of a social *role*, because they are closely connected. Following the discussion of identity and relationship above, role is a concept, like identity, that refers to the individual contribution to a transaction. I take role to be the narrower of the two, however. Role is part of the social structure, i.e., part of the generally recognized pattern of expectations in a community. Situational identity, on the other hand, is tied to a particular person in a particular situation. An individual's situational identity may well be his social role; it need not necessarily be, however.

For example, a male physician seeing a woman patient may relate to her in a purely professional manner, such that his sexual identity and hers is not involved. On the other hand, he may behave seductively, so that his situational identity is that of a male, rather than being his social role of physician. Note that if his seductive gestures are open and avowed, and recognized by both himself and the patient, the awareness context would be open. If the gestures are open but not avowed, yet mutually recognized, the situation would be that of a pretense awareness context. A suspicion context is easily visualized in this situation, as is a closed context. (In the closed context, either the physician or the patient could be perceiving the other as a sexual object, but there would be no recognition by the other, no avowal of the attribution, nor open seductive gestures.) Finally, there are relationships between physicians and patients which are not social, such as the situation where neither imputes an identity to the other. Or, in the situation that patients frequently complain of, the patient imputes an identity to the physician, but he treats the patient as a physical object only.[13]

As implied in the above example, there is a further difference between the concepts of role and identity. It is customary in sociological usage to treat role simply as an expected sequence of behavior. This usage further differentiates it from the concept of identity, since we have defined identity as the pattern of behavior that is mutually recognized as characterizing one of the participants in a transaction by those participants.

---

[13] Note that in the situation in this example, for the physician to take on the identity of a seducer casts the patient in the identity of the seducee, and vice versa. A discussion of the reciprocal nature of identity defining processes in interaction can be found in Eugene Weinstein and Paul Deutschberger, "Some Dimensions of Altercasting," *Sociometry*, XXVI (1963), 454–66.

There is, finally, a situated invariance to a social role. For example, the role of the physician is situated both physically and socially. Physically, he is attached to some base of operations, such as his office, hospital, or tele-phone-answering service. Socially, he is constrained by what he may suspect to be widely held shared doctrine, whether agreeable to him or not, as to what is expected of him.

The concept of identity refers to expectations that are far less situated and constrained. The identity of a male seducer is recognizable whatever his location in the social structure and so is less situated. It is, therefore, far more variable than that of an occupational role, because the transformation of identities may take place, and take place repeatedly, in a transaction in which the social roles of the participants remain fixed.

Returning to the example of the male physician, one might divide his potential behavior into three segments: sequences that are required, permissable, and forbidden. One way of determining an identity is simply to list all of the component sequences that fall under the three headings for the two separate identities, i.e., male seducer and male physician. A shorter way, which is probably the method that would be used by the woman patient in the hypothetical example, is simply to note which gestures are required by one identity and forbidden by the other. For example, there is a forceful and detached way of touching the body of the woman patient that is required by the physician role and forbidden in that of the seducer, just as there is an intimacy of touch that is required by the seducer and forbidden by the physician's role. In other words, the expectations that may be crucial for the determination of identities are those projected sequences of behavior that are either required or forbidden.

In the foregoing discussion, we have shown how it is possible to use the concept of the degree of shared awareness to create a unified approach to the fundamental concepts of social relationship, situational identity, and social role. We have already commented on the advantage this approach has for research, in that it is explicit and, in principal, operational. A second advantage, in this case for theory building, will now be discussed.

We have treated social relationship and identity as merely different terms for referring to the same phenomena: the establishment of mutually recognized, expected sequences of behavior in a transaction. Identity refers to the individual's sequence of acts; relationship refers to the ensemble of acts made up by the sequences of all the parties involved. We have taken social role to be a structural concept which differs in two ways from its complementary processual concept, identity. First, role is at a lesser level of complexity, since it is made up of a component part of the definition of identity, i.e., the expected sequence of acts in a transaction. Role, therefore, does not contain the added requirement of mutual recognition by the parties to the transaction. Secondly, role is treated to be part of a generalized pattern of expectations in the community, in contrast to situational identity, which is the sequence of acts expected of a given participant in a transaction by all the parties to that specific transaction.

By introducing these distinctions, we are able to discuss a particular transaction in a way that recognizes both its distinctive concrete features and its position in the institutional arrangements of the society. The interaction situation used above, of the male physician and the female patient, again provides an example. Although meeting in their officially recognized capacities as physician and patient, the actual identities in the transaction may be based on other roles, such as the man and woman as discussed above, or still other role sequences, such as kin, class or ethnic identities, etc. (In Asian societies, still other identities may be stronger than the professional one. In Japan, for example, a woman patient of advanced age may treat a younger physician merely as her junior. In Thailand, a psychiatrist seeing a Buddist priest as a patient is treated as merely an inferior, since he is not a priest.)

The approach suggested here has both promise and limitations. As indicated, the terminology attends to both the structural aspects of social interaction and to the process. It also is sufficiently precise to allow the researcher the possibility of catching some of the nuances in the elusive but basic human process of interaction. The complexity of the analysis proposed here is greater than is customary in the study of interaction: the determination of actions, attributions at three levels, and the gestures which acknowledge or fail to acknowledge them. An adequate methodology for determining attributions without unduly influencing those very attributions is by no means clear. Nevertheless, the potential of this approach for the intensive study of the structure and process of social interaction may be great enough to warrant further exploration.

One severe limitation on the present proposal is that the definitions of identity and social relationship are very much narrower than in the conventional usage of these terms in sociology. The definitions developed here are essentially one-dimensional, since they deal with a single mutually recognized sequence of behavior in only one transaction. Since the concept of identity is usually used to mean total identity, the conceptual definition offered here is called *situational identity*. In the usage proposed total identity would be constituted by the sum of all situational identities.

The issue with the concept of social relationship is somewhat more complex. Although the one-dimensional definition offered here is consonant with Weber's definition, it does not represent very well the way the concept is usually used today. In most but not all usage, social relationship is used to mean the total relationship between the parties, and not just that in a single transaction. In this broader usage, the total relationship is made up of the sum of all the situational relationships in which the parties are involved.

It would appear that the definitions of identity and social relationship offered here are sufficiently precise as to raise the issue of the exact meaning of these terms in sociological usage. If one accepts the usefulness of the proposed definitions, perhaps it would be salutary if the terms identity and relationship were never allowed to stand alone, but always used with the qualifiers "total" or "situational." One would thus be expected not to refer to the concept of identity alone, but either to situational or total identity. Similarly, one would not refer to a relationship, but to either a situational or a total relationship. Given the added precision and explicitness of this usage, it may become possible to use these basic concepts in systematic empirical research.

Summary

This paper has presented an explicit definition of the concept of a social relationship. Extending the analysis of two earlier papers, one on awareness contexts, the second on a model of the degree of consensus, the following definition was formulated. Parties to a transaction have a social relationship to the degree that they have established identities, where identities are defined as expected sequences of behavior that are mutually recognized as being applicable to the participants, each to the other. In order to establish, empirically, whether and what type of social relation exists between parties to a transaction, two types of data are needed: the accuracy of the attributions the participants are making to each other, and whether these attributions are acknowledged. Finally, it was shown how this approach to shared awareness bridges structural approaches, like role analysis, and processual ones, such as the analysis of social interaction.

15

Joan P. Emerson

"NOTHING UNUSUAL IS HAPPENING"

The societal reaction theory of deviance, disputing earlier approaches which assumed deviance to be an intrinsic quality of behavior, stresses the interaction between actor and audience. A deviant label is the product of an exchange between an actor and someone who charges the actor with rule violations, perhaps with ratification by third parties. How is social reality constructed by the participants so that an event comes to constitute a rule violation?[1]

Participants in any encounter take stances on the expectedness of the events; these stances are referred to in this paper as

---

[1] Cf. Howard S. Becker, *Outsiders: Studies in the Sociology of Deviance* (New York: The Free Press of Glencoe, Inc., 1963); and Peter Berger and Thomas Luckmann, *The Social Construction of Reality* (New York: Doubleday & Company, Inc., 1966).

"nothing unusual is happening" and "something unusual is happening." These orientations are expressed through a person's demeanor and do not necessarily reflect his private assessment of the situation. A member of the audience who undertakes labeling first must establish that "something unusual is happening" in order to define an event as a rule violation.[2] This stance sets the appropriate tone, just as the participants might effuse gaiety or being emotionally touched to carry off other events. In the framework of "something unusual," the labeler must establish the following propositions: (1) "You have committed an act of such-and-such a nature"; (2) "We recognize a prohibition on acts of this kind"; (3) "Therefore, you have committed a prohibited act." The validity of the labeler's premises may be challenged in terms of the kind of act that took place, the actor's responsibility for it, the existence of the rule, or the applicability of the rule. However, it may be more effective to prevent the establishment of the prerequisite "something unusual" framework.

This paper will consider the "nothing unusual is happening" stance as it affects the labeling of deviance. The central hypothesis is that social interaction has intrinsic properties that routinely bias negotiations toward the "nothing unusual" stance; this bias inhibits the application of deviant labels. The paper will suggest circumstances under which the "nothing unusual" stance is assumed and examine in detail two examples of negotiation. Finally, it will explore the structure of interaction affecting the outcome of such negotiations.

The "Nothing Unusual" Stance

In many situations persons assume a stance routinely. But at times it is not clear which stance to assume, or persons may not agree on how to proceed. There are two sets of circumstances relevant to labeling in which the stance is negotiated. First, persons may confront events which are particularly suitable for labeling within an acknowledged framework of rules. Second, persons may negotiate to transform an encounter from one normative framework to another.

Persons acknowledging a framework of rules must decide whether or not each particular event constitutes a violation. Although any event may be interpreted as a violation, for some events the interpretive work and winning of acceptance for the definition are easier. For such labeling-prone events the "nothing unusual" stance is particularly important. For example, a man feigning accident but deliberately caressing the body of a strange woman in a crowd trades on the woman's embarrassment, should she publicly

---

[2] Harold Garfinkel, "Conditions of Successful Degradation Ceremonies," *American Journal of Sociology*, LXI (1956), 420–24.

invoke a "something unusual" stance. Rather than call attention to the
situation at such a high price, the woman may cooperate by pretending she
thinks the touching is merely an accident unavoidable in such a tightly packed
crowd. The more a person can influence the evolving definition of what is
happening, the more he can work the system by undertaking action he thinks
would be appropriately defined as deviant and deliberately creating an
alternate definition.

When others believe that the actor did not intend to break a rule,
they may be especially ready to ignore potential violations. In any situation
where a person reveals information about himself which challenges the image
he is projecting, loses his self-control, or violates body decorum, others may
tactfully act as if nothing unusual were happening.[3] In another example,
dying patients typically are treated as though they had as assured a future
as anyone else; Barney Glaser and Anselm Strauss speak of "situation as
normal" interaction tactics in this connection.[4]

Surprisingly, persons also may react to bizarre behavior, such as
delusional statements, with similar tact. The writer repeatedly observed staff
members respond blandly to temporarily disoriented, senile, and brain-
damaged patients on a medical-surgical ward of a general hospital and later
gossip about the patients' "weird" behavior. The staff sustained an ordinary
demeanor when a patient in a leg cast and traction claimed to have walked
around the ward; when a 90 year old patient refused x-rays because her
children were too young to have the money to pay; when a senile woman
asked a young nurse, "Was the meat done when you looked at it?"; and when
an elderly man after a stroke said he was a boy scout and made a tent of his
bed sheet. On an obstetrics ward of another hospital, nurses advised the
writer not to contradict a patient who claimed John the Baptist as the
father of her baby. In everyday life as well people are inclined to acquiesce to
statements which sound incredible or paranoid. Cautious because of uncertainty about what the behavior means, persons avoid a fuss by continuing
their "nothing unusual" stance even in response to bizarre gestures.

So far negotiations about interpretations of particular events have
been discussed. Negotiations about the system of interpretation itself, however, have more radical import. When persons are invited to change their
normative framework, interpretations of numerous events may be affected
over a long period of time.

The most common circumstance in which a person is invited to
change his normative framework occurs during socialization into an unfamiliar

---

[3] Erving Goffman, *The Presentation of Self in Everyday Life* (New York:
Doubleday & Company, Inc., 1957).

[4] Barney Glaser and Anselm Strauss, "Awareness Contexts and Social Interaction," *American Sociological Review*, XXIX (1964), 672.

subculture. As persons move into new settings, they meet unanticipated experiences which initially they may regard as undesirable. Novices learn that the experiences are both customary and desirable in the new situation. Members of the subculture exhort, perhaps implicitly: "Now you see what we actually do here; I urge you to go along even though you weren't prepared to go along with such matters when you entered the situation." The "nothing unusual" stance is often a claim of expertise: "We know more about what usually happens in this situation than you do because we have been here time and time again when you have not."

A good illustration is Howard Becker's article on how experienced drug users present a "nothing unusual" definition to comrades undergoing drug-induced experiences which the latter are tempted to interpret as insanity.[5] In settings where homosexuals are dancing, flirting, and caressing, participants and heterosexual observers act as if nothing remarkable were occurring. Visitors at nudist camps remark that it seems just like an ordinary resort and that everyone seems to feel natural about not wearing clothes in public.[6] Members of occult groups, when expounding beliefs about magic, reincarnation, communication with other planets, and other matters outrageous to current scientific opinion, speak with the same casualness they use for generally accepted topics.[7]

Consider the prevailing demeanor in night clubs and topless bars. Risqué entertainment derives its impact from trifling with customary taboos, particularly about exposure of the body. Yet, while surrounded by nudity, participants strive to suggest a situation that is no different than it would be were all fully clothed. In bars where pickups occur, the participants' "situation as normal" style implies that they would be amazed to learn that the modes of introduction they were practicing would not be acceptable to Emily Post.

But it is not only in worlds generally regarded as offbeat that newcomers meet a "nothing unusual" stance. Observers in any setting, such as the medical world, find the same thing. A patient may look upon his medical condition and the technical procedures it elicits as highly unusual events, while the staff is reassuringly nonchalant. In a gynecological examination, for example, the staff members do not acknowledge as applicable the taboo exhibited in most other situations about private parts of the body; they act

---

5 Howard S. Becker, "History, Culture and Subjective Experience: An Exploration of the Social Bases of Drug-Induced Experiences," *Journal of Health and Social Behavior*, VIII (1967), 163–76.

6 Martin Weinberg, "Becoming a Nudist," in *Deviance: The Interactionist Perspective*, eds. Earl Rubington and Martin Weinberg (New York: The Macmillan Company, Publishers, 1968), pp. 240–51.

7 Leon Festinger, Henry Riechen, and Stanley Schachter, *When Prophesy Fails* (New York: Harper and Row, Publishers, 1964).

as though the procedure were as matter-of-course as an examination of the ear.[8]

Because people so frequently meet a "nothing unusual" stance from others they accept as legitimate socializing agents, they are prepared by analogy to accede to the stance under less legitimate circumstances. The "nothing unusual" stance is a claim about the standpoint of a subculture. Persons may insinuate that the suggestions they make to others are normal in a subculture when in fact this is not the case. This may happen when persons are recruited for situations they are hesitant to enter; it also may happen when two or more persons evolve private understandings. For example, the visibly handicapped, learning to manage the uneasiness of others' responses to them, attempt to negotiate a stance of "nothing unusual is happening."[9] Persons may approach each other in ways which may not fit the elaborate set of conventions surrounding introductions and the initiation of encounters. Prostitutes and clients, disattending the commercial aspect of their transaction, may attribute their encounter to friendship.

> *Moreover, much of the interaction of "john" (client) with girl (pros-*
> *titute) is specifically oriented toward the reduction of the stigma attached*
> *to both roles, each pretending that the other is fulfilling a role more*
> *obscure than that which is apparent.*[10]

Yet participants in these settings remain aware of the outsider's perspective. Thus: "Nudists envision themselves as being labeled deviant by members of the clothed society."[11] "Fringe (occult) group members are usually keenly aware of the fact that the larger culture disagrees with their view of the world...."[12] It is difficult to forget the outsider's perspective when one must continually engage in practices which implicitly acknowledge it. For example, nudist camps discourage the presence of single men, require civil inattention to nude bodies, prohibit bodily contact, and regulate photography.[13]

Underlying the overt "nothing unusual" stance may be simultaneous cues acknowledging "something unusual." Participants may devote elaborate attention to enforcing a "nothing unusual" definition, thus intensifying their interactive alertness, guardedness, and calculation. The behavior being

---

[8] Joan Emerson, "Social Functions of Humor in a Hospital Setting" (Doctoral dissertation, University of California at Berkeley, 1963), chap. 4.

[9] Fred Davis, "Deviance Disavowal: The Management of Strained Interaction by the Visibly Handicapped," *Social Problems,* IX (1961), 120–32.

[10] James Bryan, "Occupational Ideologies and Individual Attitudes of Call Girls," in Rubington and Weinberg, *op. cit.,* p. 294.

[11] Weinberg, *op. cit.,* p. 249.

[12] J. L. Simmons, "Maintaining Deviant Beliefs," in Rubington and Weinberg, *op. cit.,* p. 284.

[13] Martin Weinberg, "Sexual Modesty and the Nudist Camp," in Rubington and Weinberg, *op. cit.,* pp. 275–77.

defined as "nothing unusual" may become the intensive focus of attention, as when a person breaks down in tears in a setting (such as a psychotherapeutic one) which claims to tolerate such behavior. Even a verbal acknowledgment of "something unusual" may occur, often accompanied by a negation. For example, a man picking up a woman in a coffee house may remark, "I wouldn't be doing this except that I've been drinking all afternoon." Or before and after the event the participants may take a "something unusual" stance, as in the strained kidding which may accompany the decision to visit a topless bar and the even more forced jollity or the awkward silence on exit.

All parties may find it convenient to adopt a "nothing unusual" stance, and yet the alternate definition presses for some kind of recognition. At other times it may be possible to convince someone to accept a "nothing unusual" stance only if it is qualified by "something unusual" cues. Such cues may serve as a bargaining concession by those adamant about constructing a "nothing unusual" stance.

The Process of Negotiation

Examining the process of negotiating a '"nothing unusual" stance may provide insight into how definitions of reality are constructed and sustained in social interaction. In most settings novices quietly cooperate with seasoned participants in sustaining a "nothing unusual" stance. In the instance described below, however, the novice declined to cooperate. As a result, the process of negotiation about the framework for the interaction is more explicit than in most encounters.

Incident I. Gynecological Examination

The writer observed a highly atypical examination on the gyne-cological ward of a general hospital.[14] A twenty-six year old unmarried woman balks at one of her first pelvic examinations; rarely do patients complain about unpleasant features of the hospital to this degree. This par-ticular encounter may be viewed as a continual negotiation about whether to take a "nothing unusual" or '"something unusual" stance. The parties come to no resolution during the procedure, although shortly afterward the patient indicates to the nurse a partial capitulation.

The patient's demeanor disconcerts the staff, especially the doctor (actually a fourth year medical student), so that the staff members proceed through the episode in a guarded fashion, especially alerted to social as opposed to technical aspects, handling the patient with kid gloves, and coop-erating more closely with each other. Thus, while the staff members overtly

---

14 For the complete field account of this incident see Emerson, *loc. cit.*

assert "a nothing unusual" stance, their guardedness conveys an underlying countertheme of "something unusual." Actually, the nurse partially acknowledges a "something unusual" stance at one point when the patient demonstrates pain. This acknowledgment serves as a bargaining offer to the patient: "Okay, we'll go along with you at this point, if you'll go along with us the rest of the time." The patient refuses this offer, for otherwise she implicitly would be agreeing that the unusual element was the pain rather than the invasion of privacy in a gynecological examination.

Six excerpts from the writer's field notes on this examination will now be analyzed.

> At 8:50 p.m. the doctor enters, says "hi" in a friendly, non-professional way.
> Patient to doctor: "The blood is just gushing out of me."
> Doctor, with surprise: "Gushing out?"
> Shortly after this the doctor remarks to the nurse that the patient has her period.

The doctor opens with a casual greeting which asserts a "nothing unusual" stance. The patient counters with a remark implying that her body is in a state nonroutine to the staff. At several other points the patient makes remarks ("Shouldn't I wash before he examines me? The doctor won't be able to examine me with such a heavy flow of blood"), which hint that, because the staff members are mistakenly defining her body state as routine, they are neglecting to take action which is essential if they are to cope with her medical condition. In response the doctor expresses surprise at a move contrary to his proposed definition, attempting to discount the patient's stance. Later the doctor discounts the patient's stance more forcefully by defining her body state as routine, as he also does elsewhere in the episode.

> Patient to doctor: "Do you go through this every day?"
> Doctor: "What?"
> Patient: "This examining."
> Doctor: "Oh, yes."

The patient suggests the possibility that gynecological examinations are nonroutine to the staff. The doctor, by failing to comprehend a move so contrary to his proposed definition, refuses to validate the patient's "something unusual" stance. When the patient supplies clarification, the doctor explicitly denies the patient's suggestion.

> Doctor: "I'll tell you what I'm going to do. I'm going to take a Pap smear. This is routine test we do in this clinic."
> Patient: "Do you take anything out?"
> The nurse explains.

The doctor identifies the steps of the technical procedure beforehand, as he does at numerous other points, and directly states that the procedure is routine. The patient asks a worried question about the technical procedure, a question which implies, "Am I safe in your hands?" This move counters the "nothing unusual" stance. The nurse attempts to reinstate "nothing unusual" by a reassuring explanation.

> Doctor: "*You have some pain already, huh?*"
> Patient: "*It's just that I hate this.*"
> Doctor: "*Okay, try to spread your legs apart. Okay, I'm going to try to touch this and see where it is.*"

The doctor establishes a framework for the patient to report neutrally about discomfort. The patient ignores the suggested framework and offers a negative comment on the event in strong, emotional language. (At several other points the patient does the same thing; earlier she has said to the nurse: "'I hate this. I wish I could go home.'") The doctor ignores the patient's move and attempts to reassert his definition by neutral technical instructions and explanations.

> Doctor: "*Okay, this is the speculum and it's going to feel a little cold.*"
> Patient: "*Oh.*"
> Doctor: "*'Oh' what?*"
> Nurse to patient: "*Okay, take a few deep breaths and try to concentrate on something else. I know it's hard; that's sort of a focal point.*"
> Doctor: "*Does that hurt very much?*"
> Patient: "*Yes, very much.*"
> Soon the patient remarks: "*I won't be able to sit down for a week.*"
> Nurse with an amused air: "*You underestimate yourself.*"
> Doctor, with an amused air: "*How will you go home?*"

The doctor offers a brief explanation of the technical procedure in a casual style. The patient then demonstrates discomfort in a "something unusual" style. To negate this, the doctor claims that he fails to comprehend the patient's move. The nurse reinforces the doctor's stance by giving technical instructions, but her style and sympathetic remark constitute a compromise in the direction of "something unusual," a move that the patient has already rejected earlier. The doctor again establishes a framework for the patient to report neutrally about discomfort, and again the patient repudiates it, this time by an overt statement of pain in a "something unusual" style. Taking the offensive, the patient hints that the staff is mutilating her body. The staff attempts to discount the hint by couching the message, "You exaggerate," in a joking framework.

Doctor: "I'm going to do a rectal exam."
Patient: "No, no, no."
Doctor: "We have to do it; it's part of the examination."
Patient: "Why can't you give me a sedative first?"

The doctor announces the next step of the technical procedure. The patient protests this step in a highly emotional style. The doctor claims that both he and the patient are compelled by the standards of good medical practice: "I am merely an agent following the prescribed rules of the system," he suggests. He further emphasizes the routine nature of the procedure. The patient attempts to undermine the doctor's stance by suggesting directly how the technical procedure should be conducted. By asking that she be made insensitive to the experience via a drug, the patient implies that the staff is imposing unnecessary discomfort on her.

In each excerpt one sees a struggle over the stance to be taken. The patient insists that "something unusual is happening," and the staff tells her how routine it is. At one point the patient implies the event is unusual by asking, "Do a lot of women go through this?" Several times she challenges the staff definition by explicit references to topics taboo within the framework the staff is asserting. For example, she wonders if her body odor will repel others. The staff members attempt to establish the medical framework by discussing nonchalantly technical equipment among themselves, asking the patient technical questions in a casual style, and directly assuring the patient it will not be as bad as she anticipates.

Incident II. Attempted Holdup

Sometimes persons need to establish a "something unusual" stance in order to bring off a performance. The audience's "nothing unusual" stance in the following newspaper account undermines the robbers' performance so much that it collapses.

THEIR STORY JUST DIDN'T HOLD UP

Stockton—The worst possible fate befell two young masked robbers here last night. They tried to hold up a party of thirty-six prominent, middle-aged women, but couldn't get anybody to believe they were for real.

One of the women actually grabbed the gun held by one of the youths.

"Why," she said, "that's not wood or plastic. It must be metal."

"Lady," pleaded the man, "I've been trying to tell you, it IS real. This is a holdup."

"Ah, you're putting me on," she replied cheerfully.

> *The robbers' moment of frustration came about 9 p.m. at the*
> *home of Mrs. Florence Tout, wife of a prominent Stockton tax attorney,*
> *as she was entertaining at what is called a "hi-jinks" party.*
>
> *Jokes and pranks filled the evening. Thus not one of the ladies*
> *turned a hair when the two men, clad in black, walked in.*
>
> *"All right now, ladies, put your rings on the table," ordered the*
> *gunman.*
>
> *"What for?" one of the guests demanded.*
>
> *"This is a stickup. I'm SERIOUS!" he cried.*
>
> *All the ladies laughed.*
>
> *One of them playfully shoved one of the men. He shoved her*
> *back.*
>
> *As the ringing laughter continued, the men looked at each*
> *other, shrugged, and left empty-handed.*[15]

In order to proceed, the robbers must crack the joking framework already established in the setting; if they had been willing to escalate, as by shooting someone, the outcome would have been different. Two sequences in this story will be analyzed.

In the first sequence, the lady who grabs the gun expresses surprise that the gun is metal. Defining the holdup as make-believe, the lady checks out a piece of evidence. In a make-believe holdup the guns are also make-believe, perhaps made of wood or plastic; in a real holdup the guns are real, made of metal. By expressing surprise at evidence contrary to her proposed definition, the lady attempts to negate the challenge to her proposal. The robber immediately issues another challenge by directly stating the contrary definition: "Lady, I've been trying to tell you, it IS real. This is a holdup." The lady tries to negate this attempt by claiming the other is not really committed to the definition he is asserting: "Ah, you're putting me on."

In the second sequence, the robber opens with, "All right now, ladies, put your rings on the table." Thus, he performs an act which would logically flow from the definition he is asserting. The response, "What for?" asks for a clarification of this act, suggesting that the act is meaningless because the proposed definition from which it is supposed to follow is not accepted. The robber provides clarification by a direct statement of his definition: "This is a stickup. I'm SERIOUS!" By laughing, the ladies propose a humorous framework for the robber's assertion and succeed in discounting the definition of the situation as a holdup.

The process of negotiating the stances of "something unusual" and "nothing unusual" consists of direct assertions and counterassertions, implications and counterimplications. It also involves the establishment of frameworks for the other's subsequent moves and techniques for discounting the

---

15 *San Francisco Examiner*, April 4, 1968.

other's moves. Such techniques include incomprehension, surprise, humor, and accusing the other of a lack of investment in his own move. In the remainder of this discussion, conditions biasing the negotiations toward a "nothing unusual" stance will be explored.

Negotiating Acceptance of a "Nothing Unusual" Stance

Whoever performs a "something unusual" stance has some advantage, because his dramatic intensity is difficult to ignore. But maintaining the stance of "nothing unusual" quickly becomes untenable unless all participants corroborate it. Despite this advantage for "something unusual," however, observation suggests that a "nothing unusual" stance more often prevails in a problematic situation. Why is this so?

The "nothing unusual" advocate capitalizes on the ambiguity of events. In the movies the music swells up to signal "something unusual," the weather may change dramatically, and the crowd starts moving toward the focus of attention. Should the audience miss these cues, they can hardly miss the camera zooming in upon the actors' reactions to the unexpected event. In real life people almost expect the concomitants found in the movies, and their absence creates uncertainty about the meaning of the situation.

In the face of uncertainty, the actor may take the easiest way out. "Nothing unusual" provides a definite prescription for behavior: just continue to act in a routine manner. Actors can avoid the effort of creating a unique response. A "something unusual" definition may call for unpleasant emotions which people prefer to avoid—embarrassment and indignation, for example. People are often nonplused by events which could be defined as unusual, and they are inexperienced in managing such events. So they may be willing to take cues from others.

If one person firmly commits himself to a stand, others are likely to acquiesce. An effective strategy is to make a firm commitment to a "nothing unusual" stance immediately, without entering negotiations. An alternate strategy is to wait but decline the other's implicit "something unusual" offers, so the other concedes to "nothing unusual" to avoid a deadlock.

The ambiguity of events provides one condition favoring a "nothing unusual" stance. Conventions about maintaining social order provide another. Most social interaction is predicated on the desirability of avoiding a fuss. Many social practices rest on the assumption that it is wise to acquiesce to a person in his presence, regardless of one's private opinion. If a person has invested himself heavily in a certain definition of reality, others avoid challenging it. In particular, persons are reluctant to challenge another's claim about himself.

Since persons generally aim to maintain order in a particular situation, they invoke particular rules as relevant to the process of maintaining this situationally located order. Defining an event as a rule violation may shatter the view of reality that the participants have taken for granted. So, if invoking a particular rule would create disorder instead of maintaining order, it makes no sense to invoke the rule in that instance.

A third condition favoring a "nothing unusual" stance is the vulnerability of the would-be labeler to adverse consequences from his move. If the labeler's word must be weighed against the actor's, it may be difficult to convince third parties that a violation has occurred. In this as well as other cases, the would-be labeler's move opens him to counterdenunciation. Suppose, as in a Candid Camera sequence, a girl asks a man to help her carry a suitcase. The girl acts as if it were an ordinary suitcase, but actually it is filled with metal.[16] If the man remarks, "This suitcase is too heavy for anyone to carry," the girl might respond, "No, you must be a weak man because I have carried it myself for three blocks." Thus, a "something unusual" claim can be countered by, "No, it is you who cannot cope with this ordinary situation." Not only is a charge of inadequacy possible but, should someone persist in taking a "something unusual" stance, he could be labeled "emotionally disturbed" for displaying a demeanor too involved and for making the occasion into one more momentous than it really is.

Even if the labeler escapes counterdenunciation and succeeds in defining an event as a rule violation, this definition may reflect negatively on himself. Acknowledging the rule violation may involve a loss of face or self-derogation for the labeler. Any deviant act raises the question for observers: "Who am I that this should happen around me?" Many deviant acts are taken as an insult to others. To avoid the insult, what could be defined as a deviant act may be interpreted otherwise.

But under certain conditions others are less likely to assent to a "nothing unusual" stance. If a man comes home and discovers his wife in bed with another man, he is not inclined to accept their nonchalant invitation to join them in the living room for coffee. The following factors press for noncompliance: (1) the more persons are overwhelmed with emotion and cannot maintain the casual demeanor required; (2) the more complex the performance expected if they cooperate with the "nothing unusual" stance (civil inattention is more feasible than active participation); (3) the more certain they are of the definition of the situation that "something unusual is happening"; (4) the more committed they are to upholding rules which they think are being violated; (5) the more experienced they are

---

16 Cited in Eugene Webb, Donald Campbell, Richard Schwartz, and Lee Sechrest, *Unobtrusive Measures: Nonreactive Research in the Social Sciences* (Chicago: Rand McNally and Company, 1966), p. 156.

at imposing the definition "something unusual is happening" in similar situations; (6) the less favorably disposed they are to the "nothing unusual" advocate; (7) the higher their status is compared with the "nothing unusual" advocate, the less they are accustomed to following his lead, and the less respect they have for his judgment; and (8) the less drastic the action required by the "something unusual" stance.

The Deviant as a Monster

In the preceding section some factors inhibiting movement of the interaction in the direction of a "something unusual" stance and labeling were described. Labeling results from the application of a set of procedures for assessing situations and deciding how to proceed. From a closer examination of this set of procedures, an additional explanation for the structural inhibition against labeling emerges. The explanation is based on the inadequacy of certain commonsense conceptualizations to handle actual experience with potentially deviant behavior.

The set of procedures for assessing situations includes steps for recognizing divergent behavior. As a practical necessity any workable set of instructions singles out a few relevant features of a situation and ignores the rest. Forgetting that this selection has occurred, persons then come to think of the entire event as composed of the few features in focus. So the commonsense model has black and white categories for deviance. Both events and persons are viewed as either entirely deviant or entirely conforming.

A problematic act which persons might negotiate to define as deviant occurs in the context of numerous acts taken for granted as conforming.[17] In a bar pickup, for instance, the only questionable element may be the mode of introduction, while conduct within the exchange may be seen as entirely conforming to proper behavior for striking up an acquaintance with a stranger at a party. When one thinks about the situation in a commonsense perspective, one focuses on the offense and virtually ignores the norm-conforming context.

Because in the light of the commonsense perspective a person has been led to expect an offense to stand out markedly and overshadow any norm-conforming elements present, he is surprised at how comparatively dwarfed the possible violation is. Those pressing for a "nothing unusual" definition take advantage of this initial surprise and the moment of uncer-

---

[17] In discussing factors which impede the labeling process, Yarrow, *et al.*, make a similar point by calling the behavior of the candidate for the mental illness label a "fluctuating stimulus," at times symptomatic and at times ordinary. Marian Yarrow, Charlotte Schwartz, Harriet Murphy, and Leila Deasy, "The Psychological Meaning of Mental Illness in the Family," in Rubington and Weinberg, *op. cit.,* p. 38.

tainty it entails. Inasmuch as a person revises his expectation to take into account the norm-conforming context, he still might expect all facets of the exchange to be modified to correspond with the norm-violating note. Thus, in a bar pickup he might expect an exaggerated behavior between the couple, in which allusions to sex are blatant, the exchange has a wild, uncontrolled quality, and gestures of respect for the other person are suspended. When these expectations are contradicted by actual experience in a bar, a person's assessment procedures are thrown into confusion. Using ordinary procedures for assessing whether behavior is divergent, he is led to the conclusion the behavior is not divergent because it is obscured by norm-conforming elements.[18]

The commonsense perspective leads a person to expect that a deviant, at least in the setting where he engages in norm-violations, behaves in a way an ordinary person would not behave. Thus, victims do not suspect con men. "A deviant could not possibly be a person like you and me" is an underlying assumption. On the contrary, the deviant is a monster with whom we have nothing in common and who is so grotesque as to be incomprehensible to us.[19]

Suppose an actor has earned a reputation as an acceptable human being before he commits a labeling-prone act. Even without such a reputation, suppose he presents his act in a conforming context with "nothing unusual" cues. Such an event is experienced as not fitting the deviant-as-monster assumption. To reconcile the discrepancy, people can hold one of the following:

(1) the actor is a monster;

(2) the "deviant is a monster" assumption is not correct;

(3) the actor is not deviant; or

(4) the actor is deviant, but the case is an exception to the "deviant is a monster" assumption.

Alternatives 3 and 4 cause the least social disruption and therefore have the lowest cost. Thus, the person responding is inclined to choose 3 or 4. If he decides the actor is not deviant, then the actor escapes labeling entirely. If he decides the actor is deviant but not a monster, then the actor's total identity is not discredited.

---

[18] Jackson makes this point about labeling the alcoholic over a period of time: "The inaccuracies of the cultural stereotype of the alcoholic—particularly that he is in a constant state of inebriation—also contribute to the family's rejection of the idea of alcoholism, as the husband seems to demonstrate from time to time that he can control his drinking." Joan Jackson, "The Adjustment of the Family to the Crisis of Alcoholism," in Rubington and Weinberg, *op. cit.*, p. 56.

[19] Garfinkel suggests this view is a necessary condition for a successful degradation ceremony: "Finally, the denounced person must be ritually separated from a place in the legitimate order, i.e., he must be defined as standing at a place opposed to it. He must be placed 'outside,' he must be made 'strange.'" Garfinkel, *op. cit.*, p. 423.

To summarize, definitions of reality, such as "nothing unusual is happening" and "something unusual is happening," are negotiated. Ambiguity allows more scope for negotiations. Ambiguity is produced by over-simplified conceptual schemes contradicted by experience. The more difficult it is to use the prevailing conceptual scheme to make sense of experience, the more the social situation will be thrown into confusion and left to *ad hoc* negotiations. Negotiations provide the opportunity for persons to elude labeling when otherwise these persons might be sanctioned.

Black and white categories about deviance may at times serve to discourage behavior which risks labeling by exaggerating the horrors of crossing the line from good to bad. But when the categories are undermined, risky behavior may flourish. And the more simple any system of categories, the more likely it is to be undermined by the complexity of events.

16

Tamotsu Shibutani

ON THE PERSONIFICATION
OF ADVERSARIES

Atrocity stories abound in all intense conflicts, for combatants carry on their struggle with ruthless ferocity. Although some of the brutality can be attributed to sadists who welcome opportunities for self-expression, most vicious deeds are committed by men who, in any other social context, would regard such conduct as totally unacceptable. When the heat of conflict has passed, such acts are often condemned as depraved and inhuman. Some of the perpetrators develop a deep sense of guilt, and a few even devote the remainder of their lives to atoning for their sins. In the fervor of battle men perceive, think, and act in ways radically different from their peacetime orientations; some seem like entirely different persons. This poses a perennial question: what is it about intergroup conflict that transforms otherwise reasonable men into brutes?

One common hypothesis is that men are by nature aggressive. When customary restraints are withdrawn, they become beasts. A similar explanation is given for the ferocity of some mobs, but an alternative hypothesis is suggested in Gustave LeBon's classic study: participants in crowds are subject to a different form of social control. They are not free to speak or act as they please. Remarks that are inconsistent with the prevailing mood pass unheard or are rejected. Those who oppose a mob may themselves be attacked. Much of what happens in intergroup conflict may also be explained in similar terms: the development of another form of social control.

If what men do depends upon the manner in which they define the situations in which they are involved, one key to an understanding of such conduct is the typical manner in which conflict situations are characterized. Since World War II a number of observers have noted the tendency of enemies to form "distorted" conceptions of each other.[1] An attempt will be made in this paper to order these observations in terms of a limited set of generalizations.

The Formation of Contrast Conceptions

Men fight when values are in short supply, but viciousness does not arise from the opposition of interests as such. The central problem becomes that of ascertaining the characteristic manner in which combatants define themselves and their adversaries. Social interaction, as Harry Stack Sullivan contends, is not so much an interchange of persons as one of personifications.

There is increasing agreement among social psychologists that what men perceive is not a simple mirror image of their actual environment; perceptual objects are constructed by the perceiver in a selective process. Men become selectively sensitized to those features of their environment that are pertinent to their inclinations to act. They respond discriminatingly to cues that enable them to complete already initiated action. Just as a sexually aroused man is highly responsive to possibilities for erotic exploitation, angry men notice opportunities for attacking or justifications for their hostility. This suggests that a given situation may be defined in starkly contrasting ways by men with different orientations.

One key basis for selection is one's emotional disposition. Few objects are emotionally neutral; most of them—including categories of human beings —are evaluated in some manner. Objects that have been the source of

---

[1] Cf. David J. Finlay, Ole R. Holsti, and Richard R. Fagan, *Enemies in Politics* (Chicago: Rand McNally & Company, 1967); Herbert C. Kelman, ed., *International Behavior* (New York: Holt, Rinehart & Winston, Inc., 1965), Part I; and Ralph K. White, "Misperception and the Vietnam War," *Journal of Social Issues,* XXII (July, 1966), 1–164.

gratification are prized and coveted; objects that have been the source of
frustration are hated and attacked when possible; objects that have been
the source of pain are avoided; objects that are readily controlled are
regarded as unimportant and sometimes viewed with contempt. Because most
preferences are learned by members of an organized society, each person has
value orientations toward many objects he has never encountered directly.
He learns of them through communication. Although individual experiences
sometimes alter these appraisals, on the whole widely accepted values are
constantly reaffirmed by the consistent responses of other people. Certain
ways of assessing people are recurrent; they are found over and over in a
variety of historical contexts. It has been suggested that the manner in which
categories of human beings are appraised depends upon the relative positions
of groups to each other.[2] The estimates formed by members of groups in
conflict are consistent.

   Perception is not only selective but also seriated. It is a process in
which sensitivities depend upon hypotheses that are being constructed and
tested.[3] If an object is evaluated as frustrating or dangerous, one expects to
be attacked or inconvenienced, assumes a defensive stance, and becomes
selectively responsive to indices of further danger. Thus, the identification
of a category of people as a dangerous opponent provides a frame of reference
for subsequent perception. Consistent cues, even if they deviate slightly
from expectations, are assimilated into the developing interpretation. Cues
that are inconsistent are often unnoticed or misinterpreted in a way that
confirms expectations. When involved in conflict, one's natural inclination
is to attack, defend, or escape, and one is responsive to those features of the
environment that tend to support or justify these stances. All sensory cues
are interpreted in this manner, and the object that is constructed of the
adversary becomes chararterized by many negative attributes.

   In the construction of objects of human beings, far greater opportunities arise for the formation of diverse conceptions of the same person. The
activities of any individual are far too complex and too numerous to be
observed in their entirety. We tend to notice only those items that confirm
our expectations. Consistency with our beliefs is maintained by obliterating
distinctions and organizing cues in terms of an artificially simplified framework. Furthermore, since overt deeds are only the final phases of activities
that begin within the actor, most acts can be explained in several different
ways. The significance of a deed often depends upon the intentions of the
actor. Because inner experiences cannot be observed directly, motives must

---

   [2] Cf. Herbert Blumer, "Race Prejudice as a Sense of Group Position," *Pacific
Sociological Review,* I (1958). 3–7.
   [3] Cf. George H. Mead, *The Philosophy of the Act,* ed. C. W. Morris, *et al.*
(Chicago: University of Chicago Press, 1938), pp. 103–53.

be imputed to make observed events meaningful. The manner in which an act is interpreted is limited by the kinds of motives that are plausible to the observer. From a psychological standpoint, the explanation of human behavior by the avowal and imputation of motives is a gross oversimplification, but this is the manner in which acts are explained in the common sense universe of discourse. It is for this reason that the same individual can be seen in an entirely different light by different observers. A case to the point is infatuation; a lover is unable to see many traits in his beloved that are quite obvious to his friends, and especially to his mother.

In conflicts of all kinds, combatants form contrast conceptions of each other. The concept of *die Gegenidee* was developed by Erich Voegelin in his analysis of anti-Semitism in Germany. During the depression years following World War I, many insecure Germans constructed a negative object of Jews by attributing to them those traits that they feared and condemned in themselves. It was only by projecting these qualities to someone else that Germans could draw up a positive characterization of themselves.[4] Whether or not his account of this particular historical situation is correct, Voegelin has provided a powerful tool for the analysis of conflict situations in general. Both self-conceptions and conceptions of the enemy are objects, and both are constructed through selective perception. We tend to impute to our enemies the most foul motives, often those that we have trouble avowing ourselves: the enemy is inherently perfidious, insolent, sordid, cruel, degenerate, lacking in compassion, and enjoys aggression for its own sake. Everything he does tends to be interpreted in the most unfavorable light. If one's comrades retreat in the face of formidable opposition, they are making a strategic withdrawal; if the enemy does the same thing, he is a coward. If one's comrades fight on under such circumstances, they are credited with great courage; should the enemy do the same thing, he is dismissed as a fanatic.

Since most men involved in conflict believe in their cause, they tend to form conceptions of themselves in terms of the positive values of their culture. We seldom engage in wars because of greed. We fight for freedom and justice or in defense against unwarranted aggression. We are strong, courageous, truthful, compassionate, peace-loving, and self-sacrificing. We respect the independence of others and are loyal to our allies. Thus, men in conflict tend to form idealized self-conceptions. Should we learn that our opponents make similar claims for themselves, this strikes us as ludicrous.

If conflict is prolonged, the contrast tends to become greater and greater. More and more frustration and pain can be blamed on the adversary.

---

[4] Erich Voegelin, *Rasse und Staat* (Tuebingen: J. C. B. Mohr, 1933), pp. 181–208. Cf. Gustav Ichheiser's discussion of the "mote-beam mechanism" in "Misunderstandings in Human Relations," *American Journal of Sociology*, LV (September, 1949), Part II, pp. 51–53.

In brooding, rage is intensified. Everything the enemy does is irritating. Combatants are quick to blame and to impute foul motives, for defeats are easier to accept if attributed to the foe's unfair tactics. In time, as social distance is maximized, it becomes difficult to concede that the enemy is human. We become convinced that he lacks sentiments such as love, loyalty, a sense of fair play, or affection for children. He is a wild beast who abandons his comrades to die, attacks helpless women and children, and thinks nothing of sacrificing his own family to his fanatic dedication. He is devoid of sympathy and understanding. In Martin Buber's terms, the enemy becomes an "it" rather than a "you." Appreciating the situation from the adversary's standpoint becomes progressively more difficult. In intense conflict the foe may become a reincarnation of the devil himself—a combination of the most frightful traits imaginable.

Ordinarily characterizations of objects are tested in their use. Objects are approached and manipulated in terms of expectations. If one's hypotheses are reasonably accurate, activity is carried out successfully. If not, the situation becomes problematic, and a redefinition becomes necessary. Since firmly held beliefs tend to resist revision, many tests are inadequate; yet most objects are subject to continuous reality testing. In conflict situations, however, one encounters adversaries in contexts in which the usual testing procedures are ineffective.

In a complicated world, clarity and understanding come through simplification and emphasis, and many objects take on a stereotyped form. All prolonged conflicts tend to be transformed into a struggle between good and evil. There is a moral bifurcation of objects. The world is divided into the pure and impure, normal and pathological, decent and perverted, democratic and despotic. Because the enemy is personified as unrelieved evil, participants in the struggle see themselves as being involved in a moral crusade. This may explain why combatants so often assume a self-righteous stance, resent questions about their motives, and condemn neutralism or moderation as immoral.

Social Control in Conflict Groups

Once intergroup conflict gets under way, each side closes ranks; differences within are forgotten temporarily in uniting against a common foe. Most information from enemy sources is cut off, and such insulation plays an important part in the crystallization of contrast conceptions. Every effort is made to guard against defection. Any information favorable to the foe is suspected of being from enemy sources and is labeled as propaganda. Persons bearing such news are suspected of disloyalty. Furthermore, inconvenient reports of one's own shortcomings—adverse conditions on the front, weak leadership, corruption—are also labeled as enemy propaganda. Once the political arena has become bipolarized, all information inconsistent with contrast conceptions tends to be discredited.

As in-group solidarity develops, pressures arise toward conformity, and dissidence is no longer tolerated. Once contrast conceptions are formed, anyone who does not share them seems to be out of step. Communicative activity, like all other forms of human behavior, is subject to social control. Those who hate can express themselves freely; others must remain silent. Group sanctions are such that persons who might question the worthiness of the venture are neutralized by scorn or reprisal. Dispassionate observers, who are inclined to raise questions about the accuracy of contrast conceptions, may be accused of treason. Thus, moderate and reasonable men are virtually immobilized, and the public gets a constant repetition of a single point of view.

The stereotyped concept of the enemy is an abstract object that is constructed in social interaction. Hostile impulses that are aroused against a threatening object tend to persist until modified by further experience. Because of selective inattention and limited communication, however, opportunities for correcting false and misleading impressions are minimized. This is often costly. In belittling and underestimating the intentions and integrity of the foe, each side makes gross errors of judgment, taking unnecessary risks and making unnecessary sacrifices. Even disastrous failures often do not result in revisions. As in paranoid disorders, the possibility of rectifying mistaken beliefs is virtually eliminated.

Once contrast conceptions are established, they form the basis for new modes of group action. Mobilization for group conflict is greatly facilitated. Conflicts involve sacrifices for everyone, and especially in protracted struggles morale may become a problem. Unless men are convinced that the sacrifices are worthwhile, the fight cannot be carried on effectively. But men fight willingly against evil, especially if they are persuaded that divine justice is on their side.

Furthermore, a double standard of morality arises, making possible brutality that would never be tolerated within either community. As William G. Sumner points out, once the difference between in-group and out-group becomes accentuated, ethnocentrism becomes exaggerated and an ethical dualism develops. Since the enemy is not regarded as human, the claims and obligations that hold within one's own group do not apply to him. The enemy is outside the moral order. Moral standards are suspended, and deeds that are condemned within the community are glorified on the battlefield. Men are rewarded for treachery, bribery, and murder. Those who take unfair advantage of a situation are praised as expedient and imaginative.[5] The most

---

[5] William G. Sumner, *War and Other Essays* (New Haven: Yale University Press, 1911), pp. 10–13.

brutal carnage becomes possible because of the maximization of social distance.

Since men on both sides form contrast conceptions of one another, atrocities are committed by both sides. Those identifying with the victims are outraged. Tales of the mutilation of prisoners and the violation of women reinforce the belief that the enemy is a fiendish perpetrator of dark deeds and a violator of all rules of decency. Each act of brutality elicits retaliation, which in turn invites further retaliation, until each side becomes convinced that it has no alternative to fighting on at all cost to victory. Those who had entertained doubts about the rectitude of their cause cease to waver. Group goals are reinforced; hatred is justified; and feelings of guilt connected with violence are overcome. Mutual confirmation of one another's beliefs thus reaffirms the conceptions held by each side. Thus, contrast conceptions tend to be self-fulfilling prophecies, and all sustained conflicts tend to become escalated in intensity.

As the struggle is thus intensified, neutrality becomes impossible. Anyone who is unwilling to take an unequivocal stand on the side of righteousness becomes suspect. Those seemingly lacking in enthusiasm are scorned as slackers. In both camps moderate leaders tend to be replaced by extremists. Haters and sadists, who under other circumstances would be dismissed as eccentric, tend to win large followings. In the competition for political power in such settings extremists have a definite advantage over those of more moderate leanings. They can cite their long record of unconditional opposition to the enemy and their current dedication to his total destruction. They can assume a sanctimonious bearing, attacking those who are less militant as being soft on a vicious foe. Some moderate leaders retire in disgust and may subsequently be incarcerated; others, desiring to hold on to positions of influence, are forced to take a more radical posture.

Under these circumstances peace negotiations become extremely difficult, for the minimum confidence necessary is lacking. Combatants assume a stance that neutral observers find to be unrealistic, even foolish. Attempts at mediation by third parties frequently elicit the suspicion that anyone trying to stop the fighting actually favors the other side. Should communication channels be opened, what follows is often a case of *le dialogue des sourds*— two parties talking with neither hearing what the other is trying to say. Neither party is willing to yield, each insisting that any moderation or compromise could only lead to disastrous consequences. If a concession is proposed, it is under conditions that the adversary cannot possibly accept. Anyone within either community who suggests the possibility of an overture to the enemy is accused of appeasement, and any overture from the enemy is likely to be dismissed as a ruse. Even if some agreement that is mutually advantageous is developed, it is difficult to implement, for each is convinced that the foe cannot be trusted. Even when their cause appears hopeless, many insist on fighting to the end. Slogans such as "Better dead than Red" are not new; many prefer death to surrender.

If a bitter conflict is prolonged, the major objective is transformed. What had started as the quest for a limited aim becomes a crusade for the total obliteration of the adversary.

The Breakdown of Contrast Conceptions

If the manner in which men characterize one another depends upon the relationship between the groups with which they identify, a change in the relative positions of the groups should result in some modification of personifications. With the termination of hostilities—by conquest or through negotiation—some contrast conceptions break down. Once the fighting is definitely over, the former enemy is no longer evaluated as dangerous, especially by the victor. Contacts are gradually reestablished, and those involved in them discover that their erstwhile foes are quite different from what they had believed. In some cases, as in the period after World War II, former adversaries redefine one another with astonishing rapidity, leaving only a small core of extremists on both sides with enduring hatred.

But all perspectives tend to interfere with their own revision, and in some cases contrast conceptions do not change. Even after the fighting is over, some features of the stereotype persist. Barriers to communication sometimes become institutionalized. Even when opportunities are presented, many on both sides tend to avoid contacts with their traditional enemies. Animosities born in bitter struggles sometimes die slowly, in some instances not until the demise of the generation that participated in the fighting. Some stereotypes survive for centuries, even when overt conflict is not renewed.

Stereotyped conceptions can be broken down only with a reduction of social distance. With effective role-taking the deeds of another begin to appear reasonable, and autistic hostility may be diminished. Sometimes persons in marginal positions, such as interpreters working with prisoners of war, manage to establish initimate contacts and come to a realization that contrast conceptions are only caricatures. However, the few individuals who do see adversaries as human beings encounter difficulties in persuading their comrades.

Sometimes, after a period of continued adversity and a succession of defeats, physical exhaustion results in disenchantment and a willingness to reexamine one's own beliefs. Objects are reconstituted by failure in reality testing. New hypotheses are entertained. Men who tend to see the other side get more of a hearing, and increasing sensitivity develops for the suffering and courage of the enemy. Especially if they become disillusioned with their leaders, men begin to have doubts about their idealized self-conception and about the rectitude of their cause.

Continued defeat tends to increase friction within a combat group, and factionalism damages morale. Studies of mutinies reveal how preexisting cleavages of a community—class, ethnic, or religious—may lead to severe schisms in sustained adversity. Enlisted men disgruntled over officer privileges may identify more closely with enemy enlisted men than with their own officers. Factionalism among combatants sometimes leads to greater sympathy for a respected foe. Then, new contrast conceptions emerge; members of the other faction come to be regarded as a greater threat than the enemy.

Contrast conceptions may also be transformed if opponents are confronted with the necessity of cooperating in the pursuit of some common goal, one that cannot be achieved by either group alone. In the Robbers Cave experiment, for example, Muzafer Sherif and his associates presented competing groups of boys who had come to dislike each other with a compelling superordinate goal and found that they worked together. Although the cooperation was at first reluctant, the joint effort led to a reduction of tension and eventually to a redefinition of out-groups.[6] If faced with a common danger—being attacked by a third party or being engulfed in a catastrophe—opponents often recognize their interdependence and unite. Strikes and lockouts are sometimes terminated as the foes increasingly realize how much they need one another. Mutual trust is most likely to develop in situations in which each has a stake in the other's doing well, and effective performance in such contexts leads to reciprocal appreciation.

All this points to the importance of esteemed third parties in the termination of bitter conflicts. Just as clergymen and marriage counselors can sometimes get estranged couples to resume deliberations, federal mediators are able to resolve many labor disputes. A neutral party that is respected by both sides can open communication channels, initiate negotiations, and sometimes even induce some restraint in the exchanges that follow. But mediation is a thankless and difficult task, for mediators are attacked by extremists in both camps. The discussions that take place are often truncated, for each soon becomes convinced that the enemy is rigid and unreasonable, insisting upon points that do not make sense. As a strategem for breaking down misleading beliefs Anatol Rapoport recommends setting up a dialogue in which each side is required to state the position of the other to the opponent's complete satisfaction before either is permitted to advocate his own views.[7] This has been attempted by some mediators, leading sometimes to a breakdown of the contrast conceptions held by the negotiators, who then faced the problem of persuading those whom they represented.

---

[6] Muzafer Sherif, *et. al., Intergroup Conflict and Cooperation: The Robbers Cave Experiment* (Norman: University of Oklahoma Book Exchange, 1961), pp. 159–96.

[7] Anatol Rapoport, "Rules for Debate," in *Preventing World War III: Some Proposals,* eds. Quincy Wright, *et al.* (New York: Simon & Schuster, Inc., 1962), pp. 246–62.

Labor mediators have sometimes found it necessary to keep adversaries physically segregated, avoiding direct confrontation until after considerable groundwork had been laid. Despite all such difficulties, third parties can sometimes open doors that would otherwise remain locked. Once contrast conceptions are attenuated, some kind of negotiation becomes possible, even when conflicting interests persist.

Conclusion

What men do in the heat of battle is a manifestation of natural processes; their perception, thought, and deeds are subject to the distinctive type of social control that emerges in conflict situations. Both courage and bestiality rest on the combatants' belief that they are involved in a struggle against evil. Because men are capable of symbolic behavior, they are able to construct ogres in their imagination. Much of human conflict consists of gallant crusades to bring these monsters under control. One important implication is that aggressive action is generally directed against a scapegoat; this suggests why victims are usually dumbfounded at the justifications of those who attack them.

Contrast conceptions are found in all kinds of conflict situations— in disputes between management and labor, in revolutions, in the continuous warfare between lawbreakers and the police, in confrontations between hippies and the Establishment, and even in intense football rivalries. Adversaries are always endowed with remarkably similar attributes. Several observers have noted that in the current cold war Russians and Americans characterize one another in identical terms: *They* are the aggressors, *their* government exploits and deludes the people, *their* policy verges on madness.[8] The growing Negro hatred of the white man is also of this character. After the fighting is over, those who happen to come into contact with their erstwhile foes are invariably surprised to discover that they are human beings after all.

Because men have fought so often only to discover afterward that their adversaries were actually not what they had thought, the question arises as to why we have not learned to act more intelligently. Bertrand Russell once noted that the one lesson we learn from history is that men do not learn from history. While this may be an overstatement, it certainly holds true for intergroup conflicts. Most men realize that wars are costly. Yet, once the cumulative process gets under way, they are swept along. Even sociologists who are familiar with the theory of contrast conceptions have difficulty in

---

8 Urie Bronfenbrenner, "The Mirror Image in Soviet-American Relations," *Journal of Social Issues,* 17 (1961), #3, pp. 45–56.

exercising self-restraint when they themselves become involved in bitter campus issues. Although conflicting interests are endemic to social life, perhaps a wider appreciation of how contrast conceptions are formed will help attenuate somewhat the virulence of the hatred engendered and lead eventually to the adoption of less brutal ways of settling differences.

17

Arlene Kaplan Daniels

DEVELOPMENT OF THE SCAPEGOAT IN SENSITIVITY TRAINING SESSIONS

This paper analyzes the process of invidious social typing in a sensitivity training group conducted within a military psychiatric residency. The predominant social type that emerged in this group was the scapegoat. In the course of the group sensitivity training, or T-Group sessions, an informal structure developed which seemed to encourage the expression of hostility. The hostility was usually directed against one participant at a time. The man most frequently reported as the recipient of hostility was also one of the best students in the program, highly regarded by the professional staff. The implications of this choice appear to be that the peer group resented an outstanding member and scapegoated him; a major value shared in the group was not to rock the boat by standing out above the average. It is argued that the process of scapegoating contributed to the stability of the group and to the reaffirmation of more general values of the institution that sponsored it.

The data for the study presented were collected in interviews with the seventeen psychiatric residents and their eight supervisors at a large military hospital. (To protect the confidence of information, the hospital is anonymous and any names used are pseudonyms.) In the interviews residents were asked to discuss their educational program in detail. An attempt to discover the importance of peer interaction in the adult socialization process elicited the information that only one area of the training program provided any continuous basis for such interaction: the weekly training session for group therapy. This adjunct to the program was provided as an opportunity to learn about groups through participation.

The following history of the group was obtained from interviews with supervisors. The group had become an institutionalized part of the residency program about eight years prior to this study. It was designed to offer a nondirective experience to the residents, who met one hour per week. They could use this hour for any purpose they wished; they could ventilate grievances, practice group therapy techniques, or study communication processes. An outside (civilian) consultant was charged with maintaining group privacy and keeping its activity separate from the other faculty-directed programs.

Since other programmed duties preempted time of the residents during the latter part of their training, the group session generally included all the first year students, a smaller number of second year students, one from the third year, and none from the post third year group. At the time of this study, the number of residents continuously participating, according to informants' estimates, was about one-half of the seventeen residents in training; and of these, perhaps two-thirds to three-fourths were in actual attendance at any one meeting. A regular session, then, was attended by five or six persons.

There was very little agreement among participants about the actual purpose of this group. Some saw this group as private and personal, i.e., as "our group" and "the staff have nothing to do with it." These residents felt that the secrecy of the group was important to its integrity. They refused to speak about the group in their interview and warned that no residents would speak of these matters. Their prediction was not borne out. Eleven of the seventeen residents discussed the group quite freely. Some of these had never accepted what they saw as "the myth" of secrecy. They also did not believe that the group was really independent and thought control of the group rested with the consultant. One resident was sure the consultant talked over the activities of the group with the chief of the department. As evidence, he mentioned having observed that the consultant went into the chief's office after each weekly session and remained there for twenty minutes with the door closed.

Perhaps because of this lack of agreement about just what the group was and the conflicts this may have produced, discussion of the group meetings provided the greatest difficulties in interviewing. Sometimes the interviewer was quite abruptly cut off. Sometimes long, impassioned outbursts about this area of interaction were introduced in the interview. At first this difficulty seemed strange because, according to many, the situation was quite unstructured. Attendance was voluntary; no topic or goal was assigned for the group; the leader-trainer took the stance of a nondirective consultant. What soon became apparent was that this difficulty was probably related to the highly charged nature of the interaction of the group.

The Significance of Social Typing

As the sessions were not open to observation by the interviewer, all knowledge of the group activity comes from report. The reports were dominated by discussions of interactions with and attitudes toward one participant, a first year resident we shall call Sutter. From these reports it become clear that Sutter was treated as the scapegoat.

The scapegoat, following the usage in *The Golden Bough,* embodies within him the evil influences or ill luck of the group.[1] In this view, it is the function of the scapegoat to be sacrified in order to draw off misfortune from the community when the hardships of life—aleatory aspects suffered in any society—are confusing or intangible in their origins. The scapegoat, a visible and tangible symbol, becomes a repository and vehicle to carry these evils away. In addition, the scapegoat may embody the guilt and envy the group members feel about ideals they have not met, tasks they have not accomplished. The scapegoat who is chosen, then, may be the one who embodies the characteristics group members really wished they possessed.

The sociological value of analyzing the process of scapegoating is suggested in the theoretical formulations of Orrin Klapp, who has made extensive study of the implications of social typing. He has suggested that social types are useful indicators of normative values held within groups.

> ...*the social type is plainly a group product and group property....I think of it as a collective norm of role behavior formed and used by the group; an idealized concept of how people are expected to be or to act. Such typing may also be considered a method of social control.*[2]

> ...*a person finds a more or less deliberate effort by society to mold him in accordance with certain types that may not be the same as he has*

---

[1] J. G. Frazier, *The Golden Bough,* abridged ed. (London: Macmillan & Company, Ltd.. 1957), Vol. II.

[2] Orrin Klapp, *Heroes, Villains and Fools* (Englewood Cliffs, N. J.: Prentice Hall, Inc., 1962), p. 11.

chosen. This includes not only simple pressure but status modification.
It is plain that calling a person a "party pooper" tells him, "Don't leave
early," and subjects him to pressure not to leave and derision if he does;
"eager-beaver" says "Don't work so hard," or "What are you trying to
do, make things hard for the rest of us?"[3]

Though it is recognized that social typing fulfills the function of
social control, the particular social types chosen and the processes by which
some agreements about them are reached by all group participants remain
to be specified. When does a group exercise control by use of the villain rather
than hero type? How do those selected respond to being typed? The effort
to avoid negative typing or to type oneself, of course, also includes the effort
to type others. We are, as Klapp suggests, continually creating the other
fellow's type in our responses to his response to us. In this case it will be
shown that a variety of normative and structural group characteristics apparent in psychiatric residency training make these programs peculiarly susceptible to the development of the scapegoat. The very nature of the group
training sessions encouraged the expression of hostility and the formation of
this type.

T-Group Structure and the Expression of Hostility

The problem of organization within a free or unorganized group is
one that commonly arises in such groups as this residents' group—modeled
on group therapy, T-Groups, or sensitivity training. Participants complain
that the group has no direction, or that the direction is insidious. Many
examples of this complaint are available in descriptions of such groups.[4]
Sometimes participants quarrel among themselves because some member is
too passive—or else he is too directive. Such common complaints about
direction and leadership may be exacerbated in a group based on T-Group
or sensitivity training principles. The lack of stated instrumental purpose is
clearly acceptable in primary association; in fact it may be considered the
definition of this type of association. But there is social anxiety when the
instrumental nature of a secondary association cannot be clarified. T-Groups
attempt to mix the qualities of primary and secondary associations in one
group; the rationale used is that the primary association will provide data
for dispassionate analysis. The group provides secondary association in the
assembly of its members for the purpose of learning about group processes.
The social anxiety which occurs arises from the ambiguity based upon the
simultaneous presence of contradictory role relationships. Participants are

---

3 *Ibid.,* pp. 22–23.
4 Cf. P. E. Slater, *Microcosm: Psychological and Religious Evolution in*
Groups (New York: John Wiley & Sons, Inc., 1966).

vulnerable to instrumental criticism for primary behavior. Anxieties from such ambiguity are found in many ordinary life situations where primary associations arise in instrumental contexts—as between boss and employee— and participants are never sure which set of norms governing association are currently in operation.

These anxieties can be exacerbated where the group training session is part of a larger work setting. Although groups are purportedly free and unstructured, an underlying status system exists, and the members carry certain status attributes derived from their work position with them into the meetings. In this case the hierarchy of residents was maintained in terms of seniority. It was assumed that more experienced residents had more knowledge and could speak with more authority. Therefore, precedence or respect for colleagues tended to follow the usual understandings about deference within psychiatric and general medical settings—ordinarily accorded in terms of number of years of professional experience.[5] In this implicit value system, a likely candidate for pejorative typication was the first year resident who "spoke out of turn." But since the idea of stratification or any structure in the group was explicitly disavowed, the sanctions for ignoring implicit understandings had to be expressed indirectly.

In a situation where conflicting norms are present, development of the necessary rationale for sanctioning was found in the vocabulary and philosophy underlying T-Groups. These groups have been greatly influenced by their perception of psychoanalytic perspectives and strategies.[6] What can be seen from a study of the residents' own group is that an unforeseen by-product of this psychoanalytically oriented activity is the opportunity it offers for perfecting the technique of scapegoating through a general encouragement to express hostility.

An encouragement of aggressive behavior develops from the underlying expectations and values in T-Groups and other groups generally modeled on their pattern. In fact, the members are expected to attack and to come into conflict. "The clash which leads to change in the learner may be seen as a clash between contradictory demands of the standards of the laboratory training group and the demands of other memberships."[7]

There appear to be several reasons for this interest in the intrinsic potentiality for conflict. First, there is a presumption that everyone brings

---

[5] Cf. R. Coser, "Laughter Among Colleagues." *Psychiatry,* XXIII (1960), 81–95; and W. Caudill, *The Psychiatric Hospital as a Small Society* (Cambridge, Mass.: Harvard University Press, 1958).

[6] Cf. K. D. Benne, "History of the T-Group in the Laboratory Setting," in *T-Group Theory and Laboratory Method,* eds. L. P. Bradford, *et al.* (New York: John Wiley & Sons, Inc., 1964), pp. 80–135.

[7] K. D. Benne, *et al.* "The Laboratory Method" in Bradford, *et al., op. cit.,* p. 29.

general incapacities or personal weaknesses into the group and needs therapy. Therefore, according to the theory underlying T-Groups, conflict will be inevitably generated as self-styled "normal" individuals resist this new definition of themselves. Also it is believed that in this context "inner conflicts" will be revealed and that these conflicts, presumably, will add to individual resistances. More trouble or conflict is generated as participants are made to believe that they cannot escape examination and that their deficiencies will be revealed. Consequently, trainers or leaders in these groups try "to keep conflict alive" and to "discourage a premature or false harmony." The theoretical formulation upon which the focus on conflict rests is borrowed from psychoanalysis. In perspectives derived from Jungian or Adlerian approaches, for example, conflict is itself a useful tool for the removal of personal incapacities.

In conjunction with this perspective, T-Group theory derives some fundamental ideas from Freudian psychoanalytic theory. Examination of T-Group theory indicates a fundamental interest in sexuality and aggression and an assumption that these are the basic human impulses.[8] Therefore, one should find expressions of sexuality and aggression whenever formal, regulatory social institutions are in abeyance, as in the experimental group training session. However, these groups are in fact not really without institutional regulations. The structure of these ostensibly unstructured groups does not generally permit overt sexual expressions. "The topic of sexuality itself seems to find fairly strong taboos in training groups. . . . Sexuality is used often in pursuit of other power operations and is usually of a verbal-seductive type."[9] For example, in the group of all male military officers discussed in the following pages, no expression of homosexuality, no matter how symbolic, was acceptable; to use psychiatric vocabulary, the participants would find such expression "too threatening." On the other hand, aggressive behavior is widely accepted in a variety of public forms. Any tendencies toward aggression which may already be present in a group— for whatever reasons—are readily understood and condoned within this theoretical framework. And as the discussion of sex is curtailed, hostility becomes the sole focus of actual interaction.

As a consequence, hostile patterns of expression come to be encouraged; the T-Group training urges this expression as evidence of "real" or underlying expressions of feelings as opposed to more superficial or evasive ones. A constant theme in the literature on T-Groups is that the real person

---

[8] R. D. Mann, *Interpersonal Styles and Group Development* (New York: John Wiley & Sons, Inc., 1967).

[9] R. M. Whitman, "Psychodynamic Principles Underlying T-Group Processes," in L. P. Bradford, *et al., op. cit.*, p. 318. Cf. R. Adler, "The Thursday Group," *The New Yorker*, XLII (April 15, 1967).

and the real (hostile) feelings lie submerged and thus must be encouraged in free groups.

Recognizing that one is expressing hostility or can express it is considered a major step along the path of self-awareness, and "increased awareness of and sensitivity to emotional reactions and expression in himself and others" is a major goal for individuals in group training.

Another goal is the ability to learn through attention to one's own and others' feelings, as distinguished from what is actually said in words. The analysand is supposed to push beyond intellectualization to his deeper, more "real" feelings in order to develop self-awareness. An even more explicit expression of the psychoanalytic trend in group training appears in the statement that group training deals with personal feelings of resistance, anxiety, threat, weakness, strength, euphoria, satisfaction, and "ability to handle authority relations."[10] Therefore, ideas of progress within the experimental group are often laden with the notion of therapeutic progress for the individual participants in the groups. Group therapy for participants then readily mixes into the experimental and laboratory approach. And so it is difficult for participants to evade attack (or help) for their personal and psychological deficiencies.

Such theoretical perspectives can also be considered as potential tools for social control. The psychoanalytic interpretation is in the hands of the leader, who is acknowledged as more experienced and authoritative by the group, whether or not an explicit leadership role is denied. As long as the trainer is in command of the group, he can note when the "real" level of expression has been reached.[11] The language of psychoanalytic thought may then offer leverage to control a group when the user of that language has the final authority to interpret the behavior of others within that vocabulary.

The use of psychoanalytic interpretations thus has a significant effect on the style and organization of group training sessions. Confusion and anxiety are likely to occur because of the ambiguous structure of these groups. Difficulties are intensified when expression of hostility is encouraged. An understanding of the usefulness of psychoanalytic interpretation may become a powerful tool in the indirect control of the direction the groups take.

But given this perspective, a variety of problems are introduced in quasi-egalitarian groups where no leader is ever legitimated. First, whatever ordinary tensions or conflicts lie dormant in the training setting are magnified by the expectation that they *will* arise and that one ought not to inhibit their expression. In this way they become a special focus of attention rather than a taken-for-granted part of everyday life. Second, no legitimate authority

---

10 Benne, *et al., op. cit.,* p. 27.
11 Benne, *op. cit.,* p. 239.

exists to order the expression of hostility. Therefore, no one can openly assume responsibility for stating when "true" levels of expression are reached so that understanding may be assumed to have developed and the conflicts dissipated. In this situation the potential for magnification of minor grievances into real strife and backbiting becomes extensive. And in the case studied, the residents did in fact see these possibilities quite clearly.

The Focus of Group Interaction

The main advantage of the group, as the residents saw it, seemed to be that it provided an opportunity to ventilate general feelings of anger and hostility against anything connected with the program. This included complaints about the competence, commitment to psychiatry, and teaching ability of the supervisors, the behavior of other residents, and the general worth of the program itself. Of the eleven residents who were willing to speak about the group at all, eight mentioned the opportunity to vent grievances as of major importance. For example, one reported:

> ...there are a few (residents) that particularly get on my nerves; and it's somewhat satisfying to point out to them that they are defective (laughs), and I think they're wrong and this type of thing.... Commanding officers are criticized; the superiors in the department come in for some pretty healthy licks once in a while.... Mainly, the things that irritated us about the training program. The fact that they're not exactly what we would desire as teachers, and there are some personal foibles that some of them have that come in for commentary too.

Two of the residents said they derived intense satisfaction from the opportunity to watch aggressive interpersonal action. One of them said: "The fights that arise I enjoy. The hostility...people ventilating and blowing off ...I get a kick out of it."

The basic pattern of activity at the group sessions, as the participants saw it, seemed to be an attack on one member. "There is always a victim," one second year resident remarked. However, given the therapeutic philosophy, "victim" also meant "patient," and the attack was rationalized as an effort at education or treatment. Skowran, a second year resident, discussed this tendency: "You are putting so many people in a room, and you are saying. 'We are going to have a group therapy, so pick out a subject.' This usually means pick out a person, and we will discuss him, and the easiest way to discuss him is to start with his faults."

The power of the doctor to diagnose the ills of the patient was gradually transmuted into the power of the therapist to point out characterological and moral defects in the one who was to be therapized. "If you have a little

set of rules, you can use your training as a psychiatrist to tell how inadequate and poor somebody else is, and say, 'This is all for your benefit.' "
And so the pattern of attack was also interpreted as an inevitable tendency
to slip into the doctor-patient role—with the opportunity to choose a patient.

To the person chosen these strategies seemed of dubious value and
ethics. "I think that (the group) has been utilized as a sounding board for
grievances for people who don't have the ability to externalize what they
feel about others anywhere else...." The chosen scapegoat, Sutter, was not
the only one to question the motivation for attack. Three other residents often
in attendance were not pleased by the opportunity provided for general
release of anger. They thought it provided a chance for mischief, opportunities for scapegoating, and the eruption of tendencies destructive to
individuals and to the group. Here is how one resident expressed such misgivings:

> *Some of the reasons that have been given for having group meetings,*
> *such as therapy for the residents, I don't think are possible in there. I*
> *sometimes think that it is an example to show one-upmanship.... Some-*
> *times the people in the group use this as a method of attacking somebody.*
> *And the person is sometimes unable to respond.... I don't feel that it is*
> *for the person's benefit. It is with a malicious intent. And the other person*
> *is usually somebody who is not able to respond back.*

The structure of the group and the possibilities presented by that structure,
as the participants viewed it, clearly contained some dangers. What strategies
were generated to cope with these dangers?

Maintaining a Place in the Group

Each resident was concerned with how to present himself and what
was thought of him by the others. One resident described this defensive
position, both for himself and for the other members of the group.

> *I think I was more willing to give opinions, personal opinions, on things*
> *before my residency.... Since I started in psychiatry I'm far less willing.*
> *I'm more careful not to—spill the beans. Not to perhaps expose myself*
> *in the way that I want myself being exposed.... You're willing to admit*
> *that you have problems like everyone else, and yet, as a psychiatrist there*
> *is a certain pride, I think, in feeling more stable than other people....*
> *That is driven home when people laugh at the statements that I make*
> *and say, "Oh, boy! You know you're supposed to be a psychiatrist!*
> *What are you making a statement, a crazy statement like that, for?" It*
> *really bothers me. And I keep withdrawing. I don't say as much...become*
> *more careful in what I'm saying.*

Under these circumstances, where self-revelation is threatening, inherent conflicts in role performance were difficult to control. One possible strategy would be to behave as a patient—illustrating the psychiatric view that "everyone has problems." Yet, a desirable self-image for a young psychiatrist in training includes normality and stability.[12] So no one was very eager to play the role of the patient in group therapy. Caution and reserve provided an alternative strategy. The related skill was not sticking your neck out. Hence, the sidelines were the most attractive place to be; to get there you remained silent. There were no criticisms for silence in the group. "You can't attack somebody who is silent. It is sort of accepted that if somebody doesn't say anything, he doesn't want anything said (about him)." But the criticisms (or punishment) for sitting on the sidelines and then speaking up were sharp.

> *(Some residents) can come in and do nothing and say nothing for weeks on end, but sooner or later they'll get it. Especially if they will open up with some sort of an interpretive remark after they have been saying nothing for half a year. That is a very good way to get completely annihilated—because everybody notices.*

That the sidelines were not always entirely safe was indicated by three first year residents. One of them felt that he was criticized for being silent during an attack on another resident.

> *My personal participation hasn't been very much. I have been pretty much defensive, watching things go on in the group and making some comments on my own from time to time. But I'm not the most active person in the group. . . . There were times when I was in the spotlight briefly. . . . We were talking about Sutter and how he tends to be bombastic at times. . . . And he was being attacked rather repeatedly in several sessions for this. And (I really didn't feel that) I approved of this, yet I remained silent and did not rise to Sutter's defense. And then, later, when we had just a few people there one day, we sort of talked about this as to why we didn't rise to his defense when it seemed that things were kind of out of hand—and perhaps that one can commit the sin of omission as well as commission. And by remaining silent, perhaps (I was) doing a disservice to Sutter.*

For members of this group absence, like silence, had its problems. It did not provide an entirely comfortable escape from criticism. "(Some residents) are afraid to come knowing that they will be attacked when they do come. . . . They are told that they are talked about if they come, and they are talked about if they don't come. . . ." The strategies of avoidance were clearly not

---

[12] Cf. A. Blum and L. Rosenberg, "Some Problems Involved in Professionalizing Social Interaction," *Journal of Health and Social Behavior,* IX (1968), 72–85.

enough in themselves to maintain both the equanimity of individuals and the continuity of the group. The group was seen as important, since attendance was maintained voluntarily. But strategies of silence or avoidance contravened the purpose of group preservation. Perhaps for these reasons other strategies appeared to mitigate the extent or seriousness of attacks. As one informant explained it, a severe attack often was followed by an "undoing process." Apparently this type of behavior reaffirmed solidarity, showed respect for another's professional competence, and gave evidence of positive sentiment toward the one attacked.

Such observations indicate that informants perceived dangers in the T-Group and its potential for personal and nontherapeutic attacks. As a consequence, efforts were consistently made to avoid discussing serious personal problems likely to be disruptive for the group. "I myself have never shut anyone up (about problems with wives, drinking, affairs), but I have always felt more comfortable when they have been shut up. If they wanted to talk, I probably would have listened (if they had been allowed to speak)." Apparently, efforts were made to limit the areas in which hostility might be shown. The group participants saw the merit of limiting destructiveness to situations they felt certain they could manage. This mitigation of attack was one of the main processes at work to maintain the group. Perhaps the process occurred in recognition of the fact that too much scapegoating threatened the group's very existence. Hence, clear efforts at restoration were made regularly.

Nevertheless, the group could still be used as a strategy for attacking a deviant or disliked member. Slaughter remarked that "recently (the group) has turned into a punishing device for anyone who doesn't conform to our group standards." He argued that group attacks were a means of supporting group standards or values.

Such an argument, of course, is similar to that of Emile Durkheim. He saw that a consequence of the mobilization of a community against some deviant was reaffirmation of the values and priorities of that community. This reaffirmation strengthens group solidarity. In this way, the characteristics of the victim (or scapegoat) in the group may serve as indicators by which to examine these group standards. A discussion of the group choice for scapegoat permits just this kind of examination.

The Scapegoat in the Resident Group

At the time of this study great interest was focused upon the management of feelings about the most generally disliked participant, Sutter. All but one of his first year colleagues stated that they disliked him, though their reasons varied. Sawyer felt that Sutter's orientation to social interchange was too alien.

For example, he can see nothing wrong with telling a person they're wrong. To me, this is the type of insult that the answer...is to hit him. And we've had a lot of personality conflicts because of this. I came from, I guess you'd call it, a very inhibited society. If you told a man he was wrong, that was tantamount to saying "let's go out in the street and get it over with." In his case, he's from New York; he can say things like that and get away with it. People accept it. I don't accept it.

Scotland thought Sutter was disliked by the others because he was "self-assured, confident, powerful, although completely alone." He himself disliked Sutter because the latter was "loud, rather inconsiderate." Slaughter thought that Sutter's most irritating personality traits were that he was "flat-footed, self-assured, verbose, and unaware of others."

And the things that have drawn the most comment have been to what we call his "filibustering"; he is very verbose and repetitive, to an aggravating extent, in making a simple point. And he is very self-assured....He doesn't beat around the bush. When he comes to a conference, he slams the door, stomps to the front of the room...and is admittedly oblivious to many of the nonverbal communications you give a person.

Another resident agreed with this, and thought that Sutter talked too much and was too rambling in his exposition. In order to justify the attack on the scapegoat, other negative sanctions in the form of pejorative social typifications were leveled against him. Some of the categories applied to Sutter by his colleagues suggest this process. The selection of personality characteristics which were particularly disliked points to those group standards which Sutter threatened.

From the standpoint of the faculty that knew him, Sutter was an outstanding student. In an educational program one might reasonably look for learning and achievement in the training process as indices of value orientation. But in this program resentment and dislike with, perhaps, a shade of contempt mixed with jealousy were reserved for one who was clearly interested in such values. The fact that the outstanding student was accepted as the scapegoat tells us something about the educational values of the group and its level of enthusiasm for innovation and hard work.

The Social Type and Group Values

If we were to use Klapp's major division of social types into heroes, villains, and fools, we might say that the picture of Sutter we get from his classmates is that of a combination of villain and fool. As a villain he was a flouter, a troublemaker, a selfish grabber, an intruder, a suspicious isolate; and as a fool he was pompous—a blowhard, a showoff, a square or an eccentric misfit, a single-track mind, and an eager beaver. These aspects of the social typification process are used in this situation to justify the interaction that created the scapegoat. But these negative typifications do not describe Sutter's behavior, only the interpretations placed upon it. What prizes was Sutter grabbing, and what standards was he flouting to warrant the scapegoating he received?

Klapp suggests that certain characterizations like troublemaker, intruder, and eager beaver are invidious distinctions applied to those who symbolize a threat to the social order. In this light Sutter can be seen as a threat to the golden mean or the normative connotations of "average." In professional worlds this standard is often expressed as "colleagueship."

Second, the scholarship or excellence shown by Sutter in the program pointed to inadequacies in the majority. These inadequacies were recognized by the other residents to some extent, and the comparison with Sutter could not help but rankle.

An alternative picture of scapegoating presented by Klapp is one which emphasizes the conflict of value systems. Invidious responses may be elicited in pluralistic or shifting social orders from those who "feel insecure and defensive, or alienated and offensive, toward the order of which they are a part."[13] From this view the scapegoat may be only temporarily disadvantaged. One set of values—such as colleagueship—may be exposed when challenged by another—such as scholarship. One resident, Shipley, felt the price of resolving these conflicts was seen in the resistance to change and innovation in the program.

> *I was kind of interested in getting as much out of the program as I possibly could for myself. And I was also perhaps idealistic in thinking that the program could be improved; and if everyone kind of pulled together, we could get a better program going...and the patients would get more from us. I was...led to believe...that many people were not interested in rocking the boat, and they weren't willing to do any more work than they absolutely had to.*

From the following (admittedly jaundiced) view of Sutter, the resulting atmosphere is seen as stultifying and antithetical to learning:

> *A lot of the enthusiasm is missing in the (military).... The talk that goes on at the dinner table is what kind of a house somebody is renting, or if they are buying a house, or if they are on the promotion list. There doesn't seem to be much intellectual topics or even technical topics related to our work.... If you try to talk about your experience or what you have done, there seems to be a certain degree of resistance.*

In the conflict between scholarship and collegialities, it appears that the resolution favors collegiality. However, this does not mean that all

---

13 Klapp, *op. cit.*, p. 55.

members of the group must accept this resolution. Sutter, for example, protested and reaffirmed his own values even under the attacks by his colleagues. He made it clear that he perceived his vulnerability to attack.

The Response of the Scapegoat

Sutter saw that an invidious evaluation is a weapon that group members can use in the construction of a scapegoat. Here is his analysis of that invidious evaluation:

> *I have rather strong feelings about this because I have been the focal point of a lot of discussion there about being the kind of aggressive New Yorker. And a lot of people have strong feelings about New Yorkers, whatever that means. As a result of which, I have learned a lot about people from these groups.... I have felt threatened during these things, and I don't find this to be unexpected, when you spend week after week being bombarded with criticism. It has been going on for a couple of months. But—I don't know if you are familiar with the expression that "you won't give them the satisfaction"—I won't give them the satisfaction of not going.... I feel threatened, but I won't give the satisfaction.... There are comments on my ability to get along with people, to relate, to pick up nonverbal stimuli, to essentially—like we say in school— "respect the rights of others."...There are a lot of preconceived ideas, there, about New York people; and I think that in parenthesis this also says "Jewish."...When I discussed it with my wife...she said, "What do you think of the idea that when they are saying New Yorker, they are saying Jew?" One guy said, "It's not so much that you are Jewish...." You know, it is not so much. Well, all right, it's not so much; but it is something.... As I pointed out in a conference a while back, that, when I was a kid in the neighborhood I grew up in, there were very few Jews; and I used to run away (from the Gentiles) when they came (in) hordes.... I'm not going to give them the satisfaction of running away (now).*

When Sutter decided to stand and fight, he opened up the possibility for countertypifications. His rationale provided him with the stance from which to launch an attack on collegiality and from which he might defend scholarship.

The basic rules of the group can be used by the attacked as well as the attackers. Once Sutter grasped the principles, he felt that he became a formidable opponent in his turn. First he raised questions about the motivation of his attackers.

> *The people who have given me the roughest times in terms of these psychotherapy sessions have been a little clique made up of (three second year residents). They are the guys who have really given me the*

business left and right....I have told them they are utilizing the confer-
ences as a means of showing how sophisticated they were...and that
they didn't give a damn if it helped me or...hurt me.

Then Sutter began to construct his counterattack. "But I have learned how
to deal with them now. I gave them a pretty good sample of that yesterday.
...It occurred to me yesterday that when I walked in there with a format I
could clobber them."

Sutter's analysis of his own situation illustrates some of the problems of social typing as a collaborative process. If, as in his case, social
typing is resisted, the typers may be forced to view their own efforts in a
pejorative light. To the extent that one successfully resists the typification
process, he may turn the tables and contribute to the process himself by
villifying his attackers. (In Sutter's case, the suggestions that his chief
adversaries were unfair, personally vindictive, cowardly, lazy, philistines, and
racial bigots were not without their effects on the less committed observers,
who saw themselves as *tertius gaudens* for the group.)

Conclusions

The utility of the scapegoat as a social type is illuminated by the
example of Sutter. A voluntary group that focuses on the expression of
hostility is in danger of self-extermination. After each person has had a taste
of victimization, and refuses to return for more, the group is gradually
decimated. The only possibility is in the emergence of a tough-minded individual who can take it or who, in Sutter's terms, "won't give them the
satisfaction" of giving up. Sutter, though he resisted, reinforced the troublemaker role that was assigned to him. His refusal to give them the satisfaction was in fact giving them the satisfaction. It put him in the position of
the one who comes back again and again to renew a quarrel on the same
terms. It gave a grudge, or feudlike, stability to the situation. Such a target
for hostility continues to divert attention from potentially more disrupting
problems in the structure and priority system of the group. In these two ways,
then, the scapegoat can support the maintenance of the group.[14]

Another conclusion that may be drawn from this case study is that
the scapegoating of Sutter led to support of the status quo in the residency
program. Sutter did in fact moderate some of his more blatant and irritating
criticisms of the conduct or management of the program, and thus the other
residents were not continually bombarded with implicit and explicit attacks

---

14 Cf. E. F. Vogel and N. W. Bell, "The Emotionally Disturbed Child as the
Family Scapegoat," in *The Family,* eds. N. W. Bell and E. F. Vogel (New York: The
Free Press of Glencoe, Inc., 1960), pp. 382–97.

on their own system of values. Here are the steps Sutter said he took in order to adapt to the value system he thought he saw in operation.

> *I was at a conference about two weeks ago, and I made some comment. A guy who I know was there said to me—he was new to this department— "It amazed me no end that while you were making this comment, and you were the only one who made this comment about the dynamics of the case, why you were so apologetic about it?" Well, the reason is this. If you say anything, or exhibit that you have any understanding for something, or if you have had an experience, or what-have-you, or not, you are going to run into feeling that you are too pushy. So I don't say much at the conferences any more. I think a thousand times before I make a comment or ask a question.*

Scapegoating, when effective, inhibits change in the group which uses this tactic as well as in the victim. The group is able to disallow the criticisms of the victim and the problems he creates.

In summary, what can we learn about the nature of a group from the social types it produces, the particular kinds of individuals it elects for these types, and the relative docility or resistance to typing by the elected? The role of the deviant may be costly for himself and others. Nevertheless, as numerous social analysts have shown, the effect of the interaction between deviant and attackers often tends to stablize the group, maintain cohesiveness, and divert attention from underlying problems. However, one aspect of this process that becomes clear from the case study presented is that certain underlying and potentially nonsanctioned aspects of interaction may be revealed when the deviant label is resisted. The counterattack or argument from the potential deviant can expose inconsistencies in the normative structure. The process of scapegoating may serve the function of maintaining a precarious system. When a troublemaker is put down, his resistance jeopardizes the structure (or rocks the boat) even if the boat doesn't tip over.

18

Francis E. Merrill

LE GROUPE DES BATIGNOLLES:
A STUDY IN
THE SOCIOLOGY OF ART

"In New York," remarked a well-known surrealist painter, "there are Artists, but no Art."[1] By this *boutade,* Max Ernst meant that Art (with a capital A) is not only the individual product of a single artist but also the collective product of a number of artists in inter-action. The exchange of ideas, the mutual criticism, the friendly (or unfriendly) rivalry, and, above all, the presence of a cultural setting in which art is a vital matter—these and similar considerations lend sociological validity to the above aphorism.[2] In commenting upon

---

[1] Quoted by René Passeron, *Histoire de la Peinture Surréaliste* (Paris: Livre de Poche, 1968), p. 83.

[2] D. W. Gotschalk, *Art and the Social Order* (Chicago: University of Chicago Press, 1947), p. 239.

the presence of artists but the absence of Art, Ernst was not so much criticizing American society, which was good to him and his fellow surrealists during World War II, as he was calling attention to certain of its structural characteristics. One of these is its comparative decentralization, which means that the artist has tended to be a solitary worker, living on farms or in remote villages, far from urban centers. Hence the interaction of the European scene—whether in Munich, Zurich, Berlin, Rome, or Paris—has often been lacking to the American artist.

Times have changed, of course, since Max Ernst made his original remark. The peaceful invasion by European artists during World War II set in motion changes in the American scene that modified, if they did not eliminate altogether, some of the force of his observations. In the two and a half decades since the war, New York has become the world center for a new and dynamic movement, Abstract Expressionism. Under the initial leadership of such men as Jackson Pollock and Franz Kline, New York has assumed many (although by no means all) of the artistic functions that Paris held during the nineteenth and early twentieth centuries. The American pioneers in this new movement went through the lean years of the Depression together and painfully worked out their own style, which in a few years became a truly international expression. In this activity, they stimulated each other in the gritty but heady environment of New York City. For perhaps the first time, the serious artist was no longer alone in the United States.[3]

The Group as a Creative Medium

The artistic enterprise, despite its apparently solitary quality, is also a corporate process, involving not only the individual but the milieu in which he works, the fellow artists with whom he communicates, and the public with which he hopes to come in contact.[4] Under the impulse of an internal creative necessity, the artist comes to terms with his setting. This setting is both social and cultural and the artist interacts with the stimulation provided by each. On the social level, he takes the role of other artists and observes himself as an object through their eyes. His conception of himself and his work is in large measure a product of this interaction between self and other.[5] On the cultural level, he reacts to the cultural heritage, notably

---

[3] Bernard Rosenberg and Norris Fliegel, *The Vanguard Artist* (Chicago: Quadrangle Books, Inc., 1965), Chap. 1.

[4] R. G. Collingwood, *The Principles of Art* (London: Oxford University Press, 1938), p. 324.

[5] Francis E. Merrill, "Art and the Self," *Sociology and Social Research,* LII (1968), 185–94. Cf. George H. Mead, *Mind, Self, and Society* (Chicago: University of Chicago Press, 1934).

the work of artists who have gone before. As André Malraux wryly puts it, Giotto learned to paint by looking at the frescoes of Cimabue, not by looking at sheep.[6]

The creative process is thus a form of communication involving the origination, organization, and expression of meaningful symbols. In Susanne Langer's words, "Art is the creation of forms symbolic of human feeling."[7] The exchange of such symbols is the essence of society, and without it society could not exist. As John Dewey pointed out many years ago, "Society not only continues to exist *by* transmission, *by* communication, but it may fairly be said to exist *in* transmission, *in* communication."[8] In all societies and at all times, the artist plays an important role in this process. In this sense, art is not marginal to society, but is basic to it. This is one reason why we can speak of a sociology of art.[9]

Creation may therefore be considered in terms of its social setting. This essay deals with a particular social setting, namely, the system of interpersonal relationships wherein a single group of artists took each other into account and produced something new. It is obviously impossible to consider all—or even a small number—of the social systems, large and small, that have been an inspirational source of creation in every age and society. Any such discussion would necessarily range from the Platonic Academy, through the Pléiade, down to the aforementioned group of abstract expressionist painters in New York in the 1940s. It is not enough, however, to speak grandly of the relationship(s) between art and society. The creative process may be approached on a more manageable level. This I propose to do.

In and around the year 1869, a group of young artists were in the habit of meeting nightly at the Café Guerbois on the Rue des Batignolles, now known as the Avenue de Clichy. These men were, with one or two exceptions, virtually unknown to the art public and not at all to the general public. Their work, furthermore, had been consistently rejected by the official *Salon*, without whose sanction the artist could neither adequately display his paintings nor find buyers for them. In order of age, the group included Pissarro, Manet, Degas, Cézanne, Sisley, Monet, Renoir, and Bazille. It was supplemented by a number of critics, *amateurs* (in the French sense), and journalists, the most notable of whom was the rising young author Emile Zola, a boyhood friend of Cézanne. Because of the street on which stood the

---

6 André Malraux, *Les Voix du Silence* (Paris: Pléiade, 1951), p. 276.

7 Susanne K. Langer, *Feeling and Form* (New York: Charles Scribner's Sons, 1953), p. 40.

8 John Dewey, *Democracy and Education* (New York: The Macmillan Company, Publishers, 1916), p. 5.

9 Cf. Hugh D. Duncan, *Communication and Social Order* (New York: The Bedminister Press, Inc., 1962), pp. 437–38; and Jean Duvignaud, *Sociologie de l'Art* (Paris: Presses Universitaires de France, 1967), p. 37.

unpresuming Café Guerbois, the young men became known as *le Groupe des Batignolles*. Recent generations know them as the Impressionists.[10]

The Café Guerbois became the scene of nightly reunions that were destined to last, with interruptions, for almost a decade. A history of art, indeed, might be written about the modest institution of the café, which has served as intellectual forum, post office, and home-away-from-home for generations of European artists. Such a history would include The Mermaid Tavern, the Cheshire Cheese, La Nouvelle Athenes, the Flore, the Deux Magots, and the Dome. The important characteristic of the café in general and the Café Guerbois in particular is that it provides a "clean, well-lighted place" (the phrase is Hemingway's) for the creation, encouragement, and criticism of art. Here it was that an important school of art was generated by a group of men who combined to "carry out a common idea."[11] In this seminal atmosphere, supplemented by sessions *en plein air,* a dozen men gradually emancipated themselves from the traditional schools and evolved many of the theoretical and technical principles of the movement that was soon to be called (at first in derision) Impressionism.

The Goals of the Group

A group consists of two or more persons who interact over a certain period and share a common goal. More explicitly, a group is a social system whose members are (a) in contact over a more or less continuous interval, (b) mutually aware of each other as members, (c) able to communicate effectively, and (d) established in a patterned relationship. In the course of its development the group (a) establishes regular channels of communication, (b) evolves different roles for its members, (c) agrees upon certain functions, (d) sets its goals, and (e) works out accepted standards of behavior (norms) for its members.[12]

The group comes together because it satisfies (or appears to satisfy) some need or needs of its members. These needs may range from the comparatively uncomplicated one of simple sociability to the infinitely complex ones related to marriage. These motivations may or may not be conscious, for the individual is often unaware that he has needs and, if so, exactly what they are. Group participation has been analyzed in terms of the following needs: (a) *Personal attraction.* Individuals join with others because they

---

10 In the following discussion I am heavily indebted to John Rewald, *Histoire de l'Impressionisme* (Paris: Livre de Poche, 1965).

11 This remark was made by Van Gogh in referring to the Impressionists. Quoted by Rewald, *op. cit.,* Vol. II, p. 190.

12 Robert F. Bales, *Interaction Process Analysis* (Reading, Mass.: Addison-Wesley Publishing Co. Inc., 1950).

like them and want to be with them. (b) *Group Prestige*. Individuals join groups because it is an honor to belong and their self-images are enhanced thereby. (c) *Task Performance*. Individuals join groups, finally, because they wish to perform a task that is facilitated by their membership. They realize that they cannot solve a particular problem or reach a certain goal without the aid of others.[13]

Le Groupe des Batignolles was animated by all of these motives. In addition to friendship and mutual aid, the task performance goal was twofold: (a) to perfect their art, and (b) to effect its acceptance by the interlocking publics of the Jury, individual collectors, and art fanciers in general. Not the least important corollary of the latter was the eminently utilitarian one of selling their work. Most of the young men were poor, and with certain exceptions (e.g., Manet, Degas, and Bazille) they needed to realize something directly from their painting. Monet was in the direst straits in 1869 and for some time thereafter, even though he ultimately received comparatively large sums for his work. With a wife and child to support, he often had no bread in the house and (what was worse) no money to buy paint and canvas.

In pursuance of the first goal, the members engaged in extensive discussions of the theory and techniques of the new art. Harrison and Cynthia White describe this general activity as follows: "Painting is a process of discovery in which the questions to be asked are defined more and more clearly and the chosen form and techniques are investigated in more detail."[14] The central technical problem involved the depiction of light on various surfaces—i.e., still life, the human body, snow, and (above all) water. Considerable differences of opinion existed as to the relative importance of this problem, with Manet and Degas less interested and Monet, Renoir, Pissarro, and Sisley more so. Among their joint discoveries, the members found that zones of shade were not without any light at all, but merely had *less* light and hence less striking colors than those exposed to the sun. With regard to water, they found that the application of small particles of paint in different colors gave the effect of vibrations and hence the impression of light, movement, and life itself. Finally, they were beginning to stress the whole, rather than the details, of a picture, in contrast to the emphasis upon design stressed by such men as Ingres.[15]

Commenting long afterward upon this heady process of discussion

---

13 Kurt W. Back, "Influence Through Social Communication," *Journal of Abnormal and Social Psychology*, XLVI (1951), 9–23.

14 Harrison C. White and Cynthia A. White, *Canvases and Careers: Institutional Change in the French Painting World* (New York: John Wiley & Sons, Inc., 1965), p. 117.

15 This essay makes no pretense at analyzing the Impressionist movement as a whole, either technically or historically. The emphasis is, rather, upon its group aspects.

and experimentation, Monet recalled the passionate interest with which he and the others participated in the conversations on the terrace of the Café Guerbois. In these relationships, he continued, the members stimulated both each other and themselves to examine the new problems and, afterward, to try them out *en plein air.* Monet would thus return to his native Le Havre; Pissarro would retire to Louveciennes; Cézanne would go home to Aix-en-Provence; Sisley would install himself near Fontainbleau; and Renoir would set up his easel on the banks of the Seine below Paris. In addition to their technical discoveries, Monet recalled, the members of the group gave each other courage to persist in the long and arduous road to improvement and eventual acceptance. One left these meetings, he concluded, with thoughts clarified and will strengthened.[16] Both technically and morally, these effects were collective in the most literal sense. They indicate once more that art is, in final analysis, a social enterprise.

The second aspect of the common goal of *le Groupe des Batignolles* was, as we have indicated, to bring their work to the attention of the various publics upon which their success ultimately depended. In the spring of 1867, when the group was in its initial years, Bazille wrote to his parents in Montpellier that "some young men" (himself included) were trying to organize a joint exposition of their painting, which would be entirely separate from the official Salon and would represent their work as a group. The financial means for this enterprise—modest as they were—could not be found, and the venture had to be abandoned. The artists were forced to rely upon a few benevolent or farsighted *amateurs,* who were willing to gamble on their work and thereby keep them going, albeit modestly.

By 1873 things began to improve, although in a manner that was far from spectacular. The young men were becoming better known, their paintings were bringing higher prices (perhaps a few hundred francs), and they seemed a bit nearer to financial security, even though their works were, in general, still refused by the Jury. They decided to try again and, after considerable deliberation, took the momentous step of organizing an exposition at their own expense. This was the famous Exposition of 1874, the first in which the Impressionists exhibited as a group. A number of other artists were invited to participate in order to make the show seem less radical and also to keep down individual costs. Among the group itself Cézanne submitted three paintings; Degas, six; Monet, five; Sisley, five; and Pissarro, six. In all some 165 paintings were hung. The Impressionists were quantitatively in the minority, although qualitatively they dominated the exposition. Monet submitted several paintings under such prosaic titles as "Entrance to the Village," "Exit from the Village," and "Morning in the Village." When

---

16 Quoted by Rewald, *op. cit.,* Vol. I, p. 246.

asked to make these titles more dramatic, he replied simply, "Call them Impressions."

The Exposition of 1874 by no means solved the problems of the Impressionists, either in terms of critical acceptance or the sale of their paintings. The critics continued to laugh at them, and the public continued to ignore them. In all, some eight expositions were attempted by the group, the last in 1886. On each occasion, the original group was depleted, sometimes by the decision of individual artists and sometimes by death (Manet died in 1883). By the early years of the 1880s, the members had begun to settle farther from Paris, thereby making their encounters increasingly rare. Monet bought a property at Giverny; Sisley established himself at Moret; Cézanne returned more or less permanently to his native Aix-en-Provence; and Pissarro came to rest at an increased distance from the capital.[17] In addition, the group began to take on new members, notably Gauguin, Seurat, and Signac, and the original Impressionists (e.g., Pissarro) found themselves in the unaccustomed role of "masters" for a new generation. At the same time, Renoir, Monet, and (especially) Cézanne were going their separate artistic ways to a greater extent than ever before. Much of the greatest work of the Impressionists (now in middle age) was done after they had ceased to function as a group. But the creative interaction at the Café Guerbois had left its mark upon these men who were themselves destined to leave their mark upon subsequent generations of painters.

The Roles in the Group

In the continued process of interaction, a group evolves various roles, reflecting the personalities of the members and the goals of the group. In *le Groupe des Batignolles* definite roles developed as each individual took his part in the group activities. We will indicate briefly the nature of these roles and the individuals who played them. The roles applied to the group as it was constituted around 1869. In later years, many of the roles changed with the development of the individual personalities and the evolution of the group.

1. The Role of the Intellectual Leader

The intellectual leadership of the group was shared by several men, notably by Manet and Degas. They were both interested in the historical and theoretical aspects of painting, which reflected their sound educations in general culture and the history of art. Sons of wealthy bourgeois families,

---

17 *Ibid.,* Vol. II, pp. 143–44.

they were both proud of their background and seldom let anyone forget it. Manet was inclined to be dogmatic and did not take kindly to contradiction. He was intelligent, witty, and sometimes acerbic in his relationships with his fellow artists, who nevertheless respected his knowledge and talent. Degas was also interested in theoretical questions and defended his ideas with raillery, irony, and (sometimes) intolerance. His culture was so extensive that he could present arguments in defense of his position that were beyond the competence of many of his companions, who were largely self-taught.

2. The Role of Spiritual Leader

The doyen of the group, both in age and attitude, was Pissarro, who was always welcome because of his calm, kindness, and benevolence. He was also the social conscience of the group because of his passionate interest in social problems and in the relationships between art and society. The struggle for artistic recognition by the group was for him a part of the class struggle as a whole. Despite the radical quality of his opinions, especially to such staunch bourgeois as Manet and Degas, Pissarro was never intransigent and his good will was never questioned. Forced to live entirely by his brush, he helped others in every way—materially, by constructive advice, or through moral encouragement. His role, in short, was that of spiritual and moral leader of *le Groupe des Batignolles*.

3. The Role of Cooperative Friend

A fourth member of the group came from a wealthy family in the south of France. Alone of the original group, Bazille was destined to die young in the War of 1870, his promise largely unfulfilled. At the time of the early group meetings around 1869, however, he was one of its leading members. He had received a broad education, which enabled him to hold his own intellectually with Manet and Degas. Unlike them he was shy, modest, and generous, often helping his less fortunate friends with money, meals, and the use of his studio. His arguments were calm, reasoned, and sound, and he was one of the best theoreticians of the group. In addition to his theoretical and material contributions, Bazille offered a personal kindness which, coupled with that of Pissarro, made the nightly circle at the Café Guerbois a more friendly place.

4. The Role of Independent Listener

Another young man from the *Midi* took a less active part in the group and was often content to retire into a corner, both literally and figuratively, and listen to the conversation. Although his parents were well-to-do, Cézanne had little of the personal fastidiousness of Manet, Degas, and Bazille. Indeed, he seemed to enjoy shocking his companions by his uncouth manners, his thick meridional accent, and his unceremonious departures. From time to time he would deliver himself of a few pungent remarks when the conversation touched upon a problem that interested him. Of the group, Cézanne was the last to perfect his style and was likewise the last to receive widespread recognition. Rejected by the official Jury long after the others had been accepted, Cézanne took a savage pleasure in insulting this august body by submitting the paintings which he thought would most annoy them.

5. The Role of Innovator

Monet and Renoir were closely connected both personally and as members of the group during the early years of Impressionism. In many ways their innovations were the most characteristic of the movement. They often worked together and painted the same scenes, using such identical techniques that they sometimes had difficulty in identifying their own work. Monet was in some ways the most advanced of the group and consequently was, along with Cézanne, one of the last to be widely accepted. Monet was largely self-taught, and his lack of general culture made him shy in the presence of Manet and Degas. For the most part, Monet was content to sit quietly and listen to the others expound their theories, all the time remaining fixed in his own ideas. Despite many years of poverty and neglect, he never lost faith in himself and, with Renoir, perfected many of the most important innovations in the treatment of light.

6. The Role of Comrade

Renoir was, in some ways, the most gifted of *le Groupe des Batignolles,* with a facility that enabled him to follow any style he chose. Like Monet, Renoir was self-educated; he began his life as a painter of porcelain dishes in his native Limoges. His overflowing gaiety and sense of humor made him one of the most popular members of the group. Life was good for him, and painting was his way of showing it. The things of this world were rewarding, and his work was infused with this feeling. He was a devoted advocate of painting *en plein air* and, with Monet, perfected many of the techniques of showing the impact of light upon snow, water, and flesh. In his early days, Renoir worked in the studio of a conservative artist who had no sympathy for the efforts of the young man to discover new worlds. When the master inquired sarcastically if Renoir painted solely for his own pleasure, the latter replied gaily that this was as good a reason as any and that, if he did not get pleasure out of it, he would certainly never do it.

7. The Role of Group Spokesman

When *le Groupe des Batignolles* began to meet, Emile Zola was a rising young journalist with a passionate interest in painting, although he had neither training nor talent in this direction. He saw the movement as a new form of communication and hence as another aspect of his own *métier* of symbolic communication. He had not yet published any of his celebrated series of novels, *Les Rougon-Macquart*, frankly modeled after Balzac's *La Comédie humaine*. In one of these novels, *L'Oeuvre*, Zola described a group like that of the Café Guerbois, with a character very much like his friend Cézanne as the chief protagonist. The crusty Cézanne was not amused and growled that he (Zola) might possibly be a good writer but that he certainly did not know much about painting. In any event, Zola early became the self-appointed spokesman for the group and tirelessly employed his journalistic talents to further the cause of Impressionism. However lacking he may have been in the refinements of appreciation, he more than made up for it by his great heart.

The group, then, is composed of several persons in interaction who share a common purpose. In the course of this interaction different roles appear that reflect both the personal qualities of the members and the requirements of the group. From the interaction as a whole, furthermore, something new emerges that is more than the sum of the individual contributions. This something is the group culture, which may be nothing more lasting than a few common memories, attitudes, and behavior patterns. Most groups, both in real life and those experimentally formed in the laboratory, seldom produce any cultural element that has a permanent impact upon their own or subsequent societies.

Unlike the majority of other groups, *le Groupe des Batignolles* did produce something of lasting importance—namely, a body of painting that is a precious part of our cultural heritage. We do not know how much of the work of these young (and ultimately old) men was the result of their genetic qualities and how much was the result of these qualities in interaction with their sociocultural environment. We can assume, however, that the group interaction as such was not unimportant. We have here another documentation of the lasting importance of art as a form of human enterprise or, in Malraux's words, a triumph of man over his destiny.[18] In the century since these young men began to meet around the marble topped tables of the Café Guerbois, few groups have contributed more richly to the never-ending struggle of man against oblivion.

---

[18] Malraux, *op. cit.*, p. 637.

19

Leo Zakuta

ON "FILTHY LUCRE"

lucre: gain or money as the object of sordid desire
(from the Latin: *lucrum* gain)[1]

NO CLERKS OR SELLING IN RICH BOND STREET

London (AP)—*Bond Street's very name is the trademark of
quality.*

*Extending from Picadilly to Oxford Street, its quarter-mile of
glassed and gilded windows, doorways, and showcases constitute a tight*

---

[1] *The American College Dictionary* (New York: Random House,
Inc., 1947).

*little enclave of richness without ostentation that exudes luxury, crafts-
manship, good taste—and altitudinous prices.*

   *Bond Street is, in fact, so high class that to refer to its estab-
lishments as stores or shops seems almost an affront.*

   *Within deep-carpeted interiors are fastidious but highly knowl-
edgeable men and women dealing with the public (some of them would
probably faint if you called them clerks) who won't even use the word
"sell."*

   *They avoid that crass, commercial verb with such circumlocu-
tions as:*

   "We recently supplied one of our clients with...."
   "One of our patrons obtained from us...."
   "We were able to provide Her Royal Highness with...."[2]

Bond Street's many counterparts have made its distaste for "commerce" thoroughly familiar. Equally well-known is the charge that it is carefully cultivated, that mercenary and snobbish motives combine to extract
the money of the rich by creating the pretense that its establishments are
something more than businesses. The newspaper story shows how vulnerable
Bond Street's claim is. For all of its sympathy, the story's point is that a shop
by any other name is newsworthy, meaning that these are really stores in
which hired clerks sell.

   But why are these terms "almost an affront"? And what makes the
word *sell* so "crass" and "commercial" that it is carefully avoided? Why, in
brief, is commerce "crass," not only on the world's Bond Streets but almost
everywhere?

   The answer is plain when we note who else, according to the convention, does not "sell." Among the models which come immediately to mind
are the arts, which are supposedly dedicated to beauty and self-expression,
and even more, the professions, which ideally are more concerned with
"service" than with "profit."

   Are business, the professions, and the arts fundamentally different
activities? And do their practitioners approach their work with different
pecuniary motives? Sociologists have been inclined, like people at large,
either to accept such distinctions at face value or else to deny their validity,
but, in either case, to regard these as important and answerable questions.
For our purposes, however, they are neither answerable nor relevant. This
paper will treat these claims and beliefs as data to be analyzed rather than
as questions to be answered, on the grounds that it is the general assumptions
about these matters, and not their "real" nature, that determine how people
view these pursuits and therefore treat their practitioners. To explain people's behavior, we must find the "reality" which they think exists.

---

[2] *The Globe and Mail* (Toronto), October 12, 1964, p. 10.

For us, accordingly, a pursuit will be whatever people, including its own, think it is. And our terms—business(man), profession(al), selling, service, profit, and many others—will represent the popular classifications rather than an endorsement of them.

The relatively low standing of commerce seems to be both ancient and general. The Bible, if not inveighing against trade directly, is a storehouse of injunctions against the pursuit of money, which, in the popular mind, is closely connected with commerce, an association largely responsible for trade's low standing.

In his first epistle to Timothy, Saint Paul warns that "the love of money is the root of all evil" and that therefore to enter God's service one must be "not greedy of filthy lucre." Even if one succeeds in amassing it, Jesus serves notice that "It is easier for a camel to go through the eye of a needle, than for a rich man to enter into the kingdom of God." Money is also central in such symbolic events as Jesus' "cleansing of the temple"—"(he) cast out them that sold and bought in the temple, and overthrew the tables of the money changers"—and his eventual betrayal "for thirty pieces of silver."

Many centuries later a similar aversion to trade, money-handling, and usury among Christians and Moslems facilitated the concentration of Jews in these activities, thereby confirming their pariah status. As might be expected, where animosity towards them waned, many Jews turned from their fathers' occupations in trade towards those of higher standing, especially the professions and the arts. (Perhaps because it is the chief weapon with which Jewish "success" is attacked, the sociological explanations of their rapid rise in America have made relatively little of their base in trade as a source of literacy, wealth, and familiarity with the world around them.)

The medieval contempt for the moneyhandler in the West had its parallel in the East, especially in China and Japan, where the merchant often ranked beneath the artisans and even the peasants. In Europe, despite industrialism, being in trade continued to represent a social comedown in most "elevated" circles.

Commercial and industrial society changed rather than destroyed these ancient attitudes. Business careers became more acceptable, but reservations about commerce remained. The traditional Jewish and Christian belief that it desecrates the sabbath may be dying, but is not yet dead. Dramatic events, as usual, reveal these familiar feelings most clearly. Immediately following the two Kennedy assassinations, for example, television commercials were banned, doubtless out of the feeling that they would—or would be thought to—profane the sacred nature of these occasions. Similar rules are attached to sacred personages, as Canada's Governor-General, the Queen's representative, recently joked:

> *I'm glad I wasn't fined for some misdeameanor tonight, because I couldn't have paid. Ever since I became Governor-General, I haven't had a dollar*

in my pocket. Royalty and its representatives just don't carry money. That's what aides-de-camp are for.[3]

What accounts for these qualms and reservations about money, an object supposedly of such universal desire? The rich and varied vocabulary of everyday life provides part of the answer. The terms which disparage an "inappropriate" or "excessive" interest in, or talk about, money range all the way from "indelicate" through "materialistic" and "vulgar" to "crude," "boorish," and "gross." But it takes the unusual to lay bare the heart of the usual, in this case someone daring to speak what many others thought or feared. Some years ago a leading Canadian businessman told a parliamentary committee on prices that his company's policy was "to buy as cheaply as possible and to sell as dearly as possible." The hue and cry among his interrogators and the public at large expressed the belief that underlies all of these other instances—that pursuit of money, especially of "profit" or "gain," is a clear manifestation of self-interest.

Although self-interest and altruism are obviously value judgments passed on behavior and therefore cannot be regarded as motives by the social scientist, they are seen as among the most powerful and persistent of motives by people at large. And it is to this social, rather than sociological, classification of motives that we must direct our attention.

In general, "self-interest" takes a low place in the human classification of motives; and "'selflessness" or "altruism," a high one. The reasons for this distinction seem unfathomable, but its consequences constitute our basic data. For example, it is the belief that the professions offer or ideally should offer a "service which goes beyond self-interest" that contributes to their higher standing.[4]

This does not suggest that people classify individuals so simply. Whether they see particular businessmen as "idealistic" or certain professionals as "money-grubbers" is beside the point. What matters is that they feel that, in business, the pursuit of wealth is so natural and inevitable that only outsiders can control it but that, in the professions, the practitioner himself must restrain it to avoid conflict with the ideal of service. Accordingly, the public protests "excess" business profits on the grounds that "the government shouldn't let them get away with it" but resents the doctors' "preoccupation with money" because "they shouldn't be like that."

Why people make these distinctions is intriguing. Why do they demand a service ideal from some occupations and not from others? Once they expect it, they consider that work to be a profession or to be worthy of

---

[3] *Ibid.,* March 25, 1969, p. 2.

[4] Accuracy suggests that terms such as self-interest, altruism, pursuit of money, and provision of service be preceded by such phrases as "what is defined as" or "what is believed to be" or, at least, that they be set in quotes. Simplicity of style requires, however, that this idea should henceforth be assumed.

that "honor." Some occupations designate their work as a professional service but encounter strong resistance to that claim.

All of this suggests that the sociological penchant for using external (objective) criteria to distinguish between occupations and professions is essentially barren. It does not mean, however, as some conclude, that classification is unimportant. What does matter is the classification that people— including the incumbents—make, the reasons they make it, and the consequences that follow. Our aim will be to answer these questions.

In general, people distinguish between "higher" and "lower" wants, and they label activities and pursuits accordingly. One example is the stereotype of the *nouveau riche*. He not only pursues the higher wants "insincerely" or indulges the lower ("tasteless") ones "conspicuously", but he allegedly does so for social self-aggrandizement, that is, self-interest. This combination makes his spending "ostentatious, vulgar, and unrefined," a common way in which money is thought to lose its luster.

In contrast, those activities that supposedly cater to the higher wants are labeled professions. Traditionally they have concentrated on such matters as health and life (physical as well as moral and spiritual); legal protection against the loss of freedom, reputation, and wealth; knowledge; and, perhaps stretching a point, the safety of the country.

Because these wants are more highly valued, people are unwilling to entrust them to just anyone. For example, the higher wants are thought to require rare and hard-to-acquire skills, which the consumer (here, a patient or client) therefore feels unqualified to judge. Because of this sense of inadequacy and because he places so much stock on these matters, he turns to those whose skills and motives he feels he can trust.

Thus, if a man believes that his life is in his doctor's hands or that his salvation is in those of his priest and that he cannot judge the services they provide, he draws considerable comfort from the faith or trust that their ultimate concern is his well-being rather than their own. (The same reason may lead him to resent as "impersonal" a show of "brisk efficiency" by the doctor which he would welcome in the department store.)

Out of the ideals of service and trust a distinctive set of rules and expectations arises governing the relations between practitioner and patient, one that can be seen more clearly by comparing it with its counterpart in business. If the professional's skill is thought to require trust, his motivation is supposed to justify it. In trade, however, the time honored maxim is *caveat emptor*. Furthermore, the ideal of service is supposed to restrain the ways in which patients and clients may be sought, thereby ruling out the "blatant" advertising and self-promotion open to business.

Other patterns of control in the two areas are even clearer manifestations of these rules. The store and the medical office will serve as our illustrations. The customer is expected, and, in any case, is considered free, to shop around for goods and services. To shop in a comparable way for a doctor, especially on the basis of price, is "unthinkable" (even if some people do so). The seller is not ordinarily thought to have the right to refuse to sell goods and services which he has available. While the doctor also has no right to refuse his services if he judges them necessary, that judgment is his, as is the form which they should take.

The word that is used in both cases is revealing. It is the customer and the doctor, not the patient, who "order." Three types of people normally give orders: superiors in a hierarchy of authority, doctors, and customers. The last, it is true, order goods and services rather than command people. Nevertheless, there is some parallel in the patient's placing himself under doctor's orders and the businessman or seller taking orders from customers.

The rules define the seller as subordinate to the buyer in additional ways. He "waits on," "helps," and "serves" customers. (In this context, "serves" carries a meaning far different than the presumably voluntary and lofty service referred to previously. Its general sense is closer to servitude and subservient.) His "May I help you?" is expected to show at least a suggestion of deference. He is, after all, thought to be playing this role primarily to earn a living, that is, for money.

The rules about dominance—about who is thought to have the greater right to control the relation—in business are neatly summarized in the oft-stated ideal, however attenuated it may be in practice, "The customer is always right." By contrast, even the cynical phrase that "Doctors bury their mistakes" implies that they are never known to be wrong.

The patterns of control in the two areas differ in still other ways. The customer may buy at any time during store hours; indeed, he usually finds delays in service extraordinarily irritating. The doctor, on the other hand, fixes the time at which he is available to the patient, and the latter usually feels not only a compulsion to appear on time but little resentment and less surprise if he spends some time in a "waiting room" before the doctor "takes" him. (Many business enterprises also have waiting rooms where, however, it is the sellers who usually wait for the buyers to "see" them.) Unlike patients, doctors are seldom "late." They often keep patients waiting, but it is because they are "very busy" and therefore running behind schedule. (The concept "late" is but one more example that the subject matter of sociology is not physical events, but states of mind.)

The phrase which is expected to conclude both transactions is perhaps the most revealing of all. The offering and acknowledgment of thanks is a sensitive index of social structure. The seller is usually expected to thank the buyer, but it is the patient who generally thanks the doctor even if the latter has just pronounced a sentence of death. This particular pattern indicates which party formally defines himself to have been in greater need of the other and therefore the greater beneficiary of the exchange.

TABLE 1

PERCEPTION OF OCCUPATIONS

Profane occupations	*Sacred occupations*
Impersonal relations	Personal relations
Lower wants	Higher wants
Lesser skills	Greater skills
Responds to the wishes or orders of others	Control of the relation
Open payment	Indirect payment
Strong pecuniary motives	Financial motives secondary
Self-interest appropriate and/or inevitable	Self-interest secondary to the service of others

The medical office and the store represent two of the further points on a continuum representing that cluster of ideas on the basis of which people make moral distinctions among occupations.

The polarities shown in Table 1 represent ideas or images which people attach to particuler occupations in a general way. Even if they do not expect to find them in a crystalline form in any particular instance, they nevertheless rate occupations and organizations on the basis of the degree to which they think they either do or should approximate these models. That the models themselves exist in people's minds becomes quite clear from the sentiments aroused when elements of both are thought to be intertwined. Bond Street, as we have seen, is a case in point, although its great prestige almost permits it "to get away with it." Before analyzing this type of establishment we must return briefly to the doctor's office.

Money, we have noted, is widely regarded as a symbol of almost naked self-interest, in contrast to the sacred services and ideal of disinterest of the medical profession. The feeling that money contaminates this image seems to be strongly built into the devices for handling it. One is generally not expected to ask the doctor about his fees, nor, except perhaps in the poorer districts, to pay him directly. Instead, one either pays his nurse—outside of his presence—or, more often, upon receipt of his (unitemized) "statement," mails a check, which his nurse presumably receives, credits, and deposits, thereby sparing him from any direct contact with it. (A similar gingerly approach to money appears in universities and other circles which speak of stipends, honoraria, emoluments, and increments.)

This suggests one more reason for the medical profession's resistance to medical insurance plans, including its coolness to arguments that such schemes would bolster the doctor's income by guaranteeing payment. They would also thereby end his practice of seeing patients without charge in hospital clinics, thus depriving him of a personal sense of *noblesse oblige* and the profession of a major symbol of the ideal of disinterested service.

What lies at the two ends of the continuum can also be detected by examining the cases in the middle. Instead of Bond Street our example here will be its close relative, the "first class" restaurant, since their patterns of control are fairly similar.

The greater its prestige, the more the restaurant seems to exert, or try to exert, control over the customer or "patron." The time is often arranged by appointment (a reservation), though here the "guest," unlike the medical patient, has the greater say. The establishment imposes rules of dress which lesser restaurants could not hope to get away with, although the recent controversy about pantsuits has demonstrated the problems of enforcement. Similar difficulties may arise in the seating of its clientele, which this kind of place also attempts to control. However, here too it finds itself uncertain and uneasy when these efforts meet with resistance.

Thus, the authority that these restaurants try to assert is usually discreet and gentle. Lacking much force, it relies on the decorum of the guests for its main support. When challenged, it tends to yield, with signs of discomfort, or to be reasserted in a form which makes a show of deference.

Some establishments of the highest prestige offer the "diner" little if any choice of foods. Food, indeed, is an unacceptable term for dishes which emanate from "culinary art." (One comes here not to eat but to dine.) Where choice is available, the waiters often feel free or are expected to make "suggestions." While these are far from the doctor's orders, lesser restaurants would hardly dare to make such overtures for fear of arousing the suspicion that they were prompted by self-interest.

Money, of course, is kept discreetly in the background. Sometimes the prices appear nowhere on the menu, which is hardly an invitation to inquire about them, or they may appear only on the menu of the party's host. After the meal the check in nearly all restaurants is presented face down, but in these the handling of the money is carefully avoided. The check, the payment, the change, and the tip all travel on a tray. Cash registers are either nonexistent or inconspicuous. Credit cards increasingly facilitate a type of billing not unlike the doctor's. Mints, matches, and endless cups of coffee are offered to the "guests," who upon departure are likely to exchange thanks with their "host." (The owner of the exclusive shop may summon his subordinate to take the customer's money and wrap his parcel while he continues to chat with him.)

The care with which money is handled in these instances has many parallels where the sacred and profane are thought to be mixed. Obvious examples are contributions to the collection plate in church and the groom's or best man's anxiety about "slipping" the clergyman money (in an envelope, naturally) after the wedding. The latter is likely to be accompanied by the giver's profuse thanks, which are designed to convey the thought that the money hardly begins to compensate for the service rendered.

As an arch-symbol of the profane, money arouses a sense of incongruity and hence discomfort, not only when it accompanies the ideal of service but also when the relations involved are felt to be personal. Tipping provides some excellent examples of this combination.

Formally, even the most customary tips imply a recognition of special service—something personal beyond the minimal requirements of duty. That this occasions at least mild discomfort is evident from the rule that tips should be both given and received unobtrusively.

Tipping is also complicated by questions of status.[5] Our sense of status difference tells us when we may tip, so that it seems easier to tip the young boy who delivers our newspaper or medicine than the mature or elderly man. Should one tip the barber who owns his establishment, for example, or the waiter or cab driver who happens to be one's friend or, perhaps more interestingly, the father of a friend? In her column of advice, Amy Vanderbilt cites some of the rules.

GIFTS FOR NURSES

Q: I do shopping for an elderly lady in a nursing home. I have a most difficult time finding Christmas gifts for her to give to people I don't even know. It is especially difficult with the nurses, for there are quite a number of them and she cannot spend a large amount of money on any one. I have suggested an attractive card with a bill enclosed, but have been told that this is socially wrong. Perhaps it is, but these days one tries to be somewhat sensible, and it seems to me the nurses would far rather have the money to spend as they like, or perhaps to combine with similar gifts.

A: I think your suggestion is excellent. One does not tip nurses; this is an offense to their professional standing and is frowned upon by their professional societies. However, a Christmas gift of money is not really a tip, and would be much more acceptable than some little gadget you choose without knowing the preference of the person to receive it. Money gifts at Christmas are a little "iffy." Money may certainly be given to employees; children love getting it; and sometimes it is the best gift for a relative who can really use it. But if there is any chance that offense might be taken, it is safer to send a gift certificate, or, of course, a gift itself.[6]

Thus, the higher the status of the recipient, the more discreet and doubtful tipping becomes until it passes through this zone of mounting uncertainty into one in which tips begin to give way to gifts.

---

5 Status here also refers to how those involved perceive it.
6 *Ladies' Home Journal,* November, 1966.

Thus, another major consideration affects the transmission of money —the question of status. As Amy Vanderbilt's advice indicates, sentiment generally favors the flow of money down the status hierarchy. This becomes especially apparent when the direction of the flow is reversed. The latter is made tolerable only by the feeling that something of immeasurably greater value has descended in return. The thanks which the doctor and clergyman receive may testify to the "inequality" of this exchange, but, as we have seen, they do not completely erase its "indignity." Not too distant parallels are the feelings aroused when wives support husbands and children parents.

Beliefs about personal relations raise problems similar to those which stem from the ideal of service and considerations of status. All three are closely connected—the first two because one's friends and relatives are supposed to have one's interest close at heart, and the last two because the protective and caring role of superiors often involves the downward flow of money. Combined, they create ticklish problems.

All three may deter the doctor from charging his friends, relatives, colleagues, and other professionals. Other combinations create those familiar dilemmas of everyday life in which we wonder how to repay the neighbor who has spent considerable time repairing our car or money entertaining our children or, in general, those whose "generous" gifts, gestures or favors we feel unable to reciprocate.

The most troublesome cases, of course, are when we dare not assume which of the two—friendship or business—was the other's main motive. If we do not offer payment, will he think that the love of money led us to take advantage of him in the name of friendship? On the other hand, will offering it give offense by implying that he acted out of mercenary rather than friendly motives or that we are treating the "favor" of an equal as the work of an employee?

A common way in which people try to get around the difficulty of deciding between money and thanks is by giving gifts. The symbolism and understandings surrounding gifts cleanse and transform the money and make it acceptable.

Among the considerations, therefore, that restrict or at least direct the flow of money are fear of ostentation, the ideal of service, the view of the relation as personal, and concern about status. Its alleged power to contaminate these ideals is what makes money "dirty."[7]

The connection between these ideals and the "cleanliness" of money shows up clearly in what was once called charity and is now called philanthropy. Charity, of course, is a classic virtue. But "it is better to give than to receive" not only because giving is considered morally ennobling, to say noth-

---

[7] The late Clint Murchison, one of the world's wealthiest men, is reported to have said, "Money is like manure. When you stack it up it stinks, but when you spread it around it makes things grow." *Time,* June 27, 1969, p. 62.

ing of socially elevating, and, it is sometimes darkly hinted, a means of cleansing the money, but also because receiving charity is so often seen as humiliating and debasing.

Thus, the status gap between giver and recipient which, in the case of the buyer and seller, was so narrow as to be barely discernible grows in the measure that the giver of money is defined as receiving less than an equivalent return. This principle extends beyond money payments, as the expressions of gratitude to the doctor and clergyman indicate. The moral superiority of giving to receiving thus seems to run through social relations in general. (The reverse is equally true—the greater the status difference the less the giver is expected to receive in return.)

This principle becomes clearly apparent as we move out towards the ends of the continuum where God, in his majesty and goodness, gives everything of value to man, who is so base and insignificant that he can offer only gratitude, praise, and promises of obedience in return. On the purely human level one of the lowest places is occupied by the beggar, particularly the one who, in asking for himself, does not make even the gesture of offering pencils or a tune in return. In seeking "something for nothing" he upsets the people he approaches because whether they give or not, they feel put in the position of having to degrade him so openly.

This explains why the beggar and the priest have figured so largely in religious symbolism. The eastern religions have tended to combine the two roles, but in the Christian imagery they have represented mutually dependent polar opposites. The beggar, whose social position is so base, seeks only to satisfy his material wants and can offer nothing in return, while the priest, God's representative, out of compassion for the beggar gives him all that he has.

The sacred office of the priest offers our final reminder of the "contaminating" effect of money. To enter totally into the service of God, a man must renounce forever the "corrupting" attractions of money and sex. These similar images of money and sex are no coincidence. Both are seen as sources of enormous pleasure and thus as among the most powerful of motives but also as the essence of the profane or dirty. As we have seen, this combination restricts their expression with many barriers, legal and moral.

The "low" character of these alleged motives leads, of course, to denials of their importance, at least in one's own behavior. The strength of these disavowals varies, of course, with the spirit of the times. It is therefore curious that the twentieth century should have been so shaken by the "discoveries" by two nineteenth century, middle European Jews—Marx and Freud—that these hidden motives are what makes the world turn.

20

S. Frank Miyamoto

SELF, MOTIVATION, AND SYMBOLIC INTERACTIONIST THEORY

Current theoretical interest in social psychology is directed mainly at three orientations: balance theory, exchange theory, and symbolic interactionist theory. Of these three, the symbolic interactionist view is the oldest, dating back as it does to George H. Mead, but paradoxically it is also the one that remains least developed as a systematic theory. That is, it has not received the kind of systematic development that Leon Festinger has given to balance theory[1] or that George Homans, and J. W. Thibaut and H. H. Kelley, have given to exchange theory.[2]

---

[1] Leon Festinger, *A Theory of Cognitive Dissonance* (Evanston: Row, Peterson and Company, 1957).

[2] George C. Homans, *Social Behavior: Its Elementary Forms* (New York: Harcourt, Brace and World, Inc., 1961); and J. W. Thibaut and H. H. Kelley, *The Social Psychology of Groups* (New York: John Wiley and Sons, Inc., 1959).

The usefulness of a theory ultimately depends upon systematization —basic propositions need to be articulated and their interrelations specified—and because this requirement is widely recognized, there generally is pressure toward formalizing any approach that lays claim to a theoretical function. Why then has symbolic interactionism, the oldest of the current views in social psychology, remained relatively poorly systematized? Tentative efforts in the direction have not been lacking, for example in the works of Leonard Cottrell and Arnold Rose.[3] But nothing has appeared in symbolic interactionism since Mead that has mobilized research as have the works mentioned above for the other points of view.

One important reason for its slower development is its greater complexity. Mead's social psychology, which still remains the fount of ideas for symbolic interactionists, was an effort to elucidate how significant features of society and the social process become incorporated into the behavior of interacting individuals, a larger undertaking than that of most social psychological theorists. Concepts such as the self and other, roles, taking the role of another, communication, and organized social attitudes were necessary for Mead's account, but they have proved complex and difficult to handle in systematic theorizing.

A second difficulty in systematizing symbolic interactionist theory, I believe, is its lack of a relatively explicit or uncomplex conception of motivation. The central thesis of my article, in fact, is the argument that a relatively clear motivational conception is necessary as the foundation of any systematic social psychological theory which would be understandable to present-day students, but that such a motivational conception has not been developed in symbolic interactionism. My further purpose is to outline a motivational scheme appropriate to symbolic interactionism and to show that the self provides a suitable focus for such a scheme.

Before proceeding to these arguments, however, it is of interest to consider why symbolic interactionism has persisted as a major orientation despite its weak integration. The viability of the approach appears to lie in its nice fit with sociological facts; no other theory provides so admirable a social psychological basis for analyzing the problems of social organization or the processes of interpersonal relations and collective behavior. That the adherents of the view are predominantly sociologists is no accident. Not the least of other reasons for persistence is the strong influence that Herbert Blumer has exerted in propagating the view among successive generations of graduate students. His success in the propagation, of course, in part reflects

---

[3] L. S. Cottrell, "Analysis of Situational Fields in Social Psychology," *American Sociological Review,* VII (1942), 370–82; and Arnold M. Rose, "A Systematic Summary of Symbolic Interaction Theory," *Human Behavior and Social Processes: An Interactionist Approach* (Boston: Houghton Mifflin Company, 1962), pp. 3–19.

the validity of the orientation. But, had he lacked the ability to persuade students of its validity and potentiality, the theory very likely would have far fewer advocates today than it has.

Considering Blumer's central role in propounding and developing symbolic interactionism, we need to ask what his views are regarding its systematization. The answer, I believe, is that he has eschewed the kind of systematization I am proposing; his efforts have been directed toward a different theoretical objective. As early as his 1931 article, "Science Without Concepts," he defined the first task of science and of theory construction as one of establishing concepts which are faithful to the significant features of the empirical world and relevant to the given science.[4] Indeed, he has devoted most of his lifetime to this purpose. At the same time, he makes it clear that premature efforts at systematization with concepts bearing poor correspondence with empirical facts will yield mistaken interpretations of the social world and produce mischievous consequences.

I find no grounds for disagreement with Blumer on his basic position. The difference between us is my greater readiness to utilize the existing conceptual tools, as crude as they may be, to see what theoretical structure may be made with them. The basic ideas employed here are not alien to his views—in fact, many are drawn directly from his lectures and writings. But the way in which they are drawn together may be unlike his mode of thought. One justification for my effort is that some symbolic interactionists are now seeking to systematize the theory and, in view of these efforts, it seems desirable to offer some guidelines for the development of a useful theory. The value of Blumer's persistent emphasis on maintaining correspondence between concepts and the experiential world is that no serious student of Blumer's can set sail on a variant tack without awareness of the hidden shoals which may lie across his chosen course.

What follows is not the presentation of a systematic theory, but a discussion of one guideline for such a development.

Theories of Motivation

To develop the argument that a relatively clear, or perhaps I should say simple, motivational conception is necessary as the foundation of any systematic social psychological theory, we need first to explicate the main views regarding motivation. This is no simple task, for no other concept in social psychology has given rise to more disagreements concerning its referents and meaning. Some authors have even repudiated it as useful or

---

[4] Herbert Blumer, "Science Without Concepts," *The American Journal of Sociology,* **XXXVI** (1931), 515–33.

necessary for psychological theorizing. Despite its difficulties, the concept of motivation in one or another form keeps reappearing. I shall later try to explain its persistence, but first it will be useful to consider the principal usages which occur.

Defined in its most inclusive sense, motivation may be regarded as referring to: (1) a state of the organism that energizes action, (2) that which facilitates responses, (3) that which gives direction to action, and (4) that which gives intensity and persistence to the directed action.[5] The variations of usage have resulted largely from the different emphases given to these components and also the different ways in which the components are conceived. The instinct theorists, for example, emphasized the first component, conceived as biologically structured states which are energized by particular stimuli. By emphasizing the dominance of the biological states, they minimized the need to analyze the remaining components of motivation. Freudian theory adopted a similar conception but emphasized the conflicts of instincts which occur, and used the other components to explain the resolutions of conflicts which individuals adopt. Drive theory likewise bears a similarity to instinct theory, as various writers have noted, but in drive theory the activating states of the organism are defined narrowly as stemming from tissue deficits. Their occurrences are inferred from observations on the second and fourth components. The direction and patterning of behavior, the third component, is treated under a separate learning theory. The homeostatic model of motivation identifies the energizer of action as a state of imbalance, conceived as organic disequilibria in the original conception but including psychological disequilibria in later formulations. Action is then seen as moving toward the reestablishment of equilibrium.

The foregoing scarcely does justice to the great variety of motivational conceptions which exist, but it may suffice to suggest the features of individual behavior which tend to be emphasized in motivational schemes. In social psychology, where the behaviors under observation are generally more complex than in psychological studies, the concept of motivation is employed to account primarily for the directionality of behavior, the other features of motivation being mainly assumed. Moreover, the directions of action attended to are not so much the detailed directions in an action stream, but the longer segments of the stream for which a persistent directional flow can be identified.

The argument that motivational conceptions play an important part in systematic social psychological theorizing may be illustrated for the cases of balance theory and exchange theory. Cognitive dissonance theory, or balance theory as it is more generally called, obviously has a kinship to

---

5 C. N. Cofer and M. H. Appley, *Motivation: Theory and Research* (New York: John Wiley and Sons, Inc., 1967), pp. 7–17.

the homeostatic model of motivation. In Festinger's treatment of cognitive dissonance, he is quite explicit about the motivational role of dissonance. He declares, "The existence of dissonance, being psychologically uncomfortable, will motivate the person to try to reduce the dissonance and achieve consonance."[6] Similarly, Theodore M. Newcomb speaks of a strain toward symmetry or toward equilibrium. And Fritz Heider, who gives rather careful consideration to contrary evidence, also concludes that there exists a strong tendency of behavior toward balanced states and unit formation.[7] In all these views, states of imbalance or dissonance are considered to be tension inducing, and the removal of imbalance as tension reducing. The point of interest for the present discussion is that the assumption of the tendency or motive toward balanced states is crucial to the theory, for lacking the assumption, there is no balance theory that can be stated.

Exchange theory is no less firmly grounded in a motivational conception of human behavior, for its basic principle is that the individual over the long run will tend to behave so as to maximize the rewards he receives from others and to minimize costs. Thus, the theory assumes directionality of behavior, a movement toward rewards and away from costs.

Homans, a chief exponent of exchange theory, would deny that a motivitional theory is required, and B.F. Skinner, from whom Homans draws, makes the denial explicit. Skinner, who employs the operational term *reinforcement* in place of *reward,* regards a positive reinforcer as a stimulus, following a behavior, that tends to strengthen the behavior, and a negative reinforcer as one which weakens the behavior. The problem of reinforcers for Skinner is thus the strictly empirical one of determining the conditions associated with stimuli which strengthen or weaken behavior. Motivational concepts are regarded as simply verbal shorthands for referring to the conditions associated with reinforcing effects.[8]

Nevertheless, if these authors are seeking a general theory of behavior, especially of human behavior, it seems necessary that they develop a theoretical conception that explains rewards and reinforcers. That is, in view of the differential effects which reinforcers may have in different situations, valid generalizations about behaviors occurring in these situations would require, it seems to me, a theory about reinforcers. Such a theory, in our terms, would constitute a theory of motivation.

Although an elaborated theory of motivation is lacking in current exchange theory, an elemental theory of motivation is nevertheless very much present. The entire exchange scheme is built upon the assumption of direc-

---

[6] Festinger, *op. cit.,* p. 3.

[7] Theodore M. Newcomb, "An Approach to the Study of Communicative Acts," *Psychological Review,* LX (1953), 393–404; and Fritz Heider, *The Psychology of Interpersonal Relations* (New York: John Wiley and Sons, Inc., 1958), pp. 176–212.

[8] Cofer and Appley, *op. cit.,* pp. 514–18.

tionality in behavior, a movement toward rewards and away from costs. As I remarked about balance theory, if this assumption were lacking, an understandable exchange theory could not be stated.

By contrast, symbolic interactionism adheres to no such simple assumptions about motivation—has no simple statement regarding the direction of action—as those adopted in balance theory or exchange theory. Its underlying theme regarding motivation was stated long ago by John Dewey in his celebrated paper, "The Reflect Arc Concept in Psychology."[9] Dewey opposed the view of the reflex-arc advocates that the stimulus is the beginning of action. He argued rather that the organism is an active organism, the activity is already there and requires no explanation, and the problem of the stimulus concerns the way in which it redirects an ongoing action and not how it starts a line of action. Mead accepted a more formal view of action than Dewey. Mead conceived of the action stream as divisible in the abstract into acts, in which the act is seen as beginning with motivation and ending with the consummatory response; but his use of the term *impulse* to describe motivation—a term signifying a general tendency of action more than a specific direction—reflected his agreement with Dewey's emphasis on the fact of activity rather than on the specificity in the direction of action.[10] A lengthy account would be required to show how this nondirectional conception of motivation shaped the formulation of the symbolic interactionist scheme, and how, as a result, later symbolic interactionists have come to interpret the idea of motivation in the manner that they do. It suffices here to say that in symbolic interactionist theorizing, the nondirectional assumption regarding impulse still tends to be maintained.

Earlier I asked why the concept of motivation persists in the face of its difficulties. The answer, I believe, is that behavior cannot be well understood unless its underlying motivation, its directional tendency, is defined. D. O. Hebb and W. R. Thompson have described the difficulty experienced in understanding animal behavior from straight descriptive accounts of behavior until an overlay of motivational conceptions was introduced, and they remark on the danger involved in handling chimpanzees without the use of motivational conceptions.[11] Similarly, Heider and Simmel report, concerning a study of perceptions of moving geometrical figures, that subjects were unable to make sense of the movements until an anthropomorphic interpretation of motives was imputed to the figures.[12] These difficulties of

---

[9] John Dewey, "The Reflect Arc Concept in Psychology," *Psychological Review,* III (1896), 357–70.

[10] George Herbert Mead, *The Philosophy of the Act,* ed. Charles W. Morris (Chicago: University of Chicago Press, 1938), pp. 3–25.

[11] D. O. Hebb and W. R. Thompson, "The Social Significance of Animal Studies," in *Handbook of Social Psychology,* ed. Gardner Lindzey (Reading, Mass.: Addison-Wesley Publishing Co., Inc., 1954), Vol. I, esp., pp. 543–52.

[12] Heider, *op. cit.,* pp. 31–35.

understanding behavior *qua* behavior are surely no less true of the human case as well.

Because the primary purpose of any social psychological theory is to explain human behavior, a motivational conception must be interwoven into its fabric if the theory is to be an understandable one. Indeed, there are good grounds for arguing that every social psychological proposition that illuminates human behavior has an explicit or implicit motivational conception as its underpinning. Erving Goffman's *Presentation of Self in Everyday Life,* for example—which many students agree is a highly illuminating account of human behavior—would lose much of its significance for a reader who approached it with total ignorance of human motives. The account is illuminating to the extent that the reader assumes certain directional tendencies in human behavior, for example, the tendency of individuals to seek social approval of others or to command their respect.[13]

If the foregoing argument holds, it follows that any systematic social psychological theory that may be attempted with our present state of knowledge requires, as a basic premise underlying the theory, some scheme that specifies a general direction or directions of behavior. Such a scheme, by my definition, constitutes a motivational conception. I have tried to show that a motivational conception that serves as an integrating premise is to be found in both balance theory and exchange theory. And I have argued that the lack of an explicit motivational conception in symbolic interactionist theory has been a major sources of difficulty in the attempts to systematize this theory.

In the following sections, an attempt is made to outline a motivational scheme that may serve as the major premise for any effort to systematize symbolic interactionist theory. The conception focuses on the self as the source of motives appropriate to the latter point of view.

The Self

I shall mean by the self what George H. Mead meant by it. Mead declared, "The self has the characteristic that it is an object to itself," and added that it has the unique quality of "that which can be both subject and object. This type of object is essentially different from other objects."[14] Operationalized, the self might be defined as the verbal statements which an individual may offer regarding his own person, except that the definition fails to stress the feature that Mead emphasizes—that the self as object is

---

13 Erving Goffman, *The Presentation of Self in Everday Life* (New York: Doubleday & Company, Inc., 1959).

14 George H. Mead, *Mind, Self and Society,* ed. Charles W. Morris (Chicago: The University of Chicago Press, 1934), pp. 136ff.

possible only because of man's capacity to take the point of view of others with respect to himself. So conceived, the self is a product of social experience.

The last point requires some elaboration. When a person sees himself as kind or honest, or when he defines himself as a teacher in relation to students, the social view that enters into self-definition is evident. On the other hand, when an individual sees himself as being hungry, or having a headache, or having a radio receiver in his abdomen, it is not clear that the social view of self is involved, since these events may not be observable to others. Nevertheless, that the self is treated as object even in these situations is apparent, for example, from the manner in which a patient reports such experiences to a doctor. And, it should be noted, the social view enters via language, for in articulating these wholly subjective experiences the individual symbolizes them in ways understandable within the linguistic community and sees them in the terms of that community.

Special attention is called to the relationship between body phenomena and the self because motivational theories usually incorporate a biological component in motivation, and the foregoing is intended to suggest how bodily processes enter into a self theory. Body and self are not the same thing, as Mead argued, but body images play a part in self images.

Tamotsu Shibutani, in "A Cybernetic Approach to Motivation," has foreshadowed the scheme of motivation which I wish to elaborate, except that I propose to push his line of thinking beyond his point of closure. He begins with the assumption that motivation is defined by that which determines the direction of behavior. He then argues that behavioral direction in human beings is determined by a typical cybernetic pattern: the individual acts in response to an impluse; a feedback response to the action by the environment or other persons occurs; the individual interprets the feedback, and the interpretation becomes a guide for adjusting further actions. The direction of action, or motivation, is thus "something that is constructed in a succession of self-correcting adjustments to life conditions."[15] This is a minimal sketch of Shibutani's view, but it suffices for the present purpose. Although Shibutani is not explicit on this point, the servomechanism in this cybernetic process must be the self. And to understand how the self guides the line of action, it is necessary to indicate the features of the feedback information to which the self is particularly sensitive, that is, indicate to what criterion or criteria the self as servomechanism is adjusted. The thermostat as a servomechanism is adjusted to temperature variations; the governor on an engine, to variations of velocity. To what environmental changes or responses is the self adjusted?

---

15 Tamotsu Shibutani, "A Cybernetic Approach to Motivation," in *Modern Systems Research for the Behavioral Scientist,* ed. Walter Buckley (Chicago: Aldine Publishing Company, 1968), pp. 330–36.

It may be that the self is so constructed that it is responsive to infinitely variable features of feedback responses, and therefore is infinitely variable in its response. But if so, the cybernetic model of human behavior is not helpful in predicting or explaining the directions of behavior, since the direction will be infinitely variable. There is, however, a fair amount of predictability about the directions of human behavior. To the extent that directions of behavior are determinable, and assuming also that the cybernetic conception of motivation is valid, it should be possible to specify criteria to which the self as servomechanism is adjusted.

The singular quality of the self that Mead identified is its capacity to be an object to itself. What is true of other objects, therefore, should tend also to be true of self as object. In any action with respect to an object, as Talcott Parsons and Edward Shils have stated, a person is likely to assume one of three possible orientations: evaluative, cognitive, or affective.[16] Thus, the individual's orientation toward the self is likely to fall into one of these three modes.

In addition, the actor as an object is likely to be perceived in one or another of different perceptual settings. Three such settings typical for socialized individuals are: role, task, and nonrole nontask settings. A minister rendering a Sunday service would tend to see himself in a role setting; when preparing his sermon, he would see himself in a task setting; and when regarding himself as a person who is kind or unkind, jolly or morose, tall or short, he may no longer see himself in either a role or a task but as an object with attributes. Clearly, the three orientations overlap with each

TABLE 1

PERCEPTIONS OF SELF AS OBJECT,
BY THREE MODES OF ORIENTATION AND IN THREE PERCEPTUAL SETTINGS

Modes of orientation toward self	*Perceptual settings of self as object*		
	Attribute object	*Task object*	*Role object*
Evaluative	Good or bad qualities	Good or bad task performance	Good or bad role performance
Cognitive	Definable or nondefinable qualities	Definable or nondefinable task activity	Definable or nondefinable role
Affective	Gratifying or nongratifying qualities	Gratifying or nongratifying task activity	Gratifying or nongratifying role performance

16 Talcott Parsons and Edward A. Shils, eds., *Toward a General Theory of Action* (Cambridge, Mass.: Harvard University Press, 1951), pp. 4–6 and 53–76.

other, as do the three perceptual settings. But there tends to be a dominance of one orientation or setting, and in any case there is analytical advantage in distinguishing among them. If the three orientations and three perceptual settings are shown as a matrix, as in Table 1, the resulting pattern of cells suggests the different ways in which the self may be perceived.

Mead also emphasized that the self as object is essentially different from other objects. The essential difference to which he referred is that because the person is both subject and object, the self as perceived object has a capacity to respond directly to the assessment made by self as perceiver. It should also be noted that self as perceiver has the capacity of viewing an object from his own perspective or that of others and that these alternative perspectives also apply to self-perceptions. Finally, the process of perceiving self and responding to self-perceptions is obviously a very complex one. But it is a most thoroughly practiced skill, for no other action pattern is more continuously employed by social beings from infancy on. Indeed, it seems not too far-fetched to suggest that the self is the primary mechanism linking the person to his environment and that it is, as such, the fundamental mechanism determining his survival in that environment.

Consider how an individual survives. First, he must avoid those conditions which are biologically harmful and seek those which tend to perpetuate him as a living organism. Second, most of the conditions for survival in the first sense depend on the support he receives from other human beings, and the latter in turn depends on how well he fits into the matrix of group relations. Finally, perhaps because of the adaptations made to the second requirement, as a socialized being he finds that isolation from social contact, entirely apart from its effect on his biological survival, may be threatening to his survival as a psychic being. The thrust of our argument is that the survival of the human organism as a social, and therefore also a biological, being depends on his ability to fit into some set of social relations. And how well he fits will be registered for the individual by whether he can see himself as desirable, cognitively definable, and gratifying. It remains to explain how these modes of orientation toward self may become motivational for the individual.

The evaluative orientation implies that an object is being perceived as desirable or undesirable. In the economics of social relations, it is apparent that persons who are considered desirable are drawn into groups, while those not so regarded are ignored or rejected. Inasmuch as membership in groups is important to human beings, we conclude that an individual will wish to have others see him as desirable. Assuming that the self is a servomechanism for testing environmental responses to one's behavior, we further conclude that the individual is likely to behave in such a manner as to maximize social approval of self and minimize disapproval. This principle, that people desire approval of self in the eyes of others, is one of the oldest motivational notions in social psychology, and no claim is made that anything very new or profound has been offered. If anything new is added, it lies in the fact that the principle is stated within a more general analysis of self processes.

Two caveats must be stated, for it is not clear that the principle holds consistently. First, persons do not demand a uniformly favorable view of all aspects of self. One must admit to many shortcomings—a scholar may not be a good social conversationalist or athlete, a sociologist may not be much of a mathematician. There is no advantage in seeking a favorable assessment of one's known weaknesses. But one needs to see oneself as socially desirable in some respects, and the latter are the aspects regarding which the individual seeks to maximize social approval and minimize disapproval. Moreover, the individual on the whole selects for his main areas of activity those where he will show to best advantage, and this too is consistent with the idea of maximizing social approval.

A second contradiction of the principle occurs among people who act in ways which are calculated to arouse a maximum of social disapproval and who may even take pleasure in flaunting their socially disapproved behavior. This is often true of rebels, reformers, criminals, Bohemians, and other deviants. It will be noted, however, that deviants generally are far from being insensitive to social disapproval, that they sustain their self-esteem by selecting reference groups which approve of their behavior. One needs to see oneself as approvable in the eyes of some significant others, and the evaluations of self by all others may then be a matter of indifference. In the last analysis, it is only the psychopath, the idiot, and the utterly degraded who are unresponsive to evaluative social attitudes.

The evaluative orientation toward self is only one possible mode; there is also the cognitive view of self. The cognitive orientation implies a concern to define the object, understand it, or determine its meaning. Such a concern may exist entirely apart from an evaluative one. All behavioral enactments which occur in a social matrix require that the individual assume a cognitive orientation toward self, that he identify the part within the social relational pattern which the self is to play. The necessity of such self-knowledge for all group relations tends to make it motivational in human behavior. We assert, therefore, that an individual tends so to behave as to maximize meaningfulness of his relations with others and minimize meaninglessness of self. The meaning of an object arises from the experiences with it, especially from experiences with it as a mediating object within a stream of goal-directed action. The individual has a meaningful self, then, when he perceives that he fulfills a useful function in the goal-directed actions of a group, provided, of course, that he accepts his position and the goals of the group.

The so-called identity problems are more problems of cognitive than of evaluative orientation toward self. The concerns of the person faced with the problem are related to such questions as who am I, what is my place in the group or society, or what useful function do I serve, and have less to do with societal approval or disapproval of him. The youths of our times who are said to suffer an identity confusion seemingly have no difficulty recognizing that conformance to middle class norms would produce a socially approvable self. But insofar as they reject the middle class goals, the roles involved in such goal pursuit tend to be viewed as meaningless. The rejection of existing roles leads to the cognitive problem of defining new roles which have functional relevance in the ongoing social process. The attraction of the hippie movement to many youths appears to lie precisely in the sense of ennui associated with middle class roles and the potential offered by the movement for involvement in more meaningful self roles. The student revolts against the Establishment reflect a similar rejection of institutional goals and reflect also collective efforts to create new action goals and new identities which would yield greater meaning for selves.

Cognition of an object is essential for its control. Hence, the individual who is unable to define an appropriate place for himself in the social process is in general unable to control the effectiveness of his own actions, and there follows that sense of powerlessness that has been associated with the concepts of alienation and anomie.

Finally, human beings have a capacity for assuming an affective orientation toward the self. This orientation is less clear than the other two; yet it seems obvious that one can have affective responses to oneself. For example, one is pleased with oneself or displeased; one feels good about self or the contrary; or one becomes angry at self or generates an abnormal love of self. To simplify the variety of self-orientations which may be held, we shall borrow an idea from Harry Stack Sullivan and say that these affective orientations may vary between absolute euphoria and absolute dysphoria.[17] The affective orientation is motivational to the extent that individuals seek euphoric rather than dysphoric orientations toward self.

How the affective orientation toward self influences an individual's motive patterns is particularly well illustrated, it seems to me, in Sullivan's analysis of the uncanny emotions—awe, dread, loathing, and horror—and their function in the development of dissociative processes. Sullivan finds that parents and other adult figures sometimes respond to a child's behavior with severe censorship and produce in the child the intense anxiety associated with the uncanny emotions. By an empathic process, the child learns to regard certain instances of his own behavior spontaneously with dread, loathing, or horror. To avoid the extremely unpleasant feelings which occur whenever the impulse toward the condemned behavior is aroused, the individual, through a process of selective inattention, learns to disclaim the

---

[17] Harry Stack Sullivan, *The Interpersonal Theory of Psychiatry* (New York: W. W. Norton and Company, Inc., 1953), pp. 34–45.

impulse as a part of himself—shunts it into a "not me"—and this Sullivan believes is the origin of the dissociative processes. The example clearly illustrates the operation of an affective orientation toward self and offers an extreme case of the effect of this self view on the individual's direction of action. It is particularly worth noting that Sullivan distinguishes between the source of the "not me" and that of the "good me" and the "bad me," which are evaluative self-conceptions. The evaluative conceptions occur at a cognized and therefore analyzable level, but the "not me" is attributed to a level of feelings (parataxic level) that is more difficult to apprehend.

In Table 1, not only the modes of orientation toward self but also the perceptual settings of self as object were distinguished. The reason for considering the latter is that the criteria for judging the self under the evaluative, cognitive, and affective modes vary for the different settings. In the role setting, the criteria for judging self are in general the institutionalized expectations adhering to the role; evaluative judgments of good or bad role performance or cognitive judgments as to what the role entails would be made with reference to the institutionalized expectations. In the task setting, institutionalized criteria may again apply, to be sure. But because task performances tend to vary greatly even within given institutional settings, other more general criteria of effectiveness, such as the pragmatic one of whether an outcome is useful or has an intended effect, tend to predominate over institutionalized criteria. Finally, it is postulated that the self may be viewed in a nonrole and nontask setting, simply as an attribute object. The criteria employed in the latter situation are likely to be general societal categories for assessing human objects, independent of specific roles and tasks in which an individual may engage. The affective orientation, of course, may apply to any of the three perceptual settings and be registered by the euphoric or dysphoric affect that are called forth.

In the foregoing, the criteria for judging self have been emphasized because, in a view of self as servomechanism, the criteria must be regarded as the basic instrument necessary for the functioning of the mechanism. Given a criterion for self-assessment in a particular perceptual setting and particular mode of orientation, the self may serve as a regulator of action to move it along a specified course.

The Scheme of Motivation and Symbolic Interactionist Theory

The idea of multiple criteria to which the self is sensitive, although a complicating feature for a theory of motivation, appears to me an advance over previous formulations of motivation related to the self. The motive of self-esteem, for example, has been cogently urged by earlier writers. Yet this emphasis by itself strikes one as offering a truncated view of human motivations. One can readily think of situations where the concern for social approval recedes in significance in comparison to the concern for self-identity or for self-gratification. Contrariwise, the writers who have urged self-actualization as the dominant motive of man appear to confound the three modes of orientation toward the self which we have distinguished, and by so doing have derived a theory that is unnecessarily ambiguous. The scheme of multiple criteria to which the self is responsive, however, will be useful only if the conditions are specified under which one or another criterion of self-assessment, and therefore regulation of behavior in certain directions, will be employed. A brief attempt is made below to suggest some of these conditions.

Because human beings depend on the good will of others for their well being, the evaluative orientation toward the self tends to be ubiquitous. The need to see oneself as favorably viewed by others is generally the most critical of the self-orientations. An evaluative orientation, however, is relevant only where values are defined or are definable, and where they are shared between an actor and others. For example, the problem of self-esteem appears to have been much more critical in the traditional oriental societies of China and Japan, where criteria of proper personal behavior were well defined and firmly established, than in such a society as ours in which the criteria are much more variable. In addition, the evaluative orientation is important mainly when dealing with others whose value judgments of self are perceived as having significant consequences. When the consequences appear to be indifferent or unpredictable, as in a crowd, the evaluative mode of orientation tends to diminish in function.

The cognitive orientation toward self may be expected to dominate when one's position in social relations or the appropriate line of action are in any degree problematic. Such a condition would prevail when an action cannot be executed in a habitual or perfunctory manner. This tends to be true for most complex task performances. The condition also pertains when structured patterns of relations or of action become undermined, and the individual therefore feels the need to redefine his position or function. The unstructuring of patterned relations implies the unstructuring of value systems as well, and these conditions may be expected to produce a displacement from evaluative to cognitive concerns about the self.

Finally, the affective orientation toward self—which, like the other two orientations, is always in some degree present—would tend to become prominent when feeling states are regarded as offering a better guide of action than evaluations or cognitions. The state of being in love has long been seen as a situation in which an individual is prone to assess himself by the affect which the self-object arouses. Romanticists in general are perhaps especially disposed to this orientation toward the self. Also, there may be grounds for hypothesizing that when individuals lack the means for assessing themselves evaluatively or cognitively—as may be the case for those living in a time of revolutionary changes or for those suffering a schizophrenic attack—affect tends to serve as the primary guide of action in the absence of better criteria by which to judge action. The novel forms of behavior which are found in hippie culture are perhaps a reflection of conditions which tend to promote an affective orientation toward the self.

A properly integrated theory of motivation of the kind I am proposing would require a much more careful and extensive specification than I have been able to essay of the conditions under which one or another mode of orientation would tend to be called out. It would be necessary, also, to show how the modes of orientation would be differentiated for the different perceptual settings, a task I shall not even attempt here. And because all three modes of orientation toward the self tend in some degree to function in all situations, and the perceptual settings too tend to overlap, most important is the need to show how the different criteria in our nine-celled matrix are related to each other. As crude as this formulation remains, however, it seems to me to have been sufficiently advanced to serve as a basis for formalizing symbolic interactionist theory, which it will be remembered was my original concern.

There is currently evidence of interest in formalizing role theory, as a subdivision of symbolic interactionist theory. If my earlier argument has substance, a systematic role theory is unlikely to be developed successfully unless a suitable motivational scheme is introduced; but the formulation offered above seems suitable to such a purpose. Referring to the matrix of Table 1, role theory would confine itself to the third column of the table where the self is viewed as a role object. A thoroughgoing development of the theory would then consider how role behavior would vary when self-esteem, self-identity, or self-gratification, respectively, are the dominant motives. Alternatively, one could choose to limit the scope of the role theory and consider only the evaluative mode of orientation toward self and its effect on role behavior. In that case only the motivational criteria appearing in the upper right-hand cell of the matrix would need to be considered.

A grand theory of symbolic interactionism would require a step by step canvassing of expected behavior patterns for each of the motivational conditions I have specified. Or it would require the development of a more generalized and hence more parsimonious motivational scheme, appropriate to symbolic interactionism, than I have been able to develop. In the meantime, however, there is an advantage in proceeding with intermediate goals of theory construction, that is, with efforts at systematizing symbolic interactionist theory when only one of the modes of orientation and its accompanying motive patterns are postulated, or when only one of the perceptual settings is considered for examination.

21

David N. Solomon

ROLE AND SELF CONCEPTION: ADAPTATION AND CHANGE IN OCCUPATIONS

In the sociology of occupations there have been two apparently competing approaches. Some studies in the field emphasize structural phenomena in explaining behavior in occupational roles—role sets, normative orientations, and the like. In other studies, more attention is paid to social psychological aspects—self-conception and the internalization of norms, for example, as explanations of behavior in occupational roles. The notion of role, of course, enables one to tie together these two strands, but this is seldom done.

In studying a number of occupations I have myself moved back and forth between these two approaches. This paper consists of summaries of four pieces of research which exemplify the use of social structural and social psychological approaches, and the last of which attempts to integrate the two approaches. In my study of physicians in Chicago, I was mainly interested in structural phenomena. The infantry recruit studies, which followed, emphasized the social psychological aspect of becoming a soldier. The study of scientists in industry started with assumptions about the self-conceptions of scientists but ended with the view that structural features, that is, the roles they were playing, were the more important aspect. Finally, the study of Canadian officers in peace-keeping roles led to a consideration of the way in which changes in roles and self-conception go hand in hand as aspects of much broader processes of social change.

Chicago Physicians

The primary concern of this study was to describe medical practice in the different social worlds of medicine which were shown to exist in Chicago.[1] The medical community, reflecting the social structure of the community at large, is segmented along ethnic-religious lines, and each ethnic segment is stratified along class lines. In the Protestant sector were a few hospitals at the top of the pyramid—the four or five teaching hospitals— which I designated the *Elite Protestant Hospitals*. The remainder form a residual and quite heterogeneous category of about forty hospitals, designated *Other Hospitals*.

Elite are different from *Other Hospitals* in the sense that the relationships of doctors with each other and with the hospitals are very different in the two sectors. I wish, at the moment, to emphasize the difference in access to certain types of reward and consequently in the processes of social control over practice.

Elite Hospitals are closed in the sense that only physicians formally appointed to their staffs can practice in them. There is no such thing as casual practice, and no others can introduce patients or make use of the facilities. There are many advantages to being able to practice in one of these hospitals. They are the most prestigeful in the city. Because they are associated with the medical schools, they are close to the sources of the most recent advances in knowledge and technique on which practice is based. Their physical facilities and equipment are probably among the best, because they represent the largest capital investments. Many of their patients are among the wealthiest and consequently probably pay the highest fees. In general these are the best and most congenial environments for practice.

---

[1] For a fuller account see David N. Solomon, "Career Contingencies of Chicago Physicians" (Ph.D. dissertation, University of Chicago, 1952); and "Ethnic and Class Differences among Hospitals As Contingencies in Medical Careers," *American Journal of Sociology*, LXVI (1961), pp. 463–71.

Moreover, most of the honorific rewards sought by doctors—appointments to medical schools, for example—are controlled by the senior members of the staffs of these hospitals. These features probably contribute to higher incomes for doctors on these hospital staffs; they constitute advantages in the competition for monetary rewards.

Since these privileges are valuables which one would only very reluctantly relinquish, the closed and exclusive nature of the hospitals results in a very tight system of social control. While doctors are protected from interference from nonmedical people—administrators, boards of governors, and the like—and their independence of lay people is thus increased, they are very dependent on each other and thus subjected to a considerable degree of professional social control by their colleagues.

Standards of practice—both ethical and technical—are sustained by these close knit systems of colleagueship. The exclusiveness of these hospitals enables them to create an environment in which it is easier to practice according to the established rules than to be deviant; that is to say, there is little advantage to be gained from deviance. It is thus unnecessary most of the time for formal sanctions to be applied. The available rewards for conformity are such that negative sanctions are rarely invoked, but their existence is a reminder to those who may be tempted.

Other Hospitals are a rather heterogeneous set. Some are rather like *Elite Hospitals* in that they attempt to establish advantages for those who practice in them and to maintain the exclusiveness that makes professional control possible. Many, however, do not. The only advantage they can offer the physician is that he may introduce patients, that is, he has access to beds and other facilities from time to time. While they have formally organized staffs, a great deal of practice is in fact on a casual basis. Doctors not on staff may bring in patients provided they are willing to refer cases to the doctors who own the hospitals or control access to them, which amounts to the same thing. It is to the advantage of doctors in these positions of power over scarce resources to have a large rather than small set of others who need access to beds. Thus, in the extreme case the only rule becomes that those who wish beds occasionally for their own patients must refer patients to the specialists, usually surgeons, who control the hospitals.

Strictly medical, honorific rewards, are monopolized by *Elite Hospitals*. *Other Hospitals*, then, have little to offer in the way of rewards. The only scarce resource they control is beds. Their power to be exclusive is used only as a bargaining point. Social control rests more on day to day exchanges which, although they may not directly involve cash, do result, in both the long and short run, in gain or loss of advantages which are primarily monetary in character. The system of social control is thus tenuous rather than tight and does not affect standards of practice—whether technical or ethical—

very much. The physician may, if he is so inclined, pursue excellence. But the conditions of practice for the most part do not put any premium on excellence and leave standards to the inclinations of individual doctors, or of small groups of doctors.

In both *Elite* and *Other Hospitals* the systems of social control ensure the continuance of social systems which maintain the mutual advantages of the parties, and the bonds between doctors rest on exchanges between them. In the one, however, it is an exchange between colleagues who are bound by rules of colleagueship as well as mutual advantage, and whose situation in general gives many incentives for certain forms of professional behavior. In the other, it is more an exchange between competitors, certain of whose interests from time to time converge, and who are bound mainly by the *quid pro quo* which is involved in each exchange. In the one case there is a system of social control which, along with other features, maintains standards of high quality, ethical medical care. In the other, the system of social control leaves these matters more to the individual physician, and in fact there are incentives which work against or obstruct such standards, or perhaps make them irrelevant.

The description and explanation of the role of the physician in private practice is thus, in this study, almost entirely in structural terms. Explanation or understanding of behavior arises from the description of the two different systems of social control. Had I obtained the data, I might also have seen differences in the socialization process, in self-conception, and consequently in self-discipline in the different sectors of practice. Had I started with the hypothesis that the socialization of physicians results in a conception of self which is sufficiently durable to influence practice in all sectors, I should probably have been wrong. The most one can say is that if some internalization of standards does occur during the socialization process— which is usually thought of as the training period in medical school and hospitals—this internalization seems not to be very durable in those sectors of the medical world where it is not daily supported by social structure.

The focus of attention in this study was on structural aspects, not on self-conception, and the data could not be analyzed in these terms. However, the starting hypothesis for such an analysis would be that doctors in *Other Hospitals* tend to see themselves as entrepreneurs of a sort, in competition with, or sometimes in business with other physicians. The self-conception of doctors in *Elite Hospitals* is probably more in keeping with the image of the physician presented by the professional ideology. These doctors probably tend to see themselves cooperating as well as competing with other doctors. Although they, too, have a business orientation towards practice, this is not the predominant feature. They see themselves also as persons with a considerable commitment to high quality ethical medical care.

The Infantry Recruit Studies

        Three studies of Canadian Army infantry recruits were carried out during the summers of 1950–52.[2] The practical problem which initiated these studies was the view of military authorities that too many men who had voluntarily enlisted withdrew from the services relatively early in what it was thought, or hoped, should have been lifetime careers. At the least, the Army wanted men to serve out the term of their first enlistment, which at the time was either three or five years. The costs of recruiting and training those who did not and other problems generated by this wastage were regarded as excessive, even though turnover rates were far less than those accepted in other industries employing the same types of men.

First Study

        The first study, carried out just before the outbreak of the Korean War, concerned infantry battalions in static positions in permanent camps. Almost all senior officers and noncommissioned officers had served during World War II, and many had enlisted as regular soldiers previous to the War. On the other hand, almost all junior officers, junior NCO's, and private soldiers had joined since the War, and most of the young soldiers had between one and a half and two years service.

        The striking feature of this situation, which gave the clue that led us to select a framework for interpretation, was the contrast between senior officers and NCO's compared with junior NCO's and men. The seniors seemed to have internalized a conception of themselves which formed a very important aspect of identity for each person and to which they were deeply committed. This conception of self appeared to provide a set of guidelines for behavior in each of the various roles the senior officer or NCO was called upon to perform. The internalization of the soldierly image pretty much defined almost every situation with which they might be confronted, except for those which were so completely novel that there was no possibility of finding a precedent. This does not, of course, mean that there was no room for creative or innovative behavior. No role is ever fully specified, no situation completely defined. The soldierly self-conception provided a framework within which adaptation and, when necessary, improvisation could go on. These men were self-disciplined in the sense that they had internalized a

---

        [2] The infantry recruit studies were carried out while I was a member of the scientific staff of the Defense Research Board of Canada. My associates as consultants and field workers were Oswald Hall, H. W. F. McKay, William A. Westley, Frank E. Jones, Jacques Brazeau, T. S. F. McFeat, Bruce A. MacFarlane, T. E. Rashleigh, Hyman Rodman, and Audrey Wipper.

structure of values and norms which defined a considerable range of behavior in quite a variety of situations.

This does not mean to suggest that these "old" soldiers were always satisfied and never dissatisfied. On the contrary they were often dissatisfied, and some of the officers and NCO's upon whom we looked as model results of the process of socialization were, at the time, themselves dissatisfied. Yet they regarded the military career as one to which they were committed and as one in which they had, at times, to tolerate the dissatisfactions of the immediate situation. Although none ever put it quite that way, one had the impression that they regarded the good of the service as more important than immediate personal satisfaction. The question of dissatisfaction or satisfaction was for them irrelevant to the long-run outcome. Nor does this suggest that none ever thought of leaving the service. In fact a few subsequently did. But for most the notion was that one would continue in the service no matter what the dissatisfactions of the moment. This attitude was similar, I suppose, to that of the dissatisfied doctor who may think of changing hospitals or changing some aspect of his career or even of moving to another country but, by and large, does not seriously consider ceasing to be a doctor.

Many—perhaps most—of the young soldiers, on the other hand, appeared to have a civilian self-conception which we referred to as being particularly "adhesive." This self-conception, which clung to them or to which they clung, made them resistant to the efforts of the Army to transform them from civilians to soldiers by giving them a new image of themselves as so self-disciplined that conformity to military requirements would be more or less automatic. The Army wanted men to think of the service as a career to which they would be bound by their own conceptions of self. They wanted a lifetime commitment and involvement. Many young soldiers, however, remained oriented to civilian life. They looked upon the service as casually as they would any job to which they were neither attached nor committed and in which they had little involvement other than the desire for more or less immediate satisfaction or dissatisfaction. Some were actively seeking discharge. Some were applying for transfers to other kinds of duty which they hoped would be more satisfying, and some were making plans for civilian life on termination of their engagements. Few, however, showed much sign of undergoing the transition from civilian to soldier which would ultimately have made them more like their seniors.

Second and Third Studies

The subsequent studies were done in camps where recruits were being trained as reenforcements for battalions in Korea. We were thus able to observe the first six weeks or so of a man's military experience under the conditions that prevailed at the time. The result of the first study had been that the Army felt that, in terms of inculcating in the men the appropriate self-conception, it was not succeeding in transforming a sufficient number of recruits into soldiers. And so we now turned our attention to attempting to discover what went on during the first few weeks that was relevant to this process.

We found no indications that any of the recruits had begun to change their conceptions of themselves, that they had begun to internalize the standards required by the Army. In general they were eager to learn, particularly about weapons and other technical matters, but also to get along with others and to fit into the schedule of daily activities. They knew what the Army regarded as a "good soldier," what forms of behavior were regarded as undesirable, what aspects of training were regarded as most important, and the differences in the ways in which they were expected or permitted to behave in three very different situations: on the parade square, in field exercises, and in their own living quarters.

All this required considerable learning, but one had the impression that there was little personal commitment to the activities involved. The recruits learned to perform roles in the various situations which training presented. Although they expressed affect about training and other aspects of experience, they seemed to be learning roles as a job that had to be done. They looked upon themselves as persons who had signed up to do a job for a few years, but not as persons who were becoming soldiers.

Although we have no systematic evidence beyond this very early period of training, it seems likely that most men go through the first term of enlistment with very much this view of themselves—as being in the Army but not of it. The hypothesis proposed for further study, however, was that once the decision for a second term of enlistment is taken, then the soldier does begin to develop an internalization of the military schema which becomes part, perhaps the central part, of his attachment to the career. It may be that during the second and subsequent terms of enlistment—incidentally almost no one gets out after reenlisting—the demands of the service are such that most individuals, in order to sustain themselves, require a rationale that is characterized by what we have referred to as the military self-conception. The longer a man stays in, the more he is committed in the sense that he has accumulated valuables which he is reluctant to sacrifice.[3] He may look back, but it becomes almost impossible to turn back. Being committed in this sense to a life which from time to time makes very

---

3 Cf. Howard S. Becker, "Notes on the Concept of Commitment," *American Journal of Sociology*, LXVI (1960), pp. 32–35. The term "valuable" is from Blanche Geer, "Occupational Commitment and the Teaching Profession," in *Institutions and the Person*, eds. Howard S. Becker, *et al.* (Chicago: Aldine Publishing Company, 1968), pp. 221–34.

exacting demands, the development of a conception of self which is consistent with the demands may be the essential core of the rationale a man requires in order to explain his life to himself and to others—and also as a guide to behavior in the varied situations in which a soldier finds himself.

This kind of process leading to commitment only after a number of irrevocable decisions have been taken, and the subsequent development of a self-conception built around the occupational role, may be characteristic of other occupations as well. The part of the career which is formally designated as training is usually regarded as the phase in which secondary socialization takes place and a new kind of self-conception is formed. The military case suggests that the socialization process continues beyond the training stage and that the development of an occupational or professional self-conception may not in fact occur until relatively late in the career.

Scientists in Industry

The literature on scientists and engineers in industry suggests that persons with this sort of training have conceptions of themselves which are at odds with the requirements of their roles in industry. While some companies seek more or less immediate returns from the work of their scientists, others are willing to wait longer, perhaps as much as ten years or more. But in the final analysis the profit motive is paramount. On the other hand, it is believed that young Ph.D.'s during their years of graduate study internalize a set of values of science and develop conceptions of themselves as scientists which make it difficult for them to adapt to the demands of profit-making enterprises. During their first few years in large companies many young scientists are reported to experience a great deal of disturbing tension. They see themselves as persons who ought to be concerned with discovery and the advancement of science, with carrying out elegant or innovative experiments and the like, while the company wants them to do only things which are likely to be profitable either in the long or short run.

With these notions in mind, we interviewed all Ph.D. chemists employed in the pharmaceutical and other industries in Montreal.[4] It appeared from the interviews that most of these men had always looked upon chemistry as a way of getting along in the world and as a way of having a reasonably good life doing interesting work. In one or two cases they saw their jobs as opportunities to achieve quite great ambitions—to be a university president, for example—which had little or nothing to do with the advancement of chemistry or with the devotion to science which is regarded

4 The studies of scientists and of peace-keeping officers were supported by grants from the Defense Research Board of Canada. My associates in the scientists project were Colette Carisse, Silvia Lamb, James N. McRorie, and Lionel Tiger.

as part of the scientist's self-conception. Interviews with chemistry graduate students showed that a proportion also regarded chemistry as an avenue of social mobility rather than as something to which they were committing themselves. While they put great store in having an interesting job, it was not always felt that it had necessarily to be a job in chemistry. The general feeling was put by one who said that he regarded himself as a nine-to-five chemist, but not as the devoted type who sees himself as a potential Nobel Prize winner.

They readily accepted the goals and requirements of their companies. Since they were paid by the companies, they felt it quite proper to direct their efforts to doing things which seemed likely to result in profit for the company. Moreover, when we interviewed a number of Ph.D. chemists who had become senior executives—presidents, vice-presidents, and research directors—none gave evidence of having shed more than the most cursory tears upon leaving the bench and moving away from chemistry into management.

In understanding these careers, structural variables seemed more useful than the notion of a conception of self which included the internalization of some set of values and was durable over a long period of the career. The kind of company a man worked in and the kind of role he played in it seemed more relevant variables. Those who worked as bench chemists in companies which produced antibiotic drugs, hormones, or isotopes were more likely to think of themselves as chemists and to express some hesitation about the coming stages of their careers, which they could see leading them away from chemistry to managerial roles. Those who were in companies which produced soaps or cosmetics did not emphasize the research content of their roles. Rather they saw themselves as contributing to the company in other ways—for example, by modifying products so that they could be used in arctic or other special conditions. Those who were performing managerial roles—as directors of research, in a few instances vice-presidents in charge of research, and in one as president of a chemical company—saw themselves as managers, and some even questioned whether their scientific training was really of much use or relevance in their present roles. The work situation and work history seemed more important than some internalization which resulted from a period of early training and indoctrination.

Canadian Peace-Keeping Officers

The final study to be discussed concerns Canadian military officers who had served in United Nations peace-keeping missions.[5] The basic assump-

---

5 For a more complete report see David N. Solomon, "The Soldierly Self and the Peace-Keeping Role: Canadian Officers in Peace-Keeping Forces," in *Military Profession and Military Regimes,* ed. J. A. A. van Doorn (The Hague: Mouton & Co., 1969), pp. 52–69.

tion was that these officers conceived of themselves in terms suited to the more traditional wartime soldiering roles. Some, for example, described the objective of training as the production of "rough, tough killers." The intention of the study was to explore how officers whose self-conception was that of the fighting or war-making soldier had adapted to the demands of the peace-keeping role.

While a number of features of the peace-keeping officer's role are of interest, the focal one in terms of the present discussion centers around the use of force. The objective of all UN peace-keeping missions has been to keep or restore peace between contending parties. This could be done by negotiation, by forceful means, or by some combination of the two. For many of these officers, the basic issue was how much force they ought to have been permitted to use in order to keep the peace.

One of the central features of the traditional role of the professional soldier is the notion that you must forcefully impose your will on anyone who opposes or attempts to restrict measures which appear necessary to the achievement of defined objectives. If you are fired on, you fire back. If the enemy interferes with your freedom of movement, you attempt forcefully to prevent him from doing so. In the UN peace-keeping role, as it was defined in most of the UN operations in which these officers had participated, the policy on the means of achieving objectives was precisely the opposite. In the peace-keeping role, force and threats of force are replaced by negotiation and other modes of behavior which do not involve force, since the UN did not define itself as an agency attempting to enforce peace.

Some of the officers interviewed experienced these conflicting views as a conflict or tension at the psychological level. Their own training and experience, and indeed the military style of life, suggested one line of behavior, while the immediate situation demanded another. The feeling of tension indicated that there was a degree of role conflict—they were being asked to perform in ways which went against their own internalized notions of the nature of the military role. Looking at it another way, two sets of norms were involved in defining the situation of the peace-keeping role: first, the traditional definitions of the appropriate ways for a soldier to carry out his duties, even the duties it is appropriate for a soldier to carry out; second, the definition of the role given by the peace-keeping situation.

Probably every occupational role has in it features which make for flexibility and adaptation. In this particular case four features facilitated adaptation. First, the professional soldier is accustomed to having policies and objectives set for him. Senior officers may debate objectives among themselves or with their political masters. But once the decisions have been taken, once the policies have been laid down, once the officer has received his orders —whether from UN headquarters or from his own superiors—then, in terms of the professional definition of the role, he regards it as his duty to seek to achieve the objectives within the limits set by policy. The professional

soldier is committed to doing what he is told in the way that he is told to do
it. Occasionally officers resign, as did a number of Canadian senior officers
who disagreed with cabinet policy over the reorganization of the Canadian
Armed Forces and tried to take their case directly to the public. For the most
part, however, for the serving officer the compulsion to be loyal to set policies
is very strong, even though he may privately continue to protest to his superiors.

Second, the professional officer has a strong inclination to be loyal
to the command to which he is attached, whatever it may be. There is evidence in the interviews that these Canadian officers regarded themselves as
UN officers as well as Canadian officers. Their mandate was thus to achieve
the goals of the UN by means specified in UN policies. In some cases the
senior commanders appointed by the UN were Canadian officers; in others,
not. But once the officer becomes part of a UN force he sees himself as a
UN officer and obligated to follow the dictates of the UN command.

The inclination of these Canadian officers was thus to accept directives from and to direct their loyalties to the UN command. These inclinations
were facilitated by a third consideration. These officers believed that Canada
had no political interest in UN operations, that is to say, that Canada had
no desire to make use of these operations or the situations which made them
necessary to further her own national interests. Believing that there was no
Canadian national interest made it easier to accept directives and feel like
UN officers, while still, of course, maintaining a good deal of pride in
Canada and Canadian soldiers.

Finally, the Canadian officer conceives of himself as a person who
remains detached both from political considerations and from self-interest
which would lead him to attempt to exploit the situation to enrich himself.
The military is a service occupation in that it serves the national society.
Armed forces in Canada and elsewhere are referred to as "the services," and
the term "serving officer" is frequently used. As is the case in other professions, the notion of service implies detachment. Talcott Parsons and others
refer to the physician as having a detached concern for his patients. He is
concerned for the welfare of patients but is detached in the sense that, in
the ideal at any rate, he puts aside his own motives of financial gain or
other personal considerations. The same ideal holds, but probably much
more strongly, for the military profession, which may in fact be one of the
last to retain the service ideal as a real force in motivating behavior. This is
referred to in some interviews as a strong "sense of purpose," the purpose
being to serve the UN and the contending parties. Although the parties to a
dispute may not always be entirely appreciative of this service, the conception of Canadian officers is that they *are* serving these countries, if only by
maintaining peace for a time and saving a few lives. It is in a way a strange
paradox when military people justify their presence in terms of saving lives.

The notions of accepting objectives and policy, of being loyal to their own command, of Canada being disinterested politically, and of the individual officer being disinterested or detached from immediate self-interest all interlocked to make it relatively easy for Canadian officers to adapt themselves from the war-maker to the peace-keeper role. However, in the process many had to live for a time with their own psychological tensions, which arose from the military predisposition to use force rather than negotiation in the settlement of disputes.

Since the demands of the peace-keeping role were so readily incorporated into the professional soldier's role by these respondents—they did after all learn and perform the roles of negotiator and diplomat as well as, on occasion, policeman—one suspects that the feelings of conflict and tension reported indicate not only role conflict but also that this is a role in transition. Little more than a decade ago peace-keeping operations were unknown, except that countries with colonial empires frequently used their military forces to maintain peace, law, and order in the colonies. While these operations were not identical with UN operations, there are points of similarity. The UN type of operation can to some degree be legitimated in the image of the professional soldier by a tradition which receded into the background during World War II but which is now capable of being revitalized. The peace-keeping role is perhaps not as novel as it seemed to most respondents. In any case, by the time these officers, who served as lieutenants and captains in the first series of UN peace-keeping operations, have become majors, colonels, and brigadiers and the present colonels and brigadiers have become generals, one might predict that the transition will have moved a stage beyond the present state of moderate tension and role conflict. The peace-keeping role then will have become one of the roles regarded as appropriate for the professional soldier.

Discussion

The four studies discussed in this paper rest on two sets of concepts in terms of which behavior can be interpreted: those which have to do with the situation of action, and those which have to do with the internalization of certain aspects of experience. At times I have treated these concepts as if they were in opposition to each other, at others as if there were an interplay between them.

The Chicago doctors study was couched entirely in structural terms, but I later returned to speculate about the possible implications in terms of self-conception. The first infantry recruit study emphasized the resistance of the civilian self-conception to the military situation. The subsequent studies described recruit training in terms of the structure of the training situation but led to speculation about long-term implications for the development at a later stage of the career of a military self-conception. The Montreal chemists study discounted the significance of self-conception in favor of the demands of the work situation. Finally, in the peace-keeping officers study the data are interpreted in terms of changes in both role and self-conception. What these studies, especially those of the military, demand is some integration of the two sets of concepts dealing with role imperatives and self-conception. Consideration of a few concepts may help move in this direction.

Role can be seen as a performance which includes a set of imperatives, that is a set of definitions of behavior appropriate or required in given situations. Whether these are spelled out in terms of role obligations or expectations which participants have of each other, or whether they arise from the nature of the exchanges involved in the situation, or in some other way, a role consists in essence of behavioral imperatives which have one degree of force or another.

Self-conception is in part the internalization of some of the imperatives of a role. The person who sees himself as a doctor or a soldier sees himself as one who ought to behave in certain kinds of ways in certain situations, and who feels entitled to expect others to behave towards him in certain ways.

Role and self-conception are linked in a number of ways, but I wish to draw attention only to two. First, the performance of a role may require that the incumbent be a certain kind of person in the sense that he have a conception of himself which is consistent with the demands of the role. This can, and no doubt does, occur partly through a process of natural selection. But on the other hand—and this is the second linkage—experience in the role may result in the incumbent becoming a certain kind of person, that is to say, developing a self-conception appropriate to the role. If one performs the role long enough, there may be good reasons for developing the self-conception that goes with it.

While these comments apply generally to all kinds of roles and self-conceptions, they seem particularly well suited for dealing with occupations. *Occupation* is a label for a social category, that is for a set of persons for whose behavior the label has implications—there is a set of roles which are ordinarily performed by persons who bear the label. Not all who are so designated perform all the roles, nor are all the roles performed only by persons bearing the label, but in general the roles are associated with the social category.[6] There is usually some normative feeling, and often a statutory prescription, that those who are entitled to the label have an exclusive

---

[6] The ideas in which this interpretation originated are in S. F. Nadel, *The Theory of Social Structure* (London: Cohen and West, 1957), pp. 24–25, *et passim.*

right and duty to perform the roles and that, conversely, those who perform the roles have an exclusive right to the label.

While the occupational label invariably has implications for role performance, only in some occupations is the link between role and self-conception clearly apparent. There is a continuum at one pole of which, from the point of view of the occupational role, the nature of the conception of self matters little. At the other extreme, it is very nearly true that the roles involved can be performed only by persons with the appropriate self-conception. The contrast is between the roles of unskilled workers and those of persons we ordinarily classify as professionals, but a full discussion of these ideas would take us far afield. Suffice it to say that there are many occupations where roles and self-conception are closely linked, and possibly this is true of all occupational roles.

In many occupations there is a *career:* a sequence of roles performed over time and linked in an orderly fashion. The sequence is typical of persons bearing the occupational label. It is also normatively approved in the sense that it is expected that persons in the occupation will follow the career. Since there may, of course, be more than one typical and approved sequence of roles for a particular occupation—for example, the scientist in industry and the academic scientist—it is better to refer to careers as modal sequences.

The existence of careers has two important implications. First, since the career ordinarily extends over a considerable period, frequently the entire work life, it becomes much more likely that there will be a strong link between roles and self-conceptions. Second, a person in an occupation is, at different stages of the career, called on to perform roles which are slightly or very different. If being in the occupation requires or results in a certain conception of self, passing through the sequence of roles which make up the career will require or result in a series of changes in self-conception. As the career unfolds, the conception of self undergoes a series of changes.

On the other hand, the way a role is performed depends partly on the kinds of people coming into it. The successive roles of a career may be influenced by the self-conceptions formed at previous stages. A career should thus be regarded as consisting of two linked sequences, one consisting of roles and one of self-conceptions.

Since most occupations nowadays consist essentially of roles in formal organizations, anything which causes an organization to change may be reflected in an internal demand for changes in roles. Conversely, changes in the self-conception of members of an occupation may originate outside the organizations in which their roles are performed and yet have implications for both role performance and organizational arrangements.

At first glance the notions of role imperative and self-conception appear to be concepts which represent behavior as being resistant to change, and no doubt it is under certain conditions. The studies of doctors, scientists, and soldiers, however, have led me to use these concepts as if they were part of a theory of social change. One must conclude that, as was the case with officers in peace-keeping roles, there are probably in the roles and self-conceptions of most occupations some features which facilitate change or make it possible. Every role and every conception of self contain the seeds of innovation.

22

S. Kirson Weinberg

PRIMARY GROUP THEORY
AND CLOSEST FRIENDSHIP
OF THE SAME SEX:
AN EMPIRICAL ANALYSIS

Friendship as a pervasive human relationship exists on the margins of institutional functions. It indicates a sense of belonging that relieves man's supposed aloneness. It endows a personal dimension to behavior amidst the vast impersonality of urban life. As a criterion of personality development it points to stability in contrast to the pathology of social isolation. Its relevance to the scheme of human relations cannot be denied; yet, as an object of sustained inquiry it has generally eluded interest.[1] This study reports on one type of friendship, closest friendship of the same sex among college stu-

---

[1] S. Kirson Weinberg, "Social Psychological Aspects of Schizophrenia," in *The Sociology of Mental Disorders,* ed. S. Kirson Weinberg (Chicago: Aldine Publishing Company, 1967), pp. 133–42.

dents. It deals in sequence with: (1) the formation of such friendships, (2) the characteristics of intimate relations, and (3) the degrees of social intimacy between closest friends.

Closest Friendship as a Referent of Study

My interest in closest friendship arose from a study of social isolation among adolescent schizophrenics. I found it necessary from this inquiry to ascertain the modes of friendship among normal adolescents. My pilot inquiries of friendship generally revealed that because this concept lacked boundaries the modes of social intimacy were difficult to determine. I then limited my study to closest friendship.

Literature on closest friendship is relatively scant. One concern pertains to the homogeneity in background and personality of friends.[2] Another interest is represented in Theodore M. Newcomb's experimental analysis of acquaintanceship from a perception-balance model involving attraction and liking between the acquaintances.[3] Added illumination on the interpersonal process of friendship has been shed by Robert K. Merton, George C. Homans, Fritz Heider, and Harold H. Kelley and John W. Thibaut.[4]

However, the conceptual antecedent to closest friendship that I have selected is Charles H. Cooley's conception of the primary group, but with my heuristic revisions.[5] Cooley's loosely drawn conception of the primary group included: (1) cohesion, (2) physical presence or face-to-face relations, (3) intimacy, and (4) collective identification expressed as a "we" feeling. His elaboration of this concept included almost any small society in which members were familiar or personal. Edward Shils, Morris Janowitz, Robert Faris, Alan Bates, Nicholas Babchuck, and Elton Mayo and other investiga-

---

    2 Cf. C. E. Izard, "Personality Similarity and Friendship," *Journal of Abnormal and Social Psychology,* LXI (1960), 47–51; and Helen M. Richardson, "Studies of Mental Resemblance Between Husbands and Wives and Between Friends," *Psychological Bulletin,* XXXVI (1939), 104–20.
    3 Theodore M. Newcomb, *The Acquaintance Process* (New York: Holt, Rinehart and Winston, Inc., 1961); and Theodore M. Newcomb and Everett K. Wilson, eds., *College Peer Groups* (Chicago: Aldine Publishing Company, 1966).
    4 Robert K. Merton, "Friendship as a Social Process: A Substantive and Methodological Analysis," in *Freedom and Control in Modern Society,* eds. M. Berger, T. Abel, and C. Page (New York: D. Van Nostrand Company, Inc., 1954), pp. 18–66. Cf. George C. Homans, *The Human Group* (New York: Harcourt, Brace and World, Inc., 1950), and *Social Behavior* (New York: Harcourt, Brace and World, Inc., 1961); Fritz Heider, *The Psychology of Interpersonal Relations* (New York: John Wiley and Sons, Inc., 1958); and John W. Thibaut and Harold H. Kelley, *The Social Psychology of Groups* (New York: John Wiley and Sons, Inc., 1959).
    5 Charles H. Cooley, *Social Organization* (New York: Schocken Books, Inc., 1962), pp. 23–31.

tors of primary groups in industry have sharpened the concept of the primary group but not the interpersonal dimension of social intimacy.[6] This version of the primary group emphasizes its positive features. It differs from the version of the primary group as composed of ambivalent relations, as prevails in clinical writings, where affection and hatred coexist. A third, or macro-organizational view of the primary group, alluded to by Robert E. Park and W.I. Thomas as well as Cooley, pertains to small groups as contrasted with large, impersonal, and utilitarian bureaucracies or secondary groups.[7]

I have selected the first version as a point of departure because closest friendship as a voluntary relationship tends to deteriorate with hostility. Since I stress the interactional dimension of closest friendship, this position reverses the group-relationship sequence of the primary group. This bond is not a group property but a relationship generating a consensual group or unit. Moreover, the consensual network may lack group closure. A subject with two very close friends who do not know each other constitute a dual dyad, while three close friends who know each other comprise a solidified clique with group closure.

This relationship-group sequence also differs from the organicist or holistic position of Cooley in which the primary group and its individual members denote collective and distributive facets of a seamless whole. The attention to peer group uniformity and cohesion, in fact, has obstructed the view to closest friendship as well as to diverse relations in the peer group, as is illustrated in the following:

> There are six or seven of us in our merry little group who have been together for about five years. Most of us have worked at summer camp, so naturally the topic of what we did that year at camp is our favorite. In this context, Perry and I are not two isolated friends but part of a group of close friends. We never think of having a party without inviting one and all in the group. In this group, I consider Perry one of my closest friends. I confide almost equally to other members, and they, in turn, confide almost as fully in me. But my relationships with

---

6 Cf. Edward Shils, "The Study of the Primary Group," in *The Policy Sciences: Recent Developments in Scope and Method,* eds. Harold Lasswell and Daniel Lerner (Stanford: Stanford University Press, 1951), 44–59; Robert E. L. Faris, *Social Psychology* (New York: The Ronald Press Company, 1952), pp. 250–80; and Nicholas Babchuck and Alan Bates, "Primary Relations of Middle Class Couples," *American Sociological Review,* XXVIII (1963), 377–84.

7 Cooley, *op. cit.* Cf. Robert E. Park, "The City: Suggestions for the Investigation of Human Behavior in the City Environment," in *The City* (Chicago: University of Chicago Press, 1925); and W. I. Thomas, "Persistence of Primary Group Norms in Present-Day Society and Their Influence in Our Educational System," in *Suggestions of Modern Science Concerning Education,* ed. H. S. Jennings (New York: The Macmillan Company, Publishers, 1917), pp. 157–97.

each member, although on the same informal level, at times differ. With one member of the group I might assert my authority. I might be very critical of one and hardly critical at all of others. This is not to say that I act as if I am a different person to each member, but I am compelled to act a little differently with each member of the group. With some members my relationship is joking or kidding; with others, serious minded and critical. Sometimes I feel closer to some than to others, including my best friend, Perry. But with Perry I enjoy a particular kind of "emotional conflict" that I do not share with other members.

My operational conception of a closest friend is one so designated by the subjects. Their implicit criteria of selection of closest friendship varied, of course, but there is no substitute for this kind of initial selection. The subjects themselves, within the cultural definition of friendship, are the only ones who can designate their closest friends, but an analysis of their manner and degree of intimacy would determine the extent to which intimacy characterizes this relationship.

Since I limited the study to pairs of closest friends, those subjects who have two or more closest friends were asked to describe their relations with one representative closest friend. Although 60.5 per cent of the subjects have one single best friend, 36 per cent who had several closest friends selected one for study; the 3.5 per cent who admittedly lacked a closest friend were included only in selected aspects of the study. In analyzing these friendship pairs I may have omitted the interplay that arises from more than two friends, but I could also focus more intensively upon basic friendship processes.

Our subjects are single college youths, eighteen to twenty-five years old, American born or in this country since age ten, and of broad middle class status, as determined by father's occupation, their own aspirations, and self-rating. As students at a commuter college, Roosevelt University, many reside at home. But some have been to campus residential colleges where they formed their closest friendships; others formed closest friendships in high schools and places other than Roosevelt University, so that their friendship formation was not restricted to the University.

The subjects' age range, coupled with the marital status of never-married, is not an arbitrary category but characterizes late adolescence— the interim of becoming disengaged from one's family but not yet becoming socially committed through marriage. Friendships in this period may reach a peak of social intimacy, for with marriage closest friends are superseded predominantly by the spouse.

I have limited the subjects to those in the country from age ten or younger, for foreign-born persons would not have had the opportunity to cultivate the closest friendships with perhaps the same facility as persons who have lived in this country from childhood.

The first group of subjects consisted of 100 males and 100 females. These subjects completed a self-administered series of questionnaires. Selected subjects were then interviewed, and/or composed personal documents on their closest friendships. From these interviews I was able to discern the components of social intimacy. I then composed several miniscales for the analysis of social intimacy among another group of 140 students with similar characteristics.

As I intend to identify the processes of social intimacy in closest friendship as one type of primary relationship, it is necessary to sift the generic from the particular. The probabilistic findings pertain to the particular conditions of the subjects in the academic setting. For instance, the formative processes of closest friendship, as well as the components of social intimacy, would have basic similarities for diverse subjects in other situations, such as coworkers in a factory, soldiers in a camp, or neighbors in a city block.[8]

Formation of Closest Friendship

Closest friendships of the same sex are likely to emerge from (1) a situation which facilitates frequent face-to-face and informal encounters (2) between persons predominantly of like social categories and background[9] (3) who express and share personal interests, experiences, values, and problems so that (4) one of them acquires a personal attraction for the other and (5) differentiates this personal peer relationship from other peer relations.

The social situation may impede or facilitate the formation of closest friendship. Stigmatized situations which are inimical to reciprocal trust—such as prison, the mental hospital, or skid row—will discourage friendship formation.[10] By contrast, the school setting encourages the formation of friendships and is more instrumental than the neighborhood in the formation of closest friendships, as is shown in Table 1. Within the academic setting the participants are more likely to have frequent meetings and to com-

---

[8] A. Zaleznik, C. R. Christensen and F. J. Roethlisberger, *The Motivation, Productivity and Satisfaction of Workers* (Cambridge: Harvard University Press, 1958). Cf. Roger Little, "Buddy Relations and Combat Performance," in *The New Military,* ed. Morris Janowitz (New York: Russell Sage Foundation, 1964) ; and William F. White, *Street Corner Society* (Chicago: University of Chicago Press, 1955), pp. 255–68.

[9] I have omitted discussion of the homogeneity of social categories between closest friends because of lack of space. This will be included in the larger study in progress, entitled *Closest Friendship: A Study of Social Intimacy in a Primary Relationship.*

[10] Donald Clemmer, *The Prison Community* (New York: Holt Rinehart, E Winston, 1958). Cf. H. Warren Dunham and S. Kirson Weinberg, *The Culture of the State Mental Hospital* (Detroit: Wayne State University Press, 1960) ; and Donald Bogue, *Skid Row in America* (Chicago: University of Chicago Press, 1963).

TABLE 1

SITUATIONS WHERE CLOSE FRIENDSHIPS
WERE FORMED, BY PERCENTAGES

Situation	Total (N = 156)	Male (N = 63)	Female (N = 93)
Neighborhood	12.7	12.6	12.9
School setting	78.8	77.7	79.5
Grade school	(23.1)	(25.4)	(21.5)
High school	(26.9)	(41.2)	(17.2)
College	(28.8)	(11.1)	(40.8)
Camp, Work and other	8.5	9.7	7.6
Total	100.0	100.0	100.0

municate their common interests and activites. Thus, 78.8 per cent of the subjects formed their closest friendships in the school setting, as compared with 12.7 per cent who formed them in the neighborhood. The remaining 8.5 per cent formed their friendships in camp, job, and other situations. Although residential proximity per se is not conducive to the formation of closest friendships, it tended to reinforce an association already cultivated in school.

Some subjects who associated with their friends in school had frequent associations in the neighborhood because of residential proximity. Also, persons of like ethnic groups and social class tended to reside in similar areas. The neighborhood also served as a convenient context in which the friends participated in common activities, such as athletics or social life. Thus, 70.5 per cent of the subjects and their friends resided within a five mile radius, and 76 per cent within a ten mile radius. Ninety-four per cent of all respondents resided within a fifteen mile radius; 6 per cent did not respond.

Frequent face-to-face encounter is a crucial determinant in the formation of closest friendship among adolescents. No subject in this study formed a closest friendship by letters or phone calls. Although Ellsworth Faris has indicated that a close friendship between scholars may be expressed by correspondence, adolescents form this primary relationship by frequent face-to-face encounters and tend to sustain it in this manner.[11] Eighty-seven per cent of the subjects associated with their newly-formed friends one or more times weekly. Only 7.5 per cent visited their friends less than once weekly, while 5.5 per cent of the friends were physically inaccessible and were,

---

11 Ellsworth Faris, *The Nature of Human Nature* (New York: McGraw-Hill Book Company, 1937), chap. 4.

of course, not visited. Although many encounters were involuntary, the meetings offered opportunities for improvised and informal conversation. On this level, although closest friendship is voluntary, it emerges within a social matrix in which the principals meet frequently and informally and have the leeway to communicate spontaneously about their personal experiences.

The situation must permit informal leeway so that the interactants can digress from formal matters and improvise in conversation about their personal problems and experiences. On the other hand, frequent and informal interaction, while necessary, is not a sufficient condition for germinating closest friendships. Roommates who interact frequently may become estranged without becoming close. The mode and substance of interaction then becomes crucial in this formative process. In the initial or subsequent conversations amidst social congeniality, one companion may disclose self-involving experiences in which the other becomes interested; in sharing experiences they sustain a reciprocal personal bond.

The interactants discover common forms of participation as well as a common outlook and values. They may feel rapport in each other's views as they reciprocally attract and become socially closer. Their awareness of their common informal interests and personal values becomes mutually reassuring and the basis for a self-enhancing friendship.

> *I first met Loren only weeks after I entered college as a freshman in the fall. At that time I was 18 years old. I had met a friend from grade school in the halls, and she invited me to join her for lunch. At the time, she was with two other girls with whom she had graduated from high school. This lunch was the beginning of almost daily noon meetings. Since three of us had two hour breaks in our class schedules, we usually played cards after lunch and got involved in long discussions. It is difficult to remember just when Loren and I began feeling close to one another, but I know there was some mutual attraction at our first meeting.*
>
> *Though it was a gradual process, I think it happened very rapidly, because within one month we began spending more time with one another. We began taking walks between classes, and these seemed to have been the initial periods of the most friendliness. We were both the same age, same religion, and had similar family, economic, and educational backgrounds. Perhaps the fact that we had a common friend helped initiate our interest in each other. But we also had a rapport that I never had experienced with anyone in so short a time. We seemed to have somewhat similar philosophies about school and careers; we were in a common situation with our initiation into college and our feelings concerning it. It seemed as if we were in the initial stages of a maturation period of which we were both acutely aware. We seemed to be able to perceive each other quite objectively, analyze our faults and merits, and give advice quite freely. We were both concerned with getting*

our degrees, traveling as much as possible, and in general experiencing life to the fullest. This we discussed, along with other topics, at great length. Often I came over to her house in the evening, since she lived within walking distance from me, and we could talk for hours—sometimes until two or three in the morning. I think that within three months we considered each other best friends, and this feeling we confided quite freely.

Two acquaintances amidst strangers in a new college may draw closer; two companions who experience common anxieties may penetrate their formal reserve and generate common loyalties and greater cohesion. Thus pledges in a sorority may collectively react to a strange and hostile milieu and become closest friends.

Nina and I were known as "pledging out of the house." This meant that as pledges we were required to go to the sorority house several times during the week for things such as phone duty or meetings. We often met to go over to the house together. Throughout our first semester, Nina and I shared a liking for each other, but we had not yet become "best friends." Each of us was still closest to our original friends. In fact, throughout the following summer I rarely spoke to Nina on the phone. Once the five pledges met downtown for lunch.

The following semester we moved into the sorority house. From the five girls in our pledge class, Nina, Judy, and I were the only freshmen. The other two were sophs whose greenness had faded. We felt insecure in the house because we did not feel a part of it. I think it was at this point that my relationship with Nina began developing into a really close friendship. Judy was in this relationship and I still am very close to her, but I feel closest to Nina and call her my "best friend." The three of us had become dependent upon each other. Living in the same house provided a very conducive atmosphere for the intimacy and confidence we needed to overcome our feelings of inadequacy. This feeling of inadequacy probably stemmed from the fact that we had a previous over-idealized concept of sorority living and sorority girls. We found instead that there were several cliques that often gossiped about one another. During the entire first semester Nina, Judy, and I more or less isolated ourselves. We formed a clique of our own. We waited for one another before going to meals, sat together at meetings and gong practices, even picked beds next to each other in the dorm.

Closest friendship may be accelerated by a personal crisis of one companion who, in a plea for aid, bares his private problems; the other friend responds so that both become reciprocally involved. The substance of this crisis may be estrangement from a parent, an academic predicament, difficulties with other peers, or the opposite sex. Closest friendships may also be catalyzed by predisposing situations, such as the focused interaction and interdependence between remaining members of a disbanded peer group or between companions insulated from a larger peer group.

> *Richard and I lived on a block which had a group of about twenty fellows ranging in age from eleven to fifteen, but we were twelve at the time and the only two who attended the same grammar school; this gave us something to talk about and more or less excluded the others. After school the group usually played cards or fought or just wasted time. At night, they went to the movies or walked to the park to look for trouble. Richard and I were aware of our closeness too because we would not take chances like the others or fight like the others, and we realized that we were not as mean; this realization formed a closer bond between us. On some nights when the group looked for trouble and threw stones at windows, we would run to a safe place, then isolate ourselves from them; and this practice made us become closer with each other.*

Social Intimacy Among Closest Friends

Although closest friendship frequently is characterized by social intimacy, these two aspects of interpersonal relations are distinct. Closest friendship denotes a relationship between the subject and a designated peer whose common interests and values range from the intermittently personal to the very personal. Social intimacy between adolescent peers, however, denotes a very personal relationship expressed basically in self-disclosure and trust from which identification and informal and cathartic expression may emerge. This may intensify solidarity and thereby emotionally insulate the friends from others. Closest friendship and social intimacy intersect when the principals confide and share private experiences. In this very close friendship the interactants may evolve an argot and norms governing their behavior, including the informal manner of approachability, trust, obligation, and the sharing of common experiences. Thus companions lack social intimacy when they do not disclose private and personal experiences, despite their common participation in sports and games, their mutual congeniality, and mutual attraction.

Social intimacy denotes a specific interpersonal process. It socializes private feelings, conflicts, ideas, and anxieties by confidential communication. It deteriorates when the friend is indifferent or reacts negatively to the other's self-disclosure, as is illustrated in the following relationship.

> *The things we discuss are not too personally involving. We have had only a couple of arguments, and nothing came of them. We talk about sex, and sometimes we will discuss his girl friend. I'm touchy about my girl friends. He has quite different ideas about his female companions, which is why I don't double with him. He asks my advice about his*

family, sort of. I mean he cries on my shoulder. I try to give him my suggestions because I think he will do something like hit his father. Jim has a temper quite a bit like a kid. He is self-centered; "me" or "I" seems to stand out, and he exaggerates often. We don't talk much about money except to remark on how cheap the other is. If we have something to get off our chests, we can tell each other, but other than Jim and his family we only occasionally discuss something we consider personal.

Social intimacy inheres in sharing confidential experiences or problems, as is illustrated as follows:

Our friendship is expressed in our complete confidence with each other. We tell each other everything, all of our problems, mostly, and ask for help and sympathy. Our problems stem from school and parents to boys and clothes. We hide nothing from each other except things which we are told in confidence. On this point I find Helen tells me more secrets of others than I tell her. This is probably because Helen needs to talk to people and to tell her problems more than I do. As I said before, I am basically shy and find it hard to say what I really mean. Also, I feel that things told me in confidence should stay with me. I feel very much at ease with Helen. If I did not, I would not be able to talk so freely with her. I feel she feels this way with me also. It would be because she feels more of a need to be so. Our relationship is mostly built on confiding in one another.

From and with self-disclosure, social intimacy is expressed by informality; and by uncritical, spontaneous, and cathartic behavior it may lead to hilarity and playfulness that may become regressive in a manner which I call the "intimacy jag."

Carol and I are amazingly alike. We're both white, middle class. We live about a mile apart and went to high school together. We have the same major—education. We're both avid sports fans; right now we enjoy watching college basketball. We both have a basically optimistic outlook on life and are idealistic. We both become excited over little things; and when we get in "rummy" moods, especially after finals, we don't do anything but laugh at everything and regress when we are together.

Again,

Whenever possible one of us would spend the weekend at the other's home. We followed a pattern of activities each time. We ate, danced to the latest records, set each other's hair—then eating some more and reading "Mad" comic books until all hours of the night. After laughing ourselves sick, we would turn off the light and talk and laugh some more. Most of the time we were in hysterics over absolutely nothing. One of our parents would then tell us to stop acting like a couple of kids. We tried to settle down and go to sleep.

Closest friends who in a confidential way disclose and share their personal conflicts and experiences tend to grow closer. Their focused mutual attraction encourages reciprocal ease and social rhythm which, combined with common secrets and emotionally-involved activities, insulate them from others. They reinforce their insulation by idiomatic words or phrases which have been derived from their idiosyncratic experiences and from which may evolve a framework of singular meanings of words or phrases that an outsider would not understand completely. Although even intimate friends lacked any intricate idiomatic speech, some did use specified words which were corruptions of colloquial and profane expressions or were abbreviated terms or word combinations at times with a regressive quality, as are represented in the following characteristic statements.

> *Since our speech is very informal, there are naturally certain special phrases which we are familiar with. Through the years we have picked up certain odd little sayings which are only known to us.*
> *Since we have known each other for four years, certain incidents have come up which accompanied significant phrases. These are known to us, and we use them appropriately.*

This solidarity between pairs of closest friends who become socially intimate and cohesive has been characterized by Philip Slater as an interpersonal process in which "the greater the emotional involvement in the dyad, the greater will be the cathartic withdrawal from other objects."[12] This insularity is most intense between lovers who are "all wrapped up in each other," but with lesser intensity it has characterized some closest friendships.

> *Our relationship during the major part of our friendship was somehow characterized by a mutual exclusion of other friends. I spent most of my spare time with Diane and participated in few activities or groups without her. Besides Diane I had no other close friends, though I knew some Girl Scouts. But these friends did not know Diane, who was not a Scout. So most of the time I spent with Diane was unaccompanied by others. I remember sharing secrets with her which we pledged never to repeat to others. Since neither of us had other close friends, it was very likely that we confided to a great extent. We also devised a*

---

[12] Philip E. Slater, "On Social Regression," *American Sociological Review,* XXVIII (1963), 349–50.

code by which we could relay messages through the classroom. The code was known to no one but us. Because of the way we acted we recognized each other as best friends and were identified as best friends by all our schoolmates.

From frequency of association and insularity arose an awareness of the distinctiveness of the friendship. For some, this distinctiveness was verbalized; for others it was implicit and fluctuated between crests of social closeness and troughs of widened social distance. Some friends became identified as a unit and were recognized as such by others.

I will never forget our wonderful times together. On one occasion I decided that Sara's hair was too long and that I was going to save her money by trimming it. Well we cried for hours over the new short hair cut, and I was sure she was never going to forgive me. But she managed to get even with me when she plucked my eyebrows out one night. There was the time she stayed up all night trying to teach me how to stand on my head so I could pass my gym class. We had dozens of shopping sprees and diets and all night study sessions. People always associated us together and never a day went by when someone wouldn't ask me how she was or if I had seen her. I will always feel for her, and I am sure this is not a one-sided thing because we have a sense of loyalty towards each other that nothing will ever spoil.

This distinctive unity of a friendship in exceptional instances may have strangely hostile components which operate to the detriment of one who seemingly does not recognize the effects of hostility upon her as the supposed friend. This type of friendship represents a primary relationship because of the personal involvement of the two friends but also is an instance of pseudo-intimacy which in diverse form has been discerned by psychiatrists in family relationships.[13]

Rose and I formed a close relationship that was probably the most unique one any person could have. By that I mean it was cutthroat friendship. Rose and I never got along in grammar school, but in high school we became friendly. She was the most two faced person I hope ever to meet. Pretending to be my friend, she was talking behind my back. Yet for four years we were inseparable. I was Rose's only friend. The kids at school would talk to her, but when it came to being really friendly they didn't want anything to do with her. I never was asked in a girl's club because they refused to have Rose but they did want me. Yet they thought that I would never join if Rose wasn't asked. I would have refused to join; I was just that stupid. I always felt that I wasn't wanted,

---

[13] Cf. L. C. Wynne, *et al.*, "Pseudo-Mutuality in the Family Relations of Schizophrenics," *Psychiatry*, **XXI** (1958), 205–20.

and the only person I had was Rose. I guess that was the real reason why I held on to her. She was making me nervous. My parents would constantly tell me to stop associating with her. It was all take and little give with her. She deceived me with my boyfriend; she encouraged me to talk back to my parents. The minute I stopped being friendly with Rose, I became a different person.

Based upon the aforementioned components of social intimacy, to what extent were adolescent subjects and their closest friends intimate? The components of social intimacy which I examined for this purpose are degrees of (1) confiding, (2) ease in the relationship, (3) cathartic expression and hilarity, (4) identification, and (5) awareness of the closest friendship as distinctive. In addition to a questionnaire I have used miniscales to ascertain the degree of closeness in these varied forms of socially intimate behavior.

Since confiding is a crucial criterion of intimacy, the extent to which the subjects confided and the manner of their friends' response indicated the degree of their social closeness. Thus 83.5 per cent of the subjects made self-disclosures to their friends, particularly when discouraged or confronted with a personal crisis, and 78.5 per cent were reassured by their friends. It appears that 21.5 per cent, or about one in five subjects on this communication level, had not an intimate relationship with their closest friends.

As indicated in the miniscale of confiding and common participation

TABLE 2

DEGREES OF CONFIDING AND COMMON PARTICIPATION AMONG SUBJECTS AND THEIR CLOSEST FRIENDS, BY PERCENTAGES

Degrees of confiding and common participation	*Percentages* $(N = 140)$
I communicate impersonal but not personal experiences to my friend	6.43
I participate in common activities and communicate impersonal experiences, but not personal experiences to my friend	8.57
I confide individualized personal experiences to my friend which have not been experienced by him	8.57
I share common activities (e.g., games) and confide individual personal experiences which have not been experienced by my friend	6.43
I share in common personal activities (e.g., dating, club, school, work) and confide contemporary as well as past common personal experiences to my friend	70.00
Total	100.00

in self-involving activities, 85 per cent of another group of 140 selected subjects confided personal experiences to their closest friends, and of this category 70 per cent confided personal reactions from common personal experiences, such as going out on a double date. As can be seen from Table 2, however, 15 per cent did not divulge personal matters to their closest friends.

Although some subjects claimed that they divulged all personal experiences to their closest friends, the topics most frequently withheld dealt with family experiences, and episodes of personal humiliation and stupidity which might cause the subject to appear demeaned in the eyes of his friend.

Another facet of intimacy pertains to the ease of the relationship as well as to its cathartic expression and unrestrained hilarity. For this markedly informal behavior which indicates trust and lack of defensiveness, 71.43 per cent of the subjects felt completely at ease with their closest friends. However, the remaining 28.57 per cent of the subjects were defensive at times with their closest friends because of their friends' latent or implicit hostility, competitiveness, or criticism.

Related to this form of interpersonal behavior, 72.46 per cent of the subjects experienced episodes of complete relaxation and spontaneous hilarity with their closest friends.

Identification with the closest friend is consistent with the view that the friendship is an end rather than a means. Although ingratiation and simulated friendliness with persons in strategic roles is pervasive in this mobility-oriented society, identification differs from this behavior because it regards the friend as an end in himself and not as a utilitarian means to self-advancement or self-aggrandizement. One operational way for ascertaining the degree of identification was the subjects' reaction to a slur against his closest friend.

The vast majority of the subjects—71.2 per cent—did not regard a slur against their friend as a slur against themselves, even though they would

TABLE 3

DEGREES OF EASE WITH CLOSEST FRIEND, BY PERCENTAGES

Degrees of ease with closest friend	Percentages (N = 140)
I feel at ease but must be on guard most times because of my friend's critical or hostile reactions	2.14
I feel at ease sometimes but must be on guard at other times because of my friend's criticisms or competitiveness	26.43
I feel completely at ease with my friend without reservations	71.43
Total	100.00

TABLE 4

DEGREES OF RELAXATION AND SPONTANEOUS HILARITY
BETWEEN SUBJECTS AND CLOSEST FRIENDS, BY PERCENTAGES

Degrees of relaxation and spontaneous hilarity	*Percentages* *(N = 138)*
I have episodes when my friend and I can relax completely and engage in spontaneous hilarity or unrestrained self-disclosures	72.46
I feel relaxed with my friend, but am not so relaxed that I engage in unrestrained self-disclosures or confidences	15.94
While I feel at ease with my friend, I do not recall any episodes in which I have engaged in unrestrained hilarity or in complete self-disclosure	11.60
Total	100.00

defend their friend from such a slur. But 12.9 per cent of the subjects identified closely enough with their friends to regard a slur against their friend as a slur against themselves; on the polar extreme, 15.9 per cent of the subjects would not defend their friends against a slur. The modal reaction of the subjects is to identify with the friend only to the point of self-interest without an intrustion into his distinct identity. Self-interest as the boundaries of identification characterizes the manner of social intimacy between closest adolescent friends in our society.

TABLE 5

IDENTIFICATION: DEGREE OF SUBJECT'S DEFENSE FOR CLOSEST
FRIEND WHO HAS BEEN SLURRED, BY PERCENTAGES

Degrees of subject's defense for closest friend who has been slurred	*Percentages* *(N = 139)*
I do not see any need that I should sympathize with my friend when he is slurred; he is a distinct individual in his own right, and should defend himself	6.48
I would not defend my friend against such a slur, but would sympathize with my friend	9.35
I do not regard a slur against my friend as a slur against me, but I would defend my friend against such a slur	71.22
I regard a slur against my friend as a slur against me	12.95
Total	100.00

I have pointed out that in closest friendship social intimacy involves a tacit or verbalized recognition of the friendship as distinctive. Thus, 36.2 per cent of the subjects felt that the friendship was distinctive, but 41.85 per cent—the modal category—regarded the friendship as fluctuating and as limited to episodes of distinctiveness. About 22 per cent either did not feel the friendship to be distinctive or felt it only in degree.

TABLE 6

DISTINCTIVENESS OF THE CLOSEST FRIENDSHIP:
BY PERCENTAGES

Distinctiveness of the closest friendship	*Percentages* *(N = 141)*
I feel that my relationship with my friend is not distinctive from that with others	7.10
I feel some measure of distinctiveness with my friend which sets him off from others	14.85
I feel that my relationship with my friend is at times distinct from others and at times not	41.85
I feel that my relationship with my friend is distinct from that with others	36.20
Total	100.00

When combining the scores of the components of social intimacy, including degree of confiding about personal matters, ease of relationship, unrestrained behavior, and identification and distinctive relationship, I found that out of a possible range, 5–19, the actual scores ranged from 9–19. The average score was 15.4 ± 2.25, with 64 per cent and 34 per cent above and below the average respectively.

In terms of the aforementioned criteria of social intimacy, a definite percentage of closest friends were not intimate. Thus, 2.1 per cent of the subjects did not feel at ease with their closest friends; 6.48 per cent of the subjects did not identify with their closest friends; 7.1 per cent of the subjects did not consider their closest friendship as a distinctive relationship; 11.6 per cent of the subjects did not experience unrestrained hilarity with their closest friends; and 15 per cent did not disclose personal matters to their closest friends. Since confiding is one basic criterion of social intimacy between peers, it means that this proportion of subjects did not experience an intimate relationship with their peers, even though some of these subjects may have experienced other components of social intimacy in some measure.

Although about 4 per cent of the subjects lacked closest friends, 15 per cent of the subjects were not intimate with their designated closest friends. Of the remaining 85 per cent, as can be seen from Tables 2 though 6, about 70 per cent seem to be socially intimate, while the other 15 per cent tend to fluctuate in their degree of social intimacy with their closest friends. In short, although the majority of the subjects had a sustained social friendship during their college stay, a definite proportion of college students lacked or had a transient if relevant closest friendship.

Conclusions and Implications

In this essay, I have aimed to sharpen the connotation of social intimacy in closest friendship as one type of primary relationship. This relationship has been viewed on the interactional dimension rather than as group function or as a reduced motive such as love, trust, or admiration.

The hypothesis concerning the formation of closest friendship that has been developed is that such interpersonal attachments emerge in (1) a situation of frequent and informal face-to-face encounter (2) between adolescents predominantly of like social categories and background (3) who participate in common activities and/or (4) who express and share common interests, values, and outlook.

There are other relevant findings in closest friendship between adolescents. (1) The academic setting, particularly high school and college, more readily than the neighborhood, contributes to the formation of closest friendship. (2) Residential proximity, however, may facilitate or reinforce a closest friendship by convenient accessibility. (3) Frequent physical presence or face-to-face encounter in common activities is crucial to the formation of closest friendship. In frequent association private experiences are communicated, so that a common responsiveness and interpersonal attachment arises. (4) Friends may concentrate their attention upon each other and draw socially closer when they are residual members of a disbanded peer group or are amidst a strange or hostile milieu.

Closest friendship and social intimacy intersect but do not coincide. On the one hand, closest friendship denotes a peer relationship designated by the subject but ranges from a relatively superficial contact to a very close and sustained attachment. On the other hand, social intimacy denotes a composite of interpersonal components which is crucially expressed in confiding and the sympathetic reaction to confiding, accompanied by trust, rapport, informality, attachment, and expansiveness between two or more persons. These persons may experience episodes of unrestrained hilarity and regression, called the "intimacy jag," may cultivate a set of idiomatic expressions, become reciprocally involved with each other, may become socially insulated from others, and regard the friendship as distinctive.

These components of social intimacy tend toward an empirically derived and plausible conception of human relations, specifically of adolescent closest friendship of the same sex. This heuristic formulation of social intimacy serves as a basic point of departure for further inquiry. As a genre of human relations, the mode of social intimacy in closest friendship has similarities as well as differences to other types of primary relations, including parents and children, siblings, courtship partners, and mates. A validated conception of social intimacy in primary relations would emerge by analyzing empirically and then abstracting the recurrent and similar features of intimacy in these diverse primary relations.

When viewed from the perspective of the life cycle, closest friendship during adolescence seems to contribute to personality stability and even to socialized growth. In the sequence of personality development I found that the three successive closest confidantes are the mother, the closest friend, and the fiancé or mate. The closest friend during adolescence tends to supersede or equal the mother as a closest confidante, while the prospective mate tends normally to supersede both closest friend and mother as the closest confidante.

Social intimacy between friends also has a therapeutic effect upon the participants. In fact, closest friendship, because of the processes of intimacy, represents a natural form of therapy which seems to be built into the society. Thus, social intimacy can have an emotionally supportive value because it reinforces the subject's self-estimate through peer acceptance. It can contribute to the subject's stability, because the friend may impart techniques and practices which facilitate social participation in the culture of the age-group and in the larger milieu. It can serve as a catharsis and release, for the subject can express and verbalize his inner conflicts and lessen his tensions. It can lead to the subject's greater insight into his situational and personality problems. It should also be mentioned, on the other hand, that a hostile closest friend can mislead, dishearten, and frustrate a credulous and trusting companion.

Because social intimacy between friends can contribute to a growth experience, it differs and may even be preferable to formal psychotherapy with an adult; the adult psychotherapist represents a protective and benign parent figure who provides the means for rehabilitating the adolescent so that he can foster close friendships more easily. This would signify a goal of rehabilitation. The closest friendship per se is the reality of adjustment. Social intimacy contributes to the adolescent's capacity to confront his complicated and at times bewildering world with greater confidence, and it stimulates a feeling of belonging to counteract a prevalent reaction of confusion and alienation.

The early symbolic interactionists emphasized that human nature grows in the matrix of the primary group. Their concern was with socialization during early life. This presentation reveals that socialized growth of the adolescent continues by the process of social intimacy between closest friends.[14]

---

[14] For a discussion of socialization beyond infancy and toddlerhood see Orville G. Brim and Stanton Wheeler, *Socialization After Childhood* (New York: John Wiley and Sons, Inc., 1966) ; and John A. Clausen, ed., *Socialization and Society* (Boston: Little, Brown and Company, 1968).

IV

SOCIOLOGY AND SOCIAL POLICY

23

Ernest Becker

THE SOCIAL ROLE OF
THE MAN OF KNOWLEDGE:
A HISTORICAL AND
CRITICAL SKETCH

What can we say in a few pages on a topic as broad and involved as the one we have chosen? What can we say that has not already been said, in a wealth of scholarly detail, and by leading minds? If we were to put our question this way we would not write. But let us put the question another way. Let us ask: What can we say that would sharply point up the problem of the man of knowledge in relation to society, so that this problem becomes most clear to our groping, idealistic youth? If we ask the question this way, not only can we write, but because of the social crisis of our age we can perhaps write more relevantly in a briefer space than ever before.

The striking thing about the social role of the man of knowledge is its sameness down through history, and even in prehistory. He has usually been a servant of power, a simple reflection of the needs and desires of his society. On the primitive level, the man of knowledge is the shaman, who tries to make sense out of his peculiar experience and translate it into terms that are meaningful to the other members of the tribe. If he is a bit more odd than the rest, the shaman must find a role that offers to his fellows the benefit of his own uniqueness. His experiences in the trance, and even in psychotic behaviors, become respectable only as they can be made socially meaningful.

Perhaps we might call this the original paradigm of the man of knowledge: From the time when the first individuals discovered their own uniqueness and the extra richness of their imaginations, this uniqueness and richness had to be converted into social coin in order to be meaningful and acceptable. The priests of the archaic civilizations followed the same tradition, and we know that the Sophists in Athens sold their talents and knowledge to all comers. Socrates was the one Sophist who gave his knowledge away free; and his knowledge differed from theirs in that it was socially critical, that it called men to think about their unique calling, about truth and justice, not about public opinion or about getting ahead in society. We know, too, the fate of the peculiar kind of oddball that Socrates was. Society doesn't want men of knowledge to turn against it. This is what Plato learned to his own disenchantment; politicians don't turn to the true philosophers to help them out of their plight.

Little wonder that the men of knowledge rarely modeled themselves on Socrates and instead preferred the original ancestor, the shaman. The Alexandrians, the theologians of the Middle Ages, they all hawked their wares. In the Middle Ages students paid teachers by individual fees, the most popular getting the highest income. And we should not be surprised if this knowledge paid for by fees was a passport to a future professional career. The same thing was true of the famous humanists and literati of the Renaissance. They were bent on their own careers, and their famous knowledge was, for the most part, the equivalent of our college sheepskin—it was a meal ticket in the larger society.

If we continued on in this vein, it would be a cynical picture indeed. Our idealistic students would have no choice but to turn away from the man of knowledge in disgust, as many of them now do. But wait. The picture of sameness that history reflects is interrupted at one critical point. I mean, of course, the Enlightenment. It was here that a new ideal sprang up for the man of knowledge, an ideal that harkened back to Socrates, and not the shamans. It was a vision of the man of knowledge as critic, as social critic, as someone who would rise above his own place and time, above the folly of his society, someone who would use reason, who would overthrow dogma and chart the way out of the Gothic darkness of superstition and error to which the masses of men had always been prone. It was a vision of the man of knowledge as someone who would cut through the unthinking habit that binds men to the automatic functioning of their social institutions, someone who would help to revise social customs in the light of scientific knowledge and who would modify that knowledge as it accumulated. There it was, *mirabile dictu:* the man of knowledge would modify morality in the light of critical reason.

We know the names of those in the eighteenth century responsible for this new vision of the man of intellect; two especially come to mind. Immanuel Kant was one of the first to pose the critical problem in modern times. In his famous essay on "The Strife of the Faculties," he saw what the promise of philosophy was, and what it was meant to do. He said that philosophy (or what we today would call the humanities or liberal arts studies) had to have a place in the university different from that of the other branches of knowledge: medicine, jurisprudence, and theology. These were what we would call today the *vocational* studies; they fit men for a role in their society. Philosophy, on the other hand, would give men a critical perspective on the roles of their society and had to be kept separate and protected in the university. Philosophy was free inquiry, no matter where it led nor who would be upset by its findings. This was the general drift of Kant's remarks.

The other great new vision that came out of the eighteenth century was that of the French, particularly Condorcet and the *ideologues*. Condorcet offered a stirring vision to the ideal of the liberation of man: he proposed nothing less than to organize science and education in the service of man. In order to guarantee continuing human liberation and progress out of the dark ages of past enslavement, there had to be proper organization and implementation. The main thing that education had to do was to protect itself from the dogma of the Church, and from the new tyranny of the State. So, said Condorcet, let the educational establishment be self-governing; let there be a supreme body for the direction of science and learning; and let them be independent of all institutions of the State, even if the State is an equalitarian political system. Let there be a National Society of Arts and Sciences, with 318 members, the most distinguished minds, drawn from the four fields of knowledge taught at the *lycees:* mathematics and physical science, technological science, moral and political science, literature and the fine arts. Let the whole educational program be planned from the lower schools up to the highest; let there be continuing adult education, comprising weekly lectures on civil rights and public duties, on scientific discoveries and new knowledge as they become available. This, and this alone—reasoned Condorcet—will prevent the citizens from becoming docile instruments in the hands of those who wield power over man. The supreme body for the direction of science and education would thus be the custodian of progress and human liberation, as well as the instrument of such progress. The members of the Society would control education by preparing and appointing teachers, insuring academic freedom, awarding scholarships to the best minds, preparing textbooks, and overseeing the quality of instruction—everything, in sum, that would have to be done to save future generations from falling into the prejudices of the past or from any new prejudices that would deprive them of their freedom and human dignity. The whole thing was designed so that "...no public power should have the authority or even the influence to prevent the development of new truths or the teaching of theories contrary to its particular policies or to its momentary interests."[1]

Here, then, was the answer to the problem of both Church and State: an autonomous, self-governing community of scholars, protected from encroachment on all sides. But what about the danger from within, what about human greed and the passion for power of the scientists and educators themselves, what about autocracy from within this autonomous structure? Condorcet proposed several guarantees for this, but the best guarantee was full publicity of elective lists and scientific work, to an increasingly enlightened public, so that the broadest opinion would always be called into play.

Regardless of what we may think today about the fine points of Condorcet's proposal, about the unfinished nature of his sketches, about his simple understanding of scientific method, about his faith in scientific honesty, in disciplinary collaboration, in reason winning out over pettiness and meanness—regardless of what we think of these, his main aim of keeping the enterprise of education and knowledge separate from the State, no matter what its form, must still remain a superb vision. Thomas Jefferson shared it, and it was his hope to give American higher education just this character of a self-governing community of free men. But this was never to be. Even his proposal for a National University in Washington came to naught; it was against the spirit of the times. If the Enlightenment as a whole was a radical break with the past, Condorcet was even too radical for the Enlightenment. His proposals, as the brilliant historian of the Enlightenment, Frank Manuel, points out, "went against the grain of the existing mores."[2] What? A State within a State! The idea went against the grain in the nineteenth century, too, when even those least radical of thinkers, John Stuart Mill and Herbert Spencer, feared that education would become a monopoly of the State. They go against the grain in our day, too, while education flounders in the miasma of mass society and swims with the huge and aimless tide of

---

[1] Condorcet, quoted in L. Pearce Williams, "The Politics of Science in the French Revolution," in *Critical Problems in the History of Science,* ed. Marshall Clagett (Madison: University of Wisconsin Press, 1959), p. 299.

[2] Frank Manuel, *The Prophets of Paris* (Cambridge: Harvard University Press, 1962), p. 84.

bureaucratic-industrial mediocrity. The proposals were the dream of guaranteeing democracy, of effecting the full ideal of human liberation; and this seems to go against the grain of the organized State in any epoch of earthly time. No Establishment wants to live with a powerful rival, no matter how benevolent and intelligent. The best hope of the Enlightenment, the basic vision of Jefferson for the American democracy, was allowed to lapse.

Condorcet was one of a group of *ideologues,* and in fact his plan failed when his successors—who tried to carry it out—were suppressed by Napoleon. Here was the consummate statist who knew the threat of a State within a State. The *ideologues* were members of the famous *Institut national,* especially of its great innovation, the section of social sciences. It was the *Institut* that promised to give social-scientific findings a central place in the national life by permitting them full leeway to influence national legislation and social reconstruction. The *ideologues* were not only scientists, they were also elected to legislative office in the national assembly. This meant that social scientists were the main lobby on the legislative and governing process! Just to mention this promise today must give one a thrill of hope mingled with despair. How proper a way to begin the modern epoch; how lamentable that this beginning failed.

The *ideologues* were the new scientific liberals, and when they functioned in their legislative posts they exercised their identity as social scientists, not as politicians. At first they went along with Napoleon, but their basic antiauthoritarianism came out when he began to use increasingly capricious power. They would not become tools of unreflective and tyrannical political power. Napoleon was thus a privileged witness to one of the great experiments of history; and when he saw the danger to himself, he turned his witness into active antagonism. He suppressed the *ideologues* in 1803, by closing their section of the *Institut.* And that was the end of the social-critical function of social science in the postrevolutionary epoch.[3]

Saint-Simon, Fourier, and their followers inherited the problem of the *ideologues.* But the agonizing question was how to unite social science for social reconstruction after the politicians had excluded it. This was the problem that dogged all the utopians: *They no longer had the proper institutional-parliamentary channels for influencing the reorganization of society.* Consequently, they had to go begging with their ideas, hoping that some industrialists of good will would adopt their schemes and build a new society based on science and reason. Comte had the same trust and suffered the same fate. He gave lectures on his system to small groups of interested people; he allied himself with the conservatives in the belief that only the established

---

[3] For a history of the German counterpart to the French tradition, see F. Lilge's wise and today urgent study, *The Abuse of Learning: The Failure of the German University* (New York: The Macmillan Company, Publishers, 1948).

authority could do anything at all. Without authority, firm authority, there is social chaos; and with social chaos how can reason run society? So said Comte, as he placed his trust in the conservatives. Alas, he found that they had little or no interst in social reconstruction, and at his death Comte was already a freak like the Saint-Simon that he came to despise. The Comtean Journal lasted only a few decades.

Lester Ward, the great American follower of Comte and the Enlightenment, tried for years to set up a National University in Washington, that would influence the legislature and the executive. It would be a central brain, right on the spot, so to speak, of the pulse of America. It would fuse heart and brain in one mighty union, guiding America to a rational destiny, rather than an irrational one. The vision, as we noted, is the one that Jefferson himself had championed earlier and had lost. There was no National University. There were only universities, each *serving* the needs of the country as best it could.

In England, the Comtean John Beattie-Crozier called for a new National Bible, a national brain composed of the best knowledge, which would be the scientific gospel truth that the country would use to run itself. The great H. G. Wells carried on this tradition eloquently: he called for nothing less than a "World Brain," a new international encyclopedia that would guide the destiny of nations by providing a base of the best scientific knowledge for all their conduct.

After Wells died the idea lost its force and its glamour. It flickered in a few minds—those of John Dewey, Horace Kallen, Morris Cohen, for example. One powerful statement of it was given by Ortega y Gasset, in his plea for a return to the authentic *Mission of the University*. The function of the university, he said, was to give knowledge "at the height of the times," knowledge that shows men their fate and how to overcome it, knowledge, in a word, that enables the members of society to meet the particular historical and evolutionary crisis that threatens to submerge them.[4]

Today we can ask, what happened to this vision of a national brain, of the university as a locus of critical intellect, examining the society critically, guiding it, influencing the legislative process, freeing the citizens from their own dogma, from the automaticity of their stale institutions and beliefs? Why did it die so totally and so quietly?

Well, two great things seem to have happened. For one thing, the trend of thought of the whole nineteenth century tore away from the synthesis and monism of the late eighteenth century. The synthesis of science in an academy such as that envisaged by Condorcet, Saint-Simon, and Comte was only a dream, never yet realized. The synthesis of philosophy, that would

---

[4] Jose Ortega y Gasset, *Mission of the University,* trans. Howard Lee Nostrand (Princeton: Princeton University Press, 1944).

include science, in the work of Comte, Fichte, and Hegel became repugnant to the nineteenth century mind. The dominant note of the late nineteenth century was the flourishing of the disciplines: new knowledge, new facts, secure data—this is the prerequisite without which any kind of thinking about man in society is pure self-defeating fancy.

I think this whole change in tone can be traced suggestively, but very clearly, after Comte and Lester Ward, just by examining the careers and work of men like Albion Small and Franz Boas in the two great disciplines of sociology and anthropology. Each founded his discipline in the hope that the accumulated knowledge would one day be brought to bear on social problems, on the national intelligence. And each lived to see his discipline flourish and forget all about the social problems. The early founders of social science in America knew what that science was for and thought that by fashioning serious scientific disciplines the freedom of man in society would be best assured. But both Small and Boas had plenty of time to look wistfully over the decades of their lives and their disciplines and see how the value-neutral specialists had taken over. The only freedom the latter cared about, for the most part, was the freedom to do more research, and to be left alone. Scientific specialism proved to be bureaucratic and inherently amoral.

We can sum up this whole problem by saying that the first great reason that the critical role of the man of knowledge failed was that fact and value came apart in science and philosophy. The Enlightenment promise of science in the service of morality simply broke in two.

The second reason that this role failed is reflected in the eighteenth century itself and in the naive beliefs of Saint-Simon, Fourier, and Comte, and their predecessors—Voltaire, Rousseau, Diderot, La Mettrie, and Helvetius. These people thought that the ruling groups of society would actually consent to diminish their power and privileges for the sake of social reconstruction of the society as a whole. This is why they didn't hesitate to sell their services to Catherine, or Frederick: they thought these people might want to govern according to critical knowledge. Alas, the men of knowledge then, like most men of knowledge today, didn't understand why the White House invited poets and artists and scientists to a party. It wanted these men to boost its own legitimation, not to consult with them to rearrange the power structure of society. The rulers of Europe wanted the great lights of the eighteenth century just as the chiefs wanted the shamans— to ally their powers into a more formidable and unshakable structure, one that appealed to reason and persuasion, and not only to naked force. It was an age-old story.

These Enlightenment thinkers did not, in a word, understand that a state was a structure of domination, as well as a miasma of unreason. Only the great myth-slayers of the nineteenth century understood this, Marx and Engels especially. That is why they scorned the naiveness of Saint-Simon,

Fourier, and Comte in imagining that the industrialists would take their schemes to heart. This was utopian socialism and not scientific socialism. However much we may today lament this scorn of utopianism by the scientific socialists, we must admit that they have given us a full consciousness of power realities.

We must admit, too, that the well-intentioned naiveness of the eighteenth century dies hard, as we witness in the writings of some of our best scholars today. For one thing, they take the weakest aspect of Max Weber—his lamentable separation of fact and value, of the university from social life, and they hold this as a continual ideal model.[5] For another thing, they carry over the old fallacy that the man of knowledge still has a crucial role to play in society, so long as that society remains open and pluralistic. This was Lewis Coser's conclusion at the end of his searching exploration in *Men of Ideas.* Let us just keep working and thinking and somehow this work and thought will be translated into the public good.

But this is the naive and false hope that begs the question. Today we are in a better position than ever before to conclude that the earlier liberal hope of society run by a national brain is dead, and it cannot be revived merely by hoping, hanging on, and "doing more" science. Since the failure of the *ideologues* there has been no way to implement such a brain, except in the most monolithic and tyrannical way. The scientist would have to get control of government, or, in the tradition of science under Stalin, find a benevolent dictator who would protect and instrument his pet scientific ideology. There is no way today for social science to influence critically government via the parliamentary process. Even worse, since the national scientific organizations consistently refuse to take a stand on social and moral issues, there is no way to influence policy-makers, even by the indirect pressure of enlightening public opinion. The net result is that not only is the early liberal hope dead, but so too is the later one expressed by those like Coser. The critical function of the man of knowledge cannot exercise itself in the babel of pluralism because—as C. Wright Mills so painfully came to realize—this very pluralism swallows up the best and most critical knowledge. Pluralism delivers the fruits of knowledge over to the uncritical social functioning, to the standard version of truth, happiness, and goodness, no matter what it might be, even to the Pentagon and war capitalism with its scientific warfare and its cultured bubonic plague. The structure is just too big and overpowering for the man of knowledge to fulfill his authentic critical role within it. If he is not actively choked off, then he is unassumingly swallowed up. As Voltaire lamented for the eighteenth century, the most terrible thing is to be hanged in oblivion. And as we are learning today, the

---

[5] The most sympathetic, rounded, brief critique of Max Weber that I have seen is by Lilge, *op. cit.*

surest way of being hanged in oblivion is to be engulfed in the monolith of so-called pluralistic society. Those of us today who lament the passing of critical dialogue and scientific confrontation may well envy a climate in which a Rousseau could be arrested three days after publication of a book on education.

Is there any way out then, any possible function at all for the man of knowledge? I think that with the death of monism and hopeful liberal pluralism the third alternative becomes quite clear: it is what I call "dialectical" or "oppositional" pluralism. In this third alternative the man of knowledge would use the findings of science specifically to show up the antihumanism and the general evils outstanding in his particular time and place. He would set up his truth as a countervision, always tentative, always developing, yet always standing in judgment on the failings of his society. Optimally, he would do this as much as possible with a body of like-minded people, in some identifiable institution or locale. This is not a naive, once-for-all utopianism in which one would hope to replace all the "bad guys" with "good guys" and would try to coerce the millenium in a decade. It is, rather, a tough realism, in which one would try to show up the sham and irrationality of his social world by carefully fashioning and trying to give full publicity to a better version of the truth and to a more hopeful and challenging critical ideal.

The way to do this was perhaps best understood by the British sociologist Victor Branford, the noted partner of the famous Patrick Geddes. It was almost seventy years ago that he called for an opposition party of social scientists, who would try to win a following in the national life for their informed and scientific countervision of the ills of their world.[6]

In fact, as we look back in conclusion over the long history of our dilemma, we can see that there are really only four alternatives for the man of knowledge:

(1) The first alternative was the vision of Condorcet and the *Institut* in France; and in Germany, of the idealists. This vision would give social science a vital and direct role in the legislative process and the national life. Jefferson hoped for a similar thing in his proposal for a National University in Washington; Lester Ward tried to revive this same idea.

(2) The second alternative is the one of Victor Branford. It would consist of a new political party of social scientists. It would come about as the social scientists acquired a collective consciousness of themselves as a social group with a definite and specific heritage. That heritage would be conceived as a *trust*. This heritage and trust would then become the idea

---

[6] Victor Branford, "Note on the History of Sociology in Reply to Professor Karl Pearson," in Francis Galton, *et al., Sociological Papers* (London: Macmillan, 1905), I, 33, note.

around which a new political party of social scientists would be formed, which would seek to advocate "such policy as the sociological doctrine may sanction"—to use Branford's words. Given the social-critical nature of social science findings, this party would have to be an active opposition party. In this way it would combine the social-critical role of the intellectual outsider with inside participation in the democratic process. Whereas the *Institut* began with the hope of immediately making science the main lobby on the legislative process, the party of social scientists would begin with the hope of gradually becoming an important opposition party, as it won support from other segments of the population.

(3) The third alternative is the one we have lived through as a consequence of the failure of the first two. It is the alternative of a metaphysic of hope that we call, euphemistically, the scientific "disciplines." The metaphysic of hope is that pursuit of the disciplinary quest would one day somehow lead to a unified science in the service of man. Comte had already shown the fallacy of this metaphysic, but for certain reasons (valid and invalid) we have chosen to ignore this.[7]

(4) The price of our unruffled scientific calm is that we must forego the active experimentation in society that would firmly establish the interrelationships of things; and so we periodically lapse into the fourth alternative, namely, the *philosophy or theology of history*. This is the substitute attempt to find the meaning of life, the causal factors of history, in the natural and historical process. We need not intervene; we can content ourselves to study and imagine. In this kind of situation the man of knowledge is relegated to the kind of alienated position that Marx decried and that Hegel typified. He becomes a passive vehicle for the automatic pulsations of the Universal Spirit. I am not saying that a philosophy or theology of history would be replaced by an active science of man—as Comte, for example, thought that it would. The tragedy and evil in the human condition would still search for a broader explanation than any science could give. My point is simply that science must take *some* of the burden of explanation of the world's evil, and not leave it all to metaphysics.[8]

And so we may conclude our brief account. We are today in a better position than ever before to understand fully the lament that Plato recorded in *Republic VI:*

> *To begin with, then, teach this parable to the man who is surprised that philosophers are not honored in our cities, and try to convince him that it would be far more surprising if they were honored.*

---

[7] These reasons and the relevance of Comte to the contemporary crisis in science are treated in some detail in Ernest Becker, *The Structure of Evil: An Essay on the Unification of the Science of Man* (New York: George Braziller, Inc., 1968).

[8] *Ibid.*

We need no convincing today. When we look at the four alternatives of the man of knowledge, we must share Plato's pessimism. Perhaps for the intellectual there may be some joy in drawing unitary circles across a span of history as long as 2500 years. Who better to join hands with across history than Plato? But there is more in our situation than the satisfaction of company, of mutual disillusionment. There are twenty-five centuries more, and at no previous time have we so well understood our true fate, or so well scrutinized the full face of our adversaries. We can offer them an accusing and shaming opposition, based on a magnificent edifice of sober knowledge. We are called upon to affirm our calling and this knowledge with courage and dignity, with the heroism of the underdog who represents the liberating human cause. This idealism we can offer to our youth. Perhaps we may begin by speaking out in the councils of science. I have long shared the belief that if we could bring ourselves to see the evils, and to speak out authoritatively against them, that this alone would change the world. Admittedly, it requires no small passion and honesty to see evils, and no little courage to speak out against them. If this is a gigantic task, at least it is now clear that it is our task; and if we do not move in this direction, our scientific work can have no substantial meaning. This is the authentic self-exposure of our time.

24

Irving Louis Horowitz

THE ACADEMY AND
THE POLITY : ON SOCIAL
SCIENTISTS AND FEDERAL
ADMINISTRATORS

The burgeoning literature on the relationship between the academy and the polity is both serious and sophisticated. I shall not attempt here either an omnibus review of the literature or an explanation of present data on the subject. Instead, I prefer to confine my remarks to those aspects of the subject which have been relatively obscured in the shock of recognition that many academies are directly linked to federal policy research and dedicated to narrowing the gap (whatever the larger consequences) through the selective support of sensitive research.

The area we are getting into is the sociology of political mobilization. What we have is essentially a two party relationship, and the problem is to locate either the mutuality or incompatibility of interests which are involved in any interaction between the academy and the polity. To construct a satisfactory framework we should focus on problem areas which are decisive for both groups: initially, a study of how the interaction is perceived by political men. Apart from the interaction itself, there is the shadowy area of the consequences of the network of proposals and responses following from the relationship between the two contracting parties. Not only do social scientists and politicians interact with one another, but the professional ideologies they arrive at and the norms they establish also guide present and future interactions as well.

How Social Scientists View Politicians

(1) Money

The first and perhaps most immediate experience that social scientists have with politicians, or at least with their counterparts in various federal granting agencies, relates to the financial structure of contracts and grants. First, the difference between contracts and grants should be explained. As an operational definition we can speak of contracts as those agreements made with social scientists which originate in a federal bureaucracy. Most research on Thailand and Southeast Asia or on Pax Americana is contract work. Grants can be considered as those projects which are initiated by the social scientists.

A frequently heard complaint is that there is often a great deal of money available for contract work but comparatively little for grants for scholarly research. This can be attested to by the relative size of social science budgeting by the Department of Defense, as compared with such a grant awarding government agency as the National Science Foundation or even a high status but poorly endowed division of government as the Department of State.

At another level but within the same general scope is the fact that most contracts issued, in contrast to grants awarded by agencies such as the Department of Health, Education, and Welfare or the National Institutes of Health, have little funding allocated for free-floating research. Funds are targeted so directly and budgeted so carefully that, with the exception of the overhead portion—which administrators rather than scholars control—there is little elasticity in the contract for work which may be allied to but not directly connected with the specific purpose of the contract itself. This contrasts markedly with the case for many physical scientists, and even researchers in the field of mental health, who are often able to set aside a portion of contract funds for innovative purposes. Allowance for serendipity is, moreover, built into many physical science projects.

Related to this question of financial reward for hardware and high payoff research is the amount of funds available for social science research as a whole. Social scientists often state that the funding structure is irrational. Government funds are available in large sums for big team research, but little spillover is available for individual scholarly efforts. The government reinforces big team research by encouraging large-scale grants administered by agencies and institutes and by its stubborn unwillingness to contribute to individual scholarly enterprise. Large-scale grants are also made because they minimize bureaucratic opposition within the government, and this eliminates responsibility for research failures. But at the same time, this approach contributes to the dilemma of the scholar who is concerned with research at modest levels or research which may be far more limited than the grant proposal itself indicates. The present contract structure encourages entrepreneurial hypocrisy, which is often alien to the spirit of the individual researcher and costly to the purchase of ideas and plans.

Finally, another dilemma of the financial structure of federal contracts is that awards are usually made only to a single team or a social science institute to do research in a set area. Few funds are available for competitive research in the same areas of work. Moreover, virtually no funds are set aside for contingency researches, such as the possibility of any single grant study requiring a great deal more money on a short-term basis than originally anticipated. It might well be that the competitive issuance of grants would be just as heatedly opposed by social scientists as by federal economists preparing a budget. But it is also clear that the absence of this kind of competition in the government research and development network reduces the potency of any particular piece of research, since the element of independent verification is often lacking. Instead, powerful agencies tend to underwrite powerful research institutes. The rewards are mutual, and the risks of intellectual (or financial) competition are minimized.

(2) Secrecy

Social scientists have been increasingly critical of the government's established norms of secrecy. While most officials in government have a series of work norms with which to guide their behavior, few forms of anticipatory socialization have applied to social scientists who advise government agencies. The professionalization of social scientists has normally been directed toward publicity rather than secrecy. This fosters sharp differences in opinion and attitudes between the polity and the academy, since the reward system for career advancement is so clearly polarized.

The question of secrecy is intimately connected with matters of policy, because the standing assumption of policy makers (particularly in the field of foreign affairs) is not to reveal themselves entirely. No government in the game of international politics feels that its policies can be candidly revealed for full public review; therefore, operational research done in connection with policy considerations is customarily bound by the canons of government privacy. But while scientists have a fetish for publicizing their information, as a mechanism for professional advancement no less than as a definition of their essential role in the society, the political branches of society have as their fetish the protection of private documents and privileged information. Therefore, the polity places a premium not only on acquiring vital information, but on maintaining silence about such information precisely to the degree that the data might be of high decisional value. This leads to differing premiums between analysts and policy makers and to tensions between them.

Social scientists complain that the norm of secrecy oftentimes involves yielding their own essential work premises. A critical factor reinforcing an unwilling acceptance of the norm of secrecy by social scientists is the allocation of most government research funds for military or semimilitary purposes. Senate testimony has shown that 70 per cent of federal funds targeted for the social sciences involve such restrictions.

The real wonder turns out to be not the existence of the secrecy norm but the relative availability of large chunks of information. Indeed, the classification of materials is so inept that documents (such as the Pax Americana research) designated as confidential or secret by one agency may often be made available as a public service by another agency. There are also occasions when documents placed in a classified category by sponsoring government agencies can be gotten without charge from the private research institute doing the work.

But the main point is that the norm of secrecy makes it extremely difficult to separate science from patriotism and hence makes it that much more difficult to question the research design itself. Social scientists often express the nagging doubt that accepting the first stage—the right of the government to maintain secrecy, often carries with it acquiescence in a later stage—the necessity for silence on the part of social researchers who may disagree with the political uses of their efforts.

The demand for secrecy has its most telling impact on the methodology of the social sciences. Presumably social scientists are employed because they, as a group, represent objectivity and honesty. Social scientists like to envision themselves as a wall of truth off which policy makers may bounce their premises. They also like to think that they provide information which cannot be derived from sheer public opinion. Thus, to some degree social scientists consider that they are hired or utilized by government agencies because they will say things that may be unpopular but nonetheless significant. However, since secrecy exists, the premises upon which most social scientists seek to work are strained by the very agencies which contract out their need to know.

The terms of research and conditions of work tend to demand an initial compromise with social science methodology. The social scientist is placed in a cognitive bind. He is conditioned not to reveal maximum information lest he become victimized by the federal agencies that employ his services. Yet he is employed precisely because of his presumed thoroughness, impartiality, and candor. The social scientist who survives in government service becomes circumspect, or learns to play the game. His value to social science becomes seriously jeopardized. On the other hand, once he raises these considerations, his usefulness to the policy making sector is likewise jeopardized.

Social scientists believe that openness is more than meeting formal requirements of scientific canons; it is also a matter of making information universally available. The norm of secrecy leads to selective presentation of data. The social scientist is impeded by the policy maker because of contrasting notions about the significance of data and the general need for replication elsewhere and by others. The policy maker who demands differential access to findings considers this a normal return for the initial expenditure of risk capital. Since this utilitarian concept of data is alien to the scientific standpoint, the schism between the social scientist and the policy maker becomes pronounced precisely at the level of openness of information and accessibility to the work achieved. The social scientist's general attitude is that sponsorship of research does not entitle any one sector to benefit unduly from the findings—that sponsorship by federal agencies ought not place greater limitations on the use of work done than sponsorship by either private agencies or universities.

(3) Loyalty

The third major area that deeply concerns the social scientists is that of dual allegiance. A charge often expressed is that government work has such specific requirements and goal-oriented tasks that it intrudes upon the autonomy of the social scientist per se by forcing upon him choices between dual allegiances. The social scientist is compelled to choose between participating fully in the world of the federal bureaucracy or remaining in more familiar academic confines. He does not, however, want the former to create isolation in the latter. Thus, he often criticizes the federal bureaucracy's unwillingness to recognize his basic needs: (1) the need to teach and retain a full academic identity; (2) the need to publicize information; and above all (3) the need to place scientific responsibility above the call of patriotic obligation—when they may happen to clash. In short, he does not want to be plagued by dual or competing allegiances.

The norm of secrecy exacerbates this problem. Although many of the social scientists who become involved with federal research are intrigued by the opportunity to address important issues, they are confronted by some bureaucracies which oftentimes do not share their passion for resolving *social* problems. For example, federal obligations commit the bureaucracy to assign high priority to items having *military* potential and effectiveness and low priorities to many supposedly idealistic and far-fetched themes in which social scientists are interested.

Those social scientists, either as employees or as consultants connected to the government, are hamstrung by federal agencies which are in turn limited by political circumstances beyond their control. A federal bureaucracy must manage cumbersome, overgrown committees and data gathering agencies. Federal agencies often protect a status quo merely for the sake of rational functioning. They must conceive of academicians in their midst as a standard bureaucratic type entitled to rise to certain federal ranks. Federal agencies limit innovating concepts to what is immediately useful, not out of choice and certainly not out of resentment of the social sciences but from what is deemed as impersonal necessity. This has the effect of reducing the social scientist's role in the government to that of ally or advocate, rather than innovator or designer. Social scientists begin to feel that their enthusiasm for rapid change is unrealistic, considering how little can be done by the government bureaucracy. And they come to resent involvement in theoryless application to immediacy foisted on them by the "new Utopians," surrendering in the process the value of confronting men with the wide range of choices of what might be done. The schism, then, between autonomy and involvement is as thorough as that between secrecy and publicity, for it cuts to the quick well-intentioned pretensions at human engineering.

The problem of competing allegiances is not made simpler by the fact that many high ranking federal bureaucrats have strong nationalistic and conservative political ideologies. This contrasts markedly with the social scientist, who comes to Washington not only with a belief in the primacy of science over patriotism but also with a definition of patriotism that is more open-ended and consciously liberal than that of most appointed officials. Hence, he often perceives the conflict to extend beyond research design and social applicability into one of the incompatible ideologies held respectively by the social scientists and entrenched Washington bureaucrats. He comes to resent the proprietary attitude of the bureaucrat toward "his" government processes. The social scientist is likely to consider his social science biases a necessary buffer against the federal bureaucracy.

(4) *Ideology*

A question arising with greater frequency, now that many social scientists are doing federally sponsored research, involves the relationship between heuristic and valuative aspects of work. Put plainly, does the social scientist have the right not only to supply an operational framework of information but also to assist in the creation of a viable ideological framework —does he have the right to discuss, examine, and predict the goals of social research for social science?

Many social scientists, especially those working on foreign area research, bitterly complain that government policy makers envision social science as limited to heuristics, to supplying operational codebooks and facts about our own and other societies, and generally to viewing the social scientist as a performer of janitorial services for military missions. Social scientists, however, also consider their work in terms of its normative function, in terms of the principles and goals of foreign and domestic policy. But given their small tolerance for error, policy makers cannot absorb mistaken evaluations. This inhibits the social scientist's long-range evaluations and renders empiricism the common denominator of investigation. Factual presentations become not only "value-free" but "trouble-free."

This does not so much arise from the question of the relationship between pure and applied social research. Rather, it stems from differing perspectives on the character of application. Social scientists working for the political establishment realize that applied research is clearly here to stay. They are the first to announce that it is probably the most novel element in American, in contrast to European, social science. But federal bureaucrats operate with a concept of application which often removes theoretical considerations from research. Designing the future out of present-day hard facts—rather than analyzing types of action, interests, and their relations in the present—comes to stand for a limited administrative Utopianism and satisfies the illusion that demands for theory and candid ideological commitment have been met.

The social world is constructed like a behavioral field, the dynamics and manipulation of which are reserved for policy makers. But social scientists are aware that interests and their representative values are contending for influence on that field, and that social planning is often a matter of choosing between these values for the sake of political goals. Thus, tension arises between social scientists—who consider their work set in highly political terms, and federal bureaucrats—who prefer to consider the work of the social scientists in nonpolitical terms. Indeed, federal administrators particularly go out of their way to depoliticize the results of potentially volatile social research, so as to render it a better legitimizing device for their own bureaucratic activities. Social scientists come to suspect that their work is weighed for efficiency and applicability to an existing situation. The adequacy of the social system to confront large-scale and longstanding problems is left out of reckoning.

(5) *Reward*

Federal bureaucrats measure the value of social science involvement in the government in terms of payoffs. These are conceived to be the result of big team research involving heavy funding (like the model cities program). Moreover, the high status of individuals is appreciated when they are at the center rather than the periphery of policy performance—when they have an opportunity to influence policy at high levels, to secure valuable information, and give prestige to projects in which they participate. And, it might be added, many social scientists who contract research from the government seek just such power rewards.

Even those social scientists most involved with the government—as employees rather than as marginal consultants—express profound reservations. First, as we have noted, social scientists operate under various degrees of secrecy which stifles their urge toward publicity for the work they do. It goes instead to the men for whom they work. Second, social scientists must share responsibility for policy mistakes. Thus, they may be targeted for public criticism under difficult conditions more frequently than praised when they perform their duties well. Finally, those social scientists closest to policy agencies are most subject to congressional inquiry and to forms of harassment and investigation unlike anything that befalls strictly academic men.

The government employed social scientist runs risks to which his colleagues at universities are not subject. It is often his particular contention that these risks are not properly understood by academicians or rewarded by policy makers. (Salary scales, for example, are adequate in federal work but not particularly high in comparison with academic salaries.) Consider also that marginal financial payoffs resulting from publication are oftentimes denied federally sponsored social scientists. This is a vital area for more than monetary reasons. Social scientists' fears concerning their removal from channels of professional respectability and visibility seem to increase proportionately with their distance from the academy. They often point out how few among those in federal work receive recognition from their own professional societies and how few gain influential positions within these professional establishments. This produces a great deal of marginality in federal work. Scholars willing to get funded through government agencies, or even to accept consultantships, will reject primary association with a federal administration.

While outsiders may accuse federally sponsored social scientists of "selling out," they in turn respond to their tormentors by pointing out that

they make sacrifices which need to be made for the sake of positively influencing social change, that far from "selling out," they have not "copped
out." This self-defense, however, is often received skeptically by their colleagues in the academic arena (as well as by their would-be supporters in the
federal bureaucracy), who regard such hypersensitive moralism with suspicion. The upshot of this matter of rewards is, then, that status derived
from proximity to sources of power is offset by isolation from the actual
wielders of power—academic no less than political.

How Administrators View Academicians

The complaints of social scientists about their difficulties with government sponsored research have received so much attention as to overshadow
administrative complaints against social scientists. This has been fostered by
the fact that social scientists tend to be more articulate than other scientists
in examining their feelings and in registering their complaints about the work
they do. Also, relations with bureaucrats have a greater import for the social
scientist than those with social scientists have for the bureaucrat. It is thus
small wonder that government complaints about social scientists have been
poorly understood.

Federal agencies and their bureaucratic leaderships remain skeptical
about the necessity for employing basic social science data in their own formulations. Among traditionally appointed officials, the local lawyer or party
worker is the key means for transmitting information upward. For many of
the sectors of the military, expertise comes mainly from military personnel
performing military functions. Hence they do not require outside social science validation. And as we witnessed in the military response to the Department of Defense "Whiz Kids," they often consider outside efforts as
intrusions. High military brass (as well as a number of politicians) sounded
off hotly against the Defense Department and echoed in their critiques a
traditional posture which juxtaposed military intuition and empirical proximity to the real world, against mathematical techniques and ivory tower
orientations.

When social scientists attempt to assuage political or military doubts
and allay suspicions by preparing memoranda and documents which prove the
efficacy of social science for direct political and military use, they sometimes
do more to reinforce negative sentiments than to overcome them. When the
academy responds that way to the polity (as it did in its recommendations
to the Defense Science Board), it underwrites its own lack of autonomy if
not in fact its own ineptitude. The academy cannot prove its worth by moral
declarations and public offerings to bureaucratic agencies. The total service
orientation to social research, in contrast to the independent "feudal" aca-

demic orientation, is one which breeds contempt for the performer of such services and a lack of faith in the outcomes. This helps to explain the broad resentment toward social science research extending from the Joint Chiefs of Staff to the Senate Foreign Relations Committee. Suppliers of raw labor might be well paid if they have a powerful union, but they hardly command high status in a society which strains toward quick and inexpensive solutions.

(1) Waste

The first and perhaps foremost criticism made by administrators against the academy is that social scientists make excessive demands for funds and special treatment while working on projects that frequently have little tactical value. This is translated into a charge of impracticality. Typical is the critique made by the General Accounting Office against the Hudson Institute, headed by defense strategist Herman Kahn. Underlining charges made by the Office of Civil Defense, the work of the Hudson Institute in the area of the behavioral sciences was charged with being "less useful than had been expected" and to require "major revision" before the reports were acceptable. Various social science reports, particularly those prepared by semiprivate agencies, have been criticized for their superficiality, for their tired thinking, for their sensationalism, and above all, their lack of immediate relevance.

In response, social researchers claim that the purpose of a good report is imaginative effort rather than practical settlement of all outstanding issues. Government agencies should not expect a high rate of success on every research attempt. One reason for the persistence of this line of criticism is the infrequency with which demands for high payoff utilitarian research are ever contested. The questionable practicality in much social science research remains a sore point in the relationship, which cannot be resolved until and unless social scientists themselves work out a comfortable formula governing the worth of relevance in contrast to the demand for relevance.

(2) Inutility

Another criticism made by federal sponsors issues from the first, namely, that there are no systems for insuring that results obtained in research are usable. A gap exists between the proposal and fulfillment stages of a research undertaking. Proposals which are handsomely drawn up and attractively packaged often have disappointing results. And while many sophisticated agencies (such as the National Institutes of Health, National Science Foundation, or Office of Economic Opportunity) are aware of the need for permissiveness in research design, those agencies more rooted in hard science and engineering traditions are not as tolerant of such experimentations.

Moreover it is charged that academicians, when they do government research, "over-conservatize" their responses to placate a federal bureaucracy. This may come, however, at the point when it is trying to establish some liberal policy departures. The chore of the federal agency becomes much more difficult, since it must cope not only with the bureaucratic sloth and conservative bias of top officialdom, but with reinforcements for it in research reports by social scientists from whom there might have been some expectations of more liberal formulations. Thus, not only is there a gap between proposal stage and fulfillment stage in the research enterprise, but some reports may structure conservative biases into the programs assigned to the federal bureaucracy by congressional committees or executive leadership.

(3) Elitism

Federal administrators point out that academic men often demand differential and superior treatment on grounds other than those accorded most government employees. The charge is that social science personnel do not really accept their role as government employees but see themselves as transiently or marginally connected to the government. Particularly in areas of foreign affairs, the academician appears to want the advantages of being privy to all kinds of quasi-secret information and of being involved in decision making, yet he wants to avoid normal responsibilities which are accepted by other government employees.

To federal officials such attitudes smack of elitism, an elitism built into the structure of social scientific thinking. Social scientists are trained to analyze problems rather than to convince constituencies. They become impatient with the vagaries of politics, preferring the challenge of policy. One reason adduced by elected officials for their preference for legal rather than scientific advisors is that the former have a far keener appreciation of mechanisms for governing people and in turn being governed by them. The legal culture breeds a respect for the popular will rarely found among social scientists attached to government agencies. Indeed, the resentment expressed by many House and Senate committees against Defense Department and State Department social scientists is a direct response to the elitist streak which seems to characterize social scientists in government.

This is the reverse side of the involvement-autonomy debate. The government pushes for total involvement and participation, while the social scientist presses for autonomy and limited responsibility in decisions directly affecting policy. Elitism rationalizes the performance of important services while maintaining the appearance of detachment.

(4) Access

Although social scientists view their own federal involvement as marginal, they contradictorily demand access to top elites so that they may be assured that their recommendations will be implemented or at least seriously considered. But access at this level entails bypassing the standard bureaucratic channels through which other federal employees must go.

The social scientist's demand for elite accessibility, while often said to be inspired by noble purpose, thus tends to set the social scientist apart from other employees of the federal government. He sees himself as an advising expert, not an employee. The social scientist takes himself seriously as an appointed official playing a political role in a way that most other federal workers do not. But the federal bureaucracy finds great presumption in the fact that the social scientist has come to Washington to set the world on fire, without considering the flame that burns in the heart of staff administrators.

The desire for easy access to leadership stems from notions of the superior wisdom of the social scientist; however, it is precisely this claim that is most sharply contested by federal administrators. Largely reflecting popular feelings of resentment, these administrators claim that the easy admission of social scientists to the halls of power assumes a correctness in policy judgments not supported by historical events and not warranted by mass support from popular sectors. The duality of science and citizen roles often disguises precisely a lack of citizen participation. The scientific ethos thus comes to serve as a basis for admission into a system of power by circumventing the civic culture, and this is precisely why federal bureaucrats feel they are defending their political constituencies (and not incidentally their own bailiwicks) by limiting social science participation in the decision making process.

(5) Marginality

If social scientists chafe at being outside the mainstream of academic life during their period of involvement with the political system, the federal bureaucrats are themselves highly piqued by the degree of supplemental employment desired and enjoyed by the social scientists. This too is in clear contrast with other federal government personnel. Social scientists also are able to locate supplemental positions in the Washington area. They work as teachers and professors; they do writing for newspapers and magazines; they edit books and monographs; they offer themselves as specialist consultants capitalizing on their government involvement. They become active in self-promotion to a degree which falls outside the main reasons for their being hired in the first place.

In the more loosely structured world of the academy, such self-promotion not only goes uncriticized, but is rewarded. Royalty payments for textbook writing, involvement with publishing firms in editorial capacities, honoraria connected with membership in granting agencies, and payments for lectures on American campuses are all highly respected forms of supplemental employment. But federal government employment involves twelve months a year and twenty-four hours a day. This condition and its demands is very different than the nine months a year with fluid scheduling that govern the relations of most social scientists with academic institutions.

Federal agencies not only disdain the marginal aspects of the academicians' involvement in political life, but the awareness of agency officials that men involved in government effort are oftentimes *not* representative of the most outstanding talent available in the social sciences also disturbs them, particularly since they traffic in the status spin-off of both the academy and the polity. The anomaly exists that men who may not have been especially successful in academic life make demands upon the federal bureaucracy as if in fact they were the most outstanding representatives of their fields. And while the same problems might well arise in connection with outstanding representatives from the social sciences, the situation becomes exacerbated precisely to the degree that federal bureaucrats are dealing with second and even third echelon federally employed social scientists.

Patterns of Interaction and Accommodation

In this profile the academicians and federal administrators alike have been presented as more uniform in their response to each other than is actually the case. It should not be imagined that the two groups spend all their time in bickering criticism of each other, for then certainly no stable relationship worth speaking of could exist. Still, the roles acted out by both parties make it clear that we are in a period of extensive redefinition. The criticisms that academics and politicos have of each other often have a mirror image effect, with each side sharply focusing on the least commendable features of the other.

It is significant that the political context and content of this issue has in the main been unconsciously suppressed by both sides. The academicians have preferred to emphasize their scientific activities in objective and neutral terminology, whereas the politicians express their interests in organizational and bureaucratic terms. The strangest aspect of this interaction, then, is that in the world of politics it seems nothing is more embarrassing than political analysis and synthesis. As if by common consent, social scientists and policy makers have agreed to conduct their relations by a code of genteel disdain rather than open confrontation. The gulf between the two groups requires political distance as an operational equivalent to the social distance between competing tribal villagers.

(1) The Contract State

There may be cause for concern that federal government sponsorship corrupts the character of social science output because it emphasizes big money, an overly practical orientation, and limited dissemination of information, and fails to realize the potentially subversive nature of any research. But ironically, the government does not go in search of social scientific personnel who are timid or opportunistic. Most often the social scientist seeks the federal sponsor and becomes overly ambitious in pressing exaggerated claims for unique research designs and high payoff promises. The chief threat in this is not financial. Rather, the academician who has come to depend on the federal bureaucracy for research funds and its variety of career satisfactions may begin to develop the loyalties and cautionary temperament of the opportunistic civil servant per se.

Many interlocking appointments between the academy and the polity have occurred at the organizational level without resolving persistent questions as to what constitutes legitimate interaction between the academy and polity. This indicates that the line between the academy and the polity is blurred enough to require determination of precisely who is stimulating what kind of research and under what conditions. And as it becomes increasingly clear that academicians are the stimulants and administrators the respondents in the majority of instances, the need to become self-critical of social science participation rather than critical of federal practice becomes pressing.

To appreciate fully the sources of tension in the interaction between academicians and administrators, it is necessary to indicate the range of attitudes about connection between the government and the academy. This range extends from advocacy of complete integration between administrators and academics to complete rupture between the two groups. We now turn to the spectrum of positions available on this matter.

(2) Policy-Science Approach

The quarter of a century from 1943 to 1968 constitutes something of a spectrum along which are ranged attitudes from complete integration to complete rupture. From World War II (and even prior to that, during the

New Deal), optimism prevailed about an integrated relation between academicians and administrators. This was perhaps best expressed in the "policy-science" approach frequently associated with the work of Harold Lasswell.

In this view the relationship between the academic and the political networks would be an internal affair, with political men involved in academic affairs just as frequently and as fully as academic men would be involved in political affairs. The policy-science approach was a noble effort to redefine familiar departmental divisions of labor. Sociology, political science, economics, and the other social sciences would be absorbed by a unified policy-science which involved a common methodological core. The difficulty, as Lasswell himself well understood in later years, is that in the exchange network federal administrators spoke with the presumed force of the "garrison state," while academicians (even those temporarily in government service) spoke with the presumed impracticality of the "ivory tower."

The policy-science approach did in fact have direct policy consequences. The end of World War II and the fifties saw the rise of new forms of institutional arrangements for housing social science. But more than organization was involved. A new emphasis cut across disciplinary boundaries. Area studies emerged in every major university. Communism was studied as part of the more general problem of the role of ideology in social change. This was followed by centers for urban studies and for the study of industrial and labor relations. But despite the rise of institutionalized methods for uniting specialties, university department structures had a strange way of persisting, not just as lingering fossils but as expanding spheres of influence.

It soon became apparent that in the struggle for influence over the graduate student world and for decisions about who shall or shall not be appointed and promoted in university positions, the department held final authority. It was through the separate departments of social sciences that the disciplines retained their vitality. At the same time that the policy-science approach was confronting departmentalism, disciplinary specialization was increasing. The postwar period witnessed anthropology insisting on its own departmental arrangements apart from sociology and theology, while other areas such as political science and social work became more sharply delineated than at any time in the past. The policy-science approach was thus successful in institutionalizing all sorts of aggressive and at times even progressive reorderings of available *information,* but at no time did it really establish the existence of a policy-science *organization.* And this proved fatal to its claims for operational primacy.

The policy-science approach was supplanted by the "handmaiden" approach dominant in the early fifties. That is to say, the academy was to supply the necessary ingredients which would make the political world function smoothly. The reasoning was that the social sciences were uniquely qualified to instill styles in federal decision making based on confirmed data. But this did not entail complete integration of services and functions. The handmaiden approach was more suitable to the nature of both the social sciences and the policy making aspects of government. This approach was materially assisted by the rising emphasis on applied social research. With this new emphasis on application and on large-scale research came the theoretical rationale for providing janitorial mop-up services. It was argued that application made possible a search for the big news, for the vital thrust, and that participation in this intimate consensual arrangement would not deprive the social sciences of their freedom but on the contrary would guarantee its relevance. The "theoryless" service approach was thus wedded to the action orientation.

Advocates of the handmaiden approach, like Ithiel de Sola Pool, vigorously defended the necessity for social scientists to do meaningful research for government. It was noted that an organization like the Department of Defense has manifold needs for the tools of social science analysis as a means for understanding its world better. It was pointed out that since the days of World War I the intelligence test had been an operational instrument in manpower management and that the Defense Department and other federal agencies had become major users of social psychology in military and sensitive areas. As the world's largest training and educational institution, the United States government also has immense needs to acquire exact knowledge for use in the selection and training of human subjects. Equally significant is the federal government's needs for exact foreign area information. The thirst for exact knowledge of the cultural values and social and political structures of foreign countries increased as the world was carved up into potential enemies or potential allies of the United States.

The ironic aspect in this drive for meaningful research is that, although the handmaiden approach ostensibly left social science autonomy intact, it reduced that autonomy in fact by establishing criteria for federal rather than social science pay-off. High yield research areas uniformly involved what the social sciences could do for the political structures and not necessarily the other way around. Thus, while the policy-science approach gave way to the service industry orientation of the handmaiden approach, the latter also was unable to achieve any real parity between the academy and the polity.

(3) Selective Participation Approach

A new kind of approach, considerably removed from both the policy-science and the handmaiden approaches, has been finely articulated by David B. Truman. In theory at least, it has expressed a renewed sense of equity and parity between social scientists and administrators. Under this arrangement there would be frequent but largely unplanned interchanges between federal bureaucratic positions and university positions. This alternation of roles would prove valuable and could be explored and encouraged in the future on a systematic basis. But for the time being, the selective participation approach holds that the less formal structure in the system the better.

The most important aspect of the selective participation approach is that it rests on a norm of reciprocity. There would be a partial interchange of personnel which could be accomplished primarily through regular seminars and conferences mutually attended by social scientists and government administrators. Each cluster of men would represent carefully designed combinations, or there might be alternating presentation of scientific development and policy problems. This would be unlike the normal consultant relationship involved in the handmaiden style, since it would guarantee some kind of equity between the academy and the polity. Selective participation would also involve securing grants and promoting federal research, particularly for multidisciplinary teams of academicians working on political problems, instead of the usual outright political employment of social scientists or academic talent. This, it was hoped, would provide a flexible arrangement of specialties which would fill the gap between scientific knowledge and public purpose without detriment either to social scientists or political policy makers. Operationally, it would mean a greater flow of funds from government agencies to research institutes housed on university campuses—a not inconsequential change from the policy-science approach which projected a much more intimate ecological, as well as ideological, network.

(4) Forms of Nonparticipation

The dilemma was that the exchange network implicit in the selective participation approach assumed a parity of strength between political decision makers and academicians. It assumed rather than demonstrated that the academician would be on a par with the administrator, since the latter had financial inputs while the former had the informational outputs. Yet, in point of fact, it is the government agency which does the hiring, even in the selective participation approach, and it is still the academic who participates in a policymaking role without much expectancy of a payoff for social science theory or methodology.

This has given rise to what might be called the principle of "nonparticipation." In this framework, which is increasingly being adopted in the present period, social scientists would continue to write and publish in areas of foreign research or in sectors vital to the national political arena, but not under government contract nor as a direct response to a federal agency. The sentiment spread that if the autonomy of the social sciences meant anything at all, it signified that uses and findings legitimately arrived at would be incorporated into federal policy making whether or not there was active or critical participation by the social scientists.

Many conservative as well as radical social scientists have tended to adopt the principle of nonparticipation. They saw in the growth of federal social research a threat to the standard forms of status advancement in the professions and also a movement toward applied social planning which violated their own spirit of the generalizing nature of social science. Thus, on organizational and intellectual grounds, the principle of nonparticipation serves as an effective response to the policy-science approach. Underlying the notion of nonparticipation is the assumption that the federal government has more to gain than does the social scientist by the interaction between them. There is further implication that interaction remains, but that the order of priorities is changed so that the social scientist no longer has the onerous task of providing high payoff research for others with low yields to themselves.

In many ways the principle of nonparticipation suggests that the university department remains in fact the primary agency in the organization of social science, rather than the federal research bureau. The nonparticipant in federal programs has often found himself to be the critic of bureaucratic research in general and of bureaucratic agencies attached to universities in particular. He does not want to have his research controlled by federal decision making; and more important, he does not want a federal agency to usurp what was properly a judgment customarily in the domain of a university department.

At the same time, the principle of nonparticipation has spilled over into the principle of active opposition. This too, in the main, has been registered by younger scholars in areas such as history and among graduate students in the social sciences—that is, those often involved in student protest movements. From their point of view the matter can not be resolved on the essentially conservative grounds of selective use by the government of the best of social science. What is needed instead is a conscious attempt to utilize scholarship for partisan or revolutionary goals which could, under no circumstances, be employed by the establishments linked to government agencies. In this sense, as Hans Morgenthau indicated, there has been a movement away from the belief that the social scientist and the federal administrator merely inhabited mutually exclusive worlds to the belief in active opposition between them because they occupied mutually hostile positions with antithetical goals.

In one sense, the radical posture accepts the policy-science appraisal of a political world dominated by the "garrison state," but rejects its remedy of social science immersion to reorient government away from its predatory world missions. The policy-science view assumed the educability of military-minded rulers. The antiparticipation view assumes the reverse, namely, the ease with which social scientists become incorporated into the military and political goals of men of power.

The assertion has been made by radical critics like John McDermott that in practice the goals of the academy and the polity have become antithetical. But even further it is said that, theoretically, they ought to be antithetical. A transformation of the dream of action into the nightmare of federal participation was brought about in which the academy became in effect an adjunct of the federal establishment. The dream that academic social scientists had of position and prestige has in some sense been realized by their transformation into men of action: academic men have become high priests of social change. The desire for social change has, in effect, overwhelmed the goals toward which such change was directed.

The move toward active opposition involves a critique of the way in which the university, no less than the government, is structured. Those who moved away from federal participation simultaneously turned their energies on the university system. It is held that the academy itself, as beneficiary of federal funds, has become the political party of the academic man. In this sense the rash of student attacks against the university can be considered, in part at least, as symbolic attacks against the notion of integration of policy making and academic performance.

(5) *Surrogate Politics*

The best guarded nonsecret of the present era of university relationships to the government, at least insofar as they bear upon this notion of active opposition, has to do with the general political and ideological climate which now prevails.

During the 1941–1945 period, when the United States was engaged in a world conflict in which the overwhelming number of citizens felt involved in the very survival of civilization itself, there were no pained expressions about government recruiting on campuses. There was no feeling of resentment toward the retooling of universities to satisfy military research needs and psychological warfare, propaganda research, or conventional bombing surveys. Nor were any scholarly panels held at professional meetings concerning the propriety of social scientists who accepted appointment under the Roosevelt administration in the Office of War Information or in the Office of Strategic Services, although there are now discussions about the propriety of relationships between social scientists and the Federal Bureau of Investigation or the Central Intelligence Agency.

The present level of controversy, then, over the relationship between the academy and the polity, spills over into a series of surrogate discussions over the legitimacy of the war in Vietnam, or Latin American self-determination, or civil strife in American ghettos. Unable to address such issues directly and unprepared to design structures for future alleviation of such world and national pressures, social scientists exaggerate the politics of inner organizational life. Professional societies engage in mimetic reproduction of central social concerns on a low risk and probably a low yield basis.

Organizational struggles also receive the encouragement and support of corresponding professional men and societies from the Third World and from minority groups. It is no accident that federal projects which had Latin American targets have come under particularly severe assault. The counter social science establishments in countries such as Mexico, Chile, Argentina, and Brazil provide vocal support for domestic United States academic opposition and to firming up such opposition by posing the threat of total isolation from foreign area research for a failure to heed the dangers of certain kinds of political research. Increasingly, Negro militants in this country have adopted a similar posture of nonparticipation in social science projects without clearly stated preconditions of nonimpingement on the "rights" of the subjects or sovereigns.

The risks to both social science and public policy from the predetermination of research designs are not part of this paper. Suffice to say that surrogate politics has now become a rooted pattern in American academic affairs. It stems partly from the fact that academicians come to politics by way of moral concern, whereas politicians come to moral concerns by way of political pariticipation. Surrogate politics is also a reflex action of the expanding and articulate but impotent social sectors against what have become the dominant political trends of the United States at this time.

Surrogate politics has its place in national affairs. Indeed, the question of the relationship between the academy and the polity is exactly a question of surrogate politics. Precisely, this common undercurrent of moral revulsion for professional hucksterism and amateur gamesmanship has forced the present review of the status between social scientists and policy makers. This same reexamination should have taken place a quarter of a century ago, despite the difficulties of the situation. But precisely because of the optimal consensus which existed in the past concerning the political climate, the issues now being discussed were considered improper topics for social scientists in pursuit of truth. Now we all, hopefully, know better. We can only conclude by noting that in science as in sex it is better to be late than never at all.

25

Ethel Shanas

SOCIAL RESEARCH
AND SOCIAL POLICY
IN THE FIELD OF OLD AGE

Social scientists are now being called upon to study issues pertinent to social policy, to speak up in areas of their competence, and to make their views on public affairs a matter of public knowledge. For many social scientists this concern with social policy is new and strange. For others, however, the current vogue to relate research to policy is a reinforcement of what they have been doing all along. For some years now, persons engaged in sociological studies of old age have been investigating an area which is pertinent to public policy, making their research findings known, and then, in many instances, engaging in efforts both to have the implications of their findings understood and to have these acted upon. It is the belief of these scholars that whether one's emphasis be on old age or on youth, sociology is the study of human beings in a social setting. This social setting is the real world in which people live, and progress in coping with the real world calls for an accurate assessment of that world whether it be congenial or not.[1]

As students in the field of old age have learned more about the life of the elderly, many among them also have come to realize that having social science knowledge available does not always mean that such knowledge can be immediately useful. The social policies which in large measure determine the condition of life of old people in the United States are based on many other factors besides available information. Further, and perhaps most disheartening to the academic scholar with little experience in the development of policy, the basis of policy is often social myth, not facts. To bring policy makers to accept and act on research findings which destroy social myths is no less difficult than convincing sociologists that much of what they take for granted is nonsense.

In this paper I shall consider social research and social policy in the field of old age. The paper begins with a general discussion of the differences in the viewpoints of scholars and policy makers and how these differences affect social policy. It then considers some of the myths about old age which have been and continue to be the basis of social policy in this country and presents some of the research findings about old age which challenge these social myths.

The Research Specialist and the Social Policy Maker

The research specialist and the social policy maker view the world from different perspectives. C. P. Snow, the British scientist and novelist, has developed the theme of the interaction between scientists and policy makers in a long series of novels. He and others talk of the scientist's "culture." Yet, it is a shock to the producer of research when he discovers that what is obvious to him is not necessarily obvious to the potential research consumer. This is as true in the field of old age as it is in many other areas of investigation.

The producer of social research and the consumers of such research do not necessarily see eye to eye. Research specialists and research users often differ on program goals, on the need for haste in the introduction of programs, and on the merit or lack of merit of contradictory research findings. There is often conflict between the two on what research should be done, how this research should be carried forward, and whether available research findings have any relevance for program operations.[2]

---

[1] Donald P. Kent, *Aging—Fact and Fancy* (Washington, D. C.: U. S. Government Printing Office, 1965), p. 1.

[2] Cf. Ethel Shanas, "Social Research in Aging and its Programmatic Implications," in *Government and Aging: Prospects for Creative Federalism*, ed. Robert Binstock (forthcoming).

To begin with, the producers of social research and the potential consumers of such research do not necessarily agree on what research should be done. The interest of the research worker may be in the research problem itself, not in its practical implications, and he may make no effort to communicate his findings to those who could use them in practice. The policy maker, for his part, does not approach his task in a spirit of scientific inquiry. He, in turn, may be concerned with general issues and the implementation of governmental programs. Further, he may be unable to grasp the implications of a piece of research unless these are pointed out to him, and even when this is done he may brush the implications aside as irrelevant or impracticable.

The producers of research and the consumers of research operate with different standards of expediency. The research worker needs time to develop his thesis, to polish his argument, and to demonstrate the fine exceptions to his conclusions. The policy maker or practitioner operates within a different field of reference. The day-to-day demands of the job may call for instant decisions based on limited evidence. The need to do something, to appear to go forward, takes precedence over contemplation or even over the review and evaluation of what is already known. Often policy makers and program planners ask for evaluative research into program operations, but before the evaluative research can be completed or even designed, they introduce new programs based on assumptions about the efficacy of existing or past operating programs.

The producers of research and the consumers of research have different standards of what constitutes good research. The research specialist thinks in terms of study design, sample size, and limitations of his findings. He is aware of the exceptions to his conclusions, his possible range of error, and of data which he should have but which is somehow missing. The policy maker who wishes to utilize the results of social research has no basis for knowing what is good research. As he sees it, he is confronted with a veritable jungle of findings, some of them contradictory. What often happens in such situations is that personal preference makes a given set of research findings appealing to the policy maker, while another set of research findings is ignored. Good research then becomes that research which the policy maker finds congenial. At other times, the policy maker may be convinced that, research or no, he knows the field better than any research specialist. In these instances all research, pertinent or not, is pushed aside.

It has become fashionable for policy makers to call for more research into problems for which there are no ready answers. Such calls for knowledge have many different motivations, some of which are not related to knowledge at all. The social scientist would do well to realize that in most instances, however pertinent he may think his research findings to be, there is only a slight chance that these findings will affect social policy.

The Roots of Social Policy

The roots of social policy are rarely found in social research. Developments in social policy grow first out of past policy, second out of existing social myths, and finally out of the evaluation which policy makers and administrators make of what the public wants and is ready to accept.

Policy makers tend to draw on past policy in planning future social policy. The usual policy maker does not want to be responsible for introducing a radically new idea. New ideas are strange; they are unproven; they are apt to fail. Policy makers are more comfortable when that which is newly proposed can be related to that which has been done before.

In the same way, social myths provide much of the rationale for social policy decisions. Such myths form a body of collective beliefs which everyone knows to be "right" and to be "true." It is easy for a policy maker to accept such myths. They reinforce what he already knows. They are reassuring rather than threatening.

And finally, policy makers in the United States base social policy on what they think the public will accept. The policy maker, as a leader, must be sensitive to public expectations. He can only function as a leader if others follow him. Social policies which the public is not ready to accept are doomed to failure.

Medical insurance for the aged, Medicare, is the most revolutionary change in American social policy in the field of old age since the enactment of the Social Security laws in 1936.[3] The roots of Medicare can be found in past policy, in social myths, and in political judgments about the public mind and what the public wants.

A variety of research studies dealing with the health needs of the aged were available at the time of the congressional debates on Medicare, but these studies had little or no effect on the passage of the legislation. The major use made of the findings of these studies was as ammunition for one side or another in the extended debate.

The Medicare legislation was an outgrowth of various attempts, going back a score of years or more, to enact some health insurance scheme for needy sections of the American people. It was based on the dual assumptions that the aged were the poorest section of the population and those most likely to be sick. Its proponents called up a vision of tottering old ladies

---

[3] Extensive public hearings were held on this topic. See, for example, Committee on Ways and Means, House of Representatives, *Medical Care for the Aged,* Parts I-IV (Washington, D. C.: U. S. Government Printing Office, 1964). Eugene Feingold, *Medicare: Policy and Politics* (San Francisco: Chandler Publishing Co., 1966) gives a selection of pertinent quotations in this area. A thought provoking discussion of how the Medicare legislation was steered through the Congress is given in Richard Harris, "Annals of Legislation: Medicare," *The New Yorker,* July 2, 1966, pp. 9, 16–23.

pushed into the poor house by medical bills: its opponents argued about rich widows with limitless resources feeding at the public trough. What finally convinced the Congress to enact Medicare, however, was the failure of the Kerr-Mills legislation previously enacted to be implemented by the states, the economic decision by powerful segments of the insurance industry that medical care for the aged could not be financed through the private sector, and a feeling on the part of congressmen that the public expected the Congress to do something about the sick and impoverished aged.

To repeat, the available research studies which estimated the proportions of sick and impoverished aged played very little part in the final decision of the Congress to introduce Medicare.[4] Medicare had its roots in past social policy, in folk belief, and in a general congressional feeling that "the public expects us to do something."

Social Myths About the Aging

It is a sociological platitude that social myths act as a cohesive force in a society. Such myths, however, may also serve to obstruct both thought and action by encouraging persons to accept as fact that which is really fiction. The aged in Western urbanized societies, like the juvenile delinquent, the teenager or the industrialist, are the subject of a number of social myths. The origins of these myths vary. Many of them probably result from viewing contemporary society with a set of presuppositions that William Goode has called "Western nostalgia." At the same time the reasons for the persistence of these social myths also vary. It is interesting to speculate how many of the myths about the aged remain in force because opinion makers and opinion leaders have a vested interest in their continuance. Sociologists who have spoken widely about the nuclear family, for example, do not even bother to review the evidence for the existence of an extended family in contemporary Western society.

From the vast network of social myths about the aged which have been the bulwark of American social policy, I shall select only a few to consider here. They come from the areas of health, family relationships, and housing. They are: (1) Most older people are in poor health. A related belief is that most older people are in institutions or would be in institutions if adequate institutions were available. (2) Most old people are rejected by their adult children. A related belief is that most old people are also physically isolated from their children as well as isolated from all social interaction. (3) Adequate housing is a major concern of the aged. A related belief is that most old people prefer to live in a housing environment where there is

---

4 Cf. Ethel Shanas, *The Health of Older People: A Social Survey* (Cambridge: Harvard University Press, 1962).

age integration, that is where a broad spectrum of age groups is represented.

The reader who accepts some or all of these myths is in good company. As collective social facts, they constitute the ideological basis of much of American social policy in the field of old age. They are widely believed not only by the general public and the Congress, but also by scientists.

Scientists, like other people, are products of the culture in which they find themselves. It should be no surprise, therefore, to read in the magazine *Science* that "What we have done, mainly, is to lengthen life in relation to retirement age, and to curb diseases of youth without curing those of age, thereby insuring that our aged will be not only bored and alienated but poor and ailing as well."[5]

Life has been lengthened in relation to retirement age. Most medical advances that have been made control the diseases of youth. The statements about length of life and disease control are the only parts of the above quotation which are facts. Contrary to *Science,* while many old people are living in poverty and others in near poverty, the majority of the aged are not included among the poor. Whether the majority of the aged are ailing or not depends upon one's definition of the term "ailing." I shall say more about this later in this paper. Further, there is no evidence that the aged are any more or less bored than the remainder of the population. There is not even any good evidence that they are alienated.[6]

Collective social myths have resulted in a picture of the old in this country as enfeebled, decrepit, and isolated. It is an uncomfortable vision to use as a basis for social policy. Just as the policy maker may be motivated to do something for those pitiful objects, the elderly, he may be equally tempted to ignore them. As some government officials have said informally, "Old people have had their day. With limited resources, we have to concentrate on the young." What statements such as these suggest is that policy makers assume that since the nineteen million persons aged sixty-five and over are probably enfeebled, isolated, and decrepit, they are also powerless. Recent research findings about the health, family relationships, and housing of old people contradict many of the social myths which form the basis of contemporary social policy and constitute a challenge to the policy makers.

Research Findings About the Aging

Old people may be found in every society. In those societies where most persons do not live very long, anyone who survives into his forties will probably be considered old. In the United States where, on the average, a

---

5 Elinor Langer, "Growing Old in America: Frauds, Quackery, Swindle the Aged and Compound Their Troubles," *Science,* CXL (May 3, 1963), 470–72.

6 Ethel Shanas, "A Note on Restriction of Life Space: Attitudes of Age Cohorts," *Journal of Health and Social Behavior,* IX (1968), 86–90.

child born today can expect to live to be over seventy, we use a calendar definition of old age. For convenience, we say that those sixty-five and over are old people. The choice of the calendar age sixty-five to symbolize the beginning of old age is a cultural definition. There is no evidence that the onset of old age is related to any particular year in the life span. In this country age sixty-five as the beginning of old age was institutionalized by the Social Security Act of 1936, in which age sixty-five was selected as the age at which persons could receive old age pensions and retirement benefits.

Age sixty-five then entered popular thinking as the year which symbolized the beginning of later life. It must be stressed that a generation separates the sixty-five year old from the ninety year old. They may be as unlike as the twenty year old and the forty-five year old. When we use calendar age as an index of aging, a great variety of people—the active and the inactive, the healthy and the infirm, the working and the retired—are all grouped together.

Other definitions of old age are possible. However, since most social research on old age accepts a calendar definition of aging, the findings which follow are largely based upon studies of people aged sixty-five and over.

Are Most Old People in Poor Health?

Old age is not the same as illness. Although most old people exhibit signs of pathology upon physical examination, the presence of disease, especially of chronic conditions, may have very little effect on the day-to-day functioning of older people. What is suggested here is that it is really degree of fitness rather than extent of pathology that determines whether old people can manage by themselves and the amount of service which they will require from the community.[7] The health of older people, then, should be measured in terms of their ability to function rather than in terms of disease entities. Perhaps an illustration will make this point clearer. A man retires from a physically demanding job because he has a heart condition. He is unable to get to work in bad weather. Once retired he moves to a mild climate. He develops a pattern of life in which the physical strains on him are nominal. To all intents and purposes he lives a full, normal life. Should he then be described as being in poor health?

Using a measure of capacity based on the ability of the old person to perform the minimal tasks needed for his personal care, about two-thirds of all old people in the United States report that they have no functional incapacity.[8] The majority of old people in this country, then, behave as though

---

[7] World Health Organization, *The Public Health Aspects of the Aging of the Population.* Report of an Advisory Group Convened by the Regional Office for Europe (Copenhagen: World Health Organization, 1959), p. 8.

[8] The data on the health and family relationships of older people reported here are drawn largely from Ethel Shanas, *et al., Old People in Three Industrial Societies* (New York: Atherton Press, 1968).

they were well. Further, when asked to describe their health, the majority say their health is good, and most even think their health is better than the health of other old people. Only about one in every six old people living outside of institutions say their health is poor.

Most old people, then, are both functioning well and think they are in good health. Some old people, however, are obviously experiencing problems related to their health. Using the same measure of health described earlier the question becomes: How many old people in the United States are limited in their functional capacity?

About 3 to 4 per cent of all old people in this country are in institutions including hospitals, nursing homes, and homes for the well aged. Let us assume, however, that most of these institutionalized persons are unable to take care of themselves and form a hard core of sick persons. But what of old people living in the community? How many of them are unable to accomplish the minimal tasks required for their self-care?

About 2 per cent of the elderly population are totally bedfast at home. About 5 per cent of the elderly are housebound. An additional 5 per cent of the elderly are able to go outdoors only with difficulty. Adding these proportions together, about 16 per cent, or about one in six, of all persons aged sixty-five and over are sick or ailing, including in this 16 per cent all those institutionalized, those bedfast and housebound at home, and those housebound because they are unable to go outdoors without help. In general, then, the picture which emerges of the American aged is not of an ailing and enfeebled group of individuals or of a group of persons who would seek institutional care if it were available. Rather, one finds the majority of the aged in fairly good health. Many may have chronic diseases, but they have accommodated to these diseases. Most carry on their daily activities without assistance.

Incapacity in the elderly increases with advanced age. The most seriously incapacitated old people in this country are those aged eighty and over. The most incapacitated aged can be categorically described as very old women, either single or widowed. Yet, even among the very old, while many over eighty are quite frail, others are active and mobile. The comments of Elaine Cumming and Mary Lou Parlegreco based on their study of old people in Kansas City are pertinent here. These investigators say:

> There is some evidence that living to be over eighty...is associated with being a member of a biological and possibly psychological elite. Furthermore, very old people often have a surprisingly high level of social competence and seem able to maintain high spirits....[9]

---

9 Elaine Cumming and Mary Lou Parlegreco, "The Very Old," in *Growing Old: The Process of Disengagement,* eds., Elaine Cumming and William E. Henry (New York: Basic Books, Inc., Publishers, 1961), p. 201.

The majority of old people in the United States are active persons under seventy-five. They can scarcely be described as ailing. The feeble aged are largely found among the very old. Most old people in the United States, social myths and *Science* to the contrary, are not in poor health.

Are Most Old People Rejected by Their Adult Children?

It is difficult to know whether most old people are rejected by their children. While, as we shall see, there have been a number of studies of related topics, the quality of the relationships between old people and their adult children is still to be carefully investigated. What evidence is available indicates that the quality of the interaction between older parents and adult children varies from family to family. In general, the relationships between aged parents and adult children continue to have much the same sort of emotional content as did earlier relationships between them. What this suggests is that when older parents are rejected, the phenomenon is not a product of the age of the parents. It usually has its roots in patterns of family interaction originating far in the past.

Implicit in the belief that old people are rejected by their children, however, are several assumptions which have been carefully investigated. These assumptions are: that older parents and their children live at great distances from one another; that parents and children rarely see one another; and that aid between parents and children is nominal or nonexistent. None of these assumptions are validated by the existing evidence. Instead the evidence overwhelmingly supports the position of Sussman, who states that "...there exists in modern industrial societies...an extended kin family system, highly integrated within a network of social relationships and mutual assistance that operates along bilateral lines and vertically over several generations."[10]

About four of every five persons aged sixty-five and over in the United States have living children. Older parents and adult children do not necessarily live in the same household. In contemporary society with present means of transportation and communication the extended kin network is not dependent for its existence upon a common roof. Nevertheless, the members of the network continue to see one another frequently and to assist one another in meeting the demands of daily living.

Most old people in the United States live apart from their children and relatives. In western cultures this is what old people want—to live independently in their own homes as long as possible. As the Austrian soci-

---

[10] Marvin B. Sussman, "Relationships of Adult Children with Their Parents in the United States," in *Social Structure and the Family: Generational Relations,* eds. Ethel Shanas and Gordon F. Streib (Englewood Cliffs, N. J.: Prentice Hall, Inc., 1965).

ologists, Leopold Rosenmayr and Eva Köckeis have put it, old people want "intimacy at a distance."[11] Old persons of middle class or white collar backgrounds, whether married or widowed, are the least likely of all persons to live with children. It is old people of working class background who tend to share a home with their children. Living together in a joint household is often the way in which adult children and other relatives assist in support of aged persons.

Although old people live apart from their children, this does not mean that old people are isolated from their children. Of all old people with children, two-thirds either share a household with a child or live within ten minutes distance of a child. Only 16 per cent of all aged persons with children say that their nearest child lives an hour or more distant from them.

Not only do most old people with children live near their children, they also see their children often. In a national sample study, about two-thirds of all old people saw at least one of their children either the day they were interviewed or the day before that. There is a minority of old people with children, however, 10 per cent, who have not seen a child for a month or more.

Kinship associations compensate old people without children by providing substitutes for children.

Thus, old people who have never married tend to maintain much closer relationships with their brothers and sisters than those who marry and have children. Persons without children tend to resume closer associations with siblings upon the death of a spouse, but, interestingly, not as close as single persons.[12]

Patterns of mutual family help are widespread among the elderly. Old people and their children and relatives share housing, see one another regularly, and visit overnight. The children and relatives of old people help them in time of emergencies, give them gifts on birthdays and holidays, help them with housekeeping and home repairs, and contribute money, food, and clothing toward their upkeep.

Old people, for their part, help their children in times of emergency, give them gifts on birthdays and holidays, help with housekeeping and home repairs, take care of grandchildren and great grandchildren, and often assist children and grandchildren financially.

The pattern of family help flows from adult children to old parent or from parent to child as needed. People in their sixties are more likely to

---

11 Leopold Rosenmayr and Eva Köckeis, "Propositions for a Sociological Theory of Aging and the Family," *International Social Science Journal*, XV (1963), 418.

12 Peter Townsend in Ethel Shanas *et al., op. cit.,* p. 166.

help their children than people in their eighties. On the other hand, the older the parent the more likely he is to receive help from his children.

Contrary to popular belief, solitude is not a predominant feature of the life of the elderly in the United States. Extremely isolated persons, in the sense that they live alone and that a week or even a day can pass without human contact, are very rare. We estimate that extremely isolated old persons are only about two persons in every hundred. Among persons living alone interviewed in a national study, four of every ten had visited friends the day before they were interviewed, and about five of every ten had had visitors. Few persons were without meaningful everyday relationships and social activities. As Townsend says, "Bereavement is perhaps the single most isolating experience in old age and yet even this, as at other ages, draws a chain of 'reintegrating' responses from family and community."[13]

It may be that the relationships between old people and their children are bitter and unhappy ones and that the proximity, visiting, and mutual aid reported by old parents and adult children is a vast national denial of rejection. This would be the argument of those who cling to the rejection myth in the face of evidence which would tend to contradict it. On the other hand, it may be that adult children accept as a natural part of the life span their increasing responsibility for providing aging parents with both social and psychological support.

Generations are not the same, and there are social barriers between them. We do not know that older parents are rejected by their children. We do know, however, that the interrelationships between aging parent and child would seem to reflect the integrative nature of the primary group in industrial society. It is to their families, not to social agencies, that old people first turn help. It is children and relatives who form the bulk of visitors reported by old people.

There is no good evidence either for or against the belief that old people are rejected by their children. There is considerable evidence, however, that the relationships between older parents and adult children remain viable into extreme old age.

Are Most Old People Concerned with Their Housing?

Policy makers and practitioners in the field of aging devote much of their attention to the housing problems of the elderly. This reflects the common belief that old people are concerned about their housing and that housing is a major problem to them. Along with the attention to the physical aspects of housing we find arguments against isolating old people with their own age group, based on the assumption that in old age cross-generational ties are more desirable than peer group ties.

---

13 *Ibid.*, p. 286.

The most thoughtful research on the effect of environments, of which housing is one, upon the elderly has been carried forward by Irving Rosow. Rosow's study was made in Cleveland and grew out of the desire of the Cleveland Housing Authority to determine whether old people preferred living in age segregated housing or age integrated housing. Rosow expanded the goal of the Housing Authority into a sociological problem: What was the experience of old people in areas where many of their neighbors were their age peers as contrasted with their experience in areas where only a few of their neighbors were their age peers?

Rosow's findings emphatically refute the belief that housing is a major problem to the elderly. He states categorically that on the basis of his own research and that of others housing is "not a genuine problem to a significant number of the aged."[14] He says further: "The aged do not need special housing so much as decent housing they can afford. Indeed, what seems necessary in this context is (1) less housing *research,* (2) higher *income,* and (3) more *housing.*"[15]

Rosow's work is especially important because it contradicts the common belief that old people are happiest in neighborhoods where they can associate with persons of all ages and thus develop friendships that cut across generational lines. Rosow found that, in keeping with sociological theory, old persons tend to form friendships with people with similar status and backgrounds. Therefore, the more age peers in the immediate environment of the old person, the more opportunities he had for friendships. Rosow's findings clearly show that "Sheer generational proximity does not foster social interaction: The old are likely to become isolated in an indifferent environment of younger people."[16]

According to Rosow, the belief of policy makers that housing can solve or abate the problems of the aged is the result of several factors. Experts are mainly sensitive to material problems; they see housing as a means to social ends rather than a physical setting; and, finally, their conception of housing comes to be shared both by those in the field and by the public. It then ". . .permeates the ethos of the field. It becomes an independent value which generates vested interest in housing activity, whether of research or construction. . . . Clearly the process develops into a self-fulfilling prophecy."[17]

Social Research and Social Policy

The present paper has considered social research and social policy in the field of old age. Specifically, it has treated the differences in viewpoints

---

[14] Irving Rosow, *Social Integration of the Aged* (New York: The Free Press of Glencoe, Inc., 1967), p. 5.

[15] *Ibid.,* p. 7.

[16] *Ibid.,* p. 324.

[17] *Ibid.,* p. 8.

between scholars and policy makers and certain myths about old age which have affected social policy. Three social myths were selected for consideration—that most old people are sick, that old people are rejected by their children, and that old people are concerned about their housing. In two instances—that of health and that of housing—the myths were proven false. In a third instance, the rejection of older parents by their children, direct evidence is not available, but related evidence would tend to suggest that this myth, too, is false.

As many persons concerned with the elderly have found, the scholar who wants to affect social policy must venture into the real world. If one then hopes to influence events, one's assessment of the real world must first of all be accurate. How does one attain such accuracy? Like Herbert Blumer and others, I would argue that one begins by "observing nature rather than interpeting it in a pretentious way."[18]

I am not here calling for the discarding of social theory. Quite the contrary! One is naked in the real world without a theory which serves to sharpen and guide observation. Old age, like other social phenomena, can only be studied by asking pertinent questions, by testing observed reality against theoretical constructs, and by daring to modify or even discard these constructs for others, should they prove inadequate in explaining observed behavior.

----

[18] "Matthias Selected 'Man of the Year' in Research," *Industrial Research,* January, 1969, p. 14.

26

Leon Bramson

THE ARMED FORCES
EXAMINING STATION:
A SOCIOLOGICAL PERSPECTIVE

It is a well-known fact of nineteenth century social theory that the fathers of modern sociology regarded military institutions and war itself as an archaic survival in an industrial society. Henri de St. Simon, Auguste Comte, and Herbert Spencer among others argued that there was a necessary antithesis between the military society on the one hand and industrial society on the other. The former was homogeneous, ascriptive, authoritarian, hierarchical, and self-sufficient; the latter was heterogeneous, achievement oriented, egalitarian, democratic, and interdependent. The military was identified with what Emile Durkheim called a society based on mechanical solidarity. Comte and Spencer predicted that with the flowering of industrial society, military institutions would wither away, and war itself would become anachronistic. The basis for this prediction lay in the notion that the industrial system carried with it its own ethos—the ethos of work, of social stability, and of constantly increasing wealth. As this ethos came to dominate modern society, and as political, social, and religious institutions gradually changed their character in the age of the democratic revolutions, new forms of solidarity would arise which would preclude intertribal and international strife. Free trade would encourage economic interdependence, and a global society would emerge which would not fail to percieve that its best interests lay in the avoidance of military conflict. Under the impact of this realization and the spread of the ethos of work, the military establishment itself would shrivel and disappear. There would no longer be any meaningful function which it could fulfill.

The history of the past century gives no good grounds for optimism regarding this prediction, though Raymond Aron has argued that the conditions of industrialism visualized by Comte and Spencer have not yet been realized and that therefore the argument must still be regarded as at least not disproven.[1] As I have written elsewhere, what actually ensued was in fact the partial militarization of industry and, more important, the industrialization of the military.[2] Yet the military establishment in modern society still retains elements which Spencer contrasted sharply with industrialism, though it has been quick to adapt the achievements of the industrial system in the technological sphere to military purposes. As Albert Biderman said recently in a thoughtful paper on the subject: more and more, civil society and military establishment alike have had to cope with the same basic problems—organizing large numbers of people for a wide variety of economic and social purposes.[3] As for the uniqueness of the military institution today, Biderman argues that neither conventional nor strategic warfare presents the kinds of problems which have given the military establishment its distinctive character throughout history.

> It is a matter of complete irrelevance in the event of missile war whether the men in the missile silo or the Polaris submarine perform their duty in uniform or in their underwear. The thrust of technology is to make them obsolete in any event. Most of the key functions that can culminate in the delivery of the weapon on target have been performed earlier by civilians in industrial plants, in R & D laboratories, computer centers, Washington cubicles....On the target side, the receiving end, militariness is even more inappropriate. Uniform status has nothing whatsoever to do

---

[1] Raymond Aron, *War and Industrial Society* (London: Oxford University Press, 1958).

[2] Leon Bramson and George W. Goethals, eds., *War: Studies from Psychology, Sociology and Anthropology* (New York: Basic Books Inc., Publishers, 1964), pp. 295–96.

[3] Albert D. Biderman, "What is Military?" in *The Draft: A Handbook of Facts and Alternatives,* ed. Sol Tax (Chicago: University of Chicago Press, 1967), pp. 122–37.

with being eligible to be killed. In short, the old distinctions between combatants and noncombatants, along with many of the old rules of the game, become irrelevant.[4]

The vast majority of jobs in the U. S. Army are noncombatant support roles; only about 14 per cent of the troops are in combat posts. Furthermore, it is paradoxical that the chances of a man's being killed or wounded in combat might be greater if he is a civilian who is conscripted than if he is a member of the Regular Army.[5]

The question "What is military?" helps us to break through the crust of our accepted usages and to examine the actual functioning of institutions. To what extent are military institutions like the Armed Forces Examining and Entrance Stations (AFEES) involved in tasks which are not military at all? How military does the AFEES have to be? How much anticipatory socialization is necessary in order for AFEES to fulfill its system functions? Such a question might be viewed in the context of ex-Secretary of Defense McNamara's decision to replace 75,000 military personnel with 60,000 civilians; or in the context of Army Regulation 601–270, Paragraph 11(e) which says: "Civilians will be used in staffing of AFEES to the maximum practical extent, and will be provided by the Army as Executive Agent of AFEES." Few studies of military institutions have asked questions such as Biderman's; nor have they emphasized the problem of how military and civilian institutions are articulated. Recent anthropological studies have developed the concept of "interface institutions"[6] to designate this type of situation. Such institutions are viewed as key elements in the social structure of a plural society. Individuals who play a role in such institutions are regarded as brokers (Eric Wolf) or gatekeepers (Robert Redfield). This concept of "interface institutions," developed on the basis of Meso-American anthropological field work may be quite relevant to the situation of the AFEES. It might prove useful in looking at the consistencies and inconsistencies between the military and the civilian sectors, those instances where the two sectors touch and interpenetrate—at the borders, where they have a mutual frontier. The comment of a former commander of infantry on the AFEES gives a useful perspective from the military side of the border:

What is most remarkable to me is the extent to which these stations are divorced from the real gut life of military organization. They may indeed be "interfaces" between military organization and the larger society; but insofar as military organization is concerned, they would appear to be

---

4 *Ibid.,* p. 125

5 *Ibid.,* p. 132: "With respect to the current scene of combat, the Army calculated that a draftee currently entering the system has a one-in-three chance of serving in Vietnam, as compared with a one-in-seven chance for a man currently in the regular Army."

6 Cf. Robert and Eva Hunt, "Education As an Interface Institution in Rural Mexico and the American Inner City," *Midway Magazine,* VIII (1967), 101ff.

*very largely remote and strange kinds of establishments. The staff of the
AFEES has only marginal participation in military organization, lives in
the civilian community, has no direct contact with the kinds of experiences
to which their clientele will ultimately be exposed. There also seems to
be a tendency in assignment policy for the administrative officer personnel to assign people of rather marginal qualifications. The administrative officer personnel are either at the command level those who are
committed to early retirement, or very recently inducted into military
organization. The same great discrepancy exists among the enlisted personnel. There are the very senior sergeants whose combat credentials
are considered exemplary, and, on the other hand, the very clever clerks
and psychology technicians who administer the tests. There are also, of
course, the very senior medical corps officers, and, on the other hand,
the very fortunate and junior medical corps officers, who conduct the
medical examinations. Thus the point of contact with a newly inducted
or enlisted person is likely to be with a staff member who is not entirely
committed to military organization.*[7]

In this paper the sociological significance of AFEES will be viewed
from a number of standpoints: (1) The AFEES may be seen as the prototype
of an institution with intake functions on the border of two institutional
complexes. There are in fact many such institutions in our society; they
might appropriately be called "vestibule institutions." Erving Goffman has
discussed aspects of such institutions in connection with processing in mental
hospitals. (2) I propose to examine the actual experience of individuals
underoing processing at AFEES from the standpoint of their definition of the
situation. This will include a consideration of the larger societal context
insofar as it affects their experience. I also propose to examine the notion that
experience at the AFEES might constitute a *rite de passage* or initiation
ceremony in our society. These discussions will bear on questions of legitimacy
and solidarity in the contemporary United States. (3) I shall suggest that
new functions might be assimilated into the AFEES in addition to the ones
they already serve. Although our society is very unlike that visualized by
Comte and Spencer, there is always the possibility that we might help to
move it in the direction which they prophesied.

The AFEES as an Interface Institution

The Armed Forces Examining and Entrance Stations (AFEES) have
the manifest function (as defined in AR 601–270) of giving physical and
mental examinations to all volunteers and draftees for all branches of the
armed forces and determining their elibigility. They are responsible for all

---

[7] Roger Little, personal communication.

the clerical work associated with these examinations. Although theoretically members of all the armed forces work in these stations and the commanding officer may be from any branch, headquarters responsibility rests with the Army, and most military personnel attached to AFEES are Army. There are seventy-four AFEES in the continental United States, Hawaii, and Puerto Rico. During the fiscal year 1968 the cost of operating the AFEES was about thirty-five million dollars, with a military personnel authorization of 2,121. In addition, 2,051 civilians perform various duties connected with AFEES processing; half of all those employed at AFEES in fiscal 1968 were civilians. This writer was a participant-observer at an AFEES in Memphis, Tennessee, for seventeen months from August, 1953, to January, 1955. The opportunity to study the operation of the AFEES as an Army enlisted man in the Mental Testing Section was granted through the courtesy of the Selective Service System. More recently, through the cooperation of the Department of the Army he was permitted to refresh his memory of AFEES procedures and observe changes which have taken place since 1955 at the AFEES in Philadelphia, Pennsylvania.

In one of the few papers in the entire sociological literature which is relevant to the situation of the AFEES, Erving Goffman speaks of the moral career of the recruit in the total institution and the significance of its initial stages:

> *The recruit comes into the establishment with a conception of himself made possible by certain stable social arrangements in his home world. Upon entrance, he is immediately stripped of the support provided by these arrangements. In the accurate language of some of our oldest total institutions, he begins a series of abasements, degradations, humiliations, and profanations of self. His self is systematically, or often unintentionally, mortified. He begins some radical shifts in his moral career, a career composed of the progressive changes that occur in the beliefs that he has concerning himself and significant others. The processes by which a person's self is mortified are fairly standard in total institutions; analysis of these processes can help us to see the arrangements that ordinary establishments must guarantee if members are to preserve their civilian selves.*[8]

Note that the final sentence of this quotation uses the term "civilian" as a generic term, to distinguish the world outside the total institution, be it Army barracks, monastery, convent, boarding school, work camp, ship, colonial compound, penitentiary, concentration camp, or mental hospital. This suggests the extent to which the distinction between the soldier and the civilian is prototypical and the degree to which the Army is the total institu-

---

[8] Erving Goffman, *Asylums* (New York: Doubleday & Company, Inc., 1961), p. 14.

tion par excellence. The self-concept of the recruit or inmate has its roots in the civilian world; something must happen to him in the "vestibule" to facilitate his transition to another self-concept and his participation in another social context:

> *The inmate...finds certain roles are lost to him by virtue of the barrier that separates him from the outside world. The process of entrance typically brings other kinds of loss and mortification as well. We very generally find staff employing what are called admissions procedures, such as taking a life history, photographing, weighing, fingerprinting, assigning numbers, searching, listing personal possessions for storage, undressing, bathing, disinfecting, haircutting, issuing institutional clothing, instructing as to rules, and assigning to quarters. Admission procedures might better be called "trimming" or "programming" because in thus being squared away the new arrival allows himself to be shaped and coded into an object that can be fed into the administrative machinery of the establishment, to be worked on smoothly by routine operations. Many of these procedures depend upon attributes such as weight or fingerprints that the individual possesses merely because he is a member of the largest and most abstract of social categories, that of human being. Action taken on the basis of such attributes necessarily ignores most of his previous bases of self-identification.*[9]

In the Army, which is the most relevant example for discussion here, the admissions procedures are divided between the AFEES and the reception center on an Army post to which the newly inducted soldiers are sent immediately after being sworn in at the AFEES. A serial number is assigned at AFEES after a man has been inducted. Some aspects of Goffman's discussion, such as the assignment of new clothes and even a new name (in the form of a rank joined to the last name) come only after the individual leaves the AFEES. Goffman observes:

> *The admission procedure can be characterized as a leaving off and a taking on, with the midpoint marked by physical nakedness. Leaving off of course entails a dispossession of property, important because persons invest self-feelings in their possessions. Perhaps the most significant of these possessions is not physical at all, one's full name; whatever one is thereafter called, loss of one's name can be a great curtailment of the self.*[10]

Although Goffman's observations are extremely helpful as an introduction to the nature of the experience at AFEES, a symbolic interactionist analysis of the AFEES would be inconceivable without reference to the

---

[9] *Ibid.,* p. 16.
[10] *Ibid.,* p. 18.

peculiar circumstances in which it is operating. These circumstances have a profound effect on volunteers and conscripts alike. Here the main point is that the larger societal context which frames the experience at AFEES affects not only the men passing through but the functioning of the Army itself.

Critics have pointed out that the peacetime draft is inconsistent with fundamental American ideals. Opponents of the American military posture and critics of the draft system have been quick to seize on the AFEES as the symbolic target of their protest. Antiwar demonstrators and critics of the Selective Service System have frequently engaged in peaceful picketing and leafletting at AFEES in the past few years. Such protests are symbolic in that they illustrate that some elements of the public are questioning the legitimacy not only of the Selective Service System, but also of the fundamental consensus which makes possible its operation, and which one sociologist, following Rousseau, has called an American "civil religion."[11]

Civil Religion and the Context of Military Service

It is instructive to look at what happens at AFEES from the standpoint of the civil religion. Even in our secularized and bureaucratized society, as will be seen below, there are still attempts at ceremonial and ritual which find their way into the processing at AFEES. Behind these elements stands the civil religion, which, as Bellah has pointed out, is of fundamental importance in linking the Judeo-Christian tradition and American nationalism.

> *Behind the civil religion at every point lie biblical archetypes: Exodus, Chosen People, Promised Land, New Jerusalem, Sacrificial Death, and Rebirth. But the civil religion is also genuinely American and genuinely new. It has its own prophets and its own martyrs, its own sacred events and sacred places, its own solemn rituals and symbols. It is concerned that America be a society as perfectly in accord with the will of God as men can make it and a light to all the nations.*[12]

It is easy to lose sight of the spiritual significance of nationalism but equally easy to demonstrate the all-pervasive character of the national state in the life of the individual. A number of observers have commented on the degree to which nationalism is reinforced through ceremony and ritual in the civil religion. Carleton Hayes, for example, has argued that nationalism has become a functional equivalent for the medieval Christian world view, providing a framework of self-transcendence for the individual. Not only the

---

11 Robert N. Bellah, "Civil Religion in America," in *The Religious Situation: 1968,* ed. Donald R. Cutler (Boston: Beacon Press, 1968), pp. 331–56.

12 *Ibid.,* p. 354. Cf. W. Lloyd Warner, *The Living and the Dead: A Study of the Symbolic Life of Americans* (New Haven: Yale University Press, 1958), pp. 278–79.

intellect but the emotions are called into play, and the individual locates himself within an historically continuous experience identified with the national past and the national destiny. Among the interesting parallels between contemporary nationalism and medieval Christianity are:

> ...*the individual is born into the national state, and the secular registration of birth is the national rite of baptism. Thenceforth the state solicitously follows him through life, tutoring him in a national catechism, teaching him by pious schooling and precept the beauties of national holiness, fitting him for life of service, (no matter how exalted or how menial) to the state, and commemorating his vital crises by formal registration (with a fee) not only of his birth but likewise of his marriage, of the birth of his children, and of his death. If he has been a crusader on behalf of nationalism, his place of entombment is marked with the ensign of his service. The funerals of national heroes and potentates are celebrated with magnificent pomp and circumstance....*[13]

Membership in the national state is really compulsory. An individual may withdraw, but it is practically impossible for him to establish himself in a country which does not practice some form of nationalistic "religion." And membership in any national society involves compulsory financial support in the form of taxation, often used to support "missionary" activities associated with the national destiny. The ritual of modern nationalism, Hayes points out, focuses on the national flag; but portraits of the national leaders "adorn both the sumptuous clubs of the wealthy and the simple cottages of the poor." It is in this sense in which the proceedings at AFEES may be regarded as linked, in their ceremonial aspects and the basic assumptions reflected in processing, with the civil religion. It is also because of its relationship to the civil religion that the problem of legitimacy associated with Selective Service is so crucial. One distinguished economist has argued recently that the inequities of the peacetime draft and related problems associated with our military posture are actually underminining the legitimacy of the national state.[14] Robert Bellah suggests that the situation constitutes a crisis for the civil religion. This has important consequences for the experience of young men at AFEES.

At the age of eighteen all American males must register with the Selective Service System at their local draft boards. Most of the men who are subsequently examined at AFEES fall into one of two categories. They are volunteers for service in one of the branches of the armed forces, or they are Selective Service registrants being examined for the draft. Because men are

---

[13] Carleton Hayes, *Nationalism: A Religion* (New York: The Macmillan Company, 1960), p. 165.

[14] Kenneth Boulding, "The Impact of the Draft on the Legitimacy of the National State," in Tax, *op. cit.*, pp. 191–96.

encouraged to explore alternatives to being drafted, e.g., volunteering for service in a special branch with a guarantee of an opportunity to attend technical schools, many individuals are channeled into volunteering who would otherwise not do so. They volunteer in order to avoid the randomness of the draft, the uncertainty attending draft eligibility, and for positive reasons associated with the desire for preferential assignments and special training. Many men who "volunteer for the draft" or who volunteer for service in one of the branches are thus only semivoluntary members of the armed forces who would not volunteer if there were no draft. It is very difficult to ascertain the facts, since no impartial studies exist at this time. Department of Defense studies indicate that four out of every ten officers, about four out of ten of all enlisted volunteers, and seven out of ten Reserve enlistees would not have entered the services if there had been no draft.[15] The important point is that of the men who pass through the AFEES, some are voluntary, some are semivoluntary, and some are involuntary participants. As Goffman observes:

> *Recruits enter total institutions in different spirits. At one extreme we find the quite involuntary entrance of those who are sentenced to prison, committed to a mental hospital, or pressed into the crew of a ship. It is perhaps in such circumstances that staff's version of the ideal inmate has least chance of taking hold. At the other extreme, we find religious institutions that deal only with those who feel they have gotten the call, and, of these volunteers, take only those who seem to be the most suitable and the most serious in their intentions. (Presumably officer training camps and some political training schools qualify here, too.) In such cases, conversion seems already to have eaken place, and it only remains to show the neophyte along what lines he can best discipline himself. Midway between these two extremes we find institutions, like the Army in regard to conscripts, where inmates are required to serve but are given much opportunity to feel that this service is a justifiable one required in their own ultimate interests. Obviously, significant differences in tone will appear in total institutions, depending on whether recruitment is voluntary, semivoluntary, or involuntary.*[16]

The fact of different degrees of voluntarism tends to complicate the aspect of AFEES processing which is significant as a *rite de passage,* to which I will now turn. Since 1948 all American adolescent males have had to take account of the draft. For those who are volunteers and who actively desire to become members of the armed forces, AFEES can represent a traumatic

---

15 *Review of the Administration and Operation of the Selective Service System,* Hearings before the Committee on Armed Services, 89th Congress, 2nd session, June, 1966. (Washington, D. C.: U. S. Government Printing Office, 1966), pp. 9935–36.

16 Goffman, *op. cit.,* p. 118.

experience culminating in a humiliating failure. It is important to realize that for every 100 men examined at AFEES, about thirty-three are labelled as mental, medical, or moral failures. Of the remaining sixty-six, almost half can be considered semivoluntary or involuntary examinees, if we extrapolate from the Defense Department figures cited above. This is a very high proportion of involuntary participants and suggests that this particular *rite de passage* must be viewed with more than the usual amount of ambivalence by participants.

AFEES Experience as Rite de Passage

I would like to give critical consideration to the idea that the experience at AFEES has elements of a *rite de passage*. At least one student of initiation rites has argued that "neither physiologically, socially nor legally is there a clear demarcation between boyhood and manhood in our society." He demonstrates a relationship cross-culturally between the presence of stringent initiation rites at puberty and intense mother-son relationships during infancy. The resultant emotional dependence and identification leads to a "cross-sex identity crisis" at puberty, frequently attended by compensatory "protest masculinity." This crisis accounts for the widespread existence of stringent initiation rites which serve the purpose of resolving the dilemma by reaffirming male identity and thus precluding open rivalry with the father and Oedipal approaches to the mother. The authors note the widespread emphasis on exclusive mother-child relationships in lower class situations characterized as "broken homes" in our society, but also not unknown in the middle classes. They observe that one way of dealing with the problem of male identity is to establish a formal, institutional way of coping with adolescent boys of this type and suggest that "the present institution of selective service would perhaps serve this purpose were the boys to be drafted at an earlier age and exposed to the authority of responsible adult males."[17] The Job Corps may represent an attempt to deal with a similar problem in a non-military context.

Without in any sense endorsing the suggestion of Whiting *et al.*, it is possible to examine the degree to which AFEES processing functions as an initiation rite. Anthropologists and sociologists have pointed out that among the changes attendant on the rise of urban, industrial societies has been an increase in secularization and a decline in the importance of sacred ceremonialism. As Solon Kimball observed:

---

17 J. W. M. Whiting, Richard Kluckhohn, and Albert Anthony, "The Function of Male Initiation Ceremonies at Puberty," in E. Maccoby, *et al., Readings in Social Psychology* (New York: Holt, Rinehart and Winston, Inc., 1958), pp. 359-70.

> *Rites of passage were often, but not necessarily, tied to supernatural sanctions and to the activity of priestly intermediaries. Although such rites focused on the individual, they were also occasions for group participation—as in the initiation ceremonies of the Australian, or burial or marriage rites in an agrarian community. There is no evidence that a secularized urban world has lessened the need for ritualized expression of an individual's transition from one status to another. Obviously, ceremonialism alone cannot establish the new equilibrium, and perfunctory ritual may be pleasant but also meaningless. One of our problems is that we are lacking the empirical studies of ritual behavior and its consequences for life cycle crises upon which we might assess the relation between crisis and ritual in its current setting.[18]*

Such observations should be viewed in the context provided by Bellah's work on the American civil religion or Lloyd Warner's study of Memorial Day as a sacred ceremony.

An early student of rites of passage, Arnold van Gennep, distinguished between three phases of such rites: the phase of separation from the old state of things; the marginal period or rites of transition; and the integration in a new condition or reintegration to the old, rites of incorporation. Van Gennep stressed that one of these three stages might be emphasized according to the situation. Thus rites of separation are stressed at funerals; rites of incorporation, at weddings; and rites of transition, in initiation ceremonies. He also emphasized the importance of "transitional periods which sometimes acquire a certain autonomy," which might be relevant to the case of AFEES.[19] A recent commentator on van Gennep has pointed out that:

> *...changes in social relations involving movements between groups, or alterations of status, in semicivilized societies with their conceptions of magico-religious bases for groups, disturbed both the life of society and the life of the individual, and the function of rites de passage was to reduce the harmful effects of these disturbances.[20]*

Regarding initiation ceremonies, Max Gluckman points out that they "mark and organize the transition from childhood to socially recognized adulthood. ...They are the means of divesting a person of his status as a child in the domestic domain and investing him with the status of actual or potential citizen in the politico-jural domain."[21] By this criterion it would seem as if elements of the AFEES experience would definitely constitute initiation

---

18 Solon T. Kimball, Introduction to Arnold van Gennep, *The Rites of Passage* (Chicago: University of Chicago Press, 1960), pp. xvi–xvii.

19 van Gennep. *op. cit.*, pp. 191–92.

20 Max Gluckman, *Essays on the Ritual of Social Relations* (Manchester: Manchester University Press, 1962), p. 3.

21 *Ibid.*, p. 16.

ceremonies in terms of the cultural norms of American society. Furthermore, as Gluckman himself points out, "The social order is so impregnated with moral judgments that it can be disturbed by any failure to fulfill an obligation."[22]

Thus, it is difficult to see why Gluckman ultimately adopts a point of view which tends to argue that "rituals of the kind investigated by van Gennep are incompatible with the structure of modern urban life."[23] Gluckman is saying that the highly bureaucratized context of modern industrial society does not encourage the rise of such rites of passage. Indeed, the highly rationalized envioronment characteristic of the American urban context is viewed as positively discouraging for the rise of such ceremonials and rites. "Ritual, and even ceremonial, tend to drop into desuetude in the modern urban situation where the material basis of life, and the fragmentation of roles and activities, of themselves segregate social roles."[24] In order to see whether a case can be made for the existence of elements of initiation ritual or *rites de passage* at AFEES, we will first have to take up the details of the experience at AFEES.

AFEES Preinduction Processing

There are two categories of examination procedure: (1) preinduction examinations and (2) induction examinations and processing. What follows is a brief description of preinduction processing, although there are obviously important differences in how the situation is defined according to socio-economic class, degree of voluntarism, race, and other variables. A typical individual will have been notified by Selective Service of the date of his examination. The notification is usually mailed. He is to appear at the AFEES early in the morning, or if he is in an outlying district, he must foregather with others at an even earlier hour at his draft board for transportation to the AFEES. A group leader is appointed by Selective Service from among the people who are to be examined. The early hour (frequently prior to 7:00 AM), the occasionally foregone breakfast, and the apprehension which accompanies the examination process usually conspire to generate a mild anxiety. There is sometimes horseplay and tension release in the group, though in the big city draft boards most of them are strangers to one another. They are received at the station in a room usually set aside for the purpose, and there is a roll call in alphabetical order. What follows is an orientation, which is described in Army Regulations as follows:

---

22 *Ibid.*, p. 29.
23 *Ibid.*, pp. 36–37.
24 *Ibid.*, p. 38.

*After the roll call, registrants will be given an orientation by a com-
missioned or noncommissioned officer. The attitudes of the preinductees
toward military life will be influenced by the manner in which they are
treated during preinduction processing. All phases of preinduction processing will be conducted in a dignified and professional manner. Registrants will be treated with courtesy and maximum attention will be given
to the preinductee's welfare and to those personal preferences consistent
with military requirements. Preinductees will be given an opportunity
to ask questions and all questions will be answered courteously. Personnel
in charge will never be arrogant, flippant, or sarcastic no matter how
absurd questions seem....Preinductees will be identified by their names.
Cards, use of stamps, or other such means of identification are considered
unnecessary. The orientation will cover the following subjects: (1) steps
in preinduction processing (2) instruction regarding mess and quarters
while at the induction station (3) approximate time and method by which
registrants will be notified of results of preinduction examination....*

It is important to see that the orientation constitutes a situation in
which individuals are made aware that what happens to them that day at
AFEES is fateful; that it will determine their future in some important
respects; that they are confronting the ineluctable authority of the state; but
also that there might be something they can do to alter this imbalance of
power and control their own destiny. For example, those found acceptable for
induction are given a talk (based on Appendix 24, AR 601–270) urging them
to consider a career in the Army, Navy, Air Force, or Marine Corps by
voluntary enlistment. What follows the preinduction orientation is an interview, where the individual sits at a desk and is queried by either a soldier
or a civilian typist regarding personal information already entered on the
form DD 47. This also includes questions determining moral eligibility—e.g.,
court convictions, felonies, criminal charges filed, etc. Thus, one of the first
situations in which a man finds himself in AFEES processing is one in which
his past is being explored for possible evidence of criminality. For many
individuals who pass through the AFEES this is sufficient to evoke considerable anxiety and guilt. The regulations state that:

*A registrant who has been convicted by a civil court (of a felony) or who
has a record of adjudication adverse to him by a juvenile court, for any
offense punishable by death or imprisonment for a term exceeding one
year is morally unacceptable for service in the armed forces unless such
disqualification is waivered by the Armed Forces Moral Waiver Determination Board, which is appointed by the Commanding General, U. S.
Army Recruiting Command.*[25]

---

[25] U. S. Army Regulations 601–270, Ch. 2, C2, pp. 2–4.

Administratively disqualified men tested under Selective Service included
3.9 per cent of the total in a study of disqualifications between August,
1958, through June, 1960. This was 3,643 men out of 271,601.[26]

What follows the preinduction interview is either a mental test, the
AFQT, or a physical examination. AFEES have a great deal of flexibility in
how they handle their work loads, but they have been beset by difficulties in
work flow which is very uneven. They have also been criticized for inef-
ficiency, though it is difficult to see the grounds for such criticisms given that
some physical defects are difficult to detect and that many lower-class
registrants have had little previous medical attention.

(1) The Physical Examination

The physical examination is an extremely impersonal example of
mass processing, since the individual must undress in the company of strangers and wait in lines at the various stations where he is tested. As Goffman
points out, many of the usual identifying attributes of the self are stripped
away, and what is recorded are attributes common to him only as a human
being. It is important to realize, however, that this will often be interpreted
differently by middle-class and lower-class individuals. A lower-class youth
might interpret the processing to indicate that he is the object of special
attention, particularly if he were a volunteer with a positive orientation
toward the proceedings. A middle-class individual who is an involuntary
participant facing the possibility of conscription stands at the opposite pole
of an alienation continuum with regard to AFEES.

The examination begins with a group filling out their Form 89
(Medical History) while they are still clothed. This form is then used as
the men go through the processing clad only in their shorts, moving from
room to room. They are weighed and measured; visual acuity is tested; color
vision, auditory acuity, electrocardiogram, blood pressure, pulse rate are
taken. Blood samples are drawn for the serology tests, which include blood
typing and tests for venereal disease. A surprisingly large number of men
experience nausea either before or after the drawing of a blood sample. Testimony from enlisted personnel and personal experience at Memphis indicates
that fainting is not uncommon, and a technician at the Philadelphia AFEES
reported that 10 per cent of the men passing through his section either
fainted or showed signs of nausea. Blood is drawn with a syringe from a vein
by a corpsman dressed in white fatigue uniform. The "blood room" accen-
tuates the elements of *rite de passage* and serves to underscore the fact that

---

[26] Bernard D. Karpinos, *Qualification of American Youths for Military
Service,* Medical Statistics Division, Office of the Surgeon General, Department of the
Army, 1962.

this experience is typically one which carries a high load of anxiety for the individuals passing through.

In addition to the above, urine samples are taken, X-rays, eyeglass prescriptions recorded, and a medical interview follows detection of any physical irregularity or problem which is brought to the attention of the examining physician either by notations on the Form 47 filled out by the pre-inductee or through the examination itself. Civilian doctors are hired on a fee basis since there are not enough Army doctors to do all the examinations at AFEES. A psychiatric interview is carried out when there is any indication that it might be appropriate.

(2) *The Mental Test*

More than 10 million men have taken the Armed Forces Qualification Test; it is the basic screening instrument of the American armed forces. The test has a hundred questions and is divided into four parts: vocabulary matching, arithmetic, tool matching, and blocks and pattern matching questions. The score is rendered as a percentile, and the results are grouped into five categories, with group I the highest and group V as failure. Scoring in the 9th percentile or below means that the candidate is not qualified for service in the armed forces. A candidate who scores in the 30th percentile or below is in mental group IV, and since August, 1958, these men must take an additional test called the Army Qualification Battery. Requirements regarding the AQB have changed several times, most recently in response to the Vietnam crisis. These changes are detailed in a recent article on test failures by Bernard Karpinos.[27] It takes a little more than an hour to administer the AFQT. The instructions include test questions, and men are encouraged to do as well as they can on the grounds that their assignments in the Army will be affected by their test scores. Tests are proctored by enlisted men or officers associated with the Mental Testing Section, and proctors roam about, checking papers to see that men understand how to use the multiple-choice materials and that they have filled out the forms correctly. This academic situation is often completely foreign to men who have had little or no schooling and they often find it terrifying. Readability tests on the AFQT indicate that what counts as fourth grade reading comprehension in the northern states frequently may require as much as eight grades in culturally deprived areas.

The experience of different types of men is obviously variable in this testing situation, according to amount of education, socioeconomic class, cultural background, degree of voluntarism, and other factors. Preju-

---

[27] Bernard D. Karpinos, "Mental Test Failures," in Tax, *op. cit.*, pp. 35–53.

diced whites who live in racially segregated communities are frequently shaken to find themselves in such close proximity to Negroes or members of other minority groups on both the AFQT and the physical examination. Highly educated men often regard the test as a farce and as further evidence that the armed forces will represent a degrading experience for them. Functional illiterates who wish to volunteer for the armed forces are terrified by the test which they fail, but return again in the vain effort to pass and improve their life chances by social mobility into the armed forces. This is particularly true of southern Negroes, for many of whom the Army represents the only hope. At the Memphis AFEES, young Negro volunteers from Tennessee and Mississippi who failed the test would plead tearfully with the Mental Testing personnel to let them into the Army. Current regulations permit only one retest after failure on the AFQT. Not all Selective Service registrants who fail the test receive a complete interview in the Mental Testing Section. Whether they do depends on a number of factors, primarily inconsistencies of performance, amount of education, or level of work experience. Men who have less than eight years of school who fail the test are not interviewed. The primary purpose of an interview following AFQT failure is to determine whether or not they were malingering. There are a tiny number of deliberate malingerers. Far more difficult is the case in which men malinger who could not pass the test even if they were not malingering! Practices vary from station to station regarding informing preinductees of the test results. In any case the scores are recorded on forms which the men will eventually see, if they know how to interpret them.

These various crises constitute the essence of preinduction processing at AFEES, and they usually take the better part of a day. When men must be held over because of scheduling problems or overload, they are usually housed in a local YMCA or similar facility.

AFEES Induction Processing

The actual process of induction has two parts. One is the required induction ceremony; the other is the optional oath of allegiance ceremony. In a secular, rationalized, and bureaucratic society these ceremonies seem quite unceremonious indeed; nevertheless many induction stations have special ceremonial rooms, decorated with flags and other symbols of national authority in which men are inducted.

Before the induction ceremony, however, men must undergo a physical inspection. If more than a year has elapsed since their preinduction physical, they must have a complete reexamination. The first phase of induction processing involves an orientation talk. This includes "the purpose and significance of induction" and an account of the processing steps he will take during the day. His reserve obligations will be explained, and questions regarding insurance, etc., are taken up. There is a roll call, and individual records are issued which each man carries around with him during his processing. Sometimes inductees need a mental test too, if processing has been irregular, records have been lost, etc.

Then they must fill out Form DD 98, the Armed Forces Security Questionnaire, under the supervision of a commissioned officer. The serious nature of this questionnaire may be gleaned from the following excerpt:

> *This security questionnaire is one of the most important forms you will ever be required to complete during your military service. Its importance has to do with both the security of the United States and your own future welfare as a citizen of the United States and as a member of the United States Armed Forces. For these reasons you must execute your questionnaire with the utmost care. Before doing so, you must fully understand its purpose and the meaning of the statements you will make in Section IV.*
>
> *Why Must You Sign a Security Questionnaire?*
>
> *The fact that you are required to sign a security questionnaire at this time does not call into question your loyalty to the United States nor your intention to serve in the Armed Forces with the honor and fidelity traditional to the American soldier. The questionnaire is simply a means of helping the Federal Government protect itself and you against those who undermine and destroy our Nation and individual freedom.*
>
> *As a member of the Armed Forces you will occupy a position of honor and trust. It is vital to our national security that all such positions of honor and trust be held by persons of complete and unswerving loyalty to the United States.*
>
> *Among the thousands of men and women coming into the Armed Forces each month, we must recognize that there might be a certain number of subversives and spies working for the Communist enemy or groups hostile to our democratic form of government. This is part of the "boring" from within tactics of the Communist conspiracy....*[28]

After they have filled out the Security Questionnaire, files of all men being inducted must be completed and checked. After this they are allocated to a specific branch of the service, usually the Army in the case of Selective Service registrants.

(1) Induction Ceremony

When registrants to be inducted are assembled, the induction officer is required to say to them:

---

[28] U. S. Army Regulations, *op. cit.*, Appendix IV, p. A4–1.

You are about to be inducted into the Armed Forces of the United States, in the Army, the Navy, the Air Force, or the Marine Corps, as indicated by the service announced following your name when called. You will take one step forward as your name and service are called and such step will constitute your induction into the Armed Forces indicated.

After the roll has been called, the inductees are informed that each and every one of them is a member of the Armed Forces, using the following language:

You have now been inducted into the Armed Forces of the United States indicated when your name was called. Each one of you is now a member of the Armed Forces concerned, and amenable to the regulations and the Uniform Code of Military Justice and all other applicable laws and regulations.

(2) Oath of Allegiance Ceremony

The oath of allegiance is not a part of the induction ceremony. It is optional and is administered by a commissioned officer as soon as practicable after the induction ceremony. The oath of allegiance reads as follows:

I, _____, do solemnly swear (or affirm) that I will support and defend the Constitution of the United States against all enemies, foreign or domestic; that I will bear true faith and allegiance to the same; and that I will obey the orders of the President of the United States and the orders of the officers appointed over me, according to regulations and the Uniform Code of Military Justice. So help me God.

(3) Outprocessing

This is the Army term for the final phase of the work at AFEES. It includes the highly significant assignment of a service number to each individual (drafted men have the prefix "US" before their numbers, while volunteers have the prefix "RA" for Regular Army). Records are completed, and travel orders are issued for the reception centers. Men are now soldiers in some respects but not in others; they have no uniforms, are still wearing civilian clothes, and are usually entirely ignorant concerning the actual details of military life. One individual is usually placed in charge of the group and carries the records; the men proceed to the trains, buses, or airplanes which will carry them to their duty stations.

Rite de Passage?

We are now in a position to review the evidence regarding those aspects of preinduction and induction processing which might be considered comparable to an initiation rite. It seems to me that it is possible to make a case for the existence of a rite of the transitional type. The AFEES experience is concentrated in the intermediate phase and does not include the final phase of incorporation which takes place at the reception center and in the basic training camp. It must also be admitted that in an initiation ritual among preliterates the participants usually know one another, and the community of which they are members is usually on hand during some phase of the rite. At AFEES men are usually strangers to one another, and their community is represented only symbolically be the draft board, whose members are often total strangers.

The argument rests on the following considerations: (1) There is an actual passage or movement from the home or dwelling place to the AFEES, sometimes under mild conditions of stress and occasionally over considerable geographical distances. (2) There is a high degree of ambivalence present among the initiates because a large proportion are involuntary participants; this argues, however, for a "quasi-rite" rather than initiation ritual because they are not looking forward to the achievement of their new status. (3) The background of legitimacy and authority symbolized by the military in association with the civil religion is manifest. To the extent that legitimacy is questioned, however, the rite will fail to fulfill its functions. (4) The medical testing and examination gives some evidence of physical manliness, since negative status is still attached to the 4-F classification, though this must be qualified, too, to take account of involuntary registrants. (5) The mental test constitutes a real hurdle for a considerable proportion of the examinees, 10 per cent of whom fail the test outright and 21 per cent of whom fail contingent on the taking of the AQB. A Negro youth is four times as likely to fail as a white youth. (6) Ritual elements also include the certification of loyalty in the filling out of the Form DD 98; failure to comply correctly is punishable by perjury charges and a jail sentence on conviction. (7) The drama of the ceremonial room in induction processing with its symbols of national flag and patriotism constitutes an obvious element of *rite de passage* and the incorporation of a new role. (8) The ritual elements of processing such as the "blood room," fingerprinting, and the criminal record all tend to generate a certain anxiety in the participants. (9) The implicit power of the national authorities to deprive one of his liberty evokes both mild anxiety and an accommodating attitude among most preinductees and inductees, and the reminder regarding the jurisdiction of military law (as well as civilian law) in the induction ceremony only helps to accentuate the fact that "they've got you." (10) Finally, the rhetoric of duty and obligation merges with the rhetoric of the "privilege" of service, as volunteers and Selective Service registrants who fail the tests are actually *excluded*.

To the extent that this evidence seems to point to the rise of an initiation rite in connection with the Armed Forces Examining Station, to that extent does it contradict Gluckman's skepticism regarding *rites de passage* in contemporary industrial society.

Implications for Policy

We must now return to the qustion with which we began this discussion: "What is military?" One assumption which will guide us here is that, in spite of discontent with the draft and interest in the concept of the volunteer army, there is a strong possibility that some form of the peacetime draft will remain a permanent feature of American society for the foreseeable future. This is not, in my opinion, a satisfactory state of affairs, and represents a profound contradiction of our ideals and traditions of individual freedom.

Given this assumption, however, it could be argued that, if young men were to continue to register with Selective Service at age eighteen and to be examined at the AFEES, the process might take place in a wider, nonmilitary context which would emphasize the assessment of the nation's human resources. The AFEES is a unique collector of data, and it could become part of a system of "social indicators" which would be of positive value in developing the potentialities of individuals. It would also function as a check on the level of health facilities and the output of educational systems in state and local communities. The cause of social justice for the disadvantaged might be aided through a demonstration that educational and health services were below the national standard. Indeed, comparative data from the Office of the Surgeon General are already available which show shocking rates of failure on the AFQT among eighteen year olds in certain regions of the country and in specific minority groups.

If the draft were eliminated, the AFEES stations could function as a clearinghouse and testing center serving a wide variety of voluntary national service programs, as well as the volunteers for the armed forces.[29] But this would mean that the sharp line between the military and the civilian sector would be blurred, and that the AFEES would be functioning within a larger societal context in assessing human resources. This points toward greater "civilianization" of the AFEES and a deemphasis of their strictly military role. It is this conception which represents a return to the vision of Comte and Spencer regarding the character of the modern society.

Finally, if the draft were eliminated, it could also lead to the development of new kinds of ritual and ceremony consistent with the more

---

[29] Leon Bramson, "The Sociological Significance of Voluntary National Service in Modern Society," in *National Service,* ed. Donald J. Eberly (New York: Russell Sage Foundation, 1968).

universalist elements of the American civil religion in its nonmilitary aspects. What is now a secular "quasi-rite" in a draft system, whose legitimacy is being widely questioned, could become a real rite of passage and manhood ceremony in a society where men volunteered for a wide variety of national and international service programs (including military service) as a matter of course. The Peace Corps, the Job Corps, and Vista may have more relevance for the present and future needs of the nation and of humanity and be more consistent with the American civil religion than the Green Berets.

Bibliography of
HERBERT BLUMER

Books

Movies and Conduct. New York: The Macmillan Company, 1933.

Movies, Delinquency, and Crime, with Philip M. Hauser. New York: The Macmillan Company, 1933.

Critiques of Research in the Social Sciences: I. An Appraisal of Thomas and Znaniecki's The Polish Peasant in Europe and America. New York: Social Science Research Council, 1939.

Symbolic Interactionism: Perspective and Method. Englewood Cliffs, N.J.: Prentice-Hall, Inc., 1969.

Articles

"Science Without Concepts," *American Journal of Sociology,* XXXVI (1931), 515–33.

"Moulding of Mass Behavior Through the Motion Picture," *Publications of the American Sociological Society,* XXIX (1935), 115–27.

"Social Attitudes and Non-Symbolic Interaction," *Journal of Educational Sociology,* IX (1936), 515–23.

"Social Psychology," in *Man and Society,* ed. Emerson P. Schmidt. New York: Prentice-Hall, Inc., 1937. Pp. 144–98.

"Social Disorganization and Personal Disorganization," *American Journal of Sociology,* XLII (1937), 871–77.

"Collective Behavior," in *An Outline of the Principles of Sociology,* ed. Robert E. Park. New York: Barnes & Noble, Inc., 1939. Pp. 219–80.

"The Nature of Racial Prejudice," *Social Process in Hawaii,* V (1939), 11–21.

"The Problem of the Concept in Social Psychology," *American Journal of Sociology,* XLV (1940), 707–19.

"Morale," in *American Society in Wartime,* ed. William F. Ogburn. Chicago: University of Chicago Press, 1943. Pp. 207–31.

"Sociological Theory in Industrial Relations," *American Sociological Review,* XII (1948), 271–78.

"Public Opinion and Public Opinion Polling," *American Sociological Review,* XIII (1948), 542–54.

"Group Tension and Interest Organization," *Proceedings of the Second Annual Meeting, Industrial Relations Research Association* (1950), pp. 1–15.

"Paternalism in Industry," *Social Process in Hawaii,* XV (1951), 26–32.

"Psychological Import of the Human Group," in *Group Relations at the Crossroads,* eds. Muzafer Sherif and M. O. Wilson. New York: Harper & Bros., 1953. Pp. 185–202.

"What Is Wrong with Social Theory?" *American Sociological Review,* XIX (1954), 3–10.

"The Sociologist Views the Problem of Old Age Retirement," *Proceedings of the Society of State and City Fiscal Officials* (1954), pp. 59–65.

"Social Structure and Power Conflict," in *Industrial Conflict,* eds. A. Kornhauser, R. Dubin, and A. Ross. New York: McGraw-Hill, 1954. Pp. 232–39.

"The Nature of Race Prejudice," *Social Process in Hawaii,* XVIII (1954), 10–18.

"Attitudes and the Social Act," *Social Problems,* III (1955), 59–65.

"Reflections on Theory of Race Relations," in *Race Relations in World Perspective,* ed. Andrew W. Lind. Honolulu: University of Hawaii Press, 1955. Pp. 3–21.

"Social Science and the Desegregation Process," *The Annals of the American Academy of Political and Social Science,* CCCIV (March 1956), 137–43.

"Sociological Analysis and the 'Variable,'" *American Sociological Review,* XXI (1956), 683–90.

"Race Prejudice as a Sense of Group Position," *Pacific Sociological Review,* I (1958), 3–7.

"Research on Race Relations: United States of America," *International Bulletin of Social Science,* X (1958), 403–47.

"The Rationale of Labor-Management Relations." (A series of three lectures.) University of Puerto Rico Labor Relations Institute, 1958. 55 pp.

"Collective Behavior," in *Review of Sociology: Analysis of Decade,* ed. Joseph B. Gittler. New York: John Wiley and Sons, 1959. Pp. 127–58.

"Suggestions for the Study of Mass-Media Effects," in *American Voting Behavior,* eds. Eugene Burdick and Arthur J. Brodbeck. Glencoe, Ill.: The Free Press, 1959. Pp. 197–208.

"Industrialization and Urbanization," *Boletim de Centro Latino-Americano de Pesquisas em Ciencias Sociais,* II, No. 2 (May 1959), 17–34.

"Early Industrialization and the Laboring Class," *The Sociological Quarterly,* I (1960), 5–14.

"Society as Symbolic Interaction," in *Human Behavior and Social Processes,* ed. Arnald Rose. Boston: Houghton Mifflin Co., 1962. Pp. 179–92.

"Industrialization and the Traditional Order," *Sociology and Social Research,* XLVIII (1964), 129–38.

"The Future of the Color Line," in *The South in Continuity and Change,* eds. John Mckinney and Edgar T. Thompson. Durham, N.C.: Duke University Press, 1965. Pp. 322–36.

"Industrialization and Race Relations," in *Industrialization and Race Relations,* ed. Guy Hunter. London: Oxford University Press, 1965. Pp. 220–53.

"Sociological Implications of the Thought of George Herbert Mead," *American Journal of Sociology,* LXXI (1966), 535–48.

"The Idea of Social Development," *Studies in Comparative International Development,* Vol. II. St. Louis: Social Science Institute, Washington University, 1966. Pp. 3–11.

"Ueber das Konzept der Massengesellschaft," in *Militanter Humanismus,* ed. Alphons Silbermann. Frankfurt am Main: S. Fischer Verlag, 1966. Pp. 19–37.

"Threats from Agency-Determined Research," in *The Rise and Fall of Project Camelot,* ed. Irving Louis Horowitz. Cambridge, Mass.: M.I.T. Press, 1967. Pp. 153–74.

"Fashion," *International Encyclopedia of the Social Sciences,* Vol. V. New York: Macmillan Co., 1968. Pp. 341–45.

"Fashion: From Class Differentiation to Collective Selection," *Sociological Quarterly,* X (1969), 275–91.

LIST OF CONTRIBUTORS

BECKER, ERNEST
Professor, Behavioral Science
Foundations
Simon Fraser University
Vancouver, British Columbia

BRAMSON, LEON
Associate Professor of Sociology
and Department Chairman
Swarthmore College
Swarthmore, Pennsylvania

DANIELS, ARLENE KAPLAN
Associate Professor of Sociology
San Francisco State College
San Francisco, California

DUNHAM, H. WARREN
Professor of Sociology and
Associate in Psychiatry
Wayne State University
Detroit, Michigan

EMERSON, JOAN P.
Assistant Professor of Sociology
State University of New York
Buffalo, New York

HOROWITZ, IRVING LOUIS
Professor of Sociology
Rutgers University
New Brunswick, New Jersey

KERCKHOFF, ALAN C.
Professor of Sociology
Duke University
Durham, North Carolina

KEYFITZ, NATHAN
Professor of Demography
University of California
Berkely, California

KILLIAN, LEWIS M.
Professor of Sociology
University of Massachusetts
Amherst, Massachusetts

KLAPP, ORRIN E.
Professor of Sociology
San Diego State College
San Diego, California

LANG, GLADYS ENGEL
Senior Research Associate, Bureau of
Applied Social Research
Columbia University
New York, New York

LANG, KURT
Professor of Sociology
State University of New York
Stony Brook, New York

LEE, SHU-CHING
Professor of Sociology
Ohio University
Athens, Ohio

LOFLAND, JOHN
Associate Professor of Sociology
University of California
Davis, California

MELTZER, BERNARD N.
Professor of Sociology and Depart-
ment Chairman
Central Michigan University
Mount Pleasant, Michigan

MERRILL, FRANCIS E.
Late Professor of Sociology Emeritus
Dartmouth College
Hanover, New Hampshire

MIYAMOTO, S. FRANK
Professor of Sociology and Depart-
ment Chairman
University of Washington
Seattle, Washington

PETRAS, JOHN W.
Professor of Sociology
Central Michigan University
Mt. Pleasant, Michigan

QUARANTELLI, ENRICO L.
Professor of Sociology and Co-Director,
Disaster Research Center
The Ohio State University
Columbus, Ohio

SCHEFF, THOMAS J.
Professor of Sociology and Depart-
ment Chairman
University of California
Santa Barbara, California

SHANAS, ETHEL
Professor of Sociology
University of Illinois at Chicago
Circle
Chicago, Illinois

SHIBUTANI, TAMOTSU
Professor of Sociology
University of California
Santa Barbara, California

SOLOMON, DAVID N.
Professor of Sociology and Depart-
ment Chairman
McGill University
Montreal, P. of Quebec

STRAUSS, ANSELM
Professor of Sociology
University of California Medical
Center
San Francisco, California

SWANSON, GUY E.
Professor of Sociology
University of California
Berkeley, California

TURNER, RALPH H.
Professor of Sociology and
Anthropology
University of California
Los Angeles, California

WEINBERG, S. KIRSON
Professor of Sociology
Loyola University
Chicago, Illinois

ZAKUTA, LEO
Professor of Sociology
University of Toronto
Toronto

ACKNOWLEDGMENTS

On August 29, 1967, during the 62nd annual meeting of the American Sociological Association in San Francisco, a luncheon was held to commemorate Herbert Blumer's formal retirement from the faculty of the University of California. It was at this gathering, overflowed with friends and well-wishers, that this *Festschrift* was first proposed. The banquet had been arranged by Arlene K. Daniels, who also bore the brunt of the extensive correspondence that led to the selection of the editor.

All the authors are deeply indebted to Carol Talpers of Prentice-Hall for overseeing so effectively the countless details involved in the production of a book of this kind. The task of recasting into a standard format manuscripts submitted in diverse forms fell to Doris Kihara, and Kerina Harada prepared the index, organized around concepts developed by Professor Blumer.

INDEX

COUNTY COLLEGE LIBRARY
3800 CHARCO ROAD
BEEVILLE, TEXAS 78102
(512) 354 - 2740